Praise for *Eiffel's Tower* by Jill Jonnes

"Ms. Jonnes does a fine job of walking us through the fair, where visitors were immersed in a typical late-nineteenth-century stew of high-minded educational exhibits and cheap thrills."
—Richard B. Woodward, *The New York Times*

"In splendid detail, Jonnes examines the importance of the tower in its own historical moment." —Caroline Weber, *The New York Times Book Review*

"Exploiting the almost magnetic attraction of the great tower, Jonnes cleverly pulls into her narrative a wide range of characters, from 'Little Sure Shot' Annie Oakley to 'art warrior' Paul Gauguin. . . . She does [a] . . . fine job of demonstrating what M. Eiffel insisted all along: that his tower was much more than just 'an object of barren wonder.'"
—Robert Cremins, *Houston Chronicle*

"Jonnes' rollicking account of the Eiffel Tower's rowdy debut is an occasion for celebration itself. . . . With flair and marvelously descriptive, 'you-are-there' prose, Jonnes gives *Eiffel's Tower* the immediacy that only a talented writer can bestow on history. Adding to the book's impact are the numerous photos of the tower, the fair, and the people who came to see them. . . . Jonnes weaves these crazy fragments into a beautiful quilt. . . . As elegant and eccentric as its subject, *Eiffel's Tower* sparkles with the power of conviction and the passion of creation."
—Jay Strafford, *Richmond Times-Dispatch*

"A colorful cast of characters descended on Paris for the 1889 World's Fair, and Jonnes (*Conquering Gotham*) offers an atmospheric overview of the celebrities who made Belle Epoque Paris their stage during the memorable event." —*Publishers Weekly*

"Jonnes' book is more then just a recap of perhaps the most interesting international exposition ever staged. With the gift of hindsight, Jonnes illuminates the roots of Belle Epoque Paris and Belle Epoque Europe, a period of peace and progress marked by technological progress and cultural advances that lasted from the 1880s to the 1914 start of World War I. . . . Big dreams and world's fairs benefit mankind and make history, and Jonnes' book proves it." —David Hendricks, *San Antonio Express-News*

"This entertaining new work chronicles the tower's storied beginnings. . . . This carefully researched book, which combines technological and social history (and offers a lively account of the World's Fair), paints a compelling portrait of Belle Epoque France." —*France Magazine*

"In *Eiffel's Tower*, Jill Jonnes (*Empires of Light, Conquering Gotham*) presents an engaging story of a great engineer, one with an 'attractive boldness, impetuosity, and natural courage.'" —James Summerville, *BookPage*

"In *Eiffel's Tower*, historian Jill Jonnes helps us travel back in time to the Exposition Universelle of 1889 in Paris . . . and tells the story of Gustave Eiffel's Tour en Fer de Trois Cents Mètres. Jonnes immerses us so thoroughly in the Exposition that when we get to her description of the Fair's final day, we're almost sad to leave." —Book-of-the-Month Club

"This is a thoroughly delightful book, built around Gustave Eiffel's Tour en Fer (iron tower), but really describing in rich detail Paris and its Exposition Universelle in 1889, coincidentally the centennial of the French Revolution. Author Jill Jonnes re-creates deliciously the Belle Epoque." —Jules Wagman, *Milwaukee Journal Sentinel*

PENGUIN BOOKS

EIFFEL'S TOWER

Jill Jonnes is the author of *Conquering Gotham*, *Empires of Light*, and *South Bronx Rising*. She was named a National Endowment for the Humanities scholar and has received several grants from the Ford Foundation. She lives in Baltimore, Maryland.

Exposition Universelle, Paris, 1889

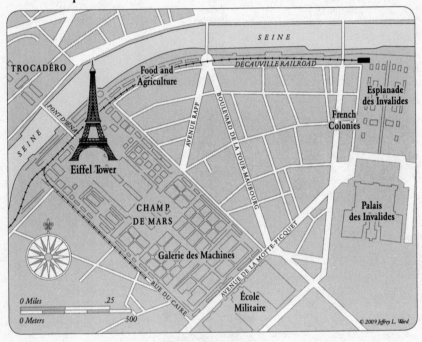

TROCADÉRO

SEINE

DECAUVILLE RAILROAD

Food and Agriculture

Esplanade des Invalides

French Colonies

PONT D'IÉNA

AVENUE RAPP

BOULEVARD DE LA TOUR-MAUBOURG

SEINE

Eiffel Tower

Palais des Invalides

CHAMP DE MARS

Galerie des Machines

AVENUE DE LA MOTTE-PICQUET

RUE DU CAIRE

École Militaire

0 Miles   .25

0 Meters   500

© 2009 Jeffrey L. Ward

Jill Jonnes

EIFFEL'S TOWER

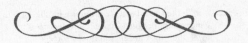

The Thrilling Story
Behind Paris's Beloved Monument
and the Extraordinary
World's Fair That
Introduced It

PENGUIN BOOKS

PENGUIN BOOKS

Published by the Penguin Group
Penguin Group (USA) Inc., 375 Hudson Street, New York, New York 10014, U.S.A.
Penguin Group (Canada), 90 Eglinton Avenue East, Suite 700, Toronto,
Ontario, Canada M4P 2Y3 (a division of Pearson Penguin Canada Inc.)
Penguin Books Ltd, 80 Strand, London WC2R 0RL, England
Penguin Ireland, 25 St Stephen's Green, Dublin 2, Ireland (a division of Penguin Books Ltd)
Penguin Group (Australia), 250 Camberwell Road, Camberwell,
Victoria 3124, Australia (a division of Pearson Australia Group Pty Ltd)
Penguin Books India Pvt Ltd, 11 Community Centre, Panchsheel Park, New Delhi – 110 017, India
Penguin Group (NZ), 67 Apollo Drive, Rosedale, North Shore 0632,
New Zealand (a division of Pearson New Zealand Ltd)
Penguin Books (South Africa) (Pty) Ltd, 24 Sturdee Avenue,
Rosebank, Johannesburg 2196, South Africa

Penguin Books Ltd, Registered Offices:
80 Strand, London WC2R 0RL, England

First published in the United States of America by Viking Penguin,
a member of Penguin Group (USA) Inc. 2009
Published in Penguin Books 2010

1 3 5 7 9 10 8 6 4 2

Map by Jeffrey L. Ward

Photograph credits appear on page 339.

THE LIBRARY OF CONGRESS HAS CATALOGED THE HARDCOVER EDITION AS FOLLOWS:
Jonnes, Jill.
Eiffel's tower: and the World's Fair where Buffalo Bill beguiled Paris, the artists quarreled,
and Thomas Edison became a count/Jill Jonnes.
p. cm.
Includes bibliographical references and index.
ISBN 978-0-670-02060-7 (hc.)
ISBN 978-0-14-311729-2 (pbk.)
1. Exposition universelle de 1889 (Paris, France)   2. Tour Eiffel (Paris, France)
3. Eiffel, Gustave, 1832–1923.   I. Title.
T803.D6E54 2009
907.4'4361–dc22   2008049839

Printed in the United States of America
Set in Berthold Garamond
Designed by Francesca Belanger

To my mother and father, Lyn and Lloyd Jonnes,
and the years our family enjoyed being Americans in Paris

CONTENTS

The Eiffel Tower and the 1889
Paris World's Fair

CHAPTER ONE

We Meet Our Characters, Who Intend to Dazzle the World at the Paris Exposition

On the cold afternoon of January 12, 1888, Annie Oakley was sitting comfortably in her apartment across from Madison Square Garden in New York, making tea and toasting muffins, when she heard a knock at the door. Her visitor was a journalist from Joseph Pulitzer's *New York World*, come to hear what America's most celebrated sharpshooting female was up to. He stepped into the cozy space to find a great jumble. "The sitting-room," he reported, "was littered with breech-loading shotguns, rifles, and revolvers, while the mantel-piece and tables were resplendent with gold and silver trophies brought back from Europe by this slender yet muscular Diana of the Northwest." Fêted and lionized by an enthralled Old World aristocracy, Oakley, twenty-seven, had returned home triumphantly three weeks earlier bearing lavish tokens of admiration, now displayed all round the apartment: two sets of silverware, a solid-silver teapot, antique sugar bowls. As for the pure-bred St. Bernard, it was en route with her horses. "I suppose a crack shot in petticoats was a novelty and curiosity to them," she said between sips of tea.

Nor was that all, she confided to the reporter: her fame as the star attraction of Buffalo Bill's Wild West show in London had inspired "four offers of marriage, including one from a French count." A Welshman had sent along his photo with his proposal. "I shot a bullet through the head of the photograph," said Annie, "and mailed it back with 'respectfully declined' on it. . . . I am Mrs. Butler in private life, although always Annie Oakley on the bills." She regaled the reporter with stories of meeting the king of Denmark and the Prince and Princess of Wales, laughing merrily as she told of a close scrape in Berlin, where she had found the avenue to her hotel closed during the Russian czar's visit. Determined to reach her room, she had dashed through a police barrier and been hotly pursued: "I rolled under an iron gate and spoiled my clothes, and the enraged guards went plumb against the gate. . . . Of course, I laughed at their discomfiture, but I tell you I was a bit scared when I remembered that I had a box of cartridges with me. Why, if they had caught me I should have surely been held as a Nihilist."

A petite, attractive woman who had started shooting game at a young age in Ohio to help her widowed mother feed the family, Annie was also a virtuoso seamstress who designed, sewed, and embroidered her own beaded and fringed cowgirl costumes. Performing with the Wild West, she had been catapulted to stardom as America's best-known woman sharpshooter. In 1884, when Chief Sitting Bull joined the Wild West for a season, he adopted her, naming her "Little Sure Shot."

"She looked innocent and above reproach," observed biographer Shirl Kasper, "a sweet little girl—yet was a sharpshooter of matchless ability. That paradox was part of her appeal. She had a pleasant, wide smile, and thick, dark hair cut close around her face and worn long in back, falling over her shoulders. There was magnetism in the way she smiled, curtsied in the foot-lights, and did that funny little kick as she ran into the wings." Of future plans after her success across the pond, Annie Oakley revealed to the *World*'s reporter only this: "I will practice horseback shooting," and that Europe might beckon once again in 1889, "as I have very flattering offers from there."

Soon enough Annie Oakley and a lively crowd of Gallic and American go-getters, artists, thinkers, politicians, and rogues would be making Belle Époque Paris their stage, for the French republican government was orga-nizing the most ambitious World's Fair yet, the Exposition Universelle of 1889. While the year marked the centennial of the fall of the Bastille, the government preferred to highlight more noble sentiments: "We will show our sons what their fathers have accomplished in the space of a century through progress in knowledge, love of work and respect for liberty," pro-claimed Georges Berger, the fair's general manager. Since 1855, the French had been holding an international exposition in Paris every eleven years (more or less), each more gigantic and wondrous than the last. This partic-ular exposition was to be "an advertisement for the Republican system, which for 18 years had kept at bay the Royalists and Bonapartists on the right and the representatives of various socialist tendencies on the left. The philosophy in power was to be seen as humanist, philanthropic, opening its arms to all of humanity." Already, the French and the Americans—republican allies but also rivals—were looking to make their respective marks at this World's Fair, each determined to uphold national honor at what might be the last great international exhibition of the nineteenth century.

As 1888 began, Parisians looking at their familiar skyline, dominated by the gilded dome of Les Invalides and the towers of Notre Dame, also saw poking up over on the Champ de Mars, the tried-and-true site of the 1867 and 1878 expositions, Gustave Eiffel's under-construction *Tour en Fer de Trois Cents Mètres*. Alternately mocked, despised, and admired, Eiffel's tower was the chosen centerpiece of the upcoming Exposition Universelle. This astonishing structure had become the most conspicuous and controversial symbol of industry's ascendancy, and the triumph of the modern. Eiffel's tower was to be the world's tallest structure, the thrusting symbol of republican France, visible from every direction, the perfect monument to preside over the rococo World's Fair rapidly rising around its four latticed legs.

Gustave Eiffel had been relentlessly pushing to ensure his tower would be finished by May 1889. A self-made millionaire, France's most successful railway bridge builder, and an engineer of global ambition, Eiffel had company offices in such colonial outposts as Peru, Saigon, and Shanghai. Attired in black frock coat, vest, and striped trousers, Monsieur Eiffel wore a high starched white collar, a cravat, and a silk top hat. His dark beard was kept neatly trimmed to a point; his hooded blue eyes missed nothing. Stolid and imperturbable, he could be found most days—sun, rain, snow, sleet—at the Champ de Mars, perched on the construction platform directing his men as they assembled the colossal wrought-iron tower. For nine months Parisians had watched in fascination as the slanting legs of the much-discussed structure rose visibly week by week. The many who loved to hate even the idea of Eiffel's tower felt quite vindicated, for the partially built tower now looked like an ugly, hulking creature.

In England, American painter James McNeill Whistler intended to make his own mark at the Exposition Universelle, for every artist of note yearned to show off his or her best work in the city where art reigned supreme and where millions of fairgoers from around the globe could admire it. And then there were the honors and awards that boosted sales and prices. However, in early 1888 Mr. Whistler was still busy in London, having embroiled himself in yet another cultural dustup. The Society of British Artists already had cause to rue bestowing its presidency the previous year upon this aging enfant terrible of the art world, for though Whistler had brought the club unaccustomed notice and prestige, he had also banished the works of most of its members and, without any consultation and at their considerable expense, transformed the club's gallery into something avant-garde. And so The Butterfly, as Whistler styled himself, was enjoying yet another public feud, albeit one not as riveting (or as financially ruinous) as those he had had with John Ruskin and Oscar Wilde.

By spring Whistler would be ousted from the Society of British Artists, but not before lecturing those leading the coup, "You elected me because I was much talked about and because you imagined I would bring notoriety to your gallery. Did you then also imagine that when I entered your building I should leave my individuality on the doormat?" To the *Pall Mall Gazette*, Whistler, apostle of the modern in art, a quasi-Impressionist ever disdainful of those painters clinging to the old ways of painting fusty historical and biblical subjects, tossed his parting shot: "No doubt their pristine sense of undisturbed somnolence will again settle upon them." This Butterfly reveled in the powerful verbal sting, and Whistler was never happier than when scrapping with the stodgy or drawing yet more attention to his own infamous, troublesome self.

Across the Channel, in France, the very much unknown Paul Gauguin would soon enough be preoccupied with the upcoming World's Fair, but for now, his problem was money. Tall, swarthy, commanding even in his red Breton beret, blue jersey, and rough work pants, he had been painting bold primitive landscapes and peasant scenes in Pont-Aven, in Brittany, while his finances atrophied. His wife, Mette, who had never expected her well-to-do stockbroker husband to become a full-time, let alone impoverished, artist, had decamped with their five children to her native Denmark. Gauguin's had been a peripatetic life. Born in Paris, he had grown up in Peru, studied at an excellent Catholic boarding school in Orléans, and then sailed the world for six years with the French navy.

During his twenties, he settled in Paris, made respectable money as a clerk-accountant and speculator at the stock exchange, married Mette, started a family, and took up art. By 1879 he had begun showing with the Impressionists. When the French economy weakened in 1884, Gauguin's stock market income dried up. He tried to make a go of it in Copenhagen, his wife's home, before retreating to Paris. He then sailed with friends to Panama, hoping for work, but when that went badly they wound up in the new French colony of Martinique, where Gauguin spent six months on that exotic island, painting.

In November of 1887 he returned to Paris still broke but excited by radical advances in his art. He had befriended the brothers Vincent and Theo van Gogh, and Theo, a dealer at the venerable firm of Boussod, Valadon and Company, had persuaded his employers to take on a few of the new Impressionists. In December Theo had shown and sold several of Gauguin's Breton paintings for 150 francs, a dispiriting contrast to the 50,000 francs routinely commanded by Boussod's top-selling Orientalist artist, Jean-Léon Gérôme.

By late February of 1888 Gauguin had returned to Pont-Aven. Soon to be forty, he wrote to Vincent van Gogh, painting in Arles: "The few works I have sold went to pay off some of my most pressing debts, and within a month I am going to find myself completely penniless. Nothing is a negative force. I do not want to pester your brother but if you could have a quiet word with him on the subject, it would calm me down or at least help me wait patiently. My God, money questions are terrible for an artist!"

Back in Paris, although the public did not know it, Gustave Eiffel's time of engineering truth was nearing, the moment when he would learn if he could properly align the four megalithic legs that would support the first-floor platform of his tower. Only a precisely aligned platform of perfect flatness could safely serve as foundation and support for the rest of the one-thousand-foot structure. Its creator continued to defend his design as utterly original: "Not Greek, not Gothic, not Renaissance, because it will be built of iron. . . . The one certain thing is that it will be a work of great drama."

In March of 1888 Gustave Eiffel, at fifty-six, was in his working prime, one of the country's wealthiest self-made men, and the celebrated engineer of the world's highest railway bridge, in Garabit, France. There his graceful four-hundred-foot-high iron arches seemed effortlessly to uphold the railway lines crossing the gigantic valley. Eiffel had also become a major colonial force. In Tan An, South Vietnam, his firm had built a long railway bridge, and much of its overseas business involved selling ingenious, easily assembled modular bridges and buildings. In Europe, Eiffel's huge, ornate train station in Pest, Hungary, was much admired for its combined metal and masonry architecture, while his ingenious design for the seventy-four-foot dome of the Nice Observatory included a "frictionless floating ring that permitted easy turning of the 110-ton dome by hand." In America, Eiffel was best known as the engineer who made possible the construction of the colossal and beloved Statue of Liberty, for he had solved the problem of the interior skeleton and then built it for sculptor Frédéric-Auguste Bartholdi.

When in late 1884 the French republic had announced a contest for a spectacular centerpiece for the 1889 Paris World's Fair, it was only natural that Eiffel's firm would enter. Two of Eiffel's young engineers, Émile Nouguier and Maurice Koechlin, and his architect, Stephen Sauvestre, created an initial design of a one-thousand-foot iron tower, one that so pleased Eiffel he made further refinements and improvements, and began promoting it as the ideal World's Fair monument. After all, it would rise nearly twice as high as the world's tallest building, the recently completed 555-foot-tall Washington Monument in America, thoroughly eclipsing that landmark.

The Eiffel Tower's first public mention appeared on October 22, 1884, in a back page of *Le Figaro*. The newspaper noted, "one of the most extraordinary [projects] is certainly a 300-meter iron tower that M. Eiffel . . . proposes to build."

The French nation badly needed to demonstrate its revived *gloire*, which had been tarnished by Napoleon III's disastrous defeat in the 1870 Franco-Prussian War, the bloody revolt of the Commune, and all the ensuing political and economic turmoil. Even now, an odd but potent alliance of the politically disenchanted—French royalists, nationalists, and leftists—was agitating to elevate to the presidency (or perhaps even to a new throne) the dashing former minister of war General Georges Boulanger. As the British journal *Engineering* noted, "Politics have done much to bring

[France] into discredit among other nations; the Exhibition will do far more to restore its prestige, and to give it even greater prominence in Art, Industry, and Science. . . . With the great mass of Frenchmen, their Exhibition is the most important object within the limit of their horizon. . . . [P]olitical strife is thrust aside for the present, and the clamour of the parties is suppressed."

Republican France had invited every nation of the world to its fête. The great European powers responded with hostility, for while the republican government might insist its fair was celebrating liberty, science, and technology, Europe's monarchs viewed it as a celebration of the downfall and beheading of kings and queens. Lord Salisbury, speaking for Great Britain, protested the very idea of the French celebration. The Russian czar bluntly denounced the French revolution "as an abomination." Germany dismissed universal exhibitions as "'out of date. Their inconveniences are not balanced by their advantages.' . . . Austria used as a pretext the Parisian manifestations in favor of Hungary. Italy said: 'The expense is greater than we could bear.'" Spain had declined, as had Belgium, Holland, Sweden, and Romania. Turkey, like Italy, had pleaded poverty. Only the Central and South American nations had enthusiastically RSVP'd, as had Japan; the United States had yet to formally accept. The French republicans dismissed the royal whiners, confident that the fair would showcase France's role "as educator, benefactor, and distributor of light and bread."

Gustave Eiffel was not the first to envision the sort of colossal tower that would be the fair's centerpiece. The original dreamer was British railroad engineer Richard Trevithick, who in 1833 had suggested erecting a one-thousand-foot cast-iron tower in London. It would have a one-hundred-foot-wide masonry base, with the tower narrowing at the top to ten feet and surmounted by a huge statue. With Trevithick's untimely death, the project, intended to celebrate passage of the First Reform Act, came to naught—a fortunate development, as later engineers declared the design fatally flawed. In 1874 the American engineers Clarke and Reeves revived the idea, proposing a one-thousand-foot iron tower for the 1876 Philadelphia Centennial Exposition. Their design was a cylinder thirty feet in diameter, stabilized and anchored by thick cables attached to its masonry base. An enthusiastic *Scientific American* championed the idea: "We will celebrate our centenary by the most colossal iron construction that the world has seen." This

hideous chimney was also never built. Now, Eiffel was building a far
sleeker version, much to the chagrin of Americans, who just four years
earlier were more than pleased to have finally completed the Washington
Monument.

Naturally, many French were swelling with pride at the mere prospect
of dwarfing the gigantic American obelisk. Engineer Max de Nansouty, a
friend of Eiffel's, had described the whole fantastic project for the first time
in great detail in the December 13, 1884, issue of the French journal *Civil
Engineer*, and he began by noting, "For a long time it seemed as if the Americans were to remain the leaders in these daring experiments that character-
ize the investigations of a special type of genius that enjoys pushing . . . the
strength of materials to their extreme limits." But now, he proclaimed, in
Eiffel and his firm, France could claim engineers undaunted by "the colossal aspects of the problem . . . they seem to have considered these aspects
as a natural extension of the enormous metal structures [Douro and Gara-
bit] that they executed earlier, and in fact they do not feel that these aspects represent the maximum achievement possible in the erection and
superimposition of metal. . . . This is the first time anyone has dared to
propose anything of this height."

Among those Americans eyeing the Paris fair for its publicity potential was
that unrivaled master of self-promotion Thomas Edison. Edison's products
had been a star attraction at the 1881 Paris Electrical Exposition, and recently the Wizard of Menlo Park, living Yankee embodiment of the genius
and potential of modern technology, had been busily perfecting his new
improved phonograph. In bucolic West Orange, New Jersey, Edison, forty-
one, was entertaining the New York press and fellow "electricians" at his
new "invention factory," an elaborate sixty-thousand-square-foot laboratory complex equipped with "eight thousand kinds of chemicals, every
kind of screw made, every size of needle, hair of humans, horses, hogs,
cows, rabbits, goat, minx, and camel." Agents for British inventors of a rival
phonograph system had had the temerity to propose that Edison consolidate interests with them, whereupon Edison cabled George Gouraud, his
longtime London-based impresario and investor, to dismiss these overtures:
"Have nothing to do with them. They are bunch pirates."

Thus galvanized, the man who had invented the lightbulb and whose companies lit up cities across America returned to the fray. On May 11, he held court in his wood-paneled library, with its ten thousand scientific volumes, puffing away at his beloved cigar while showing off the updated phonograph. "The 'talking machine' of a dozen years ago has disappeared," reported *The New York Times* in its story on the sophisticated new product: "Edison's literary and musical experiments with the invention yesterday were wonderful. Not only were words and sentences reproduced but the voices of the readers were readily recognized. The piano, cornet, violin, and clarinet were repeatedly tested singly and together with marvelous success. The phonograph has been so far perfected that next week the work of erecting a factory on the Edison plant will be begun. . . . [The machine's] possibilities are beyond calculating."

As spring gave way to summer, a weary but triumphant Buffalo Bill, strikingly handsome with his graying chestnut tresses, goatee, fringed buckskins, and jaunty scout's hat, sailed into New York Harbor on the chartered *Persian Monarch*, bringing his Wild West spectacle home to a tumultuous welcome. Buffalo Bill, forty-two, had been the toast of London, his show such an astonishment of frontier pageantry, buffalo stampedes, dazzling sharpshooting, broncobusting, and western whoop-'em-up that Queen Victoria herself had ordered up a special command performance for her jubilee.

Returning to their old showground at Erastina on Staten Island, the troupe's hundreds of cowboys and Indians and large herds of horses and buffalo debarked and set up improbable camp. Soon they were "Taming the West" twice daily before huge sold-out crowds, which arrived on special ferries. And as *The New York Times* reported, the Indians were once again indulging their taste for dog flesh: "New Shirt yesterday devoured with apparent relish an expensive poodle that had been used to much better treatment." (As for star attraction Annie Oakley, she was noticeably absent. Having declined to tour the English provinces, she had come home early and, worse yet, was now touring with a rival outfit, Pawnee Bill's Wild West.)

Buffalo Bill, né William F. Cody, had always earned big money and yet was always somehow verging on being broke. That summer he wrote his favorite sister, Julia: "I am tired out. This continual strain on mind & body is wearing me out." But after an anticipated restful October with his family at Scout's Rest Ranch in Nebraska, Cody began to plan a new show, one too fabulous for his competitors to copy, an extravaganza worthy of the upcoming Paris World's Fair. He wrote his sister: "I ain't even going to tell you & Al what it is till I spring it on the public in December—Oh I am a pretty lively dead man yet—and I ain't downed by a good deal—Keep your eye on Your Big Brother."

By 1888 James Gordon Bennett, Jr., forty-seven, publisher of the immensely powerful *New York Herald*, was one of the better known Americans in Paris, a very wealthy man, tall, imperious, with fierce blue eyes, a prominent beak of a nose, and large mustachios. Bennett had fled Gotham eleven years earlier after an infamous incident on New Year's Day of 1877. On that snowy evening, an inebriated Bennett had entered the Manhattan mansion of his affianced, Caroline May, for a party and made his way unsteadily to the crowded parlor. Feeling a pressing need to relieve himself, and oblivious to the festivities around him (not to mention the ladies), he had unbuttoned his fashionable pants, stood before the warming fire, and there directed a comforting stream of piss. The crowd's good cheer shifted to affronted wrath.

Men angrily shouting "Sir!" roughly hustled Miss May's beloved out the front door and into the falling snow, down the front stoop, and into his sleigh. The next day her brother flogged Bennett in front of his club, whereupon Bennett felt compelled to challenge him to a duel with pistols. No blood was shed, but Bennett, now persona non grata in New York society, fled to Paris.

Thanks to the miracle of the transatlantic cable, Bennett had run America's greatest and richest newspaper from Paris for more than a decade with an iron hand. He worked from one of his two luxurious apartments on the Champs-Élysées, the city's best address, where large trees shaded the bucolic beaten-earth boulevard and the palatial residences of the Duchesse d'Uzès, the Duc de Trévise, and the Duc de Massa, as well as such charming sights as merry-go-rounds and children's goat-drawn cart rides. As the favored route to reach the Bois de Boulogne, the Champs-Élysées was crowded mornings and afternoons with "fine equipages, drawn by pairs of prancing high-steppers; on the boxes, coachmen and footmen in livery;

and in the open carriages, beautiful ladies dressed in chic and costly Parisian gowns, carrying bright-colored parasols as they wended their way to the Bois."

The New York Herald, started by Bennett's father, James Gordon Bennett, Sr., had been a powerhouse of reporting ever since the Civil War, and Bennett junior gladly expended vast sums to inform and educate Americans about the rest of the world. He took great pride in *The Herald*'s foreign correspondents' routinely scooping all others as they braved the most remote jungles and tundras to report the rise and fall of empires, the spread of colonialism, the gathering might of capitalism, or simply some charming exotic scene. It was Bennett junior who in 1869 had dispatched the intrepid Henry Morton Stanley to find the missionary explorer Dr. David Livingstone in darkest Africa. As ever, expense was no object, and Bennett junior instructed: "Draw a thousand pounds now, and when you have gone through that, draw another thousand . . . and so on; but *find Livingstone*." Stanley did, becoming the most celebrated journalist of his day. Bennett also introduced the interview story, and early in his career had signed on then-young luminaries such as Mark Twain for regular columns. Bennett's own obsession with the weather and shipping news ensured that these were scrupulously covered in *The Herald*.

Monsieur Gordon-Bennett, as the French insisted on calling him (even as he once again fumed, "My name is Bennett!"), could easily have returned to Manhattan to live a few years after the scandal, but he had come to prefer his sybaritic self-exile in Paris, beauteous capital of Western civilization. Several thousand fellow expatriates made up the rather sizable American colony there, including artists such as Mary Cassatt and the famous dentist from Philadelphia Thomas Evans, whose services to the crowned heads of Europe enabled him to live in palatial splendor with his wife and a vast aviary, maintain a voluptuous mistress he shared with poet Stéphane Mallarmé, publish the weekly *American Register*, and supervise the American Charitable Fund for impecunious "unfortunates" marooned in the French capital.

Since moving to Paris, Monsieur Gordon-Bennett had startled the natives (and confirmed the French in their view of Yankees as uncouth savages) by occasionally stalking into his favorite restaurants, Maxim's and Voisin, and, thoroughly drunk, marching "down the aisle, yanking off the

tablecloths and sending a cascade of china, crystal and silver crashing to
the floor, looking straight ahead and paying not the slightest attention to the
distress that marked his passing." Despite such outrages, the finer Parisian
restaurateurs valued Bennett as a free-spending regular who spoke flawless
French (he had passed his adolescence in Paris), and as a fascinating
specimen of this new transatlantic type—the boorish American millionaire. One of Bennett's French paramours, the actress Camille Clermont,
summed him up succinctly: "Beneath his thin veneer of civilization, J.G.B.
was in reality a Barbarian." This judgment was merely confirmed by Bennett's occasional naked nocturnal rampages in his splendid coach-and-four
down the Champs-Élysées.

Still, the great publisher missed having a newspaper near to hand, and in
the fall of 1887 he had opened a Paris office to publish a European edition
of *The Herald*—a proper newspaper, with a busy city room, a staff, the smell
of printer's ink, fast-working presses, and all the ensuing glory and influence.
The timing was not accidental, for Bennett assumed waves of Americans
would soon descend upon Paris for the exposition, guaranteeing the paper's
success. A European edition of *The Herald* would both serve as an American
presence in Paris, and make *The Herald*'s publisher a man of consequence on
two continents. As in New York, the new Paris *Herald* served up high-minded
political reporting and the most lurid criminal coverage, as well as such
oddities as death by a too-tight corset at a Russian ball.

With the months ticking rapidly by until the fair's opening day in May
1889, the French fair commissioners and such nations as Argentina, Vene-
zuela, and Japan had been spending the previous year moving the prover-
bial heaven and earth to complete their respective elaborate structures and
exhibit halls in the 228 acres allotted the fair in three areas along the Seine.
Crowds coming from the Trocadéro Palace on the Right Bank would cross
the Pont d'Iéna and enter the fair by passing under the massive archways
of the Eiffel Tower. Before them they would see, in what was now a jumble of
construction, the parklike Court of Honor, its series of huge fountains
pulsating with frothy sprays of water. Straight ahead would loom the gorgeous faience-blue Central Dome, encrusted with colored tiles and statuary, a gleaming burst of color to contrast with the iron tower. Behind it the
gigantic Galerie des Machines was rising.

France intended to dazzle the world (and especially its hostile neighbors) with its shimmering city occupying the Left Bank, showcasing not just its technical and industrial prowess, but also its world-famous artists and architects, its celebrated wines and food products, its history and heroes, and the exotic cultures of Senegal, Congo, Tonkin, and Cambodia, *"les pays chauds,"* the hot nations, as many referred to the new French colonies in Asia and Africa. The Baron Delart was replicating a Cairo market street using authentic architectural bits and pieces and arranging for the market to be peopled with hundreds of real Egyptians, including many artisans—goldsmiths, weavers, sweets makers, and sculptors—who would work and sell their wares in little shops.

Undaunted by the lack of official foreign exhibits, fair commissioner Georges Berger, seasoned veteran of the 1867 and 1878 fairs, was busy wooing private foreign companies to the show. The British editors of *Engineering*, which viewed the English queen's boycott as silly and very bad for business, had no doubt the French would mount "a national exhibition as the world has never seen . . . and which will last long after the rumours of war have died away and the din of the politicians, placemen, agitators, and communards has ceased."

Although the United States had been dilatory in conveying its official acceptance, American committees, companies, and artists, fired by chauvinism and competitive zeal, were already busily concocting ways to outshine the French and all others at the fair. The United States had become astonishingly rich since the Civil War, and with its technology, industry, and agriculture reshaping the global economy, its citizens felt entitled to a more prominent place on the world stage. It was galling, as writer and expatriate Henry James complained in *The Nation*, when an American "finds Europeans very ignorant of a country, very indifferent to a country [i.e., America] which, in spite of irregularities, he may be pardoned for thinking a magnificent one."

James Gordon Bennett certainly believed the Old World required educating about the rising greatness of America, a task he intended to undertake through his new Paris edition of *The New York Herald*, which was determined "to put American ideas and American achievements on the news map of the world." The French-American relationship had long been fraught with admiration, envy, and one-upmanship. Mark Twain had caught that jousting spirit when he jibed, "France has neither winter, nor summer, nor morals. Apart from these drawbacks it is a fine country." A World's Fair was just the occasion to heat up the long-standing rivalry between the world's two sister republics, a gilded battlefield for France and America to vie for supremacy and honors.

Thomas Edison certainly intended to create a big splash this time around, making his new improved phonograph the heart of a large and elaborate exhibit at the Paris fair. In late July 1888, when Francis Upton, president of the Edison Lamp Company, received official word of the impending Exposition Universelle, he had immediately advised Edison, "I think that you should make a display, particularly of your Loud Speaking Telephone, and Phonograph, your Ore Separator; these in actual operation. Then a display of your other inventions without keeping them running.

"I strongly recommend that Mr. [William] Hammer be sent in charge of the Exhibition for you, as there is no doubt he has a genius for such displays."

And so, ten months hence, accomplished and ambitious men and women of the modern world would converge upon the boulevards of Paris to be players in this drama of the World's Fair, acting out all the passions, ambitions, rivalries, gaiety, and pleasures of Belle Époque France and Gilded Age America. This was, after all, the city that had inspired artist Thomas Gold Appleton's famous quip "Good Americans, when they die, go to Paris." But first, they would attend the fair.

~~~~~~~~~~~~~~~

CHAPTER TWO

Gustave Eiffel and
"the Odious Column of Bolted Metal"

In mid-March of 1888, Gustave Eiffel stood amid the scaffolding of his partially built tower, directing the proper alignment of its four latticed legs. What was this supremely confident engineer thinking in his chilly wrought-iron perch high above Paris? Perhaps he was simply savoring the fresh breezes and "magnificent panorama," the pure pleasure of being so high and overlooking what he loved: "this great city, with its innumerable monuments. Its avenues, its towers, and its domes; the Seine, which winds through it like a long ribbon of steel; farther off the green circle of hills which surround Paris; and beyond these, again, the wide horizon."

Or perhaps Eiffel was in a less joyful mood, remembering all the abuse he and his *Tour en Fer* had endured—insults, lawsuits, political jockeying—in the two years since fair commissioner Gen. Édouard Lockroy had bestowed upon him the coveted prize of building the fair's main attraction. Certainly Eiffel was thinking about how to ensure the perfection of the tower's first-floor platform. For if it was even "infinitesimally out of plane, the deviation would throw the tower disastrously off vertical when it reached full height." Then his enemies would rejoice, for what could he do then but dismantle his partly built tower and admit defeat? If nothing else, Eiffel had discovered during this period the joys of affronting the status quo. For as all the world knew, his magnum opus, his "dazzling demonstration of France's industrial power," this tower of unprecedented height, with its unique design of spare and simple wrought iron, had stirred up endless vitriol and controversy.

The Parisian architects had been the first to strike, outraged that a mere engineer and builder of railway bridges could imagine his iron monstrosity worthy of a central place in their illustrious city. In early February of 1885, Jules Bourdais, architect of the acclaimed Trocadéro Palace, had begun promoting *his* plan: a one-thousand-foot-tall Sun Column, a classical granite tower of elegant loggias enclosing a hollow center. Rising up from a proposed six-story museum of electricity, the Bourdais Column would be topped not only by a gigantic searchlight (combined with parabolic mirrors) that would illumine the city, but by a statue of Scientia, or Knowledge. When questioned, Bourdais declined to consider that his design was an engineering impossibility, far too heavy for its foundation, and unlikely to survive strong winds. Instead, he challenged Eiffel to show how elevators could go up and down inside his tower's curved legs. Now that, Bourdais countered, was the real impossibility!

For a year the architects quietly attacked Eiffel behind the scenes, certain they could persuade the government to choose Bourdais's Sun Column. But the fair's commissioner Lockroy, also the minister of trade in the republican administration, was clearly enamored of Eiffel's tower, and Lockroy—a swashbuckling classicist and freethinker, a veteran of Garibaldi's anti-royalist campaign in Sicily, and a man who relished drama—was not easily swayed. He was firmly committed to seeing built a "monument unique in the world . . . one of the most interesting curiosities of the capital." And so, on May 1, 1886, Paul Planat, founder and editor of the architectural journal *La construction moderne*, went noisily public, launching the first of many jeremiads against Eiffel's tower, denouncing it as "an inartistic . . . scaffolding of crossbars and angled iron" and excoriating above all its "hideously unfinished" look.

In truth, no project had yet been officially selected, and the very next day Lockroy formally invited all who wished to compete for the great honor of constructing the World's Fair tower to submit proposals by May 18, 1886. Though Lockroy suggested that the design be for an iron tower of 300 meters, many among the 107 entrants ignored that guideline. One entrant envisioned a gigantic water sprinkler, in case drought struck Paris. Another featured a tall tower built not of iron but of wood and brick. Perhaps the most historically minded design was the gigantic guillotine, so evocative of the very event being unofficially celebrated, the fall of the Bastille. Was it possible, Planat wondered in print, even as the winner was to be announced, that Monsieur Lockroy, reputedly "a man of taste," might

Gustave Eiffel

still acknowledge the error of his ways and realize that "there could be no honor in erecting [Eiffel's] monstrosity . . . [or] leaving as his legacy this scaffolding"?

By now, others had joined the campaign against Eiffel, asserting that the actual construction of a safe one-thousand-foot tower was technically impossible, as no building that tall could resist the power of the wind. Moreover, how would Eiffel find men willing or even able to work at such vertiginous heights? And what of the danger to those who would come as visitors to ascend such a structure? Of course, Eiffel knew that these nay-sayers probably understood nothing of his vast experience, the more than fifty wrought-iron railroad bridges he had built in France alone. Erecting those structures had made him thoroughly confident that his mathematical formula for shaping wrought iron would hold up to the worst possible winds. As for the labor question, his workers who had built the bridge at Garabit were already habituated to working four hundred feet above the ground. And once the tower was up, he had no doubt it would be perfectly safe. He did not bother to dignify with a reply the strange assertion that such a huge iron tower would become a dangerous magnet, drawing the nails from surrounding Parisian buildings.

Then came an entirely new line of attack, slithering out of that most poisonous undercurrent of French life: anti-Semitism. In June a hateful screed titled *The Jewish Question* charged that Eiffel, through his German ancestors, was "nothing more nor less than a German Jew." An entire chapter scourged *"L'Exposition des Juifs"* and denounced the proposed Eiffel Tower as *"une tour juive."* It was a sad commentary that Eiffel even felt obliged to respond, as he did in the republican paper *Le Temps*, stating, "I am neither Jewish nor German. I was born in France in Dijon of French Catholic parents."

Gustave Eiffel was very much a child of the bourgeoisie who'd spent his boyhood in Dijon expecting to run his rich uncle's vinegar and paint factory. But while Eiffel was finishing his education in Paris, dabbling in *la vie bohème* as a college student, a dandy who loved to dance, fence, and flirt, his ferociously republican uncle ("all kings are rogues") quarreled so violently with his sister and Bonapartist brother-in-law that relations were severed. Young Eiffel, trained in chemistry, floundered briefly before finding employment in the burgeoning new industrial field of railway engineering. The young man so impressed his employers that by age twenty-six he was entrusted with a huge and complicated project: building the first iron railroad bridge across the Garonne River in Bordeaux.

Gustave Eiffel had found his métier. He loved designing and erecting gigantic practical structures that conquered nature, he excelled at both the mathematics and the logistics of building, and he enjoyed working out in the weather with his men. His technical schooling and early training as an engineer had instilled a necessary discipline and rigor, and his brilliance and entrepreneurial spirit distinguished him even at this young age. Moreover, Eiffel also possessed an attractive boldness, impetuosity, and natural courage. When one of his bridge riveters fell into the river, Eiffel, a strong swimmer, plunged right in to rescue the man from drowning. When they were both safe, he said calmly, "Please be good enough to attach yourselves carefully in the future." Not long after, Eiffel saved yet another man and his three children from drowning when their boat capsized, this time in a raging storm.

In January 1860 Eiffel informed his mother and father that he intended to marry a young Bordelaise woman of some standing, a Mademoiselle Louise whose wealthy family owned a château and vineyards. When her widowed mother dismissed him as a mere fortune hunter whose antecedents were not of proper standing, he was humiliated. The parents of three other well-off young women proved equally unimpressed by Eiffel's considerable accomplishments and glowing prospects. Finally, about to turn thirty, his pride badly bruised, Eiffel sat down and wrote to his mother, asking her to locate a bride among the more provincial young ladies of Dijon. "I would be satisfied with a girl with an average dowry," he wrote, "a face that is kind, someone who is even-tempered and has simple tastes. Really, what I need is a good housekeeper who won't get on my nerves too much, who will be as faithful as possible, and who will give me fine children." On July 8, 1862, Eiffel married Marguerite Gaudelet, seventeen, whom he had known since childhood. Theirs proved to be a happy union, blessed over the years with five children.

Even as Eiffel was relishing his first year of married life, he made the unhappy discovery that his sister Marie's husband, Armand, a manager in the same firm as Eiffel, was an embezzler. Long the family's black sheep, Armand was banished to America, leaving behind Marie, who took up lace making to assuage her humiliation. Close on the heels of this family disgrace, Eiffel's youngest sister, Laure, was diagnosed with a throat tumor. During one of his frequent visits to her sickbed, Eiffel wrote his elderly parents, "Just in two or three days, the illness has gotten so much worse. . . . It is terrible to see." On August 11, 1864, Eiffel telegraphed his father: "Our poor Laure died this morning at 4 a.m. Come as soon as possible. I leave it to you to tell poor mother." Eiffel named his second daughter Laure in his sister's memory.

By 1867, with financial backing from his family, Gustave Eiffel had established his own firm in a Parisian suburb and immediately won an all-important contract to design and build the iron-and-glass Palais des Machines at that year's Paris World's Fair. Over the next decade, he would come to specialize in railroad bridges and viaducts—forty-two in France alone. Using his own mathematical formulas for the elasticity of wrought iron, he designed and erected strong wind-resistant structures of notable elegance, which became his industrial signature. In 1876 his parabolic railway bridge across the Douro River Gorge in Oporto, Portugal, was hailed as an aesthetic masterpiece of engineering ingenuity.

And so, by his forties, Gustave Eiffel was gaining renown and wealth, while his firm was increasingly engaged in far-flung locales outside France. At home he was a doting paterfamilias, his wife and children happily ensconced in a mansion on rue de Prony, just blocks from the beautiful Parc Monceau. His wife's frail health always worried him, and in mid-1877 she became seriously ill. Despairing, he wrote his parents: "Marguerite is suffering from a chest ailment that leaves no hope." In early September she awoke vomiting blood, collapsed, and died at the age of thirty-two. From this time on, Eiffel's oldest child, Claire, fourteen, took charge of the household. Eiffel would not remarry, and in February of 1885, when Claire wed Adolphe Salles, a tall bespectacled mining engineer, the new couple made their home with him. While Eiffel's daughters were lovely girls who made their papa proud, his two grown sons were more problematic, prone to embarrassing and sometimes expensive escapades. And so it was not Eiffel's sons who joined him at his thriving firm, but his new son-in-law, Monsieur Salles.

On June 12, 1886, the two men were delighted to learn they had won the coveted commission to build the fair's centerpiece. Despite the campaigns

of Eiffel's opponents, Commissioner Lockroy (to no one's surprise) had
selected Eiffel's *Tour en Fer de Trois Cents Mètres*, having deemed the other
projects either unworkable or—in the case of the gigantic replica of a
guillotine—simply impolitic. Eiffel's tower was praised as having "a distinctive character . . . [being] an original masterpiece of work in metal." Ultimately, Eiffel would be building a potent symbol of French modern
industrial might, a towering edifice that would exalt science and technology, assert France's superiority over its rivals (especially America), and en-
tice millions to visit Paris for the fair to ascend the tower's unprecedented
heights. After all, American and British engineers had likewise dreamed of
building a wonderfully tall tower, but they had not been able to figure out
the means to do so. Eiffel, the Frenchman, through his years of erecting
gigantic and beautiful arched railroad bridges, had solved the mystery, and
being thoroughly Gallic, he intended to build with elegance and artistry.

During this time of attacks and controversy, an English reporter who
sought out Eiffel was somewhat surprised to find that his office was located
in a modest-looking town house on a quiet street, its front door marked by
only a small brass plate engraved with Eiffel's name. Once inside, however,
the reporter found more of what he had been expecting: "The interior was
richly furnished. . . . The entrance hall was thickly carpeted, and was gay
with flowers and palms. The waiting-room was a very *salon*, most sumptu-
ously furnished, the walls being hung with plans and designs of gigantic
enterprises, accomplished or under consideration. Footmen in livery were
in attendance. An adjoining room was Eiffel's private office. It was soberly
but richly furnished, and was similarly decorated with pictures of his triumphs over iron and steel. Eiffel's table was at the far end of this room, a
plain working-table. His son-in-law sat opposite to him. Between them on
the wall were all kinds of electrical apparatus for killing time and space."

While Gustave Eiffel always spoke persuasively on the tower's design,
its safety, and its beauty, he was noticeably touchy on the subject of its
practical purpose. He repeatedly insisted that the Eiffel Tower would serve
a plethora of important needs—the study of meteorology, aerodynamics,
telegraphy, and even military strategy. "A program has already been drawn
up by our scientific men," he said, which would "include the study of the
fall of bodies through the air, the resistance of the air to varying velocities,
certain laws of elasticity, the study of the compression of gases or vapors

under pressure . . . lastly, a series of physiological experiments of the deepest interest. . . . [T]here are few scientific men who do not hope at this moment to carry out, by the help of the tower, some experiment."

After experiencing the joy of winning the commission, Eiffel entered another painful phase when he estimated the cost of erecting the tower at five million francs, or $1 million. The government, which had originally talked about underwriting that whole sum, now backpedaled, offering not quite a third, or 1.5 million francs, leaving Eiffel to raise personally the remaining millions needed to build the tower. To attract investors, he would be allowed to keep the tower up for twenty years and was assured of all profits from entry fees and restaurant concessions for the whole of that period. But after this agreement was reached, weeks and then months passed with no action and no contract. Eiffel began to worry about ever getting started with the project, much less finished.

Next, further debates arose about where best to locate the Eiffel Tower. "Was it sensible to construct the tower in the bottom of the Seine Valley? Would it not be better to place it in an elevated position, on a rise which would be a sort of pedestal for it and make it stand out more? Wouldn't the gigantic metal tower overshadow the palaces of the Champ de Mars? Should such a permanent monument be built on the site where future exhibitions would certainly be organized?" What was the point of the tower if it did not serve as a beacon to the actual fairgrounds? And how many would pay to visit a monument located on some distant hill? In the end, Eiffel once again prevailed: His tower would stand on the Champ de Mars, with the rest of the fair.

However, when the military discovered that their training ground on the Champ de Mars would be forfeited to the Eiffel Tower not just for the duration of the fair but for twenty years, it successfully agitated to relocate the tower much closer to the river. In September Eiffel was working in his office when he learned that he now was to build his tower so close to the Seine that two of the foundations for the legs would require far more complicated compressed-air construction techniques. "These foundations," he would later complain to Lockroy, "are far more onerous for me than those previously agreed to on the Champ de Mars."

Summer turned to fall, with Eiffel becoming more and more distressed at the delay. Finally, on October 22, the government committee convened to debate his contract. The powerful politicians Pierre Tirard and radical leader Georges Clemenceau both railed in now familiar fashion against Eiffel's tower, with Tirard denouncing it as "anti-artistic, contrary to French genius . . . a project more in character with America (where taste is not yet very developed) than Europe, much less France." Clemenceau balked at building the tower simply because it was "an extraordinary thing, that would perhaps be absurd, perhaps ugly, but would attract foreigners. . . . We're told we should give M. Eiffel 1,500,000 francs so all of England can ascend a thousand feet high above the banks of the Seine." Of course, as Eiffel's supporters pointed out, only their man had stepped forward with a completely original monument that he would help finance and that could be constructed in time for the exposition. But when the meeting ended, there had been no vote and thus no contract.

Once again, week after autumn week drifted by, and still there was no actual vote. The dependable gossip "Rastignac" of *L'Illustration*, while declaring himself surfeited with talk of Eiffel's tower, needled Tirard and Clemenceau for being obtuse. The French people would adore the tower, he declared, for they were "wild only about the giddy, the unexpected, the gigantic and fanciful." Nor was it just the French who hankered after the huge and amazing, he wrote; everyone wanted the incredible. For him, Eiffel's tower was just an unfortunate sign of the times.

Finally, on November 22, the committee reconvened. While certain of its members delivered the same tirades and anti-Eiffel invective, in the end, the politicians voted 21–11 to underwrite the tower. Two days later, as Eiffel sat in his office pondering how best to extricate the contract from the state bureaucrats, events took a disastrous turn. The Comtesse de Poix, along with her neighbor, filed a lawsuit to stop construction of the tower. Both were residents of the avenues abutting the Champ de Mars, and when they saw that Eiffel was about to get his contract, they went to court. "She holds that the building of the Eiffel Tower is not only a menace to her houses," reported *The New York Times*, "but that it will block up for many years the most agreeable part of the Champ de Mars, and the only one in which she has been accustomed to take her daily exercise." Many of the comtesse's neighbors imagined this wrought-iron behemoth towering over them and felt equally nervous about living in its shadow. They worried not just about its possible collapse, but that an iron tower would function as a gigantic lightning rod, attracting dangerous storm bolts. Worst of all, this overpowering structure would not disappear when the Exposition ended, but would menace them for twenty years. Eiffel's momentary sense of triumph evaporated; for the tower to be ready in time for the fair, he should be building it *now*.

Gustave Eiffel spent the cold and snowy December of 1886 in a mingled agony of frustration and indecision. It had been five months since he had won the contest, yet he still lacked the most basic building contract, much less the government subsidy. Even if he could sign a contract tomorrow, the lawsuits would prevent him from starting construction. Meanwhile, he was already expending considerable sums. At the firm's production shops out in Levallois-Perret, Eiffel's engineer Maurice Koechlin was supervising the production of 1,700 drawings of the skeleton of the tower, while other draftsmen worked on the 3,629 detailed renderings necessary to manufacture the 18,000 wrought-iron sections that would become the latticework tower. If construction did not start soon, all this time, effort, and money would be wasted.

It certainly cannot have helped Eiffel's mood to learn that on December 18 editor Paul Planat, his most vociferous opponent, had hosted a convivial dinner where the almost one hundred architecture alumni of the venerable École des Beaux-Arts drank champagne while being entertained by numerous cruel and silly skits skewering Eiffel's tower. Most hurtful, the much-admired architect of the magnificent Paris Opéra, Charles Garnier, had joined in, reportedly singing a long, ludicrous *chanson* mocking "this funnel planted on its fat butt" that dared to invade heaven. Moreover, Eiffel could look forward to seeing all this raillery in print, with biting cartoons, come the New Year.

In truth, as 1887 loomed, Eiffel had far more serious problems than the ongoing jibes, for he still had to deal with the matter of the lawsuits filed by the comtesse and her neighbor. At first, it seemed reasonable to demand a state guarantee against these legal risks, but Eiffel knew this would just present another excuse for the state to dither. Perhaps *he* should offer to indemnify the timorous state for all possible outcomes of the lawsuit and the possible collapse of his tower onto these ladies' domiciles. Should he offer to raise *all* of the five million francs needed for construction privately? As Christmas neared, he wavered between charging boldly ahead and abandoning the project.

On December 22, 1886, Eiffel sat down and wrote his longtime supporter Édouard Lockroy a letter, explaining, "Today I must tell you once again that the delays in concluding the contract are making for a very serious situation." He politely but unhappily enumerated all the roadblocks, including the litigious ladies and the state's decision that they were his problem. "Meanwhile," he pointed out, "the time is disappearing and I should have started building months ago. . . . If this situation goes on, I have to give up all hope of succeeding. . . . Still, I remain ready to start work immediately. . . . But, if I have not started work during the first part of January, I cannot possibly be finished in time. If we don't come to a definite agreement by December 31 . . . I will find it painful but necessary to give up my responsibility and take back my proposals. I would be very sorry to renounce the construction of what most agree will be one of the Exposition's principal attractions." But then Eiffel changed his mind and put the letter in a drawer, deciding not to send it.

Instead, he threw all caution to the wind. He would not give Paul Planat and his other enemies the satisfaction of seeing him retreat from the field. As the New Year neared, he decided to gamble his personal fortune for the glory of seeing his one-thousand-foot tower rise over Paris. First, he agreed to indemnify the state for the Comtesse de Poix and her neighbors' lawsuits, and any possible consequence of the tower's collapsing, hiring top lawyers to ensure the best possible solution. He would also, as previously agreed, raise all the financing beyond the state's 1.5 million francs. This bold stroke ended the logjam, and on January 7, 1887, he and the French and Parisian governments finally signed off on the long-stalled contract. The contract required Eiffel to use only French labor, materials, and technology and to submit to oversight by an exposition committee. At the end of the tower's first year, the City of Paris would become its owner, but Eiffel would still retain all income, save the 10 percent earmarked for the city's poor.

Three weeks later, on January 28, during a winter so severe that Parisians were ice-skating on lakes in the Bois de Boulogne, Eiffel broke ground at the Champ de Mars. At last, the foundations for the tower were begun. In preparation, Eiffel explained, he had made a series of borings, which "showed that the subsoil in the Champ de Mars was composed of a deep stratum of clay capable of supporting a weight of between 45 pounds and 55 pounds to the square inch, surmounted by a layer of sand and gravel of varying depth, admirably calculated to receive the foundations." As Eiffel would confess later in a lecture, he felt tremendous "satisfaction" that morning as "I watched an army of diggers start on those great excavations that were to hold the four feet of this Tower that had been a subject of constant concern for me for more than two years.

"I also felt that, notwithstanding the severe attacks directed against the Tower, public opinion was on my side, and that a host of unknown friends were preparing to welcome this daring attempt as it rose out of the ground."

The Eiffel Tower was situated to serve as a triumphant towering archway into the fairgrounds from the Pont d'Iéna, and each of its four gigantic feet marked one of the cardinal points of the compass. The east and south feet would stand firmly on deeply excavated gray plastic clay soil undergirded by a solid foundation of chalk. The north and west feet, being closer to the river, presented a more complex situation, requiring compressed-air excavation via sunken caissons. Every morning, through the snows and freezing weather of that harsh winter, great teams of laborers turned out to excavate the four gigantic foundations, with the blue-suited workmen tossing the dirt and rocky debris into large-wheeled wooden wagons to be carted away by horses.

As Eiffel and his work crews got busy, and the tower began to look like a reality, the influential *L'Illustration* continued to mock it as little better than "a lighthouse, a nail, a chandelier . . . it would never have been allowed but for politicians who have the idea it's a 'symbol of industrial civilization.'" Horrified at the scale of what they saw taking place, the tower's enemies mobilized for a last-ditch effort to stop the hated "scaffolding." On February 14, not three weeks into the digging of the foundations, forty-seven of France's most famous and powerful artists and intellectuals signed their names to an angry protest letter addressed to Paris official Adolphe Alphand, Baron Haussmann's right-hand man and principal organizer of this and the past two World Fairs. The letter, published in *Le Temps,* vehemently lamented the soulless vulgarity of such an industrial behemoth, this "dizzily ridiculous tower dominating Paris like a black and gigantic factory chimney, crushing [all] beneath its barbarous mass."

Among the signatories were France's most hallowed names—the greatest painters of the age, Ernest Meissonier and Adolphe William Bouguereau; the celebrated writers Guy de Maupassant and Alexandre Dumas *fils*; poet François Coppée; composer Charles Gounod; architect Charles Garnier; and dozens of other important Parisians—with all insisting fervently: "For the Eiffel Tower, which even commercial America would not have, is without a doubt the dishonor of Paris. Everyone feels it, everyone says it, everyone is profoundly saddened by it, and we are only a weak echo of public opinion so legitimately alarmed. When foreigners visit our Exposition they will cry out in astonishment, 'Is it this horror that the French have created to give us an idea of their vaunted taste? . . . And for the next twenty years we will see cast over the entire city, still trembling with the genius of so many centuries, cast like a spot of ink, the odious shadow of the odious column of bolted metal."

Lockroy and Eiffel had suffered through so many anti-tower attacks that this latest rarified blast served only as a high-profile opportunity to take the offensive. Interviewed at his giant noisy workshop in the suburb of Levallois-Perret, Eiffel sounded positively sanguine in his creation's defense: "I believe that the tower will have its own beauty. The first principle of architectural beauty is that the essential lines of a construction be determined by a perfect appropriateness to its use. What was the main obstacle I had to overcome in designing the tower? Its resistance to wind. And I submit that the curves of its four piers as produced by our calculations, rising from an enormous base and narrowing toward the top, will give a great impression of strength and beauty."

Eiffel instructed those clinging to the past that there was ample patriotic glory in the "tallest edifice ever raised by man . . . there is an attraction and a charm inherent in the colossal. . . . It seems to me that this Eiffel Tower is worthy of being treated with respect, if only because it will show that we are not simply an amusing people, but also the country of engineers and builders who are called upon all over the world to construct bridges, viaducts, train stations and the great monuments of modern industry."

With his tower finally launched, and the work site busy with daily progress, Eiffel could even afford to be merely amused for the readers of *Le Temps* at the artistic establishment's attack: "They begin by declaring that my tower is not French. It is big enough and clumsy enough for the English or Americans, but it is not our style, they say. We are occupied more with little artistic bibelots. . . . Why should we not show the world what we can do in the way of great engineering projects. . . . Paris is to have the greatest tower in the world, after all. . . . In fact, the tower will be the chief attraction of the Exhibition."

Lockroy, having married into the family of Victor Hugo, was well acquainted with the politics of art and literature. He, too, was fed up with Eiffel's effete critics and lambasted their after-the-fact screed, wondering if such a protest "may be used as a pretext by some nations not to take part in our celebration." Lockroy nominated the artists' letter itself as an exhibit suitable for "a showcase at the Exposition. Such beautiful and noble prose cannot but interest the crowds, and perhaps even amaze them." The authorities, however, were not interested in any further diatribes, as they had an exhibition to build.

Day by day that winter the Eiffel Tower's foundation holes grew deeper and broader. Ultimately, "each pier would rest on a massive pile of cement and stone," wrote Eiffel Tower historian Joseph Harriss, "set obliquely in the earth so that the curving columns that bore the weight of the tower would exert their thrust at right angles to the mass. Into each excavation was poured a bed of quick-setting cement twenty feet deep to serve as a nonsettling base for the masonry. Over the cement, Eiffel placed enormous blocks of limestone quarried at Souppes-sur-Loing, in central France, an area known for its solid travertine hard-cut stone from Château Landon, the quarry that had provided the stone for the Arc de Triomphe and the Sacré-Coeur basilica. Embedded in the center of each mass were two great anchor bolts twenty-six feet long and four inches in diameter, to which a cylindrical flanged iron shoe was attached; the column would be bolted to the shoe and thus locked into the heart of the stone mass."

On the fifth of May, Gaston Tissandier, founder and editor of *La Nature*, came to visit Eiffel's busy work site on the Left Bank of the Seine. On the river, barges drifted by, and laundry drying on the decks and small children were kept from falling overboard by leash-like ropes. Tissandier, whose frizzy beard was carefully coaxed into two separate points, had been a pioneering aerialist. In 1875 he and two companions had broken ascension records, reaching 28,215 feet in a balloon. He had been lucky, for he only lost his hearing from the lack of oxygen, while his fellow balloonists had both

The Eiffel Tower foundation on April 17, 1887

died. On this spring day, Tissandier was heading in the opposite direction, down below the surface of the earth in one of Eiffel's caissons, where the men were excavating a foundation in the less stable soil by the Seine. "The descent is a strange experience for the uninitiated," wrote Tissandier. "When the chamber is entered, the door is closed, and the air is compressed, producing to the visitor a peculiar sensation on the drum of his ear which a simple act of swallowing at once removes. The trap-door leading to the subterranean caisson is then opened, and the descent is made by the iron ladder. . . . In the caisson the men are at work digging away by the electric light, and filling and sending buckets aloft. The loaded caisson gradually sinks as the earth is cut away inside it, and when it is down to the required depth, it is filled with concrete, and forms an enormous mass of immovable solidity."

Convinced of the historic importance of his tower, Eiffel had engaged the renowned architectural photographer Édouard Durandelle to document its construction. In early April of 1887, Durandelle had arrived for the first time at the dusty work site and set up his bulky camera apparatus to capture the sight of the four foundations emerging from the Champ de Mars. Initially he returned every few days, but he was by no means the only photographer documenting the evolving tower. The fair commissioners had engaged Pierre Petit to follow the building of not just the tower but also the many exposition halls and palaces.

By late June the heavy masonry foundations for the Eiffel Tower's four box piers, or legs, were completed. They included at their tops an incredibly ingenious system of sixteen hydraulic jacks, one to underlie each corner of the four piers that would soon rise. "By means of these," wrote Eiffel, "each pier can be displaced and raised as much as is necessary by inserting steel wedges beneath it." These would be all-important in allowing Eiffel to fine-tune the level of the first platform, which had to be absolutely level, or the whole rest of the tower would not rise straight up.

On July 1 the wrought-iron legs themselves began to take shape, four gigantic, awkward structures whose inward slant at an angle of fifty-four degrees made them look ready to keel over. Durandelle set up his camera so that the Trocadéro was framed by the legs, and returned every few weeks to capture on film the tower's rapid upward progress. Among the crowds of the curious frequenting the tower's construction site was the writer Eugène-Melchior, Vicomte de Vogüé, onetime diplomat assigned to Constantinople, Syria, and the court of the czar. In the last posting, this scholar of Russian had met and married his wife. De Vogüé, handsome and distingué, passed by the tower almost daily in his walks, for he found these fast-rising hulking structures most evocative: "Soon the elephant's four megalithic feet weighed down upon the ground; the principal members sprang forward as cantilevers from the stone shoes, overturning all our ideas about the stability of a construction."

As the gawkers gathered to stare, horse-drawn carriages arrived from Eiffel's workshops three miles away, carrying the precisely designed and numbered sections of girders and trusses. These partially assembled wrought-iron pieces were then lifted by a traveling crane, which transported them to the four workshops at the base of each giant foot. Construction crews at each site used derricks and winches to hoist and then bolt together first the main frames, then the latticework and cross girders. Once Eiffel and his construction managers had determined that the bolted-together feet of the tower were exactly right, twenty gangs of riveters went to work removing the temporary bolts and replacing them with fiery hot permanent rivets. And so the gigantic three-dimensional puzzle began to take shape.

Each morning at dawn, with the sky just turning pink behind the city's famous domes, Eiffel's workers arrived dressed in coarse blue serge work clothes and wearing heavy wooden clogs. Every man knew his task, and one visitor watched in admiration as the "250 workmen came and went in a perfectly orderly way, carrying long beams on their shoulders, climbing up and down through the latticed ironwork with surprising agility. The rapid blows of the riveters could be heard, and they worked with fire that burned with the clear trembling flame of the will-o'-the-wisps." As the day wore on, the crowds of sightseers grew, curious to see how the tower and fair were progressing.

The very preparation of the wrought-iron pieces used in the daily assembly was a complex enterprise. Every piece had to be designed separately, taking into account the variable inclination of columns and braces along every foot of the tower's height. "The position of each," explained *The Atlantic Monthly*, "and the places for its rivets [each hole calculated to within one tenth of a millimeter], had to be decided without error. In the iron plates were drilled 7,000,000 holes, which if placed end to end would form a tube 43 miles long. There were five hundred engineers' designs, and twenty-five hundred leaves of working drawings. It was necessary to employ forty designers and calculators, for a period of about two years. It is thus seen that the iron forms a vast complicated network. . . . The large halls at Levallois-Perret had almost the appearance of a government administration."

The three-ton wrought-iron sections were delivered to the site at a steady pace, and once the legs had become too high to be assembled any longer using the derricks and winches, Eiffel designed tall, steam-powered pivoting cranes that could travel up and down the framework hoisting sections for installation. All who visited the Champ de Mars came away dazzled. "When we approach it," wrote one visitor, "the construction becomes monumental; and when we reach the floor of the colossus, we are lost in wonder at the enormous mass of metal which has been combined with mathematical precision and forms one of the boldest works that the art of engineering ever dared to attempt." The amazement was fitting, for Eiffel's Tower was truly sui generis, a structure like no other. And despite Eiffel's cool certainty that the design of his tower was feasible and completely safe, "there was virtually no experience in structural history from which Eiffel could draw other than a series of high piers that his own firm had designed earlier for railway bridges."

James Gordon Bennett, Jr.

It was as the Eiffel Tower began to take form in the summer of 1887 that James Gordon Bennett began musing about opening a newspaper in Paris. Late at night on the balcony of his Paris apartment, the occasional fiacre passing on the gaslit Champs-Élysées, Bennett had been mulling over the matter when he heard an owl hooting. He took this as a good omen, a signal to proceed, for among his many eccentricities was his utter devotion to the owl, a lucky symbol he viewed as uniquely his.

One story accounting for that talisman had Bennett senior upbraiding his son for not staying at *The Herald* until it went to press: "Young man, your future career depends upon night work on the *Herald,* and eternal vigilance. . . . [T]he owl–bird of Minerva–should be your fetish, and not the eagle or anything else." Others insisted the hooting of an owl had awakened young Bennett when he fell asleep on watch in the navy during the Civil War and saved him from running aground. Whatever the reason, all of Bennett's homes, estates, offices, and yachts featured collections of owls, hundreds of every size and material: stuffed, bronze, wooden, painted, ceramic. Owls also adorned his stationery, coaches, and newspaper masthead.

Within weeks of the persuasive hoot heard from his balcony, Bennett had purchased a small English-language paper, *The Morning News*, started in Paris in 1874 by expatriate Vermonter William Alonzo Hopkins. The city's only other and far older Paris English-language daily, the sclerotic *Galignani's Messenger* (its last moment of journalistic glory being an 1815 report of Napoleon's defeat at Waterloo), had eluded his overtures.

To serve as his Paris editor, Bennett imported the charming and often inebriated Samuel S. Chamberlain, a veteran newspaperman revered on Gotham's Park Row for his reporting triumphs and brilliant editorial sensationalism. The slim, blue-eyed Chamberlain was fastidious, a dandy who favored flowered cravats with his frock coats, a gardenia in his lapel, and a monocle, and who moved with equal ease in Newport mansions or low-rent saloons. From time to time, he plummeted into deepest melancholia and disappeared on epic drunks. "Who but Chamberlain," wondered one journalist, "could go off on a bender, wind up in Amsterdam (Holland), and return to his desk a month later as though he'd stepped out for a cup of coffee?" Bennett and Chamberlain, a well-suited pair of bon vivants, had launched themselves full force into organizing the new European edition of *The Herald*.

On September 3, 1887, as the Eiffel Tower's legs were steadily rising, Bennett issued a one-time-only French-language dummy version of the paper to mark possession of the title *The New York Herald, European edition*. He had hired a primarily English staff, rented space at 5 rue Coq-Héron, and invited the newly hired editors and reporters to his luxurious apartment for a grand luncheon. "I want you fellows to remember that I am the only reader of this paper," lectured Bennett. "I am the only one to be pleased. If I want it to be turned upside down, it must be turned upside down. I consider a dead dog in the rue du Louvre more interesting than a devastating flood in China. I want one feature article a day. If I say the feature is to be Black Beetles, Black Beetles it's going to be."

Bennett also proclaimed the arrival of this new American enterprise by opening a business office at 49 avenue de l'Opéra, at the heart of fashionable Paris and near its most elegant cafés: Café de la Paix and the Grand Café on the boulevard des Capucines, the Café Anglais on the boulevard des Italiens, and the Café de Paris. Here American tourists exhausted from a day's sightseeing could install themselves at a sidewalk table and recover while "watching the never-ending procession of fellow idlers, dandies of the day, journalists and society personalities, and the great ladies of both the *monde* and the *demi-monde* displaying the latest fashions." American visitors could now also drop in at the glass-fronted ground-floor office of *The New York Herald*, announced by huge brass letters. Inside the reception area and reading room, those who signed their names in a registry could look forward to seeing them appear in the Paris edition within a day or two.

Tuesday, October 4, 1887, a day that dawned cold with a lowering gray sky, a classic Parisian morning, was the new paper's official first day. Horse-drawn carriages had fanned out from the printer's shop at rue Coq-Héron, clattering toward the city's kiosks and more elegant hotels. Those passing in the vicinity of the Eiffel Tower could see its four slanted legs heading steadily skyward—almost ninety feet high now. In such favorite American hotels as The Grand ("The best cuisine and best wines in Paris . . . large addition to the personnel . . . No more complaints of service") many an American tourist was no doubt pleasantly surprised—and puzzled—to awake and find *The New York Herald* on his or her breakfast tray. Below the masthead was the explanation: "European edition—Paris." The price was listed as ten centimes. To the far left was the notation "Whole No. 18,670." The cognoscenti knew this marked the number of issues put out since Bennett the Elder had set up fifty-two years earlier in a basement with two barrels and a plank for a desk.

This first four-page Paris issue had arrived with neither fanfare nor formal announcement, only plenty of news, leading with "The New York Letter" ("The Anarchists were kicked out of the Labor Convention by Mr. Henry George") and moving on to such lesser matters as New York Yacht Club notices, and a roll call of notable visitors to Gotham. A separate story ("By commercial cable to *The Herald*") described President Cleveland's visit to Terre Haute (where a man clung dangerously to his carriage) and detailed the presidential travel itinerary for the rest of the month. Wall Street, the London stock market, and La Bourse were thoroughly covered on the front page, with Bennett hinting that Jay Gould was toying with the market "so that certain somebodies might get rid of their other stocks."

Also on the front page was news of the Vatican, a report that the Sultan of Morocco was very ill, and a short Paris piece titled "An enjoyable evening at the American Church," which listed every singer and pianist who had entertained. Bennett was convinced, as would be the editor of any local newspaper, that people loved to see the names of people they knew, especially themselves. From this debut issue on, page 2 was devoted to the haut monde of which Bennett was such an active member, specifically the restless comings and goings of this mobile new moneyed class ("Mr. William K. Vanderbilt will return from London to the Bristol on Wednesday") or their extravagances ("Joe Andrews, the San Francisco diamond collector, wears a $15,000 cluster of diamonds on his necktie"). And there, under the headline "American Visitors," were the names of thirty-two Americans (and their temporary abodes) who had registered at *The Herald*'s rue de l'Opéra office.

Two days later, when a reader had written to the editor perplexed by the lack of any introduction, Bennett had responded in his usual peremptory way: "This is not a new newspaper. *The Herald* is over a half century old. The fact that we have chosen to publish a European edition is a detail. We do not, moreover, believe in buncombe articles about 'long felt needs' and

The Eiffel Tower on December 7, 1887

telling what one intends to do, and what not to do. A good newspaper speaks for itself." While James Gordon Bennett viewed his core readership as the expatriate American colonies in permanent residence across the Continent, as well as the many wealthy American tourists and travelers floating about from Paris to Rome to Étretat to Carlsbad, he also intended to attract Europeans by reporting all manner of court news and the travels of European aristocracy and their followers. And so, Monsieur Gordon-Bennett and his new Paris edition began gearing up for the wave of visitors coming for the World's Fair.

By mid-October 1887, the Eiffel Tower's four inclined box pier legs had reached a height of 92 feet, and Eiffel had constructed a supporting system of scaffolds so they would not fall over as they rose farther, to 180 feet, the underside of the first platform. The legs rested not against the actual wooden scaffold, but against sand boxes that would play a crucial role—along with the sixteen hydraulic jacks down under the four legs—in the all-important alignment of the four piers.

Then another nervous neighbor filed suit, and the work was halted. After all, every French citizen of the late nineteenth century was all too familiar with such industrial disasters as the Tay Bridge collapse. Who was to say this monstrous set of metal girders would not come crashing down on them all at the first punishing wind? In fact, a French professor of mathematics "predicted flatly that if the structure ever reached the height of 748 feet, it would ineluctably collapse." Eiffel, pressed for time, agreed once again to accept liability, as well as the cost of demolition if the tower proved impossible to complete.

In November of 1887, Gustave Eiffel was surprised to hear from Ferdinand de Lesseps, the builder of the Suez Canal and president of the company now constructing the sea-level Panama Canal. "I had never believed in a sea-level canal," explained Eiffel, "and I was one of the few who voted against it at the meeting in 1879 at the Geographic Society. Monsieur Ferdinand de Lesseps had never forgotten that vote over the years. Still, I had followed the work on the canal closely." Since 1881 some eight hundred thousand ordinary Frenchmen and women had bought shares of stock in de Lesseps's Panama company, believing the national hero's assurances that, yes, there had been delays, but all in good time the Panama Canal would be finished and open, to the greater glory of France and their bank accounts. There had in fact been setbacks, troubles, and disquieting reports that the sea-level canal was a disastrous folly, which resulted in the constantly falling value of Panama Canal stock. De Lesseps had gone back into the bond markets again and again, but so much money was being wasted on a plan that was technically doomed that he always needed more. Now he began to pull all possible political strings to have the government bail him out via a state lottery.

By the time he contacted Eiffel, de Lesseps had finally admitted that his sea-level plan was a botch. "I was visited by Baron de Reinbach," said Eiffel, "who proposed I enter into negotiations with the company. Monsieur Ferdinand de Lesseps called for my help in terms that touched me." Eiffel spent several weeks mulling over de Lesseps's flattering proposal that he, Eiffel, should rescue the canal by designing and building a system of locks. "Oh, I hesitated. I hesitated a long time," admitted Eiffel later. But in mid-November 1887, unable to resist the appeals to his patriotism and pride, nor the opportunity to show France leading the world, Eiffel reluctantly agreed to bail out de Lesseps. He took over as the general contractor in Panama, plunging ahead with a new $25 million "gigantic ten-lock liquid staircase." By January of 1888, Eiffel's firm arrived in Panama, and work began.

In Paris, the first icy days of 1888 found Gustave Eiffel supervising the installation of a second huge scaffold on the Eiffel Tower to hold in place the four separate piers that would join into one giant square frame—the tower's first floor—as the four legs (or piers) rose and pressed down. Once joined together atop the piers, this four-section frame would also provide support for the iron girders and trusswork that would encircle and unite the four piers, a thick metal belt. This would constitute the first platform, the all-important foundation for the rest of the tower. However, Parisians, used to seeing the tower growing in height almost daily, now assumed the worst. The popular daily *Le Matin* declared in a headline, "The Tower Is Sinking," and urged that all "building should stop and sections already built should be demolished as quickly as possible."

As Eiffel began the months-long process of completing and aligning the first platform, he faced the critical question of whether the twenty-five-foot-deep trusswork and girders that were to belt together the four piers into a solid base could do that and still maintain an absolutely horizontal platform. The tower's four legs each had four corner columns, and each of those sixteen columns had to meet the belt at precisely the right height and at exactly the predetermined spots where the rivet holes had been bored, or the first platform would be slightly and fatally askew. In that case, the remaining eight hundred feet of the tower could not be safely built atop it. Eiffel and his men began with amazing finesse to install the girders and trusswork. By March they were minutely calibrating the four piers, each weighing 440 tons. "If a column was found to be too high by even a fraction of an inch, the plug could be pulled and the fine sand allowed to run out until the piston—and the column—was lowered to the correct position," wrote Eiffel Tower historian Harriss. "If, on the other hand, a column was too low, the jack beside the cylinder could be operated to push the column back to the proper angle. If simplicity of conception and economy of means are signs of genius, it is such touches that define Eiffel."

A reporter for *L'Illustration* dropped by the construction site at the beginning of March and came away deeply impressed. "Despite all the snow-falls and exceptionally cold temperatures of this winter, the workers at the Eiffel Tower have never eased up on their work. As of now, the tower has reached 197 feet." He watched the riveting operation in fascination. "Each team has four workers and a portable forge. A kid called the 'deck boy' is in charge of fanning the forge; he carries the rivet heated to a white heat to the worker known as the 'keeper of things,' who drives the rivet into the holes by pounding on the rivet's head. On the other side, another worker strikes, smashing the emerging rivet swiftly to begin forming a second head; the fourth man, known as the striker, finishes up the second rivet head with a snap rivet that he pounds into place with a sledge hammer weighing 13 pounds.

"At this time there are twenty teams of riveters all going strong."

On March 26, 1888, Eiffel and his engineers once again measured the first platform. It was absolutely perfectly horizontal. He would later write, "Joined by a belt of girders, the piers formed a solid table with a wide base. The sight of it alone was enough to brush aside any fears of its overturning. We no longer had to worry about a major accident, and any minor ones that might occur now could not compromise completion of the structure."

However, Eiffel still faced an entirely different but unsolved challenge of utmost importance: the elevators, a "very complex, intricate problem, full of danger and uncertainty." As no one had ever erected a tower of one thousand feet, no one had any experience with building elevators to reach such heights. If the crowds could not ascend safely and swiftly up the Eiffel Tower, what sort of attraction would it be?

The Eiffel Tower with the first platform finished

CHAPTER THREE

Troubles on the Tower

Was there any place quite so delightful as Paris in the spring, when the chestnut trees bloomed a frothy pink, the fountains in the formal parks burbled to life, and the flâneurs strolled the boulevards, twirling their canes and tipping their silk top hats to ladies in passing fiacres? Out and about on the city's bustling sidewalks, "the oyster peddler tosses shells at our legs, the distributor of broadsheets bars the passage, the perambulating salesman draws a crowd ideal for pickpockets; deprived of the sidewalk, we must hop quickly into the street, where the omnibus waits to run over us, if we have, happily, escaped the carriage." Mark Twain had reveled in Paris street life: "so frisky, so affable, so fearfully and wonderfully Frenchy! . . . Two hundred people sat at little tables on the sidewalk, sipping wine and coffee; the streets were thronged with light vehicles and joyous pleasure-seekers; there was music in the air, life and action all about us."

By May of 1888, some of those cheerful Parisian crowds had taken to enjoying the warmer days by drifting over to the Champ de Mars, drawn by the never-ending spectacle of the Eiffel Tower under construction. "M. Eiffel's Tower of Babel is rising steadily," reported the Paris correspondent for London's *Daily Telegraph*, "and the enormous mass of iron which the constructors have already piled up against the clouds is the amazement of everybody. When you stand at the base of the gigantic monument and look up to the skies through a colossal spider's web of red metal the whole thing strikes you as being one of the most daring attempts since Biblical days." Inevitably, when the weather was favorable, the photographers would be out taking yet more pictures of the already famous structure, their sequential images documenting the tower's rapid rise.

Each morning, soon after the workmen arrived, the rapid blows of the riveters could be heard, and on gray or foggy days the flames of the forges could be seen flickering red and orange in the upper reaches of the tower. "The four cranes—one for each pillar—which brought up the pieces for this vast metallic framework one by one, stood out against the sky with their great arms at the four corners of this lofty site."

Eiffel's two years of planning were now paying off. "Each piece [of the tower] had to be designed separately, taking into account the variable inclination of columns and braces along every foot of the tower's height. In addition, every rivet hole had to be drawn in at precisely the right spot, so that all the on-site workers would have to do was to place one-third of 2.5 million rivets, the rest being placed at the shops in advance . . . all calculations had to be accurate to one-tenth of a millimeter."

As soon as Eiffel had his all-important first platform balanced, he opened a canteen there to serve food and save his men the time and trouble of clambering up and down for coffee or a meal. Now on lovely spring days at noon his men had their lunch up in the open air and breezes. Here, "a chunk of coarse bread serves as the *pièce de résistance* to a toothsome bit of boiled meat, or a spoonful of mutton gravy, or an artichoke, or a trifle of chicory salad." This system also enabled Eiffel to make sure that no worker drank too much wine, thus becoming a danger to himself and others. Pay increased along with the height of the tower, ranging from eight cents an hour for unskilled labor to fourteen cents an hour for most skilled. The construction pace was relentless.

As May turned to June, the weather in Paris became far hotter than normal. July brought sweltering days, with the temperatures sometimes nearing one hundred. Although Eiffel had equipped the tower with lightning rods—twenty-inch-wide cast-iron pipes for each pier, buried sixty feet deep and rising up through the wrought-iron girders above the top portion of work—thunderstorms not infrequently swept in and forced the men working on the tower to scramble down to safety. When the lightning passed on, work resumed and continued until it was too dark to see. There could be no days off.

Some complained that Eiffel's huge metal edifice had changed the city's climate, generating the strange lingering heat and thunderstorms.

James Gordon Bennett, Jr., always obsessed with the weather, concurred, and *The Herald* asserted, "People who have watched the tower closely and attentively have remarked the large quantities of heavy rain and thunderclouds which gather round it and then, as if deprived by the lightning conductors of part of their electricity, are blown farther on and break in showers in quite another part of town."

While the originality and sheer size of the Eiffel Tower, the continuing aesthetic controversy, and its swift progress up to the heavens all made it the center of attention, the rest of the fair buildings were advancing smartly, too. Jennie June, a writer for *Godey's Lady's Book* who was spending a month in Paris that summer, reported, "Paris is making great preparations for the great Exhibition which is to take place next year." Dressed for the warm weather in a light cotton gown and one of the large straw hats that were all the fashion, Miss June had obtained special entry into the fairgrounds to stroll about the construction sites, and wrote, "The miles of main buildings have their great spaces already nearly all enclosed with [nine-foot panels of] pale green glass, a third of an inch in thickness . . . which give a lovely light. . . . The grounds are being laid out, turfed and planted; great trees have been transplanted, and vines already cover some of their trunks." That instant greenery was a welcome counterpoint to the dust, noise, and heat.

The 1889 Exposition Universelle was to be laid out in three distinct areas. The Eiffel Tower would dominate the first and most important one, the Champ de Mars on the Left Bank, and act as the grand entry arch from the Pont d'Iéna for those coming across the Seine from the Right Bank and the Trocadéro Palace (designed for the Exposition of 1878 by Gabriel Davioud). The Eiffel Tower stood at one end of the large Court of Honor park, while the under-construction Central Dome occupied the other. Flanking the court were rising twin buildings, one to hold all the painting and Fine Arts exhibits, the other to showcase the Liberal Arts. Behind the Central Dome, workers were busy erecting the gigantic Galerie des Machines. Nearby, some smaller South American pavilions of great charm were under construction, as was Baron Delart's re-creation of a Cairo street.

The fair's second area, a narrow strip along the river Seine on the Quai

d'Orsay intended for various agricultural pavilions, would serve to connect
the Champ de Mars area with the other large part of the fair, the esplanade
of the Hôtel des Invalides. Here fairgoers would find yet more agricultural
exhibits, the Ministry of War pavilion, and the exotic French colonial pavilions, featuring working native villages from Senegal, the Congo, and
Indochina. A special little fair railroad—the Decauville railroad—would
trundle along the perimeter between the many acres of the Champ de
Mars and the Esplanade des Invalides, making merely getting around not
just easier but another adventure.

Everyone had an opinion about the Eiffel Tower, and Miss June, having
now seen it up close, declared herself an admirer, writing, "it will be, when
completed, a marvel of beauty, harmony, grace, and proportion, consider-
ing its height and the strength necessary to sustain it. . . . The apparent size
increases enormously as you approach the arch, and, looking up from the
great spaces of the interior, already the workmen upon the upper sides of
the building look like specks, although the building has reached only a
third of its height."

Gustave Eiffel was pleased with the tower's rapid progress, and by July
4, 1888, was ready to welcome and woo eighty of Paris's most influential
journalists at a summer banquet to be served on the tower's first platform.
Eiffel, in a formal frock coat suit and best silk top hat, awaited his guests at
the base. Almost to a man, the writers whose words informed France on
politics, science, letters, and art appeared for their fête-in-the-sky wearing
similar outfits. A few sartorial upstarts wore dove-gray trousers, while the
more prudent brandished furled umbrellas, prepared for the possibility of
rain. They set off up the stairs amid much chattering, exclamations over the
gigantic girders creating the latticework, and high spirits at being among the
first to ascend the tower. Long trestle tables had been laid out for their meal,
230 feet up in the sky. High above their heads, the press could see and hear
workmen riveting together the half-finished second platform. In recent
weeks, the Eiffel Tower had become the tallest structure in Paris, rising
above the towers of Notre Dame, at 217 feet, the Pantheon, at 260 feet, and
the dome of Les Invalides, heretofore the city's highest monument at 344
feet.

From the first platform, the journalists gazed upon a city very different
from the Paris where the Bastille had been stormed ninety-nine years earlier.

From 1853 to 1870, Emperor Napoleon Bonaparte III and Baron Georges-Eugène Haussmann had dramatically remade the French capital, creating a modern monumental urban center arranged around new thoroughfares, squares, boulevards, theaters, and railroad stations. Haussmann's bold vision included clearing space around public monuments, establishing elegant small public gardens, and opening up and landscaping the large parks, with all the greenery and color serving to freshen and redefine the city. As part of its makeover, Paris had been subdivided into twenty arrondissements, each with its own town hall, schools, improved sanitation, and central food market. "On the Left Bank, the boulevard Saint-Germain was opened up; on the right, the older boulevards were widened. All were planted with trees, equipped with wide asphalt pedestrian sidewalks, and lined with monumental buildings. . . . The new life generated by the Haussmannian city could be seen everywhere, all along the open streets and boulevards." The city's population had by now doubled, to more than two million.

The journalists there that day savored being among the very first to see Paris from such a height, and then sat down to their festive lunch. As the meal progressed, Eiffel the proud builder arose, champagne glass in hand, and toasted his tower, saying, "The beginning was difficult, and criticism as passionate as it was premature was addressed to me. I faced the storm as best I could, thanks to the constant support of M. Lockroy . . . and I strove by the steady progress of the work to conciliate, if not the opinion of the artists, at least that of engineers and scientific men. I desired to show, in spite of my personal insignificance, that France continued to hold a foremost place in the art of iron construction."

He was, he declared, heartened by "the interest which [the tower] inspires, abroad as well as at home," and hoped it would be "a triumphal arch as striking as those which earlier generations have raised to honor conquerors." The eighty journalists present joined in the toast and, after lunch, clustered round and posed for a photograph amid the girders with their famous host. To Eiffel's left, exuding importance, sat the Buddhaesque Francisque Sarcey, for thirty years now the nation's most feared theater critic, absorbing this particular drama for *Le Temps*.

Back in the spring, Eiffel had begun cultivating the goodwill of select journalists, starting with one of his more vociferous critics, *Le Figaro*'s

powerful founder and editor, Albert Wolff. Hosting this journalistic émi-
nence grise to breakfast atop the recently completed first platform had had a
most salutary effect, to the degree that the Paris correspondent for *The New
York Times*, no fan of the tower, found himself disappointed and startled to
read Wolff waxing rhapsodic in *Le Figaro* about the *Tour en Fer* with phrases
such as "a grandiose marvel as it rises majestically in the air," "the audacity
of its conception, the mathematical precision of its execution," and "at once
graceful and imposing, having naught in common with that tower of Babel,
which, if it ever did exist, rose no higher than a fifth-story window."

Monsieur Wolff, with his well-honed journalist's sense for news, had
joined those who believed the Eiffel Tower would be the sensation of the
fair. And shrewd editor that he was, he had quietly made a deal with Eiffel
that would promote both enterprises: *Le Figaro* would be the envy of every
other paper in Paris by having an actual (albeit tiny) editorial office and
printing press on the tower's second floor, producing a special daily paper,
Le Figaro de la Tour, concerned only with the doings upon the Eiffel Tower
and at the fair.

Of course, that did not stop *Le Figaro* from publishing mocking attacks
by high-profile critics such as poet François Coppée, who in mid-July entertained the paper's readers with thirty mean-spirited verses:

> I visited the enormous Eiffel Tower,
> That iron mast with hard rigging.
> Unfinished, confused, deformed,
> The iron monstrosity is hideous up close
> A giant, without beauty or style
> It is really a metal idol,
> Symbol of useless force
> A triumph of brute reality.

And so it went, verse after verse, concluding with:

> And here is the great thought,
> The real goal, the profound point:
> –This ridiculous pyramid
> We will go up it for a hundred cents.

Presumably Eiffel, though still sensitive to such slights, was too busy to brood for long. All Paris knew that if the tower was to be open ten months hence, time was of the essence. By mid-July, Eiffel's men had completed the second platform, at a height of 387 feet. On July 14, Bastille Day, to celebrate his steady progress, Eiffel set off a fantastic fireworks display from the new apex. All around and above the tower, the night sky burst into exploding lights of many brilliant hues and shapes, all cascading down from the heavens.

At 3:00 a.m. on June 12, 1888, back in Orange, New Jersey, Thomas Edison was in his laboratory catching up on correspondence. He had been extremely busy working out the myriad problems of perfecting his improved phonograph in order to have it ready for the Paris World's Fair, while at the same time overseeing the building of his various electric companies. A fortnight earlier, in the midst of this most intense period of his inventing and business career, his lovely second wife, Mina, had had their first child. The baby girl, named Madeleine, was the fourth of Edison's offspring, for he already had three adolescent children by his deceased first wife.

Edison was writing to Col. George Gouraud, the bluff and hardy American entrepreneur who had befriended him back in 1873 when the young, struggling inventor had visited London on business. Gouraud, a decorated veteran of the Civil War now long resident in England, had first gone there to promote the Pullman Palace Car. Over the years, Gouraud had so often served as an Edison partner and promoter that he had named his West Surrey estate "Little Menlo," after Edison's Menlo Park Laboratory. Edison had naturally engaged Gouraud as his European partner and representative for the phonograph. Wrote Edison that morning:

Friend Gouraud:

This is my first mailing phonogram. It will go to you in the regular U.S. mail via North German Lloyd steamer *Eider*. I send you by Mr. Hamilton a new phonograph, the first one of the new model which has just left my hands.

It has been put together very hurriedly and is not finished, as you will see. . . .

Mrs. Edison and the baby are doing well. The baby's articulation is quite loud enough but a trifle indistinct; it can be improved but it is not bad for a first experiment.

With kind regards,

Yours, EDISON

Because Parisians were well aware that Eiffel was racing to make his deadline, they were perplexed when the month of August 1888 came and went with no visible progress beyond the second platform. Rumors started to swirl, with some saying that Eiffel had gone mad under the strain, others that he had simply given up. When those tastemakers who had been *en vacances* at their châteaux in the countryside or villas by the sea returned in September, they, too, were quite surprised to find the tower little taller than when they had decamped in late summer. "Rumors were afloat," reported *The New York Times*, "that M. Eiffel was at a loss how to construct the remainder of his gigantic structure. . . . The difficulty seems to have been the conveyance of the material up to [the second floor], but now it is stated that everything is ready for continuing work."

By mid-September, the necessary cranes and winches had indeed been set up, Eiffel's workmen were busy, and the tower was again visibly rising toward the heavens. Pay also rose, to ten cents and sixteen cents an hour. But even as the workers once again began assembling the final six hundred feet of the tower, the slender spire, they were restless and unhappy. The autumn chill presaged more bitterly cold weather, and fewer daylight working hours meant weekly pay would soon shrink. The previous winter, working outside atop the tower had been grueling. Biting winds gusted so strongly they threatened some days to send a man plunging overboard, while clinging cold fogs and debilitating hoarfrosts all exacerbated the coldness of the iron itself. "There was snow," recalled one worker, "and the frost froze our cheeks and fingers. I can tell you it was not easy. And there was not a minute, not a minute to take it easy at this work." Some men had complained in early 1888 to the City of Paris about their wages, denouncing Eiffel as an exploiter of labor. Now, as the days shortened and the air grew chilly, the workers' discontent festered.

On September 19, days after construction had recommenced, Eiffel's men rebelled. Well aware that time, deadlines, and the unfinished tower favored their cause, the disgruntled laborers confronted Gustave Eiffel, laid out their grievances, and demanded a four-cent-an-hour pay raise. Eiffel countered with a lower offer. With that, the men descended the tower and went on strike. Eiffel, desperate to avoid any delay, bargained for the next three days, finally agreeing to a compromise whereby the men would get their four-cent raise, but one phased in over a period of four months. He would also supply the work crews with sheepskin clothing, waterproof garments for protection against the coming winter, and hot wine. Eiffel heaved a sigh of relief as he watched his crew return to work and set to, their heavy sledgehammers ringing out the familiar rhythms of pounding in rivets, hour after hour. Once again the tower began to rise, looking more graceful with each passing week.

The Vicomte de Vogüé, a regular observer in his daily constitutional along the Seine, marveled at it all: "After the second platform, the slender column rose rapidly into space. Yet, you could not really see the construction work. The autumn fogs often hid the aerial work-place; though in the twilight of late-winter afternoons, you could see the red fires of the forges up in the sky and hear the hammers hitting the iron fittings. This was what was so striking—you almost never saw the workers on the tower; the tower appeared to grow all by itself, as if by the spell of a genie. The great works of ancient times, like the pyramids for example, are linked in our minds with the idea of great multitudes, weighing down on the levers and struggling with huge ropes; this modern pyramid was being raised up by the power of calculations requiring a very few number of hands, for today the necessary force for construction rests in a thought."

With Christmas approaching, and the tower nearing its halfway mark, labor trouble erupted yet again. On December 20, one of the men complained that he had worked ten hours but had been paid for only nine. A group again confronted Eiffel, agitating for further raises, citing the unprecedented heights they would be scaling and working at from here on in. Eiffel did not see the logic: "The professional risks remained the same; whether a man fell from 40 meters or 300 meters, the result was the same—certain death." More important, he worried that if he capitulated now, it would only encourage further strikes at critical moments. "To show them that I was guided far less by financial considerations than by my wish

The Eiffel Tower on December 26, 1888

to see the success of the work begun," he said, "I promised that a bonus of 100 francs would be granted to all construction workers who continued working until the flag was raised." Then he threw down the gauntlet. "All those who were not present at midday the following day would be dismissed and replaced by new workers."

The next day, December 21, almost all his men were present and working when the midday deadline arrived. The few out on strike were fired, and those who replaced them, says Eiffel, "went up to 200 meters straightaway, and after half a day were able to perform the same tasks as the old ones. Thus, it was proved that with the proper equipment a good construction worker can work at any height without feeling unwell." Eiffel had no personal experience with vertigo and had never observed it among workmen on his bridges. "Were those workmen specially trained?" he asked. "Not in the least, they were for the most part simple peasants accustomed to working at great heights. . . . [O]n the tower the men will not work swinging in the air as they did on the viaducts I mentioned; they will be on a platform. . . . In every way you see these fears are chimerical."

Eiffel then assigned those who had not gone on strike—but who had complained about the prospect of working at ever greater heights—to install the lacy decorative arches on the first level. "Their workmates laughed at them, calling them the *indispensables*, and soon afterwards they left." The work proceeded quickly, with the workmen in their sheepskins arriving in the freezing, cold dawn, ascending the icy tower, warming up at the forges, and then putting in a long, frigid day.

As the year 1888 ended, Gustave Eiffel could doubly rejoice. First, he had resolved his labor troubles. Second, and far more exciting, the Eiffel Tower had grown to surpass in height the tallest edifice in the world, the 555-foot-tall Washington Monument, in Washington, D.C., a structure that took almost forty years to build. Completed in 1884, the American monument had suffered from an inadequate initial foundation resulting in tilting that required costly fixing. One could easily forgive Eiffel's Gallic pride as he crowed about his triumph over "the Americans, [who] in spite of their enterprising spirit and the national enthusiasm excited by [erecting a still-taller structure than the Washington Monument], shrank from its execution."

The Americans, for their part, did not bother to conceal their chagrin,

ungraciously mocking the monumental Eiffel Tower as "a useless structure" and comparing it unfavorably to "the Washington shaft at Washington, D.C., which is, after all, more artistic than the Eiffel Tower. . . . If [the
Eiffel Tower's] great height does not make the shaft appear too spindling
and if the top has been designed with some attempt at art the result may
not be so dreadful as it was supposed." In truth, the higher the Eiffel Tower
rose, the more elegant it appeared, mollifying many of its most vehement
early critics. A correspondent for *The New York Times* conceded that the
half-completed tower was a grandiose marvel but, in a bout of sour grapes,
doubted whether it would be a success: "The public may go up to its summit
occasionally, but having once gazed . . . said public will go where it can find
things more interesting."

Ah, but how exactly would those curious hordes ascend to the top?
Even as Eiffel was delighting in his tower in the sky, there remained the
truly grave problem of the elevators (as Bourdais had ungraciously pointed
out). Eiffel, an artist in the use of iron, had refused to take the easy route
of simply having an elevator rise straight up through the center of what he
rightly viewed as his magnum opus, marring the uncluttered simplicity of
the tower's elegant profile. Instead, two elevators would ascend to the first
floor via the gently curving legs, and two would rise to the second floor via
the far more curved upper legs. A third elevator would rise from the second
platform of the tower to the pinnacle.

Back in the spring of 1888, James Whistler had written a chastising letter to
art collector Henry S. Theobald after he declined to loan one of his Whistler works to a show: "Your role herein, as the 'patron,'" instructed The
Butterfly, "certainly is that of the man who, owning some of the works of
the Master, takes every occasion of spreading his fame by showing them,
and is pleased and proud to do so. . . . [N]ext year, when the great International Exhibition takes place, do not the cruelty to me, and to yourself the
injustice, of proposing to hold back these dainty pictures that should take
their part before my confreres in the chapter of my work."

Not long after, Whistler had traveled to Paris to attend a Paul Durand-
Ruel exhibition that featured a half dozen of his, Whistler's, artworks.
While there he wrote in French to Comte Robert de Montesquiou-Fezensac,
a recent acquaintance, "I am burning with desire to see your beautiful

things and I have a plan which I should like to discuss with you. So do come and lunch with me." Whistler hoped that when the count saw his paintings and etchings at Durand-Ruel, he would agree to let Whistler paint his portrait. Montesquiou-Fezensac was one of Belle Époque Paris's legendary personages, an aesthete, dandy, Symbolist poet, and connoisseur who "cultivated upward-pointed mustaches, improved his complexion with make-up and spent much of each day with his tailor, hairdresser and manicurist." Yet he was also a wit and brilliant intellectual who "knew everyone in Paris worth knowing." De Montesquiou (and his jewel-encrusted pet turtle) had already been immortalized in J. K. Huysmans's novel *À Rebours*.

James McNeill Whistler

The count was also renowned for transforming the attic in his family's mansion with a novel interior décor that combined *Arabian Nights* and spare *Japonaise* style: "The room of all shades of red . . . the grey room where all was grey and for which he used to ransack Paris weekly to find grey flowers; the bedroom where a black dragon was apparently waddling away with the bed on his back. . . . It was all queer, disturbing, baroque, yet individual and even beautiful . . . a tiny fairy palace." Wandering through these refined spaces was the famous turtle gilded with jewels. As Whistler had dubbed himself The Butterfly, so Montesquiou-Fezensac had adopted the sobriquet and emblem of The Bat. The two soon became fast friends.

Whistler went on to have a typically eventful summer. Early in June he had quarreled with his friend, the poet Algernon Swinburne, who had, at Whistler's request, penned a review of a new Whistler venture: giving a formal lecture. The artist had judged Swinburne's review of his *Ten O'Clock* lecture insufficiently adulatory and dispatched one of his signature waspish letters.

Far more momentous and surprising had been his spur-of-the-moment marriage, on August 11, 1888, to Beatrix Godwin, formidable recent widow of an old architect friend. Whistler's friends had been as stunned as his public. "The Butterfly chained at last!" declared the London papers. Whistler thus broke the heart of his model and mistress of fourteen years, the beautiful red-haired Maud Franklin, who had long called herself Mrs. Whistler. With many of Whistler's old friends furious at his caddish desertion, the newlyweds decided it was a propitious moment to decamp to France on a leisurely honeymoon.

Late that September, Buffalo Bill's Wild West had concluded its lucrative sojourn on Staten Island and then headed south for a final run in Richmond. Before all the Indians dispersed home, Buffalo Bill escorted seventy-five of them to Washington, D.C., to see the House and Senate in action. They even dropped in at the Bureau of Indian Affairs to smoke a peace pipe. At the White House, President Grover Cleveland hosted a special reception in the East Room for Colonel Cody, famed for his exploits as a frontier military scout, and his more eminent Indians, solemn and resplendent in their feathered headdresses and beaded finery.

Financially flush, Buffalo Bill had then departed the capital in a blaze of glory, passing through Chicago on the train en route to his house out on the prairie, Scout's Rest Ranch, in North Platte, Nebraska. He had reunited with his beloved younger sister, Julia, and her husband, Al, who had helped build, furnish, and run the whole palatial enterprise while Cody gallivanted about trying to earn one final vast fortune. Buffalo Bill, a world-class convivial drinker, had instructed Al two years earlier: "I want a side board in the house someplace, probably just as well in my bedroom up stairs, with some nice decanters & glasses. I don't propose to make a barroom out of your home, but must have a side board. All we big dogs have a side board."

Once home in North Platte, Cody had confided that he would be taking the Wild West show to the Paris World's Fair in the upcoming year. He also engaged in his usual squabbling with his wife, Louisa, a.k.a. Lulu, about money, his philandering, and her bad temper. Some years back, Cody had discovered that "Lulu has got most if not all of our North Platte property in her name. . . . Aint that a nice way for a wife to act? . . . I don't care a snap about money but the way she has treated me." Ever since, he had had bouts of threatening divorce, making their children unhappy, but by November of 1888 he was preoccupied with organizing a hunt for Lords de Clifford and Mandeville and a handful of British nobles about to arrive at the ranch. With Buffalo Bill leading the way, they had ridden off into the southern wilderness, intending to amble through northern Mexico before traversing the Sierra Madres en route to Senator William Hearst's magnificent California ranch overlooking the vastness of the Pacific Ocean.

Annie Oakley was back on the East Coast by late 1888, trying her hand at a whole new theatrical venture, playing the star role in *Deadwood Dick: or the Sunbeam of the Sierras.* This western melodrama featured Oakley (the Sunbeam) shooting apple-sized glass balls with "unerring aim . . . leaving a houseful of smoke . . . and an astonished audience." Such were the "desperate situations and howling climaxes" played out in the theater that at the end of three acts twenty-five characters were dead. In later years, Oakley wrote of this play and of her brief foray into theater: "I never quite understood just why the press abstained from vegetable throwing but they threw not one carrot."

When not on the stage, Oakley was often busy taking part in high-stakes shooting matches, notices of which she carefully clipped for her scrapbook. On September 26, 1888: "Annie Oakley defeats John Lavett. Miss Oakley appeared in a short skirt and otherwise jauntily attired. Twenty-five birds each were liberated at 31 yards. Mr. Lavett scored 21, while his fair opponent scored 23. She broke all records." On October 5, 1888: "Annie Oakley defeated Miles Johnson, the champion of New Jersey, in a match of 50 live pigeons. Thirty-one thousand people saw, or tried to see, this match. The traps had to be moved farther out three times as the vast overflow from the grandstand closed in."

Paul Gauguin had finally made his way to Arles in Provence in late October 1888, settling in to paint with Vincent van Gogh, whose brother, Theo, was providing both men with monthly stipends. Vincent had rented and furnished a yellow house for them on the Place Lamartine, near the train station, and had covered the walls with his new paintings. On warm fall days the two men worked *en plein air*, and Gauguin, freed of money woes for the moment, wrote contentedly to Émile Bernard in Pont-Aven, "It's strange, but Vincent sees opportunities here for painting in the style of Daumier, whereas I see in terms of colored Puvis [de Chavannes], mixed with Japanese style."

Theo van Gogh hoped that the presence of a fellow painter would alleviate Vincent's dark moods and loneliness. As young men, the two brothers had both entered the art trade. Although he had health problems, Theo had flourished, but Vincent had been fired in 1876, creating a family crisis. What would he do? First he considered university, but then decided to try preaching. He found a position in an impoverished mining district in southern France, but after only a year, the Protestant minister there and many of the villagers had concluded that Vincent was mad, and they wanted him gone. In the wake of this second failure, Vincent found his own salvation in art. For two years, he and Theo lived together in Paris before Vincent struck out for the more rustic ambiance of Arles. Theo believed that his brother had real talent as a painter. "It is amazing the number of things he knows and what a clear view he has of the world, this is why I am sure he will make a name for himself. I have gotten to know many painters through him as he is very well thought of in their circles. He is one of the champions of the new ideas."

Gauguin exulted that his lot was finally improving. Theo had sold a number of his paintings for good prices, including one to artist Edgar Degas, whom Gauguin much admired. In Arles, he and Vincent developed a productive routine, which included regular "hygienic" visits to the local brothels. By late November, Gauguin had dispatched four good paintings to Theo's gallery. Next, an avant-garde group in Brussels, Les XX, had invited him to be in a show. Ebullient, Gauguin wrote painter Émile Schuffenecker ("Schuff"), "You can ask Pissarro if I am not talented. Personal hygiene and regular sex, together with work, are all a man needs to pull through."

But by early December, Gauguin's mood had soured. "I feel completely disoriented in Arles," he wrote Bernard. "I find everything so small and mean, both the landscape and the people. In general, Vincent and I do not see eye to eye, particularly on painting. He admires Daumier, Daubigny, Ziem and the great [Théodore] Rousseau, all of whom I cannot bear. And he hates Ingres, Raphael, Degas, all of whom I admire. I reply, 'Corporal, you're right,' just to get a bit of peace. He likes my pictures very much, but when I'm painting them he criticizes me for this and for that. He's a romantic, while I am more of a primitive."

Gauguin feared that if he left Arles too abruptly Theo might drop him as a client. But on December 12, as Vincent's behavior became stranger and even hostile, Gauguin advised Theo, "All things considered, I find myself compelled to return to Paris. Vincent and I find it absolutely impossible to live peacefully in each other's company; our temperaments are incompatible and we both need peace and quiet in order to work. He is a remarkable man of great intelligence. . . . I appreciate the thoughtful way in which you have behaved towards me and beg you to excuse my decision."

By December 20, Gauguin had calmed down, writing to Theo, "Please consider my journey to Paris as something imaginary and thus the letter I wrote to you as a bad dream. . . . I felt increasingly nostalgic for the West Indies, so of course as soon as I have sold a few things I shall be going there." Meanwhile, he informed Theo that he had sent an offering, "a portrait of your brother on a size 30 canvas . . . [with] the theme *The painter of sunflowers.* . . . If you have no objection, keep it, unless you do not like it."

Gauguin confided to Schuff, "My situation here is painful: I owe much to [Theo] van Gogh and Vincent and despite some discord I can't bear a grudge against a good heart who is ill and suffers and wants to see me. . . . I'm staying here now, but I'm poised to leave at any moment."

Late on the evening of Sunday, December 23, Gauguin walked out of the Yellow House, seeking fresh air and a respite from Vincent's odd behavior. Vincent followed, brandishing a razor, but fled when Gauguin fixed him with a harsh stare. An uneasy Gauguin slept in a hotel and returned to the Yellow House the next morning to find blood everywhere, and the police, called by the neighbors, accusing him of murder. Full of trepidation, Gauguin led them upstairs, where they found Vincent, covered in blood but alive. He had sliced off his ear.

Gauguin summoned Theo, who had just gotten engaged to a Dutch woman named Jo Bonger. He arrived by train on Christmas morning to find Gauguin badly shaken and Vincent in the hospital at Arles. "Will he remain insane?" he wondered sadly. Because Theo had to return to Paris, to his new fiancée and his gallery, he asked Vincent's friends, the *famille*

Roulin, to keep an eye on him while he was in the hospital. Late that night, Gauguin and Theo boarded the train to Paris. Amazingly, Vincent seemed to make a complete recovery in less than two weeks and was soon ensconced in his yellow house once again painting.

Back in Paris and at a safe remove, Gauguin resumed his epistolary friendship with Vincent, praising a recent painting of "sunflowers against a yellow background. . . . I consider [this] a perfect example of a style that is essentially your own. At your brother's I saw your *Sower*, which is very good, as well as a still-life in yellow with apples and lemons."

But Gauguin now had other matters on his mind. Like every other person in Paris, he had only to look up and see the marvel that was the almost-completed Eiffel Tower to be reminded that soon the World's Fair would be opening. He had no doubt that his art had to be displayed at the fair. The problem was where? He entrusted his artist friend Émile Schuffenecker with finding a venue.

As 1889 began, *New York Herald* publisher James Gordon Bennett was thoroughly enjoying having his new newspaper at 5 rue Coq-Héron, the "picturesque, rat-infested street near the Bourse." Here he could descend at any hour, "turning the paper upside down, ripping out stories and advertisements which annoyed him, rampaging from press room to editorial department to composing room, promoting and demoting." Despite Bennett's notorious nocturnal sprees, the *Herald* publisher habitually rose with the sun, and after a quick, light *petit déjeuner* would be off to the Bois de Boulogne to see and be seen.

Bennett's carriage, amid horseback riders and coaches heading up the Champs-Élysées to the Bois, was part of "a glittering cortège, which included high-born dandies and their female counterparts, the beautifully costumed *amazones* like the Baroness Adolphe de Rothschild who always rode escorted by two grooms wearing cockaded top hats. Duels were still being fought in the Bois, amorous intrigues would be discreetly planned there and every morning the *amazones* would gallop between the Porte Dauphine and the Champ des Courses to stop at the Pré Catalan for refreshment and to exchange gossip."

When Bennett returned from his jaunt round the Bois, he settled into his office at a second luxurious apartment at 120 avenue de Champs-Élysées, and set to work dictating cables and marking up newspapers with his long blue pencils. New visitors were always taken aback to find every surface of his office occupied by owls.

Even those who knew *The Herald*'s publisher well never ceased to marvel at the man. "His hot temper came from both parents," said one longtime editor. "Unstable in many things, in others whimsical to the point of extravagance, close and generous, optimist and pessimist, unrelenting and unforgiving, sparkling with joy or deep in the blues, he was a constant puzzle to everyone about him, yet endowed with the perception of great things; prompt, open-handed and broad in their execution, and holding on grimly to the idea that the *Herald* must be kept at the front."

Bennett maintained newsroom spies ("The White Mice") in Gotham who tattled faithfully, and the publisher thought nothing of summoning editors and reporters to cross the Atlantic immediately to see him. These commands always struck terror, for it was known that Bennett liked to do his firing in person. Some men found themselves waiting for weeks to be seen, only to be sent home without ever laying eyes on their boss. Another pair of editors recounted entering Bennett's Paris office only to be received with a curt "What in hell are you doing here?"

"You sent for us."

"Go back to New York!"

This ferocious publisher, absent a wife and children, also surrounded himself with adorable (live) tiny dogs—Pekingese, Pomeranians, pugs, and Yorkshire terriers. When a wily Irishman working in Bennett's London bureau was ominously ordered to Paris, he prepared for the encounter by tucking little slices of liver in his trouser cuffs and silk hat band. As he entered Bennett's owl-filled inner sanctum, the dogs swarmed happily about him, with the beaming Bennett observing, "You must be a good fellow or my dogs would find you out."

In early 1889 Bennett, always a ladies' man, had been haunting the salon of his neighbor, the Duchesse d'Uzès, a superb horsewoman and monarchist who had fervently taken up promoting the political career of Gen. Georges Boulanger, the wildly popular veteran of the Tunisian campaigns and former minister of war. Boulanger "was handsome, he had fine whiskers, he rode a black charger superbly at military reviews. . . . He had been idolised for the way he had faced up to Germany over a frontier incident . . . [but] his warlike fervor had made him such an embarrassment to the government that in July 1887 he had been sent to the provinces to take command of a corps. . . . [A] huge crowd came to see him leave. . . . Royalist and right-wing propaganda made him out to be a patriotic martyr sacrificed to expediency by a cowardly and corrupt government, afraid of the 'honest man.'"

In 1888 Boulanger reappeared in Paris, and was promptly sacked from the army for leaving his provincial post. Although he had become the leader of a right-wing party called The Nationalists, he made alluring promises to both the exiled Comte de France, ever hopeful of regaining the French throne, and the aging Prince Napoleon, in Switzerland, while he himself continued to insist that he was a liberal republican. By being all things to all men, Boulanger and his party managed to pick up numerous seats in these elections. His onetime patron Clemenceau denounced him, he was injured in a duel with republican prime minister Floquet, and many opposing factions united behind him, hailing him as "The Man of Destiny" who would root out corruption. Passions crescendoed as Boulanger ran to represent Paris in the Chamber of Deputies in a special January 27, 1889, election. All that month, the infatuated Bennett had thrown *The New York Herald*'s European edition behind the Duchesse d'Uzès's candidate, describing the Boulanger "boom" in an approving way and the man as "the hero of the moment."

On January 20, Monsieur Gordon-Bennett received a summons to the office of His Excellency Ernest Constans, Minister of the Interior, in charge of all police matters. Bennett arrived at the ministry to find Constans seated in his large and elaborate office. He began by flattering the publisher: "We enjoy having you with us and respect and admire you for . . . publishing here a European edition of your great American newspaper." There the friendly tone ended. Noting Bennett's unseemly enthusiasm for Boulanger, Constans warned, "We must therefore ask you to refrain from giving aid to those who are opposing us, or this Government shall find itself compelled to ask you to leave this country and take your paper along with you." Not since his father's day had Bennett received such a dressing-down, or such an ultimatum. Although his Paris paper had established his importance here, the French played by different rules; no American politician would ever have dared issue such dictates. And yet, as an American, he lived here only at the French government's pleasure. The coverage and editorials of the Paris *Herald* changed abruptly, denouncing the general and his crusade to upend democracy.

Many in Paris believed that January 27, 1889, would be the last day of the French republic, and "huge crowds gathered in the Place de la Madeleine outside the Restaurant Durand where Boulanger and his supporters were dining." When General Boulanger pulled off a stirring victory, those worshipful crowds waited breathlessly for him to seize the moment. All royalist Paris anticipated a thrilling military coup, while others awaited Boulanger's coronation as a new Napoleon. Numerous supporters, including the Duchesse d'Uzès, were among the guests at this victory celebration. "It was less well known that Boulanger's beloved mistress, Madame de Bonnemains, was also waiting discreetly for her lover in another room. . . . It was impossible to preserve order in the streets and boulevards. Carriages were stopped by the crowds and the passengers forced to cry 'Vive Boulanger!'

"In the restaurant, Boulanger's companions urged him to make his way to the Élysée in a triumphal procession and take over. . . . But Boulanger refused to march against his President. He would not even show himself to the crowd. . . . There would be no coup d'état. Instead, he drove away from the restaurant to go to bed with his mistress." The handsome Boulanger had hesitated, and the moment was lost, with the Third Republic surviving this particular challenge. The Exposition Universelle, it seemed, would still celebrate liberty and technological and social progress (and yes, the downfall of the Bastille), but not the demise of the republic and the rise of a new emperor.

The correspondent for *The New York Times* reported back to his countrymen in late January 1889 not only on the anticlimactic Boulanger drama, but also that "the late cold snap made things most uncomfortable for the workmen at the Eiffel Tower. While the aristocracy enjoyed the unusual possibility of a skating frolic . . . in the Bois, the poor devils working away at French glory in the Champ de Mars were nearly frozen. At 6 o'clock in the morning when the work day begins, the thermometer marked 25 degrees, and the cold biting wind seemed to sway the great tower. It takes a good quarter of an hour for them to crawl up 230 feet, and there they found 27 degrees. It is here that the four restaurants are to be located. . . . The workmen eat there even now, indifferent to the beehive beneath or to the landscape beyond. All they find or want is cheap food, warm stoves, and the relief from the tedious climb three times a day.

"The men working way up on the top have to face still greater severity of temperature and far more discomfort. They are about 20 in all, forming the faithful bodyguard of M. Eiffel and his son-in-law M. Salles and they are heroes in their quiet hard-working way. Luckily their labor requires blazing fire to heat the huge iron nails, and as their blows must come heavy and strong, work is fun and cold leisure pain. . . .

"And, it looks as if the first outburst of derision that ridiculed the idea of the monster construction might finally be changed into a victorious hosanna of praise, to the particular happiness of M. Eiffel himself and to the tribute also of his more obscure assistants."

The month of February delivered a nation-shaking shock when Ferdinand de Lesseps, who had been desperately trying to raise enough money to continue pushing through Gustave Eiffel's $25 million system of locks on the Panama Canal, announced that the last bond issue had not been even half subscribed. Since 1881 the company had endured many difficulties, and had repeatedly been forced to seek additional funds. Yet, after eight years and $300 million, a viable canal was only starting to be built. On December 14, the Panama Canal Company had filed for bankruptcy, but the ever-optimistic de Lesseps immediately petitioned the government to let the company reorganize and regroup. When the Chamber of Deputies voted against his proposal, de Lesseps went white and whispered, "It is impossible! It is shameful."

Even then, de Lesseps had refused to acknowledge defeat, rallying his flagging stockholders and pressing for more time, a lottery, something. In late January, he had launched a new canal company, but of sixty thousand shares of its stock, only nine thousand sold. On February 4, the end had come, and a liquidator was appointed. Gustave Eiffel could not believe France would allow a project of such transcendent strategic importance to fail, and instructed his men at the isthmus to keep working, albeit at a slower pace, while they waited for the politicians to come to their senses. Meanwhile, all over France, those who had believed in Ferdinand de Lesseps and his canal also clung to that hope, knowing that otherwise they faced financial devastation.

The Eiffel Tower on February 2, 1889

CHAPTER FOUR

"The First Elevator of Its Kind"

On February 24, 1889, journalist Robert C. Henri woke up at 8:00 a.m. and rushed to his window to see what the Paris day would be like. "Desolation on desolation!" he wrote. "The sky was black—the snow fell—the air was icy—the thermometer was at two degrees below zero." Henri, whose pen name was Hugues Le Roux, intended on that day to become the first journalist to ascend to the top of the nearly completed *Tour en Fer*. "I had an engagement to meet M. Eiffel at the foot of the Tower at two o'clock!" he would tell the readers of *Le Figaro*. "Well! We would make the ascent—even though Paris disappeared entirely beneath this cold white counterpane."

Fortunately, by the time Le Roux's carriage arrived at the Champ de Mars, which was covered in icy white drifts, the snowfall had temporarily subsided. Eiffel was awaiting him with a party of fifteen, including "several ladies who purposed going only as far as the second story, and my guide, who was to accompany me to the platform 900 feet above the earth where the riveters were at work. Four or five persons who had already made the ascent had armed themselves against the cold with close caps, ear muffs and fur gloves." And so at two thirty, with the temperature now one degree below zero, they set out. "In Indian file, preceded by M. Eiffel and the guide, we entered the right pillar of the Tower." Eiffel advised the reporter to imitate his gait. The engineer "climbed slowly," wrote Le Roux, "with his right arm resting on the railing. He swings his body from one hip to the other, using the momentum of the swing to negotiate each step. Here the incline was so gradual that we could chat as we climbed, and no one was winded when we reached the first platform."

It was now 3:05, and they stopped to look about. This first platform was like "a huge ship-builder's yard, in a perfect fever of work. Four great pavilions were going up at once. . . . They are now building almost two hundred feet of wine-cellars. At mealtimes, this vast platform will accommodate 4,200 persons—the population of a town." Down below, observed Le Roux, "the silhouettes of passers-by and fiacres are like little black spots of ink in the streets, very black, very clear . . . [like] small mechanical figures which step jerkily through the little panoramas frequently exhibited in shop windows. Only the rippling Seine seemed still alive."

At 3:25 the party of climbers, now reduced to ten, began the ascent up a small spiral staircase to the second platform, a matter of twenty minutes. There Le Roux was astonished to see "wagons mounted on rails. Yes! At this height had been constructed a railroad with its engine and cars for the furtherance of the work here." When finished, the second platform, 377 feet high, would be furnished with benches and settees so those who walked up could rest and enjoy the vistas. "To the south there is a fine view of the Exposition grounds, with the glass roof of the Machinery Hall looking like a blue lake of molten lead." The light was already starting to fade, and when Le Roux glanced through a square opening in the wooden flooring, he looked "straight down into the abyss. Far below, I could see very small ducks swimming in a half-frozen pond. A shiver ran down my spine at the thought of a possible fall from this height. It grew suddenly colder." Unlike Eiffel, here was a man with an active sense of vertigo.

At 4:10 p.m., the party set out again. "The cold now became intense," wrote Le Roux; "a terrible wind was abroad and brought with it a sudden, blinding hail. The cold railing hurt my fingers so much that I tried to climb with my hands in my pockets, but the wind buffeted me and I was blinded by the driving sleet. So I grabbed the railing again and shielded my face with my arm. All I could see was M. Eiffel's coat tails ahead." Shivering, the wind whipping round them, they climbed steadily, pausing briefly at the intermediate platform at 660 feet.

It was now 5:00 p.m., and twilight was engulfing the city. "Again to the iron stairway!" declared Le Roux. But as he began once more to ascend, he made an unnerving discovery. "The staircase was not attached to the tower except at the top. It oscillated sickeningly beneath us. This put a sudden

Artist Henri Rivière's photograph of workers up on the Eiffel Tower

damper on the zeal of many of our companions who had mounted cheerfully enough as far as the Intermediate Platform. . . . We were now only four. M. Eiffel, a M. Richard, the guide, and myself. We had passed the steps and were on the ladders. Here were neither platforms nor balconies—only the ladders poised on thick planks which rode the immensity of space! The ladders were lashed together with mighty ropes. Look not to the right nor to the left! Keep your eyes only on the rung of the ladder on which you are about to place your foot! After the third ladder we attained the platform 900 feet above the earth. Here the riveters were at work, a dozen men, lost in space. As well they might—abreast of the fearful wind—they worked under the shelter of canvas. . . . As we stood there, they lifted a huge rivet, red hot from the forge, and drove it into place. The furious wind caught up the blows of their ringing iron mallets and rushed off with them, into the night. . . .

"The wind tore spitefully at my garments as if trying to wrench them from my body. . . . I was sensible of a peculiar swaying motion, as if the planks beneath my feet were the deck of some vessel rocking in mid-ocean. . . . I was approaching the edge of the platform. Before looking down into the fathomless darkness . . . I closed my eyes as one does involuntarily, when brought face to face with a great danger. . . . Then I strained my eyes to catch the outline at the base of the tower. What a plunge that would be! How some human creature standing here, like myself, but seized with the sudden madness that lurks about high places, might fling himself out, with a horrid shriek. . . . B-r-r-r! I was going mad, myself. And forgetful, really, of where I stood, I gave myself a little irritated shake. As I did so the weight of my body seemed to slip forward, and I hung, for an instant, far inclined over the edge of the Tower. Involuntarily I extended my hand. My fingers encountered a rope—and they encircled it eagerly, grateful for the timely support.

"Horror of horrors! The rope yielded to my touch. In a frenzy of terror my grip upon it tightened, and it began slowly to descend! I felt myself descending with it! I felt myself falling! . . . Suddenly I regained possession of my hands. I found the rope was still clutched in them. Voices came to me through the wind. A voice close to me!

"'You should never touch a rope—that one is attached only to a pulley. Had you leaned more heavily on it the consequences would not have been pleasant. . . . It is now time to descend,' said M. Eiffel."

Le Roux recovered from his imagined brush with death long enough to gaze down to find Paris "swallowed by the darkness . . . night covered the world. . . . [L]ike some fabled city, Paris had sunk forever beneath the waves and no trace remained, but sometimes there came across the seas, at nightfall, a hum and murmur from her buried streets, the faint, glad voices of her children or the ghostly ringing of her church bells." The two men stared down at the metropolis spread out below. It was bitterly cold and growing late, so the four began the long half-hour descent down the lashed ladders and swaying spiral staircase through the dark.

At the second platform, they gratefully entered a canteen and warmed up with hot drinks. As they relaxed, Monsieur Richard regaled them with stories of his climb up Mont Blanc. Eiffel reported happily that "congratulations were coming in from all over, even from many of the artists who signed the famous protest. 'There are only three or four stubborn writers still holding out,' he said. 'I really don't understand why.' Conversation dragged on lazily. We were reluctant to leave the warmth of our shelter to go back into the wind which seemed to weep with the sound of human sobs in these hundreds of feet of iron stretched from earth to the clouds like an Aeolian harp."

Eiffel could only be grateful that his guest M. Le Roux, during the long ascent to the construction at the top, had not inquired about the whereabouts of the elevators. The unfortunate answer was that Eiffel still did not have functioning ones, even though the contract had called for them to be already completed. In less than three months, hundreds of thousands of people would be swarming in to visit the fair, and in the course of the summer, Eiffel hoped that a million would visit its foremost attraction, his already world-famous tower. But would anyone be able to ascend by elevator? No other problem in the tower's construction had proven so difficult, so vexing.

The fair commission supervising the tower's construction together with Eiffel had early on jointly retained an engineer named Backmann to design the tower's elevators. "The curvature of the Tower's legs imposed a problem unique in elevator design, and it caused great annoyance to Eiffel, the Fair's Commission, and all others concerned," wrote technology historian Robert M. Vogel. "The problem of reaching the first platform was not serious. The legs were wide enough and their curvature so slight in this lower portion as to permit them to contain a straight run of track. . . . Two elevators to operate only that far were contracted for with no difficulty—one to be placed in the east leg and one in the west."

The truly perplexing issue was how to safely and swiftly transport passengers the 377 feet up from the ground to the *second* platform (the north leg) and also from the first platform to the second (the south leg). These two elevators would have to negotiate the tower's most pronounced curvature, an unprecedented challenge in an era when elevators ran not on electric motors, but by hydraulic or water pressure. Then, to reach the top of the tower, passengers on the second platform would have to take yet another elevator and ascend in two stages, making a quick transfer halfway up. Monsieur Backmann chose to address himself only to designing the elevator for the ascent from the second platform to the very top, leaving the commission to seek bids elsewhere for the four elevators leading to the first and then second floors. The commission had ruled that any elevator installed in the Eiffel Tower would have to be absolutely safe, reasonably swift, and of French manufacture. The first-floor contract, a simple enough matter, was awarded to Roux, Combaluzier et Lepape, who would install a clunky articulated chain-link device that would move the cars up and down with a notable but stolid clatter.

But when the commission solicited bids for the second-floor elevators, only the Paris branch of the American Otis Brothers and Company responded. The company prided itself on its global preeminence, as Charles Otis told shareholders not long afterward: "[We] have shipped our products to almost every civilized country of the globe. We have opened a large acquaintance and trade with Australia. . . . Our London connection is promising well . . . notwithstanding the well known prejudice of the English people against American products. . . . Our business along the Pacific Slope has also been satisfactory. We have during the past year shipped elevators to China and South America."

But Otis, however global its reach, was not a French firm, and so the commission briskly rejected its interest as an impertinence, and issued another call for bids. Again no French firms came forward. By then, the summer of 1887, Eiffel was six months into his labors, and some firm would soon have to begin elevator work on what was the most difficult section of the tower. The commission reluctantly waived its own rules and in July awarded the $22,500 contract to Otis.

W. Frank Hall, the Otis representative in Paris, gloried in the challenge: "Yes, this is the first elevator of its kind. Our people for thirty-eight years have been doing this work, and have constructed thousands of elevators vertically, and many on an incline, but never one to strike a radius of 160 feet for a distance of over 50 feet. It has required a great amount of preparatory study." It soon emerged that the Otis Company had been studying the matter ever since Eiffel won Lockroy's contest. "Quite so," said Hall, "we knew that, although the French authorities were very reluctant to give away this piece of work, they would be bound to come to us, and so we were preparing for them." After all, Otis Brothers had just installed the elevator in what had been the world's tallest structure up until then, the Washington Monument. Little did the ebullient Hall of Otis or Eiffel dream of the dire troubles and conflicts ahead.

The Otis Company proposed a design of double-decked elevators that, because of the unusual incline, would operate on regular rail sections. The motive power was to be the usual hydraulic cylinder sunk in the ground and moved by water pressure. Steam engines would pump Seine river water up to a large reservoir on the second platform. When that reservoir's water began to flow back to the ground, it would power the cylinders, activating a block and tackle that would enable the counterweighted elevators to go up and down, as controlled by the elevator operator. When Hall had first presented the Otis plans, Eiffel and the commission felt uncomfortable with the fact that the elevators would be pulled by cables from the top, rather than pushed from the bottom, as was the European system. The method simply seemed less safe, when safety was paramount.

The fair commissioners and all Paris still remembered with a shudder the Baroness de Schack's dreadful death a decade earlier, when the ascending elevator in the Grand Hôtel malfunctioned, plummeting like a stone from the top floor to the basement. Eiffel accordingly demanded "a device that permitted the car to be lowered by hand, even after failure of all the hoisting cables," and when Hall balked at this feature, Eiffel then insisted that the Otis Company's chief engineer, Thomas E. Brown, Jr., come over from the United States to confer with him.

Safety, speed, and quality were characteristics on which Otis Brothers and Company of New York prided itself, but above all, safety. If an Otis elevator's hoisting cables broke or stretched out, powerful leaf springs were released, causing the brake shoes to grip the rails, thus bringing the falling car to a gradual halt. All who followed the history of elevators could cite the famous moment in 1854 when firm founder Elisha G. Otis dramatically demonstrated "the perfect safety of his elevator by cutting the hoisting rope of a suspended platform on which he himself stood." As the platform came to a gentle stop, Mr. Otis declared to his astonished audience, "All safe, gentlemen!" But almost four decades of established Otis safety were not sufficiently reassuring for Eiffel and the commission.

By the time Mr. Thomas E. Brown, Jr., of Otis had arrived in Paris on Monday evening, January 23, 1888, relations between Eiffel and the firm were already strained. Brown informed New York that it had taken two days just to hear from Eiffel, who then said he could not meet with him until Saturday. "Meantime," wrote Brown, "we examined the Tower, and I saw at once that the bracing as constructed would not be sufficiently strong to sustain the cylinders in the position assigned to them by our plans, but I thought that a small matter of detail, which could be changed." During their meeting that Saturday, there was much discussion about how best to accommodate the Otis elevators to recent changes in the curved legs, and whether Eiffel would have to eliminate stairways in those two legs, a measure he preferred not to take. Brown felt this could all be worked out.

But the next issue presented far greater conflicts, as "Eiffel stated that he had not much faith in the safeties we had shown." Perhaps worse, for the first time Eiffel indicated that the fair commission, which had yet to approve the final Otis contract, would be satisfied only with "a device known as the rack and pinion safety that was used to some extent on European cog railways. . . . The serious shortcomings of the rack and pinion were its great noisiness and the limitation it imposed on hoisting speed." (Cog railroads, in use in the mountains for more than a quarter century, featured a cog wheel, or pinion, that meshed with a toothed rack rail, usually set between the running rails, as it rolled laboriously up and down steep gradients.) But Eiffel and the commission liked this device because if all the elevator hoisting cables failed, the rack and pinion would allow the car to be safely lowered to the ground by hand.

Brown, an expert in elevator engineering, was appalled at the pointless hobbling of their machines, which would create noise, drag, and jarring as the elevators traveled up and down. "On Monday," Brown told his bosses in a twelve-page memo, "I reported to [Eiffel engineer] Mr. Koechlin that I would return to N.Y. on the next steamer, and lay the matter before the Co.; and that if they saw fit to make modified plans, the same would be sent to Mr. Eiffel. . . . In other words, it would be fatal to our projects to present [to the commission] the plans as they then were. . . . I got the impression that Mr. Eiffel and the Commission were at loggerheads."

In mid-February one top Otis executive read Brown's report and counseled president Charles Otis to stand resolute on the rack-and-pinion issue. "I should favor giving up the whole matter rather than allying ourselves with any such abortion. It certainly would be a serious damage to our elevator business in all Europe, and we would be the laughingstock of the world, for putting up such a contrivance." Worse yet, if Otis agreed to the design of such elevators and the machines failed, they would be "criticized by the public and the press as an American failure, [and] we would of course exceedingly regret that we had ever had anything to do with it." The French finally backed down only after the Otis officials informed Eiffel that if he and the commission insisted on rack-and-pinion safeties, they would withdraw from the contract.

Meanwhile, Eiffel had also decided once again to modify slightly the tower's legs, which of course meant further alterations to the elevator designs. As the Otis people later bitterly complained, "You forget that when the matter was first brought to our attention, the formation of the legs of the tower was different from that finally adopted, and that we wrought and substantially completed the engineering elements of the difficulty as then presented; subsequently you changed this form,—making an abrupt bend in the [interior of the] legs, and thereby not only rendering much of our past study and labor useless, but by such a change greatly adding to the engineering difficulties to be overcome." About this same time, Eiffel and the commission, examining their man Backmann's *second* effort to design an elevator serving the top, realized he was no connoisseur of elevators. In mid-1888, they had rejected his plans, which included the worrisome novelty of an electric motor, and fired him.

With just one year until the fair and Backmann dismissed, Eiffel had to find another provider for the elevator to the top. The problem, in this age before electric motors were the norm, was the sheer footage to be ascended: 525 feet. Eiffel turned to an old classmate, Léon Édoux, an elevator inventor and magnate who had installed a very successful 230-foot elevator in the Trocadéro Palace across the Seine. Édoux came up with "an ingenious modification. . . . The run was divided into two equal sections, each of 262 feet, and two cars were used." When one was going up to the interim platform where you changed for the final ride to the top, the other was coming down, and so no other weights were needed than the cars themselves. "When these two elevators were in operation, water was admitted to the two cylinders [that provided power] from a tank on the third platform. The resultant hydraulic head was sufficient to force out the rams and raise the upper car."

Even as Gustave Eiffel and Mr. Otis were quarreling, James Gordon Bennett and his faithful managing editor, Samuel Chamberlain, were perfecting the European version of *The New York Herald*. They engaged in all sorts of clever promotional stunts, including creating a special summary of the week's news distributed to every passenger on steamships arriving from the United States, a preemptive introduction to what was already becoming known as the Paris *Herald*. Within days of launching his new paper, Bennett floated a subtle ploy to enter the Continent's better-off households: the offer of a free year's subscription to "English governesses living in any English, Russian, French, Spanish, or Italian families." He engaged a corps of society correspondents to write in from fashionable resorts and watering holes on the doings of the cosmopolitan set.

Once Bennett junior had the European edition successfully launched, he felt ready for an autumnal Mediterranean cruise on his palatial yacht, *Namouna*. A formidable sailor (known to his staff sometimes as the Commodore), Bennett insisted that Chamberlain accompany him; after all, the telegraph would enable both men to keep close tabs on the newspapers. One glorious sunny morning some weeks into their Mediterranean cruise, as they approached the Greek port of Piraeus, they sighted an American navy cruiser on maneuvers. It was obvious that the two American vessels were on a collision course. The Commodore ordered his helmsman, "Keep right ahead. That ship has no right to cross my bow." An ashen Chamberlain, also on the bridge, warned Bennett that hitting a U.S. warship was bad policy. The Commodore roared to the helmsman to stay the course. As disaster loomed, Chamberlain leapt for the helm and swung the yacht slowly around, saving Bennett from his own pigheadedness. Bennett was not grateful and within hours he had deposited his managing editor on a desolate island (though provisioned with food and water) before steaming off. Only the imprecations of his other guests persuaded him to dispatch a rowboat to retrieve Chamberlain. At the next port, Chamberlain debarked, his editorship at *The Herald*'s European edition abruptly concluded.

At the Eiffel Tower, meanwhile, matters were not proceeding smoothly with Otis. As the months ticked by in the second half of 1888, every structural adjustment in the interior of the tower's legs required the Otis Company to make its own elevator design accommodations. Moreover, all the extra work had forced Otis to revise the price of the two elevators upward to $30,000, a 30 percent surcharge. Finally, Otis informed Eiffel that because of the constant changes the firm could no longer guarantee full operation of the two elevators by the contract deadline of January 1, 1889. However, Otis did assure Eiffel that all would be running smoothly by May 1 when the fair opened.

Eiffel was apoplectic, and in a bitter letter written on February 1, 1889, he accused Otis of not keeping its word and placing him in "a cruel situation." He followed this with an angry cablegram "reserving his rights." Why should he pay the extra charges for elevators delivered so late as to jeopardize the opening of the tower? Not long after his freezing ascent up the tower with Hugues Le Roux of *Le Figaro*, Eiffel received Charles Otis's five-page single-spaced letter acknowledging the "horror of the situation"—

i.e., Eiffel's fear that the Otis elevators would not be installed and ready on time. Charles Otis, a somber man with a biblical gray beard, had been running his company with his brother since their father's death twenty-seven years earlier. He began his letter to Eiffel contritely, expressing his regret that "you have lost all confidence in us. We are likewise embarrassed by this state of things, inasmuch as, now, whatever we tell you, we feel reasonably assured that you will not believe us." However, Otis once again tactfully reminded Eiffel that it was his own continuing changes to the ultimate interior shape of the tower's legs that were responsible for much of the delay, as

Charles Otis of Otis Brothers
and Company

was the commission's effort to impose rack-and-pinion safeties.

Charles Otis also defended his own firm's tardiness, explaining that its high standards were part of the reason things were moving slowly. When it came to the design and manufacture of the Eiffel Tower elevators, "we have been more severe in our exactions upon ourselves." They were using steel rather than cast iron, and their steel supplier had "disappointed and delayed us." He assured Eiffel that the elevators would be working by May 1 and would be ready for the great crowds, "unless unjust and unnecessary obstacles [are] thrown in our way by Mr. Eiffel himself."

Charles Otis also wished Mr. Eiffel to understand that even the new higher price did not reflect the true cost of the complicated elevators. His firm now expected to *lose* $20,000 on the contract. While he appreciated Eiffel's distress, he was himself angry about Eiffel's "threat that you will not pay us even the pittance which it pleased you to allow us." Charles Otis minced no words: "After all we have borne and suffered and achieved in your behalf, we regard this as a trifle too much; and we do not hesitate to declare, in the strongest terms possible to the English language, that we will not put up with it . . . and if there is to be War, under the existing circumstances, propose that at least part of it shall be fought on American ground. If Mr. Eiffel shall, on the contrary, treat us as we believe we are entitled to be treated, under the circumstances, and his confidence in our integrity to serve him well shall be restored in season to admit of the completion of this work at the time wanted, well and good; but it must be done at once . . . otherwise we shall ship no more work from this side, and Mr. Eiffel must charge to himself the consequences of his own acts." Eiffel and the commission had little choice but to back down; the tower had to open to the public in less than six months. Eiffel had risked his own money and reputation on making that deadline.

During that same February of 1889, not far from the Otis Brothers and Company Park Row offices in Manhattan, Annie Oakley and her husband-manager, Frank Butler, were busy negotiating their own World's Fair contract. Buffalo Bill's longtime partner and business manager, Nate Salsbury, was using all his charm to persuade Oakley to return to the Wild West as a star attraction for a planned Paris run. Certainly, Oakley's stage career with *Deadwood Dick* had proved short-lived. The traveling show had fallen apart in Chambersburg, Pennsylvania, when the assistant manager decamped with such receipts as there were. Oakley paid everyone's way home.

Now here came Salsbury, always a vision of Gilded Age elegance in his cutaway coat, fine derby hat, and fancy cane, to persuade Oakley to return to the show she had left in London with a degree of bad feelings, though she would never explain what was at issue. It was Nate Salsbury who had discovered her back in 1884 in Louisville, Kentucky, when Oakley, then twenty-four, was still a small-time vaudeville act. He had seen her practicing for her Wild West tryout in the empty arena, and afterward he had rushed over crying, "Fine! Wonderful! Have you got some photographs with your gun?" He hired her on the spot and paid $7,000 for the necessary publicity shots and posters.

Recalled Oakley years later, "When the cowboys, Mexicans and Indians got back from the parade, they were all lined up on one side. Mr. Cody and Mr. Salsbury were on the other side, and my husband and I were called upon to pass down the line, meeting all of them.

"There I was facing the real Wild West, the first white woman to travel with what society might have considered an impossible outfit."

Oakley, who had never been farther west than Ohio, where she had grown up, loved performing and traveling with the Wild West. "A crowned queen was never treated with more reverence than I was by those whole-souled western boys." New York City was always a great venue for the Wild West and one year, after a new snowfall, Oakley decided to get out into the fresh air around Madison Square Garden. "I had Jerry, the big moose, hitched to a sled and thought I'd take a spin around the block. All went swimmingly until we turned a corner about twenty feet from the entrance and Jerry's bead-like eyes espied a push cart laden with nice juicy red apples. Three of his long strides and he was at the cart and apples flew in all directions. The vendor's hair stood on end. My moose ate the apples and my $5 paid the bill."

For Annie Oakley, the Wild West's 1887 season in London had been one triumph after another. "Tons of beautiful flowers poured in upon me," she recounted happily. "Books, dainty handkerchiefs, pretty lace, ties, gloves, fans and silk for a dress were sent to me." The Prince and Princess of Wales presented framed autographed photos. "There were many receptions and teas in my honor. I was made a welcome visitor at the two gun clubs in London." Oakley, an ace shot since girlhood, also made significant money. At a time when the average annual American salary was $500, she won $750 in a single week at various private gun-club competitions. The English upper crust, who prized a good shot, could not get enough of this demure, petite wonder who could outshoot them all.

Annie Oakley with her rifle

When Edward, Prince of Wales, sitting in the royal box at the Wild West show with his wife, Alexandra, asked to meet Oakley after a performance, she expressed her disapproval of his famous womanizing by proffering her hand first to the princess. Said Oakley, she "took my hand gently in her own saying, 'What a wonderful little girl.' Nor was his highness displeased at my daring. He shook my hand warmly when I turned from the princess . . . he said loud enough for me and the entire assembly to hear: 'What a pity there are not more women in the world like that little one.'"

Was it any surprise that in March Oakley signed a new contract with Buffalo Bill and the Wild West? Paris and the World's Fair promised to be an even more wonderful, and more lucrative, adventure.

Even as Gustave Eiffel and the Otis Company engaged in their ongoing struggles over the elevators, work on the tower itself proceeded at a rigorous pace. The crowds down below could watch as the steam crane on the first platform lifted a wrought-iron section from the ground to its level. Then the operator on a second crane on the second platform lifted that same piece up to the second platform, while a third steam crane working yet farther up then leaned down and lifted up the next wrought-iron segment. "On the highest point reached there is a steam engine working day and night and two cranes bearing a weight of 24,000 pounds, to raise the enormous shafts of iron," wrote a *New York Times* reporter. "To get each shaft into position maneuvers lasting 20 minutes are required; the workers are placed on a movable floor rising with them and railed around, so that actual danger is reduced as far as possible." From the ground looking up, the human workers were hard to discern in this whole astonishing mechanized system.

Not surprisingly the relentless scrutiny to which the construction was subjected produced regular rumors. In mid-January of 1889, *The Engineer* reported "a rumor that [the Eiffel Tower] had fallen out of the perpendicular. It is somewhat remarkable that this scare did not occur at an earlier date. . . . By optical illusion, portions of the Tower appear to have shifted from their proper positions. . . . The scare in Paris this week was so great that the Exhibition authorities were obliged to send their own engineers specially to certify that everything is alright."

Journalists clamored to see the wonders of the Eiffel Tower close-up.

Not long after Hugues Le Roux had made his frigid ascent on the still-swaying ladders, Eiffel hosted the minor literary lion Émile Goudeau, whose new novel, *The Depraved*, was to be published in time for the fair. By now the riveters were working at the very top of the tower, a confined and slightly surreal work-scene-in-the-sky, and when he joined them, Goudeau, a distinctive figure with his unruly black hair, wild beard, and crossed eyes, found himself almost nine hundred feet above Paris enveloped by "thick coal tar smoke" that hurt his throat, "even as I was deafened by the horrendous clangor of the sledgehammers. One was bolting over there; workers, squeezed onto a ledge of a few centimeters, took turns wielding their iron sledgehammers with tremendous force on the rivets; elsewhere blacksmiths were calmly and rhythmically pounding on their anvils, as if working their forge in the village; but these smiths do not strike from top to bottom, vertically, but horizontally, and with each blow sparks spray forth; these blackened men, looming large against the open sky, appear to be tossing lightning bolts into the clouds."

As the tower achieved its final shape, its early critics were grudgingly coming around and conceding its comeliness. "As soon as it was possible to judge the monument as a whole, hostile opinion began to relent," wrote the Vicomte de Vogüé, whose constitutionals along the Seine had literally led him to new heights: he had received special permission from Eiffel to wander about the tower's upper reaches while it was still being built. "There was in this iron mountain the elements of a new beauty, elements difficult to define, because no grammar of art had as yet supplied the formula, but evident to the most biased art critics. People admired its combination of lightness with power, the daring centering of the great arches, and the erect curves of the principal rafters, which . . . leap towards the clouds in a single bound. What [people] admired above all was the visible logic of this structure . . . logic translated into something visible . . . an abstract and algebraic beauty. . . . Lastly, the spectators were won over by what inevitably conquers everyone: a tenacious will, embodied in the success of a difficult undertaking. Only the top was still criticized, was adjudged unfinished, a weak and complicated crown that did not hold with the very simple lines. Something was missing at the top."

Others particularly liked the top of the tower, whose summit ended in a rounded campanile. When visitors alighted at the very top from the elevator, they would step into a covered gallery. Fitted all round with glazed sashes that could be opened or shut as required, this penultimate gallery would be sixteen meters long on each side, and accommodate eight hundred visitors. Above this public gallery, Eiffel planned a series of rooms reserved for scientific purposes, and what would be the envy of many in coming months: an elegant personal apartment.

Above these rooms, at the tower's true pinnacle, was the lighthouse. Reached only by an open-air ladder, the lighthouse was encircled at its base by a small, narrow terrace with a metal handrail. This terrace, three hundred meters from the ground, was specially designed for the anemometers and other meteorological instruments that required complete isolation. Crowning the edifice would eventually be a tall flagpole.

In February of 1889 an Englishman penned a pamphlet asserting that whatever the Eiffel Tower's "merits, or otherwise, no one can deny that it is the greatest engineering work of the day, and as such it's an object of intense interest throughout the entire civilized world." Moreover, he was puzzled "why so much mud should have been thrown at M. Eiffel by part of the press, even if [the tower] turns out to have no further value. . . . Why call a man mad and a fool who has sufficient pluck and ingenuity to attempt something never before attempted? . . . It will be *something* to say you have been to the top of this enormous tower."

Gaston Tissandier, the aerialist, was likewise puzzled, and wondered, "How many times have we not heard the remark, 'What is the use of the Eiffel Tower?'

"A similar question has been asked concerning almost every new thing that appears in the world.

"In reply, it is enough to repeat that the iron monument was planned as part of the Universal Exhibition of 1889. In celebrating our glorious centenary it was desirable to astonish the world with some grand achievement, the like of which had never been seen before; and M. Eiffel's project is justified by the success attained.

"But the edifice should not only be looked at as a colossal monument for the mere attraction of public curiosity. It is an experiment in iron construction of unusual importance, and on so large a scale that at the outset competent engineers considered it to be impossible. From it the engineer's art has gained many valuable lessons to be applied in further developments.

The Eiffel Tower is in a sense the pier of a gigantic bridge, which will lead to the undertaking in the near future of works of public utility, which up to recently would have been looked upon as simply chimerical."

While the aesthetes had been finding fault with the tower, the makers of bibelots were cashing in. Happily exploiting the world's fascination with this unique structure, they manufactured endless likenesses of it. There were images executed in "pen, pencil, and brush, in photo and lithography, in oil and pastel, on paper, canvas, on wood and ivory, on china, steel, and zinc," not to mention Eiffel Towers replicated "on handkerchiefs and caps; it was eaten in chocolate and marchpane; formed into cigar cases and hand bells, inkstands and candlesticks; it dangled from the gentlemen's watch chains and was fastened in the ladies ears; it stood in hundreds of forms in the shop-windows, and made all idle hands busy in the workshops." When M. Jaluzot, director of the Magasins du Printemps, declared his intention that February of enforcing his exclusive monopoly to manufacture all such reproductions, the affected businesses threatened legal war, while the Parisian peddlers who found selling all these Eiffel Towers lucrative "came near making a riot." The French courts quickly ruled against Jaluzot and any monopoly of reproduction, citing the state's partial subsidy in building the tower.

With that, "the Eiffel Tower mania knew no bounds. Everything was *à la tour Eiffel*, from toilet tables and clocks to snuff-boxes, umbrella handles, scarf pins, and sleeve buttons. They were made to suit all prices and all tastes; they were sold on the street corners under magnifying glass for two sous, and they were built in the provinces fifteen meters high, and containing little private dining-rooms just as it stood at the foot of Iéna bridge, and everywhere on the globe the portrait of the giant was to be seen."

Gustave Eiffel was understandably rhapsodic over the nearing completion of the tower and its embrace by the masses. He basked in the rising chorus of admiration and excitement, the contrition of many of his early detractors, and the hosannas of praise. The *Revue Illustrée*, which had featured him on its cover, had lauded this giant of engineering for combining "the practicality and methodical *sang-froid* of the English engineer, the audacity of the American engineer, and the theoretical science and taste of the French engineer." Even *The Times* of London offered a mea culpa: "The

Gustave Eiffel *(left)* poses atop his tower
during the fair.

form suggested the ugliest parts of a suspension bridge, and it was predicted that the deformity would be increased with the increase of size. The result has not been what was predicted. Even some of those who protested most loudly against the proposal now admit that the effect of the structure is not what they anticipated. They acknowledge that it has a light and graceful appearance, in spite of its gigantic size, and that it is an imposing monument, not unworthy of Paris."

Out in the boulevards jammed with omnibuses and horse-drawn trams, and in the quieter side streets of touristic Paris, French hoteliers, restaurateurs, and shopkeepers were waiting expectantly: they had heard Americans would be coming to the fair in free-spending hordes, as many as half a million. Perhaps Parisians thought *Herald* publisher James Gordon Bennett was the model of a typically profligate Yankee. "Their idea of the American," confided the *New York Tribune* reporter, quoting the local press, "is that he likes to spend money, which may be true, and that he does not care what he gets in return; which also may be true, in fact." Parisian newspapers were already counseling the natives against excessive chauvinism or rapaciousness. First, they urged, it was the duty of every French citizen to "conceal his natural antipathies" to the foreigner and "to treat him civilly, and to get as much out of him as possible. He should be made to pay well, but not too well. . . . The supreme art is to pluck the goose without making the creature cry out. . . . [He should not raise] his prices beyond what even the American will stand." The *Tribune* reporter, contemplating the imminent mass fleecing of his countrymen as they came to the Paris fair to admire the triumph of the modern, offered a few words to the wise. "Every restaurant-keeper inside the railings of the Champ de Mars has sworn an oath to retire next November with a fortune." Rather than paying exorbitant prices, they could seek out the Duval establishments, cheap and reliable. Or, they could be like the French and buy from the vendors outside the railings, and picnic.

CHAPTER FIVE

In Which the Artists Quarrel
and the Tower Opens

On Thursday, April 25, 1889, James McNeill Whistler looked quite the dapper gentleman in his overlong black frock coat, white duck trousers, yellow gloves, and silk top hat as he strolled along the avenue de la Bourdonnais. He was heading toward number 27, the stately mansion that housed the Paris headquarters of the United States Commission for the Universal Exposition, handily opposite the Champ de Mars and the Eiffel Tower. Whistler adjusted the monocle firmly perched in his right eye, stilled the swinging of his slender Japanese bamboo walking stick, and passed the young Marine guard to enter.

At fifty-four, Whistler, his hair tousled with its trademark white curl, was still very much the witty troublemaker of the art world, a bantam of a man who delighted in provocations and feuds. Just the previous month, in his latest contretemps, he had slapped and kicked another American artist who insulted him at the Hogarth Club in London.

On this particular spring afternoon, Whistler was fresh off the Channel ferry and very much on a mission: he had come to find Gen. Rush Christopher Hawkins, the American commissioner of fine arts. Whistler held in his hand a printed circular that read: "Sir, Ten of your exhibits have not received the approval of the jury. Will you kindly remove them?" The paper was signed by Hawkins. Whistler was directed to a spacious office, and there found said general, a formidable-looking man of noble mien, who had been a distinguished commander of a regiment of Zouaves who fought in the American Civil War. In the decades since the war Hawkins had become a wealthy and famously irascible New York lawyer devoted to collecting art and fifteenth-century books. The general's thankless but important job here in Paris was to organize the exhibiting of the American republic's best art at the fair. The general and his compatriots felt certain that American artists, whether resident in Europe or back home, now had a thing or two to show the French, and a real prospect of winning medals and distinction. In the prestigious arena of culture, painting was America's best hope for victories. There had been two American art committees working toward this end: one in New York, judging artists working in the United States, and another expatriate committee making selections in Paris. The two American groups would be geographically separate at the fair, as they were in real life, and their work would hang in adjoining galleries.

Whistler, however tiresome and eccentric he could be, was certainly one of painting's leading figures. Raised in the United States and then St. Petersburg, where his father was building railroads for the czar, James McNeill Whistler had attended West Point, was ejected before graduating, worked briefly in Washington, D.C., and then came to study art in Paris. Fluent in French from his family's years at the Russian court, he had a charming, resolutely bohemian, and pugnacious personality that was as controversial as his modern, impressionistic paintings. After witnessing some of his antics, his artist friend Edgar Degas had said, "Whistler, if you were not a genius, you would be the most ridiculous man in Paris. It must be very tiring to keep up the role of butterfly." There was something in Whistler that relished notoriety and attention. Still, however many public feuds and fights in which he engaged, he was a serious artist who had won his share of honors and acclaim even while battling the considerable forces of reaction in art. For three decades now, he had lived in London.

"I am Mr. Whistler, and I believe this note is from you," the artist now announced. "I have come to remove my etchings."

"Ah," said the general, nodding, "we were very sorry not to have had space enough for all your etchings, but we are glad to have seventeen and the portrait."

"You are too kind," said Whistler, "but really, I will not trouble you." The general slowly realized that Whistler intended to remove *all* his work, and would not exhibit with the other Americans. Once again, the painter's famous dander was up. (Some proposed that Whistler adopt as his hallmark

The domes, towers, and bridges of Belle Époque Paris

the hummingbird, an American bird "whose daintiness and love of beautiful things are only equaled by its pugnacity.") Later Whistler confided to the Paris *Herald*, "I did not mind the fact that my works were criticized, but it was the discourteous manner in which it was done. If the request to me had been made in proper language, and they had simply said: 'Mr. Whistler, we have not space enough for twenty-seven etchings. Will you kindly select those which you prefer, and we shall be glad to have them,' I would have given them the privilege of placing them in the American section."

Whistler gathered his works and departed, leaving in his wake, as was so often his intention, ire and annoyance. What he did not mention in this brief foray to stir up trouble and retrieve his work was that he intended instead to exhibit with the British, since he was currently resident in London. Ultimately, there being even less space available in the British galleries, Whistler would hang only his large oil portrait of Lady Archibald Campbell and two etchings.

Several weeks earlier, on Sunday, March 31, 1889, the tower's overall structure was completed. The pinnacle achieved a final height of 300 meters, or 984 feet. With the addition of the flagpole, the tower reached 1,000 feet. After five difficult years, starting from the moment Eiffel first admired the initial idea for a *Tour en fer de trois cents mètres*, it had been a relentless push to get construction under way and completed on time. Gustave Eiffel and his men had, as promised, finished in twenty-two months, in time for the fair. The day after the tower was finished, on the brisk, windy afternoon of Monday, April 1, 1889, Gustave Eiffel triumphantly welcomed to the Champ de Mars select members of the Paris press, along with his champion, fair commissioner Édouard Lockroy; French prime minister Pierre Tirard, a civil engineer by training and an early critic; the Paris Municipal Council; various high officials; and curious wives and children. The occasion was the formal first ascension of the tower, followed by a champagne fête for Eiffel's men. At 1:30 p.m., 150 guests and all of Eiffel's 199 workers had gathered at the north pillar stairs, while not far off, fair construction workers toiled away, racing to complete the vast, elaborate exposition buildings, gardens, and fountains.

Eiffel once again would lead the walk up the tower's iron staircase, for even the simplest of the tower's elevators, the Roux railway-like cars to the first floor, were not yet ready. It was still not at all clear if *any* of the elevators would be ready in time, but given that it would be five weeks until the fair opened, and that it was a day of such jubilation, did their absence matter?

As Eiffel waited to lead his guests, a politician who suffered from acute vertigo used a scarf to blindfold himself, and then clutched his colleague's arm as they started upward. The group was lively and excited. The sun came in and out of the clouds racing across the sky, and at times the March wind gusted violently, whirling dust from below. Eiffel stopped not infrequently to explain this or that feature and to let the sightseers look down at the fair or up the Seine. When the party of one hundred arrived at the first platform, Eiffel indicated where the four eateries would be—an Anglo-American bar, a Flemish brasserie, and then a Russian and a French restaurant, each with five or six hundred seats. Most of the ladies in their spring silk dresses and the top-hatted gentlemen chose to go no farther.

But forty of the more intrepid followed Eiffel up the circular staircase to the second platform, more than a third of the way to the top. From this vantage point, these lifelong Parisians were delighted by the new panorama of their beloved city. The Seine had become a silver ribbon undulating through a miniature landscape. Most of them had never seen Paris from such a height. It was an exhilarating but somehow chastening sight. After their exertions and, for many, incipient vertigo, half of the group declined to ascend any higher.

Only Gustave Eiffel and two dozen others, including his son-in-law, Salles, Lockroy, Gaston Tissandier, the aerialist editor of *La Nature*, a few officials, and all the journalists (including a dogged Paris *Herald* reporter), persevered for the final half-hour climb to the top observation deck. From this lofty new perch, *Le Figaro*'s reporter (not Le Roux, on this occasion) discovered that the human landscape and enterprise were reduced to disquieting inconsequence: "Mounts Valérien, Montmartre, Sannois, all look like little gray blobs; the forest of Saint-Germain fades into the blue mists, the Seine becomes a tranquil rivulet, traversed by Lilliputian barges, and Paris appears like a tiny stage set with its straight roads, squares rooftops, and orderly facades. The tiny black dots are the crowds. Everything everywhere looks devoid of life, except for the green of the Bois; there is no visible movement in this immensity; no noise to show the life of the people who are 'below.' One would say that a sudden slumber has, in broad daylight, rendered the city inert and silent."

Up a small spiral stair was a second glassed-in floor of four rooms—one was Eiffel's personal well-furnished aerie apartment, the other three were devoted to scientific studies. Some of the men blanched as they saw they now had to climb yet another circular stair out into the open where the wind was strong. Only eleven continued up, emerging outside on a tiny windy balcony with only a slender rail fence. Here was the true, terrifying pinnacle of the tower. Eiffel exultantly unfolded a gigantic red, white, and blue French flag—fifteen feet by five feet—with the large initials *R.F.* (*République Française*) embroidered upon it in gold. He offered it to Monsieur Lockroy, who demurred, insisting Eiffel have the honor. As Eiffel was hoisting the tricolor up the waiting flagpole, one of the journalists began emotionally singing "La Marseillaise," and all soon joined in. At that moment, 2:40 p.m., as the flag unfurled and waved high above Paris, twenty-one cannon-like fireworks boomed forth from the second platform.

Up on the dizzying pinnacle, the wind was rushing by, the flag was flapping, and all bowed their heads as Eiffel's chief engineer proclaimed, "We salute the flag of 1789, which our fathers bore so proudly, which won so many victories, and which witnessed so much progress in science and humanity. We have tried to raise an adequate monument in honor of the great date of 1789, wherefore the Tower's colossal proportions." With that, a city official announced Eiffel's workers would share in a 1,000 franc bonus. The hardy few, higher up than any man (except in a balloon) had ever been in Paris, popped open champagne bottles to celebrate with toasts: *"Gloire à M. Eiffel et à ses collaborateurs!" "Vive la France!" "Vive Paris!" "Et vive la République!"* They admired the view, calculated to be almost fifty miles distant on a clear day, and then began the long descent. Forty-five vertiginous minutes later, Eiffel and the exultant flag-raisers were back at the foot of the tower, where Prime Minister Pierre Tirard was waiting.

Eiffel and all his guests sat down to "an elegant little lunch served to replace the animal carbon that the visitors had expended in mounting and descending the tower." The 199 laborers enjoyed ham, German sausage, and cheese. When all had eaten and drunk their fill, Eiffel climbed up on a chair and began to speak, declaring his great satisfaction and gratitude to all who had helped complete this colossal triumphal arch of wrought iron. He described the tower's great scientific potential as an observatory and laboratory, announcing that he had "decided to inscribe in letters of gold on the great frieze of the first platform, and in the place of honor, the names of the greatest men of science who have honored France, from 1789, down to our day. Besides all these uses, which I might have explained in greater detail, but which, even in this rapid summary will serve to show that we have not erected an object of barren wonder, the tower possesses in my eyes a usefulness of a totally different order, which is the true source of the ardor which has inspired me in my work.

"The public at large understood this, and it is also the reason for the very general and warm sympathy they have shown me.

"My goal was to demonstrate to the whole world that France is a great country, and that she is still capable of success where others have failed." Eiffel's guests and workmen joined in waves of applause.

Gustave Eiffel now also announced the installation of a plaque on the tower with the names of 199 of his workmen to honor their hard and faithful labor. While there had been the strikes, he as well as anyone appreciated the sheer physical effort, the terrible cold, the relentless pace, and the necessary precision and care involved in assembling this 7,300-ton structure. The tower had, regrettably, taken two lives: a worker who died in a fall, and another hurt in an accident who then died of gangrene.

Prime Minister Tirard now stood, a graybeard of sixty-one, a committed republican who had survived France's worst political convulsions, conceding gracefully his newfound admiration for a tower he had originally reviled. Then, as a gratifying surprise, the prime minister revealed that he had nominated Eiffel for promotion in the Legion of Honor to the rank of officer. Eiffel's boyhood friend Gustave Noblemaire, who already held this rank and was wearing his own red rosette ribbon on his lapel, stepped forward, removed his rosette, and attached it to Eiffel's lapel as the crowd cheered. Eiffel smiled radiantly, suffused with an almost childlike happiness. At this, several workmen arose holding six bouquets of fragrant white lilacs. They presented the first to Eiffel, the second to Adolphe Salles, and then one to each of Eiffel's four other assistants. As the triumphant celebration broke up, Eiffel shook hands with all the many well-wishers. Throughout this informal ceremony, the wind had been blowing stronger, the skies growing darker and threatening, and now winds lashed harder and the heavens finally opened.

For the republicans it had been a great day. The Eiffel Tower, which they had championed as the centerpiece of their World's Fair, was already a huge success. As Eiffel had said earlier in his remarks, "The tower is now known to the whole world; it has struck the imagination of every nation, and inspired the most remote with the desire of visiting the Exhibition."

Also on that day, Gen. Georges Boulanger had fled the country, fearful that he might be arrested for treason. France could now concentrate without distraction on its great fête.

Down in Pont-Aven, Brittany, Paul Gauguin was delighted to hear that his friend Émile Schuffenecker had secured a promising place within the fair itself to exhibit their paintings. "Bravo!" he wrote Schuff in April. "You have brought it off." Excluded from the official French painting pavilion, and yearning for attention, Gauguin lacked the funds to emulate Courbet and Manet, who had solved their exclusion from the 1867 exposition by building their own pavilions. Schuff had learned that Monsieur Volpini, whose Café Riche was the scene of Impressionist dinners organized by Gustave Caillebotte, had a contract to run a restaurant in the Palais des Beaux-Arts. Volpini's Café des Beaux-Arts would stand directly at the exit of the official French painting pavilion with its hundreds of paintings depicting historical and biblical tales and sweetly pastoral scenes. Moreover, Schuff had discovered that Volpini was in despair because the large mirrors for his café walls had not arrived.

Schuff accordingly persuaded Volpini to cancel the mirrors, cover the walls with pomegranate red material, and hang art in their stead. He, Gauguin, and their friends, declaring themselves the Groupe Impressioniste et Synthétiste, would provide the decor. Gauguin asked Theo Van Gogh if Vincent would like to join them. "At first," Theo later wrote Vincent, "I said you would show some things too, but they assumed an air of being such tremendous fellows that it really became a bad thing to participate. . . . It gave one somewhat the impression of going to the World's Fair by the back stairs."

Vincent had had a difficult year, battling his demons. In February, after yet another short stay in the hospital, the neighbors protested his return to the Yellow House in a petition that complained that his "excessive drinking" led to wild behavior that "frightens all the inhabitants of the quarter, and above all the women and children." In a letter to his sister, Vincent sadly confided his suffering from "moods of indescribable mental anguish, sometimes moments when the veil of time and the fatality of circumstances seemed to be torn apart for an instance." Even an invitation from pointillist artist Paul Signac to join him in Grasse did not tempt Vincent, who had resigned himself to closing the Yellow House and retreating to a sanitarium fifteen miles away in St.-Rémy.

As for Gauguin, he planned to exhibit ten works at the fair, including paintings from Martinique, Brittany, and his two months in Arles with Vincent. Gauguin warned Schuff, "Only remember it is not an exhibition for the others. So let us arrange it for a little group of comrades, and from this point of view I want to be represented there as fully as possible." Gauguin and Schuff hoped that tired fairgoers sipping coffee or enjoying a glass of wine, beguiled by the music of the all-woman Russian string orchestra, would be smitten with the bold contemporary art all about, simple scenes of the modern world, intensely colored, the paint thick and almost crude, and might even purchase a work or two.

Paul Gauguin viewed himself as nothing less than an art warrior, portraying the modern world as it was, combating stale state-sanctioned art, art that barely acknowledged the nineteenth century but harked back again and again to ancient myths, Bible stories, and battles. For fifty years, he lamented, "the State increasingly protected mediocrity and professors who suited everyone. . . . Yet alongside these pedants, courageous fighters have come along and dared to show: paintings without recipes. . . . All of XXth-century art will derive from them. . . . We would like to have seen these independent artists in a separate section at the Exhibition." As that was not to be, he, a modern artist, would await no patron, but hang his own show.

In early May, Vincent wrote his new sister-in-law from St.-Rémy, where the mental asylum was housed in a twelfth-century Franciscan convent with an austere cloistered walkway around a lovely interior garden. "The fear and horror of madness that I used to have has already lessened a great deal. And though here you continually hear terrible cries and howls like beasts in a menagerie, in spite of that people get to know each other very well and help each other when their attacks come on. When I am working in the garden, they all come to look, and I assure you they have the discretion and manners to leave me alone—more than the good people of the town of Arles, for instance.

"It may well be that I shall stay here long enough—I have never been so peaceful as here and in the hospital in Arles—to be able to paint a little at last. Quite near here there are some little mountains, gray and blue, and at their foot some very, very green cornfields and pines." A few weeks later, he wrote his brother to say he was doing fine. "I have a little room with greenish-gray paper with two curtains of sea-green with a design of very pale roses, brightened by slight touches of blood-red. These curtains, probably the relics of some rich and ruined deceased, are very pretty in design. A very worn armchair probably comes from the same source; it is upholstered with tapestry. . . . Through the iron-barred window I see a square field of wheat in an enclosure, a perspective like Van Gloyen, above which I see the morning sun rising in all its glory. . . .

"The food is so-so. Naturally it tastes rather moldy, like a cockroach-infested restaurant in Paris or in a boardinghouse. As these poor souls do absolutely nothing (not a book, nothing to distract them but a game of boules and a game of checkers) they have no other daily distraction than to stuff themselves with chick peas, beans, lentils, and other groceries."

For some time, Thomas Edison had been hearing disquieting reports from London about his old friend Col. George Gouraud, who held the European rights to the phonograph. The colonel was apparently promoting the machine as a high-profile Edison curiosity and personal cash cow rather than as a serious product of great promise. Samuel Insull, general manager of the Edison Machine Works, had once worked for Gouraud and now heard from his father in London that Gouraud was "'making a great deal of money' exhibiting the phonograph. I do not think the contract calls for such a thing." Indeed, Gouraud, besieged at Edison House by crowds anxious to hear this miraculous apparatus, had decided to charge for the privilege of listening (on one of the long earphones) to an introductory speech by Edison, followed by short recordings of Prime Minister William Gladstone, the poet Robert Browning flubbing some of his own verses, and Sir Arthur Sullivan declaring, "I am astonished and somewhat terrified at the results of this evening's experiments—astonished at the wonderful power you have developed and terrified at the thought that so much hideous and bad music may be put on record forever!"

Edison largely ignored the gossip about his old friend, for he was focused on the larger issues—above all, the coming Paris World's Fair. "Without doubt," Edison reminded Gouraud in early March of 1889, "the fair would be . . . the best opportunity, which can or will be had, to introduce the phonograph to the peoples of Europe, in fact the whole world, and as such my desire is to take every advantage of it." Back in December Edison had told him, "I have placed Mr. W. J. Hammer in charge of the whole [Paris World's Fair] exhibit and he is actively engaged in getting together everything which we propose showing. These arrangements, of course, include the phonograph. I will send instruments from here for the purpose and attend to all the details in connection therewith." Edison expected Gouraud to pay his part of the very substantial costs.

In late March, Gouraud confirmed the unpleasant rumors about himself when he blithely informed Edison that he had installed a phonograph in the Gainsborough Gallery on Bond Street, where "anyone who wishes to pay for the privilege may see it." As huge crowds waited patiently and paid the fee, the enterprise proved gratifyingly lucrative. Edison was furious, especially when he learned that Gouraud had proposed to Hammer to replicate this profitable scheme at the Paris fair. On April 8, less than a month before the Exposition Universelle was to open, Edison sent Gouraud a cablegram: "Refuse absolutely to permit charging entrance fees or the introduction of any side show or Barnum methods at Paris." Gouraud argued back that his heavy fair expenses in exhibiting the phonograph warranted "a small charge of admission to the general public and complimentary tickets can be issued to the nobility and other people of importance. . . . I quite understand that you shall not participate in the expense. . . . I will take the risk myself *and my profits.*"

Shortly thereafter, Edison cabled Hammer: "Make no arrangement with Gouraud. . . . Intend exhibit shall be my own, at my own expense, and under my control." On April 20, Edison informed Gouraud of the same and charged him with following a course that "threatens to bring the enterprise into contempt in the estimation of the public. . . . You have a very large interest in the proceeds of the legitimate enterprise contemplated in your contract with myself. . . . I expect to invest money before looking for a return. . . . I will not countenance an exhibition of the phonograph for money anywhere within the City of Paris during the time that the Universal Exposition is in progress."

Edison had perhaps less patience for Gouraud—who was, after all, an old business partner—than he might have, for earlier that year the great inventor had learned that two of his trusted American partners in the phonograph had secretly diverted to themselves $250,000 due Edison when they sold his phonograph rights. Edison, wounded and angered by this betrayal, was turning to the courts for redress.

Alas for Gen. Rush Hawkins—he, too, had his woes. As April faded into May and the opening of the exhibition loomed, Whistler's defection looked to be the least of his troubles. As late as March, Hawkins had still been desperately trying to get an official allocation of exhibition space, some actual walls for hanging art. It would be hard for anyone who had not experienced the Parisian art scene to comprehend the complex and exalted role that art played in the city. Edward Simmons, one of the expatriate artists chosen for the official American exhibition, caught its spirit when he described his first Salon in 1881. He and his art student friends would "congregate at the Palais de l'Industrie [on the Champs-Élysées] and watch the four or five thousand pictures arrive for selection. From these only about two thousand were chosen. We were a great crowd, lining the grand stairway or sitting on the balustrade, and it was everybody's business to be funny. First would come vans and wagons from which would issue twenty and sometimes forty pictures; then messengers; poor artists with their one creation." Hoots, jeers, and curses greeted the flood tide of paintings, with the catcalls pausing respectfully only when the work of an acknowledged master came through the gauntlet.

The day the Salon opened, the president of the republic, no less, hosted the opening ceremony before an assemblage of political and artistic notables, who then toured the galleries of paintings hung from floor to ceiling. That afternoon's *vernissage*, or private viewing, was so socially fraught that top Paris fashion houses vied to have their new gowns debut there. "Everyone of importance and all fashion turned out," recalled Simmons. "New

York society cannot conceive of what a place the fine arts have in France. . . . [G]reat masses of people go through the galleries together, with some such person as Sarah Bernhardt at the head and the lesser following. . . . One who always attracted a crowd was Rosa Bonheur [the animal painter] who was made famous and wealthy by American dollars. She looked like a small, undersized man, wore gray trousers, Prince Albert coat and top hat to these affairs. Her face was gray white and wizened, and she gesticulated, speaking in a high, squeaky voice. I have never seen anyone who gave a more perfect impression of a eunuch." For days, even weeks, the press devoted endless columns to critiques and discussions of the painters and their work, and speculated about who might win a medal, and thus launch or consolidate a career.

Just as there were famous artists, so were there famous collectors. One such was the self-made millionaire Alfred Chauchard, owner of the city's fashionable department store Les Magasins du Louvre. "Whenever Chauchard's tall, bearded figure was seen in the Salon, there would be a sudden hush among the public. Even the most famous painters would defer to him as he ponderously inspected the display, occasionally shaking hands, solemnly passing judgement on one of the year's 'novelties' or remarking to the critics and journalists who followed him that 'this year the Salon is of exceptional quality. . . . What a pity that weeks are needed to see it all! Too much talent!" Chauchard showed off his own art collection during lavish entertainments at his avenue Velasquez mansion.

For the many rejected from the Salon, the Refusés, having their paintings seen was so important they sometimes arranged their own shows. The so-called Impressionists, painters such as Claude Monet, Camille Pissarro, Edgar Degas, Claude Renoir, Berthe Morisot, and the American Mary Cassatt, despite occasional acceptance at the Salon, still chose some years to exhibit separately. After visiting their 1877 show, American painter J. Alden Weir had written home, "I never in my life saw such horrible things. . . . It was worse than a chamber of horrors. I was there a quarter of an hour and left with a head ache." Cassatt had shown with the Americans in the 1879 Paris World's Fair, but this year she was recuperating from a bad fall from a horse. Hawkins had heard that a few of the Impressionists—notably Claude Monet—had been accepted into the official French fair exhibit.

Three days after Whistler decamped with his works, the beleaguered General Hawkins was sitting in his office when three female American journalists known to write about art scurried past and closeted themselves with Commissioner-General William B. Franklin. There had been a great deal of complaint among the American artists whose works were rejected for exhibit at the World's Fair. Sensing trouble, Hawkins knocked on the door and invited himself to the gathering. As he listened to these "three prying scribblers" bemoan the injustice of the juries, he could barely contain his temper. When the women asked Franklin, "Could you do something for the many [rejected] painters and sculptors who are suffering?" Hawkins leapt up and barked at them, "As long as I can help it, no revision will be made in the work of the American Art Jury!" General Franklin, more the diplomat, spoke soothing words all around, assuring the ladies that he "was well aware that much distress had been created . . . and he would do what he could to right affairs, if any wrongs had been perpetrated." True to his word and to Hawkins's chagrin, Franklin tried to keep peace in the American colony by reinstating a few refused works of art.

At times, General Hawkins had wondered if there would be space to display *any* art. Finally, in late April, mere weeks before the fair was to open, he secured two spacious rooms for the American painting exhibition, the largest at the fair after the French, but he was now at wit's end in his attempt to get them properly prepared. The French fair commissioners insisted that Hawkins accept the Parisian workmen they had assigned and none other. "These workmen lagged and loitered and loafed and lounged in a perfectly incredible fashion; appeals to their pride, their pockets, their sympathy with the great trans-Atlantic republic—all alike failed. It was not permitted to beat them. . . . [O]bjurgation, entreaty, epithet, and reproach all left them unmoved."

The general watched with actual tears of rage in his eyes as once again "these white-bloused idlers" departed work to get a drink. May had arrived, and still the American exhibition rooms were not close to ready—nor, for that matter, were anyone else's. A week before the fair was to open, a *New York Tribune* reporter described "the finest exhibition ever seen of packing cases, empty showcases and machinery not in motion. No exhibition ever was ready at the appointed date. This will be the unreadiest of all, and if justice is to be done, Frenchmen will award themselves a gold medal of the highest class for unpunctuality."

For weeks, Gustave Eiffel had been basking in the wild success of his monumental tower. "Paris is going into raptures about the Eiffel Tower," reported *The New York Tribune*, "which is one of the greatest successes as a wonder of the world that the world ever wondered at . . . a grandiose symbol of the march of progress since 1789." But while the Eiffel Tower might appear finished, workmen were still laboring around the clock in two twelve-hour shifts, night and day. The tower was crawling with painters coating the wrought-iron sections with a bronze red that lightened in the higher reaches almost to a yellow. As for the elevators, the galling truth was that the machines were *still* not operational, as all three elevator companies continued to work frantically to get their machines running smoothly. The Otis representatives were irritated because they were not allowed to use American-made Worthington pumps to get the water up to the reservoir on the second platform, nor was the water reservoir covered as they thought necessary. Consequently, when they tested their elevators, they operated below expectation, a failure the company insisted was not its fault.

Gustave Eiffel, meanwhile, had endeared himself to every trinket maker and seller in Paris. Shopkeepers along every boulevard and street sold "Eiffel Towers of every size, devoted to every purpose, from tiny charms for watch chains to large clocks for halls. . . . If a tall woman goes down a street, the gamins run after her, shouting, 'Mme. Eiffel! Mme. Eiffel!'" This being Paris, a clever dressmaker in the rue Auber was soon selling a ladies' dress, *Eiffel ascensionniste*, whose several ascending collars would be just the look when one visited the tower. The world of *la mode* was already referring to "Eiffel red." Out in the suburbs, gardens sprouted Eiffel Towers complete with little flags.

The Americans and English, meanwhile, maintained a churlish attitude toward the French achievement. "As an enormous and skillful monument of metallic construction," sniffed a *New York Times* correspondent, "the French admit its originality and value, but they deplore its ugliness and regret that the time and money were not given to something of more picturesque art, and *au fond*, they are not proud to show this gigantic iron structure to strangers. . . . [T]hey vote it an abomination and eyesore."

The editors of the London *Times* persisted in referring to the "monstrous erection in the midst of the noble public buildings of Paris." In an editorial, the paper conceded that the Eiffel Tower "has a certain symmetry of its own, and as a mere effort of engineering, never equaled in its own kind, it deserves high praise, if not all that its author has claimed for himself and his fellow-workers. Yet we are bound to remember that the beauty, the excellence, the grandeur of great engineering works consist in the perfect adaptation of means to ends, while in the case of the Eiffel Tower there are no ends at all, useful or ornamental, except in the idle ostentation more worthy of Chicago or San Francisco than of Paris."

As opening day for the Exposition Universelle neared, the City of Paris was in a "fever of festivity. . . . It has been repainted and regilded, and the grime of ten years has been scraped off many vast buildings of Caen stone, which are blazing in this May sun as if just whitewashed. Bouquets of tricolor flags are hung along many a street. . . . [T]here are signs of coming illuminations. The faces of the people are illuminated already. . . . The one thing that surprises all beholders is the Eiffel Tower. The upper part, light and graceful as if it had grown there with only Nature for its architect, looks severely down on the wilderness of edifices below, some of them business-like, some fantastic, all of them, like the tower, intensely modern."

In this Paris, ready for any and all adventures, every day, it seemed, there popped up more gigantic posters of a huge charging buffalo superimposed with a handsome Col. William F. Cody proclaiming, *"JE VIENS."* What, the Parisians wondered, were these garish hairy beasts plastered on every kiosk and fence? What were the posters advertising, and who was coming? Soon enough the newspapers explained. But as the images became ubiquitous, some French commentators began to complain. Albert Wolff of *Le Figaro* asked, "Haven't we had enough of this Buffalo Bill during the last fifteen days?"

The opening day of the Exposition Universelle, Monday, May 6, dawned cool and pale blue. By noon, the American editor of *The Christian Advocate* was among the jostling crowd of two hundred thousand who had paid three francs (triple the usual admission price) to attend the fair's inaugural festivities. "We were there early," he wrote, "but had to struggle with the crowd for forty minutes before reaching the gate of entrance." At two o'clock President Sadi Carnot and numerous ministers paraded in, heralded by breastplated cuirassiers and blaring trumpets. The French president pronounced (at length) suitably welcoming remarks before processing through the Gallery of Fine Arts, as yet unready for visitors. There he pressed several electrical buttons, causing the magnificent series of fountains in the three reflecting pools at the foot of the Eiffel Tower to burst into silvery life—their waters of vertical and crossed parabolic jets shooting skyward, tumbling and foaming down, and spraying back up again and sideways over the statues. Outside, the crowd unleashed a delighted roar and then began dispersing among the 228 acres of marvels.

Conspicuous in their absence from the opening ceremony was the entirety of the British and European diplomatic corps. "[British ambassador] Lord Lytton found that he had family engagements in England," related *The Tribune*'s man in Paris. "Count Hoyos was wanted in Austria. The Russian Ambassador's health required him to take the waters at Aix, which is thought more annoying than if he had gone to St. Petersburg. General Menabrea is improving his knowledge of French scenery. Count Munster is visiting his estates in Hanover. Such is the final response of monarchical Europe to the French Republic invitation to join in celebrating the overthrow of monarchy. The French are vexed, which is natural, if not reasonable." The ambassadors of more distant realms in Asia and Africa were in attendance in all their native sartorial splendor. The retiring American minister, Mr. Robert Lane, was noticeable for the very plainness of his black suit, undecorated by medals or military honors.

The American editor of *The Christian Advocate* stood and looked around as best he could through the happy assembly. The Eiffel Tower loomed overhead, its industrial presence a foil to the dancing fountains and the 195-foot-high bronze and brilliant turquoise blue rococo Central Dome, surmounted by a thirty-foot-tall statue of the female incarnation of France. The domes of the flanking palaces of Liberal Arts and Fine Arts shimmered in complementary blue-green faience splendor. The editor moved with the throngs through the verdant, flowering grounds artfully landscaped with ten thousand full-grown trees and shrubs, including thousands of rhododendron just bursting into iridescent pink bloom. Colorful banners fluttered in the breeze as he walked toward the exhibition halls on paths graced with bronze and marble statuary. He felt adrift in a dreamscape from the *Thousand and One Nights.*

In the Palace of Fine Arts he found the French were still hanging their hundred-year retrospective of French artistic genius from Fragonard to Rodin. On the east side, the Palace of Liberal Arts would soon be filled with impressive republican exhibits on education, photography, music, medicine, and books. The editor found "the exhibits in an imperfect state . . . the articles of others not even having arrived upon the ground." Here at its Exposition Universelle, the French republican administration intended— when all the exhibits were actually installed—to serve up a carefully constructed vision of La Belle France after eighteen years of their governance: "humanistic, philanthropic, opening its arms to all of humanity. . . . The Republic in 1889 would present two faces to the world: one as educator, benefactor, and distributor of light and bread; the other as champion of France's imperial mission purveying the same benefits abroad through the division of Africa and the conquest of Indochina."

The first fairgoers were delighted to find so many exotic cultures in such convenient proximity. The American editor could barely believe the fantastical pavilions of the South American nations, above all the "palace of the Argentine Republic . . . perhaps the most beautiful building on the grounds . . . [a] glittering mass of incrusted gold and flashing crystals, with color upon color like the fairy dreams of childhood." At the Egyptian section he strolled down the rue du Caire with its many open-air shops and coffeehouses. "There are fifty or sixty Egyptian donkeys with genuine donkey boys. Yonder is a company of Moors from Morocco and Algeria, living, working, eating, sleeping, dressing, just as we have seen them in those countries. The East Indian soldiers were there on guard in their peculiar dress; the Chinese, in their native costume, are painting and decorating their houses."

The American editor now followed the crowds along the Left Bank of the Seine and found himself perusing pavilions devoted to agriculture. As he noted, "France, of course, has the largest display, and the department of wines, the exhibition of the varieties of vats, wine-making, and preserving machinery gives a stupendous idea of the ingenuity, capital, and labor of the business, and shows most depressingly the terrible forces in the way of universal temperance." The bitter fact, for the French, was that their vineyards (and thus their wine industry) had been under siege from the phylloxera aphid, an alien pest traced back to plants imported from the United States. It was little solace to French farmers watching their ancient vineyards wither that the solution seemed to be replanting with American grapevines.

And of course there was the Eiffel Tower, always drawing back visitors like a lodestar: The editor was properly awed by this "most extraordinary triumph of energy, industry, and engineering skill. . . . The various engineers and artists who opposed it, and the general public who called the projector a 'barbarian' or a monomaniac, with one accord acknowledge it to be graceful, practical, useful, and ornamental. . . . It is in one sense a veritable tower of Babel, for amid the crowds walking about at the base I recognized twenty-eight dialects and languages besides considerable jargon which I could not identify owing to my ignorance." The milling public could not know it, but up on the tower, one of Gustave Eiffel's worst fears had come true—the Eiffel Tower was not ready for the public on the day the World's Fair opened. And so, the visitors wandered about below and craned their necks to admire this edifice they could not yet ascend. Overhead, they could hear and see busy workmen.

Opening day with so many wonders ended for the editor of *The Christian Advocate* with "an amazing display of fireworks. . . . From the sound it would have been easy to believe that the city of Paris was being bombarded, and from the spectacle that the whole heavens were in a state of recrystallization . . . at 10 o'clock on Monday night as a loud explosion was heard, the [Eiffel] Tower blazed from base to summit with red Greek fire, and then was crowned by a shower of green Roman candles." The first World's Fair ever to be open at night, thanks to Edison and his electrical inventions, the illuminated Exposition was a lovely sight. "The next morning," wrote the editor, "all Paris went to work as though nothing had happened, but I felt as one might whose eyes had seen and whose ears had heard the nineteenth century in a day and a night."

Alas, as the editor had learned, few of the actual exhibits in any of the Champ de Mars buildings were properly installed, much less open. The monumental glass-and-iron Gallery of Machines had a jeweled exterior shimmering with colored glass, mosaics, and ceramic brick. Inside, however, the colossal fifteen-acre temple to engineering and industry was largely a litter of unopened crates and half-assembled machinery. Soon enough it would be devoted to "all aspects of French industry, ranging from machinery for agriculture and food processing to equipment for clothmaking, papermaking, woodworking, construction, and generating electricity. Pumps, dynamos, transformers, engines, hydraulic elevators, and even windmills [would be displayed]." Traversing it all overhead was a welcome novelty for weary fairgoers—a moving walkway.

The shining exception to the tardiness in the Galerie des Machines was the Edison exhibit, which was up and running from the very first day. "The Exposition has been opened a week and is an assured success," reported William Hammer to Edison. "On the day of opening (last Monday) we were in better shape than any exhibit in the Machinery Palace, and the only place that President Carnot and his party stopped in the building was in front of the Edison Department to examine the 'Big Lamp,' Edison's bust and picture, and we had two phonographs with loud records one singing the 'marseillais' [*sic*] and 'America' and the other shouting, 'Vive Carnot,' 'Vive la France,' 'Vive la République.' . . . Incidentally I will remark that the U.S. Commissioners have been more bother than assistance to us here and the complaints of their inefficiency and lack of attention are general, however, they did not get away with us, though they have tried to cut up our space and take some of it away on various occasions."

There were many American journalists at the Paris World's Fair in these early weeks. One reporter, Harold Frederic, was determined to review his country's painting exhibition, its best prospect for cultural glory, even though it was not yet open. He found himself sneaking past a policeman and squeezing through a boarded-up doorway. In the rooms beyond, he found but half of the 341 American oil paintings actually hung, while the rest were stacked against the walls amid a jumble of construction debris. As he poked about the mess, examining the offerings, Frederic had some severe opinions. Why, he wondered, had Henry Bacon sent "as his solitary picture a cheap and trivial daub"? And why had Walter Gay and Alexander Harrison contributed eleven gigantic canvases "with scarcely one square foot of good painting"?

But when Frederic entered another room, the gallery of the expatriate painters, he came upon the works of John Singer Sargent, whose six large portraits of women and girls proved him "easily the most distinguished and original of American artists abroad. . . . He does not know how to be commonplace or conventional." Sargent, an internationally acclaimed painter at thirty-three, had relocated his studio from Paris to London in 1884 to escape the scandal surrounding his Salon painting *Madame X*, which depicted the American beauty Virginie Gautreau in a black evening gown with one strap suggestively slipping off her chalk-white shoulder. To his and her surprise, the work was vilified as a debauched portrait unworthy of a married woman. His current paintings, while masterful, were unlikely to ignite outrage.

Although much of the actual exhibition was far from ready, the grounds alone were an amazing enough creation to satisfy most early visitors. Trilled one American reporter, "The walks are broad, the trees numerous, the grass luxuriant and green, the fountains always bursting with their stores of molten silver, the birds vocal with glad songs, and the cafés flowing with absinthe and beer. For now the Frenchman drinks his Munich beer without bitter recollections of German insolence. . . . Everywhere the finger tips are kissed at you and you breathe in the spirit of the merry chanson. The Eiffel Tower has character. It is distinctly French. It kisses its finger tips at you. It is nothing if not light, airy, volatile. It strikes one as being even effervescent. It seems as if it might in the dead hours of the night, when no one was looking, pick up its short skirts and dance the pastoral version of the can-can trimmed with the waltz."

For American tourists there were other de rigueur attractions in Paris—the Louvre, where you might buy a painting from the dozens of copyists busy at their easels; the city's ancient monuments and churches; cafés; *jardins*; the twice-daily fashionable cavalcade at the Bois de Boulogne; the horse races; and above all, shopping for all those irresistible bibelots, perfumes, and gowns from the House of Worth or the less well known Monsieur Arnaud. Gastronomes settled into leisurely meals at the Grand Véfour, Ledoyen on the Champs-Élysées, or Lapérouse.

Oddly, for decades the standard American tour had also required a grisly stop at the Paris morgue, conveniently near Notre Dame. "We stood before a grating," related the dutiful Mark Twain, "and looked through into a room which was hung all about with the clothing of dead men; coarse blouses, water-soaked; the delicate garments of women and children;

patrician vestments, flecked and stabbed and stained with red; a hat that was crushed and bloody. On a slanting stone lay a drowned man, naked, swollen, purple." It was also still possible, Americans learned from the ever-alert *New York Herald*, to see a French criminal guillotined. On Thursday, May 23, in the Place de la Roquette, a soldier who had murdered an old woman had been so dispatched before a small crowd of "horror seekers."

And then there was the somewhat more daring side of Parisian tourism, outings to bohemian Montmartre, where Rodolphe Salis ran the fashionable cabaret Le Chat Noir. Here "actors and singers kept up a stream of mockery and invective aimed at society, politicians, the rich and the demi-monde," the very audience who jammed the cabaret. Even more sensational and beloved was singer-poet Aristide Bruant, who performed at his cabaret, Le Mirliton. A burly man with thick dark locks, Bruant always strode onto the floor about 11:00 p.m., dressed in his signature look: black corduroy jacket, pants, scarlet flannel shirt, black neck scarf, and black boots. "He would gaze disdainfully at his audience for a few moments and then announce the title of his new number: 'Now, I'm going to sing you *à Saint Lazare!*' and then exhort his listeners to join in: 'As for you, herd of camels, try to bray together in tune, will you?'" One Paris critic described "an arrogant and brutal voice which penetrated into your soul like the stab of a flick-knife into a straw dummy." For several hours Bruant would keep the audience mesmerized, mixing his working-class songs with insults and an easy geniality. For tourists whose taste ran to racier entertainment, there were nightclubs such as the Folies Bergère.

An American gentleman sitting by himself at a sidewalk café might soon find discreetly slipped onto his table a scented pink visiting card with a female name and address "and the hint *'tout confort'* or 'discretion assured.' Some were more eloquent, promising such delights as *'tableaux vivants'* and all the refinements of 'modern science.'" Far more open were the city's two hundred or so *brasseries filles*, spots such as the Café du Gaulois and the Brasserie Moderne, where foreigners might drop in not just for a beer but also to order up one of the serving girls for a paid assignation in an upstairs room. The brasseries operated somewhat sub rosa, avoiding the strict government rules for brothels.

For those with more money, Paris of 1889 offered far more elaborate and luxurious sexual scenarios than waitresses of easy virtue. The city had seventy-five licensed brothels, identifiable by their extra-large illuminated street numbers. One of the most famous high-class bordellos was the Chabanais, whose reception room was decorated with "antique furniture, gilt and inlaid panelling and 18th-century paintings." Once the customer had selected his partner, he had the choice of "the Japanese, Spanish or Directoire rooms or the astonishing 'Moorish' room in imitation of the Alhambra at Granada, the Chambre Louis XVI with painted medallions in the style of Boucher, or its extraordinary 'Pompeian saloon' for which Toulouse-Lautrec had painted some medallions. Finally, as an added attraction for those drawn to the 'English vice,' it had 'the prettiest torture chamber in Paris.'"

As evening fell on Friday, May 10, Buffalo Bill and his Wild West cowboys and Indians crowded the rails on the upper decks of the *Persian Monarch*, scanning the horizon for signs of France and terra firma. After violently tempestuous days at sea, the troupe was more than eager to reach Le Havre. For many of the Indians, wrapped against the cold in colorful blankets, their long hair braided with feathers and beads, this had been their first ocean voyage. When Lakota holy man Black Elk crossed the "big water," he wrote of fears that the boat "might drop off where the water ended." When storms struck, "we were all in despair and many were feeling so sick that they began to sing their death-songs." Now the Atlantic was calm, the sky indigo blue, and the first stars just coming out.

Closer to Le Havre, a tugful of French reporters had been scanning the horizon for the *Persian Monarch* since late afternoon. The reporters had begun their day in Paris, boarding two saloon carriages chartered by the Wild West show, well stocked, reported *The Herald*, with "an elegant cold collation . . . washed down with some of Moët et Chandon's dryest. The journey was enlivened by Mr. Crawford's many anecdotes of the harassing trouble he had had with French authorities before he could obtain permission to open the show." Nate Salsbury and T. C. Crawford had been in Paris since January, negotiating a site for the Wild West camp, getting it prepared, laying the groundwork with the press, and making sure the city was plastered with the "JE VIENS" posters. Salsbury had been awaiting the reporters at the Le Havre terminal, and by midafternoon they were cruising the waters beyond the port in their tug and ready to greet the *Persian Monarch*. Ferdinand Xau of the *Écho de Paris* stared through his binoculars, raising a fuss at every fishing boat that passed off in the distance.

Five o'clock came and went. Six o'clock. The ocean was placid but empty of any sign of the *Persian Monarch*. The reporters were getting restive. At around seven o'clock Xau swore he saw smoke on the horizon. Forty-five minutes later, the Wild West's green ocean liner finally loomed into sight, steaming toward the port and the tug. The French press and Crawford and Salsbury all began to yell and wave. Colonel Cody's answering shouts set the cowboys and Indians to whooping and yelling. The Cowboy Band struck up "Yankee Doodle Dandy," and followed up with "La Marseillaise." As the tug came up alongside the steamship, its passengers were informed that no one could board before the French health authorities had inspected the ship. The reporters settled in for another wait, until finally, at eight o'clock, another tug arrived with the inspectors. The tide was now going out, and so the leviathan ship couldn't enter port until the following day. The health inspectors decided to postpone their work, saying they would return in the morning at six o'clock.

Colonel Cody was not pleased, for the delay meant he would miss that night's press banquet. Nate Salsbury had the press tug draw alongside the *Persian Monarch*, and only he was allowed to clamber up a swaying rope ladder so he could join Buffalo Bill aboard. As the press tug pulled away at nine o'clock under a rising moon, the frustrated French reporters saw the Indian men on deck starting to dance, while the women sang and chanted, making a sound the French heard as "hou, hou." Charmed and tantalized by this brief encounter, the reporters salved their disappointment at a sumptuous Wild West–hosted banquet in town, presided over by U.S. consul Monsieur Dufais, replete with many champagne toasts and uneasy jokes about Indians and scalping.

As dawn broke on Saturday, the Wild West steamship was escorted by tugs into port amid a frenzy of debarkation preparations. Le Havre's morning newspapers had stirred up a sensation with their descriptions of *Guillaume Buffalo et ses peaux rouges, garçons de boeuf et incroyable bufles*. The whole town wanted a glimpse of these mythic beings from the New World. Even the large, jovial Major John Burke, Wild West company manager, could not believe his eyes as they docked in the harbor. "There must have been fifty thousand people there. They were on all the docks, in the rigging of the ships near by, even on the nearest housetops." The Paris press was once again assembled, still anxious to board the *Persian Monarch*, its decks "crowded with strange, weird-looking Indians of all sorts of hues, wrapped in queer-looking blankets." The American correspondents watched with amusement as the French newsmen rushed up the gangplank, and Ferdinand Xau, prince of Paris reporters, boldly shouted in English as he seized Colonel Cody's hand, "How are you?"

Buffalo Bill and Major Burke squired the reporters around, starting with the menagerie in the now-pungent stalls belowdecks. Twenty buffalo were recumbent, placidly chewing their cud. "They had been the best sailors of the whole lot," said Cody. "Nothing seemed to upset them. When the ship rolled they simply lay down and rolled with her." The horses had not fared as well, with two of the two hundred dying during the storm-tossed crossing. Then Cody led the reporters back up on deck to meet several dozen of the one hundred Indians. He introduced various Sioux chiefs, strapping men wrapped up against the early-morning chill in their heavy blankets, striking with their high-cheekboned faces, stoic reserve, and many tattoos.

A century had passed since the French roamed North America as trappers and colonists, and now they mainly knew of *les Peaux Rouges* through James Fenimore Cooper's elegiac *Last of the Mohicans*, the hugely popular Western novels of the late French adventurer and author Gustave Aimard, and Chateaubriand's romantic 1801 novel, *Atala*, set in the New World. The French press gawked and marveled that the Indians really did have bronze-red skin. Meanwhile, the health inspectors asked them various questions, decided that the Indians had to be inoculated against smallpox, and proceeded to give them all shots.

The reporter for *Le Figaro* found the Indians "majestic and proud." Both men and women, he noted, dressed in much the same clothes—buckskin pants, a long loose overshirt with colorful fringe. Both favored long hair. He was startled to find, when he opened his cigarette case, "twenty hands covered with tattoos made for the case. I gestured certainly. In the blink of an eye, the cigarette case was empty. But I was repaid by the Indians' *owah! owah!* of satisfaction."

Bronco Bill Nelson, a lanky white man married to an Indian, stepped forward to serve as interpreter, making special introductions to the chiefs Red Shirt, Rocky Bear, Eagle Man, Black Hawk, and No Neck. Red Shirt, tall, handsome, and noble, and a veteran of the London trip, was in charge of the Wild West Indians. His wife was among the numerous women and children traveling with the troupe. The paternalistic U.S. Office of Indian Affairs took a dim view of Wild West shows, and had only reluctantly allowed the Sioux to go overseas, as the Indian commissioners thought their charges should be home on reservations adjusting to their new lives as farmers. Families had come along to maintain moral tone. Cody had posted a $20,000 cash bond with the government to guarantee proper treatment, while every Indian on deck that day had had to get the local Indian agent to sign off on his contract.

The French reporters then met Annie Oakley, and found this demure young woman hard to reconcile with guns or marksmanship. The press was thrilled to find a few French-speaking Canadian trappers in the troupe, reminders of the old days of French empire in America. The best known was Gabriel Dumont, lieutenant to Louis Riel, who had been hanged in 1885 for leading the North-West Rebellion in Manitoba against the British. As Cody introduced the Canadians, Annie Oakley disappeared down to her cabin, where she was soon busy filling hot-water bottles with fifty pounds of her favorite Schultze gunpowder. French customs had just informed her that she could not bring in the English gunpowder she swore by, so she was forced to improvise a smuggling scheme. When it came time to debark, each of the show's four cowgirls figured out how best to keep a powder-filled water bottle hidden under her dress bustle as she walked

Annie Oakley

smilingly off the *Persian Monarch* and onto the busy quay. "We sure did attract some attention," said Oakley later, "as we went down that gang plank, for although the bustle originated in France it was going out about that time."

The next morning in Paris, the Wild West's special train pulled into a station in leafy Batignolles, near Montmartre, a rustic quarter of cottages, gardens, and windmills popular with artists and writers. Here all the cowboys and Indians debarked before a curious crowd of onlookers and began leading the horses and buffalo off the railroad cars. The Indians boarded three large brake carriages, while each cowboy and cowgirl mounted a horse and led several others. This "curious cavalcade," reported *The New York Herald*, proceeded up "the route de la Révolte to the 'camp' at Neuilly. . . . The buffaloes were driven along in leash. A large and gradually increasing crowd assembled round the station and along the line of route. Shortly after leaving the station, one of the buffalo managed to get loose and started for a run on his own account, to the great dismay of the crowd. He was, however, deftly lassoed in the twinkling of an eye by a watchful cowboy. . . . After this . . . the whole company arrived in camp without further incident. Large furniture vans followed with the tents and baggage."

The camp, situated inside the crumbling ruins of the Porte de Ternes fort, was surrounded by towering old shade trees. All spring, Salsbury and Crawford had been preparing the grounds for this day, when the Wild West troupe would arrive to pitch its two hundred tents and fill the corrals with horses and buffalo. The whole camp had been encircled by a western-style stockade fence, and beautifully landscaped with broad red gravel paths, greenswards, and flowering bushes and shrubs. Up on the old fortifications, hundreds of curious French had gathered to watch this strange spectacle of the American West setting up camp in their suburb, the cowboys erecting the spacious square living tents and the huge outdoor mess hall, while the Indians pitched and secured their large teepees decorated with paintings of buffalo and hunting. The horses, mules, and buffalo were let loose to graze in separate corrals.

The French would soon learn that the mysterious but wonderfully handsome Buffalo Bill was one of America's more famous western army scouts, a rider for the brief-lived Pony Express, a celebrated buffalo hunter and wilderness guide, an occasional Indian fighter, and a man immortalized in hundreds of cheap dime novels about western exploits. In recent years, "Guillaume Buffalo" had been the successful star and promoter of a new kind of entertainment, the Wild West show, a nostalgic celebration of the often-brutal settling of the fast-vanishing American frontier.

Charismatic and outgoing, Colonel Cody was also optimistic, far too generous, and highly fond of a drink. "Buffalo Bill was one of the world's great men. I don't mean wise, but I do mean great," said Johnny Baker, a boy whom Cody and his wife, Lulu, took in and helped raise after they lost their own young son. Baker, a sharpshooter in the Paris show ("Petit Jean Tireur"), spoke for almost all who knew Cody. "His heart was as big as his show tent, and as warm as a ranch house cookstove. Around his supple body there was an aura that people loved to share."

And while Buffalo Bill had certainly been an Indian fighter (who proudly displayed in his luxurious tent the purported scalp of the Cheyenne Indian Yellow Hand), he had a sympathy for the Indians' plight that was rare at the time. "In nine times out of ten," Cody was fond of saying, "where there is trouble between white men and Indians, it will be found that the white man is responsible." Wrote Cody biographer Louis S. Warren, "Often, [Buffalo Bill] buttressed this political commentary with references to Indian nobility. 'Indians expect a man to keep his word. They can't understand how a man can lie. Most of them would as soon cut off a leg as tell a lie.' He routinely criticized the failure of Americans to abide by their treaties, warning that 'there is just one thing to be considered' where the 'management of Indians' was concerned: 'That is, that when you promise him anything you must keep your word; break it, and the trouble commences at once. . . . Although I have had many a tough fight with the red man my sympathy is with him entirely, because he has been ill-used and trampled on by those whose duty it was to protect him.'"

Although Cody himself was a master of organization and a natural showman, it was when Nate Salsbury came aboard as the outfit's manager in 1884 that Buffalo Bill's Wild West was catapulted into new realms of celebrity. Salsbury brought on the excellent Cowboy Band, discovered the show's biggest single draw, Annie Oakley, and created a coherent narrative that distinguished the show from a half-dozen competitors. In recent seasons the Wild West show had made significant money, which the big-hearted Cody quickly spent. "Where did the money go?" asked biographer Warren. "He invested much of it in Scout's Rest and his other properties. The rest seemed to vanish. He had a taste for fine belongings, like the extravagant four-in-hand coach which he ordered and which he drove around North Platte with crowds of elegant guests." Buffalo Bill also gave loans (rarely repaid) to almost any comer, supporting numerous family members, and investing "wildly in mines, irrigation schemes, hotels (usually in places tourists had no interest in going), and even products such as White Beaver's Cough Cream, the Great Lung Healer."

Both Americans and the British loved Cody's much-imitated Wild West entertainment formula, in which modernity and progress (i.e., white civilization) triumphed over the old and backward (i.e., the buffalo and Indians). The presence of actual Indians in his show blunted any criticism. The English had loved Cody and his show as much as the Americans. But how would the French receive it? Cody the gambler and entrepreneur was betting they would love it.

Although Crawford and Salsbury had arrived months earlier to prepare the arena and campground, a great deal of work remained before the Wild West's advertised opening performance of May 18, not the least of which was completing grandstands to accommodate fifteen thousand spectators and helping their impresario and orator, Frank Richmond, learn all his speeches in French.

Nine days after the official opening of the Universal Exposition, Gustave Eiffel was at long last finally ready for business. On May 15, at 11:50, the great engineer's *Tour en Fer de Trois Cents Mètres,* still being painted a shimmering bronze red, welcomed the paying masses. It was exactly two years, four months, and one week since Eiffel had broken ground for the foundations. Eiffel himself, fittingly, was the first to sign the official guest book: "Ten minutes to twelve, May 15, 1889," he wrote. "The tower is opened to the public. At last!" Directly below signed in Sauvestre, the original architect of the tower, with the whimsical *"Midi moins neuf, ouf!"* From up on the first platform, where three of the four restaurateurs were not ready to serve customers, Eiffel could see thousands already lined up below, waiting patiently to be among the first to ascend the stairway.

Very possibly those first visitors saw and recognized the modest Gustave

Eiffel, like the captain of a ship always on duty. He was no king, no prince, but a man of middling birth who had made the best use of his education and his democratic opportunities to build some of the leading structures of industrial civilization. He had helped his fellow men and become rich and successful in the process. Eiffel had become, as Lockroy had hoped, a living refutation of all monarchical doctrine. The gilded names engraved on the Eiffel Tower's first-floor frieze were not those of rulers, but French scientists, men whose knowledge had advanced the world. The tower was elegant, powerful, and playful, but its ultimate message was political, in a world where kings and queens still ruled much of the earth.

Above, on the second platform, *Le Figaro* had already opened its tiny office with a small staff and a printing press to publish *Le Figaro, Édition Spéciale Imprimée dans la Tour Eiffel*. On this heady occasion, the first issue was available for sale for fifteen centimes. "We have put together this number," the Eiffel Tower journalists wrote, "under rather special conditions: in a shack that barely covers our heads, amid carpenters, gas workers, blacksmiths, and painters, dizzy from the unaccustomed air, dust, and noise and tired by the climb up 730 steps (36 stories, if you please) because the tower's elevators are not working yet." The newspaper staff encouraged all visitors to drop by their aerial office to sign a guest book, as their names would be run in subsequent issues of the paper. The first person to affix his signature was a wealthy Arab in a burnoose named Si-Ali-Mahoui.

The weather was perfect—clear and cool with gentle spring zephyrs wafting through the tower's airy structure. Throughout the day a steady line of thousands gaily ascended the stairs, having paid one franc each to reach the first platform. Eiffel's workers were still rushing about painting and fixing and finishing a thousand and one details. As for Gustave Eiffel, on this inaugural public debut of his magnum opus, he "remained all day, ever active and full of contented zeal. Cheers were given a Mme. Sommer, who was the first lady to touch terra firma above. . . . All the French press came and one or two foreign journalists. Each and all inscribed their names on the *Figaro* sheet."

Only the hardier souls ascending the tower paid yet another franc to press on to the second platform, up another 380 steep spiral steps. There they signed *Le Figaro*'s book and patronized Monsieur Jacquart's little stand-up bar. It remained a most galling truth that while one could watch various persons testing the elevators of the Eiffel Tower, they were *still* not ready for public use. The tower was a marvel, but without the elevator service, no one could ascend to the top, the pinnacle of the whole experience. *Le Figaro* acknowledged that while there was no fixed date for the opening of the elevators, "it's not more, we believe, than a matter of five or six days."

Eiffel, his daughter, Claire, and his son-in-law, Monsieur Salles, and Monsieur Sauvestre, the tower's original architect, and his wife all dined at the first platform's one open eatery, La Brasserie Alsace-Lorraine on that first day. When a boy appeared with the first issue of *Le Figaro de la Tour* hot off the small press, customers rushed for copies, knowing they would be valuable souvenirs. Eiffel gallantly toasted this printed sign of progress.

Next to the astonishment of the tower, there were no greater technological marvels at the Exposition than those to be found in the Edison Company's one-acre exhibit in the vast iron-and-glass Galerie des Machines. William Hammer, directing forty-five assistants, had more than succeeded in showcasing all the Edison inventions, celebrating the still-novel miracle of electricity. It was widely agreed that "what Eiffel is to the externals of this exposition Edison is to the interior. He towers head and shoulders in individual importance over any other man. . . . His exhibits have the place of honor, the largest space given to any one interest." It took *Engineering Magazine* fourteen issues to cover them all. An Edison central generating station ran artful displays of thousands of incandescent bulbs of every size, shape, and color, and "fountains of light," luminous and lovely. Visitors admired numerous variations on the telephone and a telegraph that sent messages back and forth to a little moving train. Here people had a glimpse of a future transformed by technology: safe, easy lights for their homes and workplaces; quick, simple communication via telephones. Of course, only the most affluent could afford such luxuries.

But the unquestioned technological sensation of the World's Fair—to Edison's delight—was his newly perfected talking phonograph. While the machine was certainly capable of playing music, Edison envisioned the phonograph mainly "for business purposes only." In Paris, for the first time, the device was available to the public, who could not get enough of it. From the opening day, many thousands of fairgoers stood in long, slow lines to hear the recorded human voice—they could choose among fifty different languages—captured on wax cylinders and played back on one of the twenty-five phonographs. When someone's turn came, he gingerly took the little earbuds attached by a wire to the machine (five per machine), inserted them in his ears, and listened intently. Almost without fail, a look of astonishment soon spread over his face. With so many waiting in line, each listener was limited to three minutes.

Fair visitors sated with modern machinery or edifying exhibits on chocolate making and champagne escaped Western civilization entirely by drifting over to the "villages" showcasing France's new colonies. The nearest was the rue du Caire, the Egyptian market street, complete with crumbling minareted mosque and tall whitewashed buildings on each side, each inset with typical beautiful tiles, carved wooden doors, and arched windows. Cheeky young donkey drivers in long blue tunics added real color as they galloped up and down through the bustling outdoor bazaar. In the street's many little shops, native craftsmen hammered out brass trays, threw pottery, chiseled delicate carvings, or made leather goods, including ornate saddles. And as in any good Oriental souk, rug merchants plied customers with glasses of tea.

The exotic music of Arab orchestras wafted out from small cafés. Fairgoers tentatively stepped inside to sit at the small tables and revive themselves with tiny cups of strong bitter coffee or dishes of icy sherbet, or even the gummy dessert Turkish delight. Most were astonished in the first days of the fair to discover that these cafés featured female Egyptian dancers. The *danse du ventre*, or belly dancing, quickly became one of the fair's undisputed sensations. "A girl in half-nude dress," reported the *New York Times* reporter, "revealing a good deal of ugliness under closely-drawn tulle, rises and walks about, moving, first, her bosom, and then her hips in true Eastern fashion. . . . The girls dance in bare feet outrageously painted red and yellow."

The Egyptian women performed on the half hour throughout the afternoon and evening, in "half a dozen grimy cafés," reported William Brownell, thirty-eight, a veteran of the *New York World* and now an editor at Charles Scribner's Sons. He took a jaundiced view of this particular craze, describing the performers as "so absolutely mechanical and listless . . . that, to a reflecting person, it was the audience that was really the spectacle." To his dismay, far too many American women were shamelessly

The bustling crowds along the fair's popular rue du Caire

present in those hole-in-the-wall cafés, avidly staring at the half-naked con-
tortions of their foreign sisters. "The [American women] almost forgot decorum in crowding for a better view, in leaning over the backs of chairs, in
concentrated, absorbed attention."

Those who tired of the delights (however dubious) of this faux little
Egypt could experience France's other colonial realms over in the second
section of the fair, located on the Esplanade des Invalides, best reached by
the specially installed toylike Decauville railroad. The diminutive train, which
made a two-mile trip around the perimeter of the two fairgrounds, also
quickly became popular: "A very wobbly, rock-a-bye little railway it is, with
notices put up all over it and along its route, warning you in every known
tongue not to put out your head, arms, or legs, and if you mind this in-
junction and hold on very firmly you don't fall out. When you reach the
Esplanade you wonder why you stayed so long on the Champ de Mars; for

if anything this is more delightful. Arabs stalk majestically around in their white bournous, and permit you to inspect their tents. Chinamen with no shoes and a great deal of hat fly by bearing passengers in their *pousse-pousses*, and laughing as if it were rather good fun, not hard work at all."

On the Esplanade, "the Arabic, Moorish and Turkish manufactures draw crowds. Here men are making shoes; there a woman is weaving a blanket, drawing her thread back and forth painfully, without even a shuttle. In the Morocco pavilion dinner is being served, and two men, reclining on a carpet, dip their hands together into the dish." Many French citizens saw for the first time some of the peoples of their new far-flung colonial empire. Fairgoers were lured by "the smell of Oriental spices and north African couscous, the sound of Senegalese tom-toms, Polynesian flutes and Annamite gongs, the sight of Moslem minarets and Cambodian temples. In the bazaars of the large Algerian and Tunisian pavilions craftsmen fashioned jewelry, finely tooled leather and brightly colored tapestries." All the enchanting possibilities were overwhelming. One reporter contemplated a day in which he would "breakfast at Siam, dine in Bucharest, have his tea served by real Indians, and wind up with a Khedive cigarette at the Egyptian concert, where the dance girl Aicha does not seem to be distant, to say the least."

In early May Paul Gauguin arrived in Paris from Pont-Aven to help hang the Volpini show. He and his friends had lugged their white-framed paintings on handcarts through the exhibition grounds to Monsieur Volpini's and carefully arranged the canvasses on its pomegranate-colored walls. In the end, Gauguin chose only one of his Martinique paintings and three Brittany pastels. During the few weeks he remained in the city, he spent late nights going round plastering buildings with advertising posters for the show: EXPOSITION DE PEINTURES AT THE EXPOSITION UNIVERSELLE.

Vincent had written Theo to say, "I think you were right not to show any pictures of mine at the exhibition that Gauguin and the others had. My not yet being recovered is reason enough for my keeping out of it without giving them offense.

"I think unquestionably Gauguin and [Émile] Bernard have great and real merit.

"And it remains very understandable that for beings like them—young and very vigorous, who *must* live and try to hack out their way—it would be impossible to turn all their canvases to the wall until it should please people to admit them into something, into the official stew. You cause a stir by exhibiting in cafés; I do not say it is not bad taste to do it, but I myself have this crime on my conscience twice over, as I exhibited at the Tambourin and at the Avenue de Clichy."

Gauguin happily joined the crowds exploring the newly opened fair. Like everyone else, he had an opinion on the Eiffel Tower: "Of course this exhibition sees the triumph of iron, not only with regard to machines but also with regard to architecture. And yet architecture is at a new beginning in the sense that it lacks an artistic form of decoration consistent with the new material. . . . It's up to the architect-engineers to come up with a new art of decoration, such as ornamental bolts, iron corners jutting beyond the main outline, a sort of gothic lacework of iron. To some extent this is what we find in the Eiffel Tower."

Still yearning to travel to the tropics, Gauguin was delighted to discover the next closest thing at the Esplanade: a bamboo-and-thatch Javanese kampong complete with a headman's house on stilts, and cafés in little huts amid a grove of bamboo. Dutch businessmen promoting Van Houten cacao and Lucas Bols spirits had arranged for sixty-five Javanese to live there during the fair, including "a troupe of temple dancers, little girls aged from twelve to sixteen, dressed in exquisitely bejewelled costumes, performing temple dances whose movements mirror the Khmer figures on the temple next door," a faithful life-size plaster replica of Angkor Wat in the new French colony of Cambodia.

Gauguin was just one of many artists enthralled by these living versions of art they had only seen in reproductions. "You missed something in not coming the other day," he wrote his friend Émile Bernard. "In the Javanese village there are Hindu dances. All the art of India can be seen in them, and they give you a literal transcription of the photographs I have from Cambodia. I'm going back on Thursday as I have an appointment with a mulatto girl. Come on Thursday, but I mustn't be too late getting there. . . . I intend to leave next Tuesday and I must think about packing up my things."

Brownell of Scribner's far preferred the serpentine Javanese dances performed to gamelan music to the belly dancing, describing how "all of artistic Paris" was in thrall to one particular Javanese dancer of fourteen or fifteen. "Her skin, of which a great deal was visible, was of the most beautiful golden hue, with citron shadows, and her arms were modelled with an extraordinary delicacy. Her face was decidedly of a moon-like character with eyes wide apart." All over the fair, novel sensations, dramas, and amusements abounded.

Javanese dancers

CHAPTER SIX

Buffalo Bill and Annie Oakley Triumphant

On Saturday, May 18, *le tout Paris* streamed toward Buffalo Bill's Wild West in the leafy precincts of the Parc de Neuilly. By two o'clock a distinguished crowd, including the former queen Isabella II of Spain, princes, counts, generals, politicians of high rank, and famous artists such as Jean-Louis-Ernest Meissonier had so overflowed the grandstands (capacity fifteen thousand) that there was standing room only. The entire American colony was patriotically present, wondering nervously what in the world the French would make of such a uniquely Yankee spectacle. Col. William F. Cody was staging this first invitation-only command performance in honor of Third Republic president Sadi Carnot. The Cowboy Band struck up a lively tune as U.S. Marines marched in with American minister Robert Lane, who then waited to welcome President and Madame Carnot and escort the couple to a loge box draped with the tricolor.

With that, Wild West orator Frank Richmond strode into the huge arena, where a vast canvas backdrop of the rugged Rocky Mountains and lonesome pines evoked the American West. Richmond, whose voice had been likened to a steam calliope, gamely began to declaim *"l'histoire de l'ouest sauvage de Buffalo Bill,"* in a freshly memorized French version of the scripted narration. Up in the jammed stands, the French audience collectively furrowed its brow trying to discern what language this impressive man might be speaking. Richmond declared in his rote-learned *français* that this frontier pageant was the real and true story of modern nineteenth-century American progress, the white man's taming of the Wild West of buffalo and Indians. He then introduced *"Le Grand Défilé de*

Toute la Troupe," and Buck Taylor led in the scores of whooping cowboys, who thundered about on their horses doing rope tricks. Proceeding more solemnly, the one hundred Plains Indians presented a fearsome sight in brilliant war paint and feathered bonnets, with orator Richmond introducing each chief by name. The Mexican vaqueros in their silver-bedecked costumes and sombreros rode past, as did the cowgirls, followed by the French-Canadian trappers and their Eskimo sled dogs, and of course that famous star Miss Annie Oakley. "Last—but not by any means least," reported the Paris *Herald,* "came Buffalo Bill, who rode in like the wind on his beautifully groomed gray mustang, and stopped in splendid fashion before the Presidential box to salute M. Carnot. The American flag carried round by an old Indian fighter elicited a hearty round of applause; then the show began."

Almost every American present knew precisely who Col. William F. Cody was: Buffalo Bill, legendary all-American western scout, King of the Border Men, Indian fighter, crack shot, buffalo hunter, and showman extraordinaire. The French, however, were familiar only with the Wild West posters everywhere and the few newspaper stories, so they were fascinated but still somewhat mystified. In England, Richmond's scripted narration had helpfully elucidated such Wild West show mainstays as the running of the legendary Pony Express, an Indian ambush of the Deadwood Stage, the buffalo hunt, the war between different Indian tribes, broncobusting, sharpshooting, and the grand finale, a stealthy Indian attack on a small pioneer cabin thwarted by none other than Buffalo Bill himself. But here in Neuilly, Richmond's *accent français* was so fractured that few in the audience could fathom *what* he was declaiming when he made the opening introduction of *"L'attaque d'un convoi de Trappeurs et de Pionniers par une tribu de peaux-Rouges."*

Backstage, Buffalo Bill, show promoter Major Burke, and impresario Nate Salsbury realized something was very amiss when the audience barely responded as the Indians, their bodies vibrant in thick red, green, and blue war paint, roared into the arena, riding bareback and shrieking bloodcurdling whoops as they surrounded and attacked the wagon train pulled by eight mules. When the clarion notes of a trumpet signaled the arrival of the cavalry and the defeat of the Indians, the French again sat largely mute.

This poster promoting the Wild West show was plastered everywhere in Paris.

(Buffalo Bill Historical Center, Cody, Wyoming; 1.69.442)

Buffalo Bill thunders into the arena on his horse.

Buffalo Bill turned to Annie Oakley and told her she was going on next, well before her usual slot. Dressed in her fringed buckskin dress, boots, and cowgirl hat, she made sure her entrance was, "a very pretty one. She tripped in, bowing and waving, and wafting kisses. . . . She was a consummate actress, with a personality that made itself felt as soon as she entered the arena." On a table a small arsenal of shotguns and rifles awaited. Small, slender, with nerves of steel, Annie Oakley, Little Sureshot, coolly surveyed the grandstands. "They sat like icebergs at first," she said. "There was no friendly welcome, just a 'you must show me' air." Major Burke had a few "clackers" whose job was to get the applause going. Oakley told her husband, Frank, to call them off. "I wanted honest applause or none at all."

A hollow glass ball the size of an orange whizzed through the air and Oakley whirled into action, shooting it precisely. The air was soon alive with flying objects, and Oakley blasted each and every one, tossing her guns on the table as she used up their shots. The aristocratic crowd, ardent hunters and military veterans, could not believe what they were witnessing. Finally came the long-delayed "ahs" and then, as the shots came faster, cries of "Bravo! Bravo!" rang through the smoky air as the applause built louder and louder. Oakley was shooting as fast as the wind, absolute mistress of her guns, turning her back and whipping around to dispatch a number of clay pigeons. As the last hot gun hit the table the crowd roared to its feet, throwing handkerchiefs and sunshades into the arena. Annie Oakley had arrived. "The icebergs were ready to fight for me during my six months' stay in Paris," she said later.

"As the cheers kept up I ran to my room, made a complete quick change, jumped onto my wild little horse 'Billy' and away we went around the arena at full speed." Riding swiftly, she aimed true to blast apart yet more glass balls and pigeons and, even more astounding to the audience, shot holes straight through French coins tossed in the air. Finally, Oakley leaned over, jumped off the horse, and bowed. The audience stayed on its feet, proclaiming its delight.

Nate Salsbury, who had discovered Oakley a mere four years earlier, would always credit her with saving the Paris Wild West show, as the won-over French suddenly thrilled to the subsequent numbers involving cowboys and Indians, buffalo, fights, and chases. To the utter delight of the nervous Americans, the Parisians decided that they loved this rollicking pageant of frontier America, Colonel Cody's romanticized version of taming the West. "A great success in every way," crowed the Paris *Herald*, in a front-page story headlined "Carnot Among the Cowboys," "A Brilliant Gathering," "The American Colony and All Paris, Political and Social, Muster in Full Force." Cody himself was amused to see that "fashionable young men bought American and Mexican saddles for their rides in the Bois. Cowboy hats appeared everywhere on the street. Relics from the plains and mountains, bows, moccasins, and Indian baskets sold like hot cakes in the souvenir stores."

Under Cody's powerful spell, the French were even willing to try snacking on the pink and white popcorn balls sold at Wild West refreshment stands. This was no small gustatory concession, for the French had long held that corn was a food fit only for pigs. Many Parisian Americans had been appalled to discover that the just-opened World's Fair featured an American Corn Palace, located in the agricultural displays near the Trocadéro, where the uses of this Yankee favorite were "to be picturesquely

introduced to Europeans." As the Paris *Herald* opined of this Western undertaking, "Its success is uncertain."

Back in 1871, early on in his career, Buffalo Bill had been the western guide
for James Gordon Bennett and a sizable party of glamorous New York and
Chicago nabobs out to experience the Great Plains and buffalo hunting.
Such a "high-toned" group, decided Cody, demanded dazzle. Already
rather famous for his Indian-fighting exploits and as a character in Western
dime novels, he had donned his best fringed and spangled buckskin coat
and pants, a crimson shirt, and a broad sombrero, and then mounted a
pure white horse. Buffalo Bill coming into camp had been a vision one of
the guests never forgot: "Carrying his rifle lightly in one hand, as his horse
came toward us on an easy gallop, he realized to perfection the bold hunter
and gallant sportsman of the plains." The men adored Cody, who over a
period of ten days had shown them western life and helped them drive the
buffalo nearer to extinction—they collectively slaughtered six hundred
beasts, not to mention two hundred elk.

One view from the Eiffel Tower's first-floor promenade

Buffalo Bill possessed an innate sense of the theatrical. When the Winchester repeating rifle became known as "the gun that won the West," Bill Cody quickly allied himself with the potent weapon and its famous slogan. In the dime novels that spread his fame, he often used a Winchester. He also appeared in the Winchester Company's 1875 catalogue testifying, "I have tried and used nearly every kind of gun made in the United States, and for general hunting, or Indian fighting, I pronounce your improved Winchester the boss."

On Sunday, the day after Buffalo Bill's brilliant opening performance, happy crowds were still walking up the Eiffel Tower stairways in record numbers. Brief midday rain squalls had given way to idyllic May weather, three of the four first-platform eateries were now open and abuzz with diners, and flocks of university students, young soldiers, and military officers-in-training strolled about. Far below on the boulevards, the city's famous chestnut trees were in full pink bloom. In the tower's upper reaches, men were still working away at the as-yet-unfinished details.

At about three o'clock, a Monsieur Paul Angeray, nattily attired in a new gray redingote jacket, trousers, and fine silk top hat, was lingering on the second platform near the offices of *Le Figaro* when, to his astonishment, he found himself coated head to foot in yellowish paint. Shouts of surprise and dismay rose all about as more than a dozen other ill-fated tourists were splattered to varying degrees with the same thick paint. "We laughed a lot," wrote the *Figaro* reporters, "but the *monsieur*, he was not happy." It seemed that one of Eiffel's painters, coating part of an elevator on the intermediate platform, had knocked over his bucket, creating havoc below. The seventeen victims were reimbursed 1,563 francs for their ruined outfits.

The reporters at *Le Figaro* were far less amused when they later found part of a thin beam had fallen at the same time as the paint and sheared off a cornice by their office. "The platform was at that moment covered with people. It is astonishing that no one was hit," they observed. On Monday morning, it happened again, and this time the little beam fell near the Bar Jacquet. Then on Tuesday, at about 3:00 p.m. a bolt came hurtling through the glass ceiling of the reporters' office, piercing the very seat a man had just vacated. The journalists became incensed. "Had he been there, he would have been killed instantly," *Le Figaro* reported. "We would like to remind M. Eiffel's engineers that the tower's platforms are a promenade, not a battlefield. A fatal accident would badly mar the success of their enterprise. It is a miracle it hasn't happened yet." In fact, shortly thereafter, on Friday, May 24, Eiffel Tower worker Angelo Scagliotti died. There is no record of what exactly befell him, but on that day he became the third Eiffel construction fatality. He left behind a wife and three children under the age of five. His widow, Amelia Novarini, who said she would like to return to Italy, was given five hundred francs for that purpose, as well as a later payment of four thousand francs when she agreed to file no legal action.

A frustrated Gustave Eiffel, meanwhile, was still wrestling with the intractable elevators. On Sunday, May 26, the Roux cog-railroad elevator in the east leg had finally gone into regular operation. Eiffel had become so infuriated at the delayed opening that he had taken the firm to court for missing its February 15 deadline. The Roux made a terrible noise as it clanked its way up and down, but for those not wishing to trudge up 347 steps to the first floor, it was a civilized, modern alternative. The elevator's hydraulic workings were kept greased with a mixture of pig or ox fat mixed with hemp. On that same Sunday, at seven thirty in the morning, *Le Figaro de la Tour* proudly reported, its staff had received special permission to ride in the otherwise off-limits Otis elevator to reach their second-platform office.

Eiffel-Otis relations, however, remained badly strained. On the morning of Wednesday, May 29, three days after the Roux lifts went into full service (and a full two weeks after the tower had finally opened to the public), Mr. Brown of the Otis elevator company arrived at the tower. He had once again sailed all the way from New York, this time to be present when his firm demonstrated to the fair committee and Gustave Eiffel once and for all that his company's elevators were completely safe, for only then could Otis finally put its machines into belated service. The London *Times* Paris correspondent Henri de Blowitz heard rumors of the test run and hurried over to find workmen filling the Otis double-decker elevator compartments with three thousand kilograms of lead, to simulate a full load of people. Next, the Otis workers fastened the elevators with ordinary thick ropes, removing altogether the usual overhead steel wire cables. "What was to be done," the reporter explained, "was to cut the ropes, and allow the lift to fall, so as to ascertain whether, if the steel cables were to give way, the brake would work properly and support the lift." Thirty people were present for the all-important trial, and concern was clear on every face.

After a couple of hours, "two carpenters, armed with great hatchets, had ascended to the lift, and were ready to cut the [rope] cables on a signal to be given by Mr. Brown." As everyone present understood, if the Otis elevator plummeted to the ground, it would be ruined and there would be no means (for the foreseeable future) for the hordes of fair visitors to reach the second platform—except by foot. This, in turn, would greatly diminish the number of visitors who would take the final elevator to the top. The financial repercussions to Eiffel would be profound. The blow to reputations French and American would be severe. And the enemies of the republic would certainly crow if the tower symbolic of all that was modern offered no easy means to reach its summit. As the moment of truth loomed, Eiffel turned to Mr. Brown and asked, "Are you alarmed?"

Mr. Brown, feeling no fondness for his Gallic client, responded coolly, "Only two things can happen." He then called out to the carpenters up above, "One, two, three!"

With that, the hatchets swung, and the rope was sliced in a stroke.

Everyone gasped as the enormous fifteen-ton Otis machine began to fall. But then, "the lift began to move more slowly, it swayed for a moment from left to right, stuck on the brake, and stopped." The thirty men present cheered madly and applauded: The Otis elevator's safety brakes had stopped it thirty feet above the ground. As Elisha G. Otis had promised all those decades earlier, "All safe, gentlemen." Later, when Eiffel and Brown inspected the machine, "Not a pane of glass in the lift had been broken or cracked."

Out in Neuilly, Buffalo Bill's Wild West had become *un succès fou*. Twice each day fifteen thousand spectators packed the grandstand, while many were turned away. Among that huge audience sat Paul Gauguin, who was determined to soak up all the exotica of the fair, including these astonishing cowboys and Indians. Toward the end of May, he wrote to Émile Bernard that he must see the show, and urged him to come on Saturday: "You must get to les Ternes by 3 o'clock, otherwise there's no chance of getting a seat." Gauguin waited, but Bernard did not arrive. Gauguin later wrote him and chastised him for not showing up. "I was at Buffalo. You absolutely have to *come see this*. It is hugely interesting. So come this Wednesday to Schuff's, and we'll go in the afternoon. Let me know if you can't."

The involvement of the Indians in the show suggested they harbored few resentments. Chief Red Shirt had conceded in a London interview that yes, the U.S. government had taken away their land and "white men have eaten up our deer and our buffalo, but the Government now give us food that we may not starve. . . . Our children will learn the whiteman's civilization and to live like him." Red Shirt was himself intent on learning about the white man and mastering his ways.

For the French citizen desiring to better understand the mysteries of all things Buffalo Bill and his Wild West, the show offered a fifty-page illustrated program (in French) whose serious and solemn tone alone was sufficient to render much of it unintentionally hilarious. Between the shameless showbiz puffery and the highly embroidered version of Colonel Cody's life and times, a gullible Frenchman could be forgiven for concluding that Buffalo Bill had almost single-handedly won the American West. A two-page elegy to *"Vieux Charlie, Le Cheval qui porta Buffalo Bill 160 kilomètres en 9 heures 45 minutes,"* as well as all manner of homage to the cowboy, the Indian, the Pony Express, and the Deadwood Stage, made for a peculiar and potent literary brew. The French press freely dipped into it, happy to portray *Guillaume Bufle* as some sort of musketeer, a western D'Artagnan, complete with the flowing tresses and thigh-high soft leather boots.

Before and after the Wild West shows, the Parisians flocked to the picturesque Wild West encampment, ambling its broad gravel paths, thrilled to examine more closely this exotic slice of disappearing American frontier. The last real French encounter with American Indians had been almost half a century earlier, when artist/showman George Catlin brought twelve Iowa Indians to Paris to stir up interest in his five hundred works of art displayed as the "Indian Gallery." King Louis-Philippe was enthralled and ordered a command performance of Indian dancing in one of the ornate *salles* in the Louvre Palace.

Writer George Sand was among the guests at that occasion and was astonished by the sight of the Indians in their full war paint and feathers. Catlin's paintings she described as "hideous scenes of initiations into mysteries, of agony, torture, of Homeric chases, of deadly combat; in sum, all the testimony and all the fearfully dramatic scenes of savage life." Charles Baudelaire summed up the general French opinion: "When M. Catlin came to Paris, with his Museum and his Ioways, the word went round that he was a good fellow who could neither paint nor draw, and that if he had produced some tolerable studies, it was thanks only to his courage and his patience." In fact, asserted Baudelaire, "M. Catlin can paint and draw very well indeed . . . [he] has captured the proud, free character and the noble expression of these splendid fellows in a masterly way."

That had all been many years ago, and the French were still eager to witness the real denizens of an American West they knew only from stories and paintings. They peered at the cowboys' spacious tents and lingered about the Indian village with its towering teepees decorated with painted animals and hunting scenes, where lived many handsome women and small children. "The Parisians appear to take a great interest [in the Indians] . . . they require to examine closely the costumes of the warriors in order to be convinced that they are really nothing thicker than paint; the colors are so vivid and boldly applied to all parts of the body that the all but absolute nudity of the Indian is invisible."

The French mingled with the Indians and with cowboys such as Bronco Bill and Buck Taylor, and took a closer look at the ponies, twenty woolly bison, and the eight Eskimo sled dogs. "The prettiest women of the capital throng the tents of the cowboys," one American publication proudly reported, "and the most dandy of dandies pet the girls who shoot and ride." Indeed, wrote *The New York Times*, "The Indian tents are already a *chic* attraction, however Indian morality may suffer. The braves are courted and feted by the prettiest women in Paris." The ladies of the demimonde particularly admired the Indians. "Yesterday Valtesse and Depaix carried them cigarettes. Wherever you go you hear of nothing but 'Buffalo Beel.'"

Nor was it just the ladies of the demimonde who were taken with the Indians. When Boulanger's great patroness, the Duchesse d'Uzès, announced that she would lead a stag hunt in the Versailles woods one Sunday "for the benefit of the Berck Hospital for Scrofulous Children," part of the draw was that "Buffalo Bill's Indians are to take part." And there were

The Wild West show Indians at the camp in Neuilly, outside Paris

the inevitable scandals. Within weeks, the wife of a French nobleman had run off with one of the Wild West Indians, and the *York Weekly Post* reported their arrival in London: "The irate husband is on their track and arrived at Charing Cross on Sunday night in hot pursuit of the guilty couple, and he vows that he will kill them both. Their destination is said to be America. The wife has succeeded in securing several millions of francs in convertible securities—'to the bearer.' The couple propose to go West, buy a ranch, and settle in Columbia, where the Indian came from. The Liverpool steamers are being closely watched."

Many of the Wild West personnel held court for their fans. At Annie Oakley's tent, a cowboy served as her sentinel, maintaining decorum and raising a rope to let in visitors. After the opening show, the Paris *Herald* reported a crowd of admirers: statesmen, journalists, and soldiers of many nations, all received with notable graciousness and poise. "I am delighted with my reception," Oakley told *The Herald*, "but I am so hungry that I must go to dinner. I was a little nervous the first time in France, but I feel I have so many friends that I shall do better than ever I have done before." Inside her spacious tent, a large collection of shooting prizes and trophies—

silver cups, medals, prize pistols—covered a table. At certain times, Oakley would wear her many decorations. "She is not even 25," wrote *Écho de Paris*, "and her chest is more bedecked with medals than that of an old general." (In truth, Oakley would be twenty-nine on August 13, but in classic show-business style, she had knocked six years off her age, listing her year of birth as 1866.)

Like many another fashionable Parisian, after attending the Wild West show, Paul Gauguin bought a Stetson to wear. Within weeks, *L'Illustration*, which first acclaimed *Guillaume Buffalo* as *"le Napoléon de la Prairie,"* further declared him the social lion of the moment, the most beloved and famous American in Paris since Benjamin Franklin. Paris had abandoned Boulanger, in pouting self-exile in England, to idolize Buffalo Bill. One suspects the officials of the Third Republic could not believe this unlikely stroke of fortune.

About a week after the Wild West show opened, the *Herald* reporter arrived at Neuilly after breakfast to join Major Burke on a special sightseeing jaunt. The good-natured major, his jacket a bit tight across his ample midriff and his sombrero at a rakish tilt, was taking the Indians on a trip into Paris and the fair. Promptly at 9:00 a.m. they boarded the three brakes and headed downtown along the bucolic Champs-Élysées, traversed several tree-lined boulevards, and then passed by the Bastille and the Place de la Concorde en route to the fairgrounds. "Many of the Indians," wrote the journalist, "had been brought straight from the interior of America to New York, shipped at once on board the *Persian Monarch* and brought direct from Havre to Neuilly. . . . Major Burke promised his recruits to show them the big city which all good Americans hope to see before they die, and he has kept his promise."

As the three carriages rolled along, and the Indians took in the ornate buildings and wide boulevards lined with flowering chestnuts and busy with horsedrawn omnibuses, trams, and carriages, their excitement "was strange to witness. When passing before the Louvre and the Tuileries, Rocky Bear said he thought they had better return to camp or some of the Indians would go mad with excitement. Some of them even covered their eyes, because they had already seen too much for one day." At the fair, the *New York Times* man joined the outing and wrote in bemusement, "It would be hard to say whether [the Indians'] astonishment was greater than the delighted enthusiasm of the crowd. The American section [in the Galerie des Machines] was the scene of this first inspection."

Major Burke shepherded the Indians through the immense Galerie des Machines, with its acres of whirring machinery and overhead moving sidewalks, to the fair's painting gallery. There the Indians "stopped suddenly before some picture representing a horse in full gallop and remained wrapped in admiration," many of the Indian women and children squatting comfortably as they studied the scene. Exclaimed an artist in the gallery, "Really this is the best group I have seen at the Exhibition." Then Major Burke proposed they return to the noise and clatter of the Galerie des Machines to view the Edison exhibits. They wended their way to the always crowded phonographs, where Red Shirt listened to music and speeches recorded on the phonograph cylinders.

The Edison people then asked the chief to record a message in Sioux for Rocky Bear, including an Indian war whoop. When it was Rocky Bear's turn, he listened to the cylinder of Red Shirt's recording, his face registering utter surprise. At Red Shirt's shrill war cry, he dropped the listening apparatus and said he was ready to go back to the carriages. The *Times* man reported that the French were agog "over these dark-skinned savages. Had they tomahawked half the people Parisians would have fled, but not with surprise." In fact, the Indians settled themselves sedately into the three brakes as once again crowds gathered, and "waved their hands in farewell with as much grace as could have done a popular monarch."

That same week Gen. Rush Hawkins finally had the American painting galleries properly hung and open for viewing. At the last minute, the French had allotted part of the American space to "some of the petty Balkan states. Then the American eagle did scream and no mistake." Commissioner Hawkins informed the authorities on behalf of the American artists that "unless the space was restored to them forthwith, they would withdraw their entire exhibit. This firmness had the desired effect."

That moment of calm was brief-lived, for within days the American artists were squabbling and complaining. There was no gainsaying that those American painters who had served on the committees claimed the best places for themselves, displaying more and larger canvases. "It is not surprising that there should have been lamentation and gnashing of teeth among those who sent or brought their pictures," said one Boston correspondent. "The Parisianized Americans wanted all or nearly all the available space; but is there not the same gnashing of teeth among hundreds of *refusés* every year just before the Salon opens?"

The artists' imbroglios became a regular and entertaining feature of the Paris *Herald*'s letters to the editor. From that high-profile perch, American painters unhappy with their lot began issuing a steady barrage of verbal brickbats. On June 1, one wrote that General Hawkins "knows very little, if anything, about ancient or modern art, and how he ever secured the position he now holds is a political mystery. . . . [N]ever before in the history of Americans abroad was there such injustice, unkindness, unfairness and unmanliness shown as this Exposition coterie have been guilty of recently. . . . [N]ever since the time when Miss Gardner bravely went in to study the nude, the first American girl who dared to do such a thing, never in all these years has there been so much pain inflicted."

On Sunday, June 2, a day of bright sunshine, London *Times* reporter Henri de Blowitz, famous for his flamboyant facial hair, huge white cravat, and amazing diplomatic scoops, returned again to the Eiffel Tower to be treated to a test run in the Otis elevator, riding up with Eiffel; Mr. Gibson, chairman of the Otis company; a *Figaro* reporter; and Monsieur Édoux. As the elevator moves upward "through the transparent tower the panorama is constantly changing, expanding, taking new colours and proportions," wrote de Blowitz. "A beautiful scene is unfolded beneath them, which it would have been impossible to imagine. One of the most remarkable sensations experienced between the ground and the second stage is caused by the change in the position of the Otis lift. Up to nearly the middle of its course it inclines backwards. Then there is a change of position; it inclines forward, and those in it feel themselves bending over, and completely suspended over the abyss. However there is no feeling of danger. The great solid [Otis] machine ascends and descends majestically, without the slightest shock or inequality in its movements that could cause alarm, and the most timid of those who ascend to the second platform do so with a feeling of perfect security."

The group transferred at the second floor and rode Monsieur Édoux's elevators (in two stages) to the very top. It was a respectably swift ride, taking all told only seven minutes from the ground to the pinnacle. The Édoux vehicles, large cages essentially, were straightforward in comparison to the double-decker, tilting-one-way-and-then-the-other Otis elevators. Otis was now six months behind the original contracted date of January 1, and a month later than the revised delivery date of May 1. Just the day before, the Paris civil court had appointed an expert to determine fault in Eiffel's suit against the Roux elevator company. The World's Fair had been open for more than three weeks, and still no visitor could ascend by elevator beyond the first floor of the Eiffel Tower. The ever-optimistic *Figaro de la Tour* wrote that by Thursday, June 6, at the latest, the public could ascend to the summit by elevator.

On the subject of the Eiffel Tower, the Americans remained adamantly truculent. *Harper's Weekly* reported Americans "have flocked to Paris" and "as much as anybody else have helped to make the exhibition a success." As for the American visitor they encountered up on the Eiffel Tower, he was determinedly unimpressed by the tower, saying, "Yes, fairly lofty; but lay it flat, and it would not span the East River. As to height, well, take an elevator in any of the new buildings in New York, and if you want dizzy you can have quite enough of that kind of thing." Already citizens of New York and Chicago were on the scene, busily vying for their cities to be the site of the next World's Fair. Americans still smarting over the Eiffel Tower confided that they were planning a 1,500-foot-high tower in Manhattan "to which the Eiffel Tower would be only a walking stick." This New York Tower would be "surmounted by a figure of an angel blatantly trumpeting to the world the marvels of American industry and enterprise."

All in all, no one would deny that the Exposition Universelle was a beauteous wonder, a cornucopia of modern human achievement—the tallest tower, the strongest engine, Thomas Edison's electrical and phonographic wizardry—deliciously mixed with art, gastronomy, French historical pageants, and exotic colonial pavilions. The 228-acre fairground was an aesthetic triumph, the spare Eiffel Tower and the equally gigantic and

The Decauville train pulls up near the Algerian Pavilion.

handsome iron-and-glass Galerie des Machines serving as foils to the gorgeous and gaudy, wildly embellished exhibition pavilions.

Everyone loved the tiny open-air Decauville railroad that steamed around the perimeter of the fair. And then there was that other delightful mode of transportation: Oriental rickshaws, which came to be known as *les pousse-pousses*. One American lady explained their appeal: "These *voitures Tonkinoises* are more comfortable than the ordinary rolling chair used in the Champ de Mars, because of the hood that can be drawn up to keep off the sun. Under their umbrella-shaped shade hats, with loose, light jacket and trousers and sandaled feet, these little men look far too small for their loads; but they seize the shafts of the chaise with their well-developed, muscular hands, and off they go. . . . The little men cry 'Attention!' right and left, in very broken French, as they force their way along, and the people pass the word on and give way with smiles of delight. . . . Thirty cents an hour, with a little fee to your man pays for this diversion." The *pousse-pousse* was equipped with little cards for riders offering useful translated phrases: Straight ahead (Di-Thang), Go right (Di Duong hao), and so on.

The official American Exhibition, with its commercial glass-making, pottery, and jewelry, was judged by its own citizens to be paltry and underwhelming. The Paris *Herald* summed it up mournfully: "Our Inventive Genius Is Unsurpassable, but Our Ignorance of the Beautiful is Unpardonable." The American railway exhibit was likened to a train wreck. Sophisticated Yankees cringed both at the American Corn Palace and one U.S. firm's full-size chocolate Aphrodite sculpture, the latter provoking a French critic to scoff, "Only a Yankee could have conceived the idea of creating an edible Venus de Milo."

Americans distressed by their nation's dismal showing in the fair's official exhibitions were relieved to be rescued from ignominy by Thomas Edison's magnificent display and the miracle of his talking phonograph, and by Buffalo Bill and his Wild West. Here, thankfully, was splendid American private enterprise at its sensational best: Edison's exhibit was not only a marvel of modern technology and invention, but, as Edison manager W. J. Hammer was quick to point out, at 9,000 square feet it was the largest department in the Exhibition. "It is American! It is not a commercial display, but a scientific one. We sell nothing, give no prices, solicit no trade. Edison's exhibit costs him between seventy-five and a hundred thousand dollars."

Also, Bill Cody's show was an authentic living spectacle whose success at least rivaled that of the ubiquitous Eiffel Tower. Ultimately, when all the elevators were finally working at the Eiffel Tower, it would attract about twelve thousand visitors each day. Contrast that with Thomas Edison's recording machines, which tens of thousands came daily to hear, or with the Wild West's, where every day thirty thousand paying spectators attended two sold-out shows, jamming the grandstands to gawk and cheer on the cowboys and Indians.

Thomas Edison, delighted by the smashing success of his phonograph at the fair, was eager to start selling the device in Europe. That was, of course, Gouraud's bailiwick. The two partners had patched things up after the unpleasantness about fees and the fair, and Edison immediately began pressing the colonel: How many phonographs could Edison ship to London and when? Even as Gouraud sang the praises of the Edison machine, he parried these queries with all sorts of reasons why it would be more prudent to wait for a more perfect version before plunging into actual sales. On June 1, Edison wrote, "Phonographs are ready when you want them." Although Gouraud had successfully promoted the Edison telephone a decade earlier, he no longer seemed to be the enthusiastic go-getter.

Edison had become so suspicious of his London partner that he had dispatched Alfred O. Tate, twenty-six, his private secretary, to England to investigate. By late May, Tate had arrived and set up shop at the Metropole Hotel. It was his first trip abroad and he loved being in the land of Dickens, relishing his first stay at a big country house, and tasting gooseberries. Young Tate found Gouraud to be a "tall, handsome man whose distinguished presence would attract attention in any company." He made numerous visits to Edison House to discuss with Gouraud just exactly how and when he planned to form a Continental Phonograph Company. One day, wrote Tate, he was finishing up a meeting with Gouraud "when the card of a visitor was sent in. Immediately I rose to leave when [Gouraud] put out his hand protestingly and said:

"'No! No! My dear chap! Don't go yet! I make it a rule never to see any caller under fifteen minutes. It impresses them.'

"I could have assured him that it impressed them, but not in the way he imagined."

Tate eventually concluded, after hearing Gouraud's vague and complicated plans, "He does not intend to invest a dollar in the business personally and for the very good reason that he has not got a dollar to invest."

In those early weeks in Paris, Colonel Cody held court in his huge tent, the front entry flap crowned with a shaggy buffalo head and draped with American flags. Those lucky enough to be invited inside found a reception room furnished with chairs, a dining room, and a bedroom. Cody had on prominent display a collection of souvenirs of his Wild West life, including Yellow Hand's scalp, a trophy from their putative fight to death. The *Herald* correspondent was among the guests and he noted with pride the stream of

French generals and high army and government officials who came by, and how Buffalo Bill "received his guests with that easy urbanity. . . . Colonel Cody had an appropriate greeting for everyone."

Most amazing to the French, however, was Annie Oakley, above all her shooting skills while at full gallop astride a horse. The reporter for *Écho de Paris* marveled at how she had charged across the Wild West arena on horseback, aimed at a tossed-up ten-sou piece, and shot a hole right through it. Dazzled, he sought her out in her tent. There he was charmed by her simple friendliness. "Go see her," he wrote, "and she will give you her photograph. She even writes a few words, if you know to ask . . . and because there's no furniture yet in her tent she graciously kneels, makes two neat lines with her pencil and signs on them, *Compliments of Annie Oakley*, and then stands up and hands you her picture."

Not all the French reporters were so gallant. One wrote frankly, "I attribute her masterly shooting skill to the fact that she is not voluptuous. But if she marries and she has a child who needs to be nourished, I defy her

Annie Oakley poses in a formal gown before her tent in the Neuilly camp.

to show comparable skill. Actually, I have to confess she has a sureness. . . . [A] shooting guest of this caliber could end up destroying everything up to the last lark in France."

Oakley loved her life with the Wild West. She and her husband did not generally sleep in their luxurious tent, with its rugs and chairs and cots and many vases of flowers, but spent many restful hours there. "We could always have hot water, plenty of soap, a collapsible bath tub and crash towels. I often took a morning dip like a wild bird, my tub on the green grass in one corner of the tent.

"Eat? Everything in sight! Good coffee, bread, butter, preserves, fine steaks broiled over wood coals, with fruits and berries in season.

"I could rope and hold the strongest horse. I could smile at the torrents of rain, that drenched me to the the-the—well, never mind!

"An afternoon of rehearsal, then a rub of witch hazel and alcohol and rolled in a soft blanket I lay me down in a hammock to sleep, lulled by the wind. Then a five o'clock dinner, an hour for writing, a practice with my lariat and I was ready for the night's performance."

Among the more surprising events in those early weeks at the Wild West camp was the appearance of Sioux holy man Black Elk, who had been with the show in England but had failed to appear when the steamship departed to New York. In the intervening two years, as Buffalo Bill learned, Black Elk and several other stranded Indians had toured around Europe with Mexican Joe's, a ragtag third-rate variation of the Wild West. When the show played Paris earlier in the year, Black Elk was too ill to perform. A young Frenchwoman and her family took him in, nursing him as best they could. When he emerged from a three-day coma, the family told him, "Pahuska [Buffalo Bill] was in town again. So they took me to where he had his show, and he was glad to see me. He had all his people give me three cheers. Then he asked if I wanted to be in the show or if I wanted to go home. I told him I was sick to go home. So he said he would fix that. He gave me a ticket and ninety dollars. Then he gave me a big dinner. Pahuska had a strong heart." Soon, Black Elk was crossing the "big water" home to Pine Ridge.

Given his gregarious and charming nature, it was not surprising that Colonel Cody was more than happy to join the Parisian social whirl, sweeping from one triumph to another. The Vicomtesse de Chandon, best known as Miss Minnie Gardner before her marriage six years earlier into the champagne fortune, hosted a breakfast for Buffalo Bill so the local royalists could mingle with the celebrity of the moment. Unlike many Americans in Paris, Buffalo Bill was proud of his rambunctious young nation, and made no embarrassing efforts to emulate the French at all, thus endearing himself to both French and American camps.

It had been the custom of the American colony in Paris to maintain a strict pecking order, with expatriates long resident scorning the mere American tourist and snobbishly lamenting the gaucheries of their newly arrived brethren: "The American traveller . . . does not know his place. . . . In his ignorance of custom and etiquette he will thrust himself even upon royalty. . . . A distinguished New York politician, who misses, no doubt, in Paris his home constituency of ragamuffins, used to address the servants of his hotel, urging them to go to America, where all men were equal and labor respected. . . . The Boulevard is not like Lake Avenue, and at the cafes you cannot get pork and beans or fried ham." Buffalo Bill demolished such pretension because he was so completely at ease—as so few Americans overseas were—in his own buckskins. In him, Paris recognized that rare item: an aristocratic common man.

Nor was this a stance he adopted for the occasion. Annie Oakley, who spent years working for him, testified to Cody's bona fides as a genuine democrat. "During our travels I have had opportunity of seeing his sterling qualities put to every test. Fearlessness and independence were not a pose with him. I never saw him in any situation that changed his natural attitude a scintilla. None could possibly tell the difference between the reception of a band of cowboys and the train of an emperor. Dinner at camp was the same informal hearty humorous story telling affair when we were alone, and when the Duchess of Holstein came visiting in all her glory. He was probably the guest of more people in diverse circumstances than any man alive. But teepee and palace were all the same to him. And so were their inhabitants. He never in his life bowed lower to a king than the king bowed to him. He had hundreds of imitators, but was quite inimitable. One cannot pretend to be the peer of any company he may be in. He has to be. And Buffalo Bill was."

Bill Cody inevitably became something of an American goodwill

Buffalo Bill in a studio portrait taken in Paris during the 1889 fair

ambassador among the French. He engaged a luxurious apartment, where, reported *The Chicago Tribune*, "he entertains handsomely. He has been purchasing some fine paintings, and is really looked upon as an esthete of high standing. He is still pursued by women who have matrimonial aspirations. In one week recently he received fourteen written proposals from women, some of whom are wealthy and in good social positions." The popular colonel (a title bestowed by the Nebraska National Guard in time for his London debut) did not always bother to make clear that he was not at liberty to marry, that he had a very bad-tempered wife back in North Platte. Americans, wrote one journalist, basked in "the halo of glory that now envelops Buffalo Bill. Of course, the American minister is casually mentioned in the official gazettes, and if you get into trouble you must apply to him, but for real distinction you must proclaim yourself a countryman of Buffalo Bill."

The real American minister (as the ambassador was then called) was *New York Tribune* publisher Whitelaw Reid, who arrived in Paris the day after Buffalo Bill. An Ohio native, Reid had made a name for himself as a journalist covering the Civil War, before joining the *Tribune* in 1868 when it was still run by the great eminence Horace Greeley (of "Go West, young man!" fame). Upon Greeley's death in 1872, Reid purchased the newspaper, the nation's preeminent Republican journal. Resolutely high-toned and proudly literary, the *Tribune* had once hired as its Paris correspondent Henry James. While the paper's circulation was never more than sixty thousand, its Republican readers were influential. In 1882, Reid had married Elizabeth Mills, only daughter of gold rush millionaire Darius Ogden Mills, an alliance that elevated Reid into the ranks of the very rich. In the last election, Reid, fifty, had successfully marshaled and cajoled Republicans to drive Grover Cleveland from the White House. He had hoped to be made ambassador to England but had settled reluctantly for France.

On May 22, Reid, a slender man with a thick beard chiseled to an elegant point, had presented his credentials at the Élysée Palace to President Sadi Carnot, who was generally considered honest, capable, and dull. Jibed one politician: "The fact that a man, if you ask him to dinner, will not put your spoons into his pocket, is not a sufficient reason for making him President of a republic." (Carnot had risen to power in the wake of Prime

Minister Jules Ferry's resignation, which was prompted by revelations that Ferry's son-in-law was selling government honors.) Sadi Carnot, Minister Reid wrote to the new Republican U.S. president Benjamin Harrison, had "a kindly feeling because of our attitude towards their exposition while Europe was boycotting it;—and on their success with the exposition their official lives depend."

At his first official meeting, Reid graciously told the French: "We do not forget that you helped in the success of our Revolution." It was true that the French monarchy had once saved the infant American republic by steady rounds of financing, but as Alexander Hamilton pointed out, the French motive was "to enfeeble a hated and powerful rival by breaking in pieces the British Empire. . . . He must be a fool who can be credulous enough to believe that a despotic [French] court aided a popular [American] revolution from regard to liberty or friendship to the principles of such a revolution." Nonetheless, such was now the official myth, and so it was only fitting that a great wave of the American citizenry would now return the favor and fortify the fragile French republic with an ample infusion of dollars. A prosperous Paris was unlikely to support a revived monarchy.

Reid saw no sign of the World's Fair failing, however, writing, "Americans have been swarming here as if Paris were another Oklahoma." After settling into their hotels, many of these Americans headed to the rue de l'Opéra and the business offices of *The New York Herald*, where James Gordon Bennett had succeeded in making his Paris newspaper the signing-in place for traveling Yankees. Not only was there the *Herald* registry book, and the prospect of seeing their names in the paper, but "serried files containing almost every paper published in the United States. . . . A homesick-looking man pounces upon the Pawtucket *Chronicle*. . . . Around the register [book] of American arrivals . . . [are] a moving mass of new gowns, summer suits, smart parasols, and straw hats . . . [and a] permanent hum of conversation which is broken at intervals by the ever-recurring, sharp, staccato cry, 'Why, when did you come?' "

With Americans arriving en masse for the fair, the Paris *Herald* was flourishing. James Gordon Bennett had been adamant from the start that this new operation was more a public service than a business, stating on the third day of the paper's existence, "We do not intend to permit the

European Edition of the *Herald* to make any money. In fact, we expect to furnish so good a paper that it will cost us a trifle of 300,000 or 400,000 fr. per year, above receipts, to give Paris what it has needed so long, namely, a first-class Anglo-American daily newspaper."

And yet, even as the French had finally found in Buffalo Bill some facet of American civilization to admire (perhaps because he confirmed that Americans really *were* savages), it was clear that James Gordon Bennett and his Paris *Herald* still had much educating to do. Not long after the Wild West show opened, eight incensed Paris municipal officials proposed it be shut down because *"Les exhibitions d'Indiens and de nègres esclaves sont odieuses."* Not one member of the Paris council seemed to be aware that there had been no slaves in America since the Civil War. (One French reporter had believed briefly that the Indians in the Wild West show were Cody's prisoners of war!) However, another French politician rejoined wisely that there was really no need to deprive Parisians of their favorite pageant, since these poor Wild West slaves naturally became free the minute they debarked on good republican French soil. *The Herald* could only sputter editorially, "This is simply excruciating. It quite paralyzes us, and renders comment impossible." Such ignorance about America was trying to Bennett, who was an ardent, if idiosyncratic, patriot. As he explained to a Paris editor, "I love America, but I hate most Americans."

The phenomenal success of Buffalo Bill's Wild West should not have been a complete surprise, for he and his troupe had conquered London in similar fashion just two summers earlier. Of course, it was not good show-business politics to remind French republicans too often that the British queen Victoria had discovered Guillaume Buffalo first. But thanks to Major Burke, the colonel's longtime partner and master of promotion, many Americans knew that the Prince of Wales had persuaded Queen Victoria that she had to see the Wild West and its amazing exhibitions.

As her son expected, the queen, head of a vast British Empire at the apogee of its power, had been as delighted and mesmerized by the whoop-it-up performance as any child. Afterward, she stunned her courtiers by insisting on personally greeting Buffalo Bill and Sioux chief Red Shirt, and telling Annie Oakley, "You are a very, very clever girl." A second royal performance was ordered. England was electrified. This time Buffalo

Bill himself drove the Deadwood Coach, assigning the Prince of Wales to ride shotgun, while royals from Denmark, Greece, Belgium, and Saxony held on for dear life inside as they careened about, escaping the marauding Indians. This episode gave rise to Buffalo Bill's most famous quip: "I've held four kings, but four kings and the Prince of Wales makes a royal flush, and that's unprecedented."

All in all, U.S. minister Reid, who had come to serve in Paris only out of a sense of duty to the Republican Party, found the French friendly. Nonetheless, he quickly learned how low on the diplomatic totem pole the American minister ranked. Just before his arrival several young American ladies visiting Nice had become embroiled in a dispute with a dressmaker. On May 3 they had been set to depart the Hôtel Cosmopolitan in that resort city when a box appeared with the new clothes they had ordered. However, the package yielded up only a shirt, and not the two dresses and jacket. Angry at such a fraud, the ladies sent the box back and declined to pay. They departed for Menton, where that night they found themselves detained, arrested, and imprisoned.

The ladies paid off the fraudulent debt but were determined to have justice. Reid's first attempt to discuss the matter with the French minister came to naught as he explained to the secretary of state in a long letter, "The Russian, the German, the Turkish, the Austrian and the Italian Ambassadors came in successively and had to be received before me. I left when it became evident that I had not a chance of seeing the Minister before dark. Had I remained, the Nuncio and the Spanish Ambassador, who came in later, would also have had precedence over the Representative of the United States."

And so, Minister Reid found the American colony in fine humor, puffed up and patriotic over the Edison Company's and Buffalo Bill's triumphant debuts, and all anticipating a summer of pleasant diversions at the World's Fair. Then, in the third week of the U.S. minister's new position, the calamity of the Johnstown Flood in Pennsylvania cast a momentary pall over the Americans in Paris. A dam at the South Fork Club, a private fishing retreat owned by Pittsburgh industrialists, had given way, unleashing a solid wall of roaring water and deadly debris that destroyed the little factory towns of the Conemaugh Valley. More than two thousand people, many of them women and children, died terrible deaths. Reid immediately called a meeting of the American community in Paris to raise money for the relief fund. Hundreds of expatriates and tourists jammed into the Legation and quickly subscribed forty thousand francs. Buffalo Bill scheduled a special fund-raising show. Andrew Carnegie, in Paris for the fair, lent his support, never mentioning that he was one of the South Fork Club's negligent owners.

By early June, Paul Gauguin had returned to Le Pouldu in Brittany to paint, disappointed that, thus far, the Volpini exhibit had attracted little attention. One of the few reviewers (for a minor publication) complained that the Café des Beaux-Arts was far from an ideal art venue, noting "it is not easy to approach these canvases on account of the sideboards, beer pumps, the bosom of M. Volpini's cashier, and an orchestra of young Moscovites whose bows unleash in the large room a music that has no relation to these polychromatic works."

Understandably, Gauguin was not in good spirits when he wrote his wife, Mette, after finally hearing from her. "You want my news? I am by the sea in a little fishing village with 150 people, I live like a peasant or savage. . . . I spend one franc each day for my food and tobacco. So you cannot reproach me with living it up. I speak to no one and I receive no news of my children. Alone—all alone—I show my work at Goupil's in Paris, and they make a big sensation but they're difficult to sell. . . . I'm thinking of asking some influential friends to get me a [government] appointment in Tonkin where I hope I might live for a while and await better times."

Then, hearing that Theo van Gogh was less than pleased with the Volpini show, Gauguin took up his pen to defend the enterprise, writing, "Schuff has written to say you think my exhibition is to be regretted. I'm very surprised. . . . I organized this little show at the Universal Exhibition to show what we had to do as a group . . . what harm can it do me? None, seeing that I'm unknown and that nobody is showing my work to the public. If my paintings are bad it will change nothing, and if they are good, which is *probable*, I will get myself known. . . . There remains the question of the venue! This seems to me infantile, and I don't think (knowing your ideas) that you will find anything wrong in that respect.

"Our friends the *well-known* Impressionists are capable at any time of believing that other artists should be ignored, and it is not in their interests that Bernard and I, and the others, should seek to put on an exhibition. . . . I was anxious to give you a frank explanation of all my reasons. There you are." A modern artist in revolt against the ancien régime had no choice but to make his own way.

Eiffel drawn as his tower in the June 29, 1889, issue of *Punch*

CHAPTER SEVEN

Gustave Eiffel Holds Court
amid the Art Wars

By the second week of June, high upon his tower's third floor, Gustave Eiffel had the immense satisfaction of finally watching the public debark from the completed elevator. The event was front-page news in the Paris *Herald*, whose man reported on his own journey: "From the second floor runs a large car, holding sixty people. . . . [The elevator] is simply a square box, with the upper part of two sides glazed. . . . In two minutes and a half, the car arrives at a platform, which may be called floor number two and a half. . . . Here the guard calls out 'All change here,' and the passengers walk across a narrow bridge into a similar elevator which takes them as high as they are allowed to go. 'Mind the step as you go out, ladies,' says the thoughtful guard. Everybody, of course, looks at the step, and between a rather dangerously wide crack in the boards, sees the grounds of the Exhibition gardens, two hundred and seventy-five metres below. . . . The sensation upon going up can scarcely be described as pleasant, especially as from time to time the elevator gives strange little jerks."

The reporter from Pulitzer's New York *World* patriotically lauded the Otis lifts and their "great triumph of American skill" before describing how "975 feet above the world people become pigmies. . . . At this height the Arc de Triomphe has become a little toy and the churches are like those in the Dutch boxes of villages. It was all map-like and indefinite; the people were crawling ants; all that looked large had disappeared, excepting a balloon, which was our contemporary."

Other visitors had to contend with their newly discovered fear of heights, such as an Englishman from Manchester who said: "Though the hand rail is high enough, still there are thoughts of going over which are

anything but pleasant. However, perseverance is repaid when one steps out
on the top platform ... there is no comparison between 1,000 feet of
mountain and 1,000 feet of Eiffel. The absence of any ground falling away
from one's feet, or of any surrounding mountains, gives us a sense of isolation and unnaturalness new to any but a balloonist or steeplejack. It takes
a few moments before one can muster nerve to walk on the edge of the
platform and look over. You must have a strong head to do that. . . . [I]t
takes some time before one can realize that the winding rivulet is the silver
Seine. . . . The only distinguishable moving objects are small clouds of
white smoke traveling slowly along—the railways. . . . Above all, an almighty
silence, which is most oppressive."

In Gustave Eiffel's own elegantly appointed aerie, furnished with comfortable black velvet fringed divans, and handsome works of art, he lived
with the weather as no man ever had. The dawn was superb, unfolding ros-
ily, while the thunderstorms with their bolts of lightning crashing all about
were entirely magnificent and terrifying. In the little adjacent laboratories,
scientists came to study high in the heavens "the violence of atmospheric
currents, the chemical composition of the air, its electricity, its humidity . . .
the oscillations of the pendulum, certain laws of electricity, and the compression of gases by air." The nighttime, when all the gay lights of Paris
twinkled like reflections of the starry sky, was especially enchanting. The
great Eiffel Tower spotlight overhead in the campanile arced through the
dark, illuminating whatever it swept past. Far down below, the fountains,
too, were illuminated three times each evening with a rainbow of artistically changing colors, a sight that delighted night after night.

Gustave Eiffel soon began to be deluged with all sorts of letters from
the tower's admirers. In one, a woman propositioned him, writing, "My
request may seem odd to you but perhaps you will agree if I am the first to
suggest it. I am not ugly or old, really, but capricious. I have a dream of
spending one night at the summit of the tower that has your name. Would
you do this for me? If you answer my letter, I will be in Paris on June 5th
next and would come in person to make my request. I look forward to the
pleasure of your reply, if it is not too much to hope?" The tower inspired
not only such occasional proposals of seduction by mail but endless bad
poetry, songs, polkas, waltzes, and a forgettable symphony. A poet who

described himself as "*jeune, pauvre, inconnu,*" sent along his verses, hoping for a patron.

One American at the tower's pinnacle marveled at the citizens of many nations enjoying the tower: "a hundred Congo sailors, black as midnight, . . . Turks, Arabs, Chinese, and other less familiar nationalities, many Americans and many English, the whole clientele of a French school." The tower's public registry made for diverting reading: "When upon this tower, and reflecting upon its construction, who is not proud to be a Frenchman?" Or there was the wit who left these universally understood lines: "From the top of this tower in rapture I see / My mother-in-law only as big as a flea." *Le Figaro* faithfully reported on various silly milestones. "Spotted at 11 o'clock," read the May 25 paper, "a dog on the second platform. This is the first one to visit us. He came into our pavilion, but he did not sign his name."

Eiffel tried to use all parts of the tower to advantage. Tucked away in every available space were tiny enterprises catering to the visitors: "Women selling cigarettes, men renting opera-glasses and selling souvenirs, and curiosity dealers installed in dense crowds among the iron bars and stairs near the lifts that were forever moving up and down, and whose chains moved with a dull and regular sound like the noise of a machine. It was like a city hanging in the rigging of an immense steamer. The wind gusts came fresh and sharp like the sea breeze; one might take the sky, seen through the iron bars, for the perspective of the endless ocean."

The tower's sheer enormity and complexity, its many levels, the constantly moving elevators, the excited crowds, the delicious smells wafting from the crowded restaurants, the many little souvenir and snack stalls, the busy editing and publishing of *Le Figaro*, all combined to create an atmosphere of exhilaration. Eiffel was gratified to see how people wished to experience his tower, to be part of something so new, so gargantuan, so modern, which he viewed as an affirmation of technology, of progress. The reporters at *Le Figaro* had become enamored of the young female help at the Alsatian restaurant, and liked to see these young women each morning chattering away while peeling radishes and cutting asparagus for salads, a lovely sight in their colorful hair ribbons and traditional costumes. An enterprising lark even established a nest on the tower.

On Monday, June 10, the English bank holiday of Whitmonday, it seemed as if all of England had crossed the Channel en masse to visit the World's Fair, including no less a royal personage than Queen Victoria's son and heir, Arthur Edward, Prince of Wales. He was accompanied by his wife, Alexandra, the Princess of Wales, and their five adult children. For the French, the prince's visit was especially gratifying, for all Paris knew that Queen Victoria had recalled her ambassador to France, Lord Lytton, just to make sure he did not attend this Gallic centennial celebration of monarchical downfall. Yet here was her own son come to Paris "privately" to tour the World's Fair officially snubbed by his own government. The prince, forty-seven, a genial man known as "Bertie," liked his amusements, hunting, and mistresses. His royal love affairs had tended toward famous beauties, such as Lillie Langtry, and celebrated actresses, including in his younger years that Parisian favorite, the inimitable Sarah Bernhardt. Perhaps Prince Bertie had come to the Eiffel Tower because he understood better than his aging mother the critical role that technology already played in the wealth of nations and modern power.

The Eiffel Tower, the Bolivian Pavilion (black and white),
and the Nicaraguan Pavilion

The British royals, diplomatic entourage in tow, appeared at the foot of the tower at 10:30 a.m. The press wrote approvingly of the Princess of Wales's rather simple lightweight dark blue and white silk gown and bonnet of black lace trimmed with lilies of the valley. Gustave Eiffel, along with his son-in-law, Monsieur Salles, and various French ministers and fair officials, greeted them (the prince spoke good French) and provided an escort up to the second floor, which was mobbed with the prince's countrymen. With great difficulty, a path was cleared for their majesties to enter the Édoux elevator, specially furnished for the occasion with garden benches and footstools. Atop the tower, advance officers from the British embassy awaited. The prince and his family were aloft barely ten minutes, just long enough to admire the view and sign Gustave Eiffel's new *Livre d'Or*, a handsome, oversize green leatherbound book with watered-silk end pages. The royal signatures featured impressive flourishes and occupied the entire first page. Theirs would be but the first of many illustrious autographs and messages to come, mementos of this summer when the Eiffel Tower was new. Later Eiffel would say proudly, "We gave the monarchies the spectacle of democracy happy by virtue of its own effort."

Safely returned to the second platform, the British royal party was steered to the *Figaro*'s pavilion, where the prince spied the paper's *Guide Bleu* to Paris and expressed an interest in having one. As the editors inscribed the guidebook, the prince and his entourage were already being swept away toward the elevator. A daring reporter tossed the gift volume toward the vanishing prince, who caught it, smiled, and waved jauntily as he disappeared into the Otis lift.

On that same most crowded day of the 1889 World's Fair, American Susan Hayes Ward, a writer for *The Christian Union*, steered clear of the worst crush at the foot of the Eiffel Tower and instead walked along the Seine and through the History of Habitation, "an interesting group of buildings designed by M. Charles Garnier to illustrate human habitation from the stone and bronze age down to the time of the Renaissance, together with dwellings from many of the ruder races of the present day." Bypassing the uninviting "cave of the troglodyte," she lingered in the replicas of civilized dwellings from ancient times, including the "Egyptian house, time of Sesostris; Assyrian, 700 B.C., Phoenician, Hebrew, and Etruscan, each

1,000 B.C.; Hindu, 300 B.C.; Persian, 400 B.C., Greek, time of Pericles, Roman, time of Augustus."

Even off in St.-Rémy, Vincent van Gogh had heard about Garnier's clever homage to the architectural past, and wrote Theo, "I should so have liked to have seen an Egyptian house at the exhibition . . . painted in red, yellow, and blue, with a garden regularly divided into beds by rows of bricks—the dwelling place of beings whom we know only as mummies or in granite." Meanwhile Vincent had also seen an actual announcement for the Volpini show and asked Theo, "Was that the exhibition you spoke of? What storms in teacups."

Susan Hayes Ward was charmed by the History of Human Habitation, with its picturesque houses built and staffed by the "Esquimaux, Laplanders, Indians, Chinese, Japanese, Russians, Bulgarians, Central Africans, Aztecs, [and] Incas," appreciative that "each house, too, is surrounded by appropriate vegetation; tea plants, bamboo and azaleas grow in the little Chinese garden and other sharp-leaved plants surround the Aztec and Inca dwellings." In many of the houses, she sampled the native cultures, buying "Russian tea from a samovar, or Turkish coffee in tiny cups; baby canoes of birch bark, made and sold by Canadian Indians, Venetian glass, blown and shaped after ancient models under the visitor's eye—each house has its own attractions." She did have one complaint: "the modern American house, with its comforts, improvements, and conveniences, has been strangely overlooked."

Ward then joined the crowds surging toward the Esplanade to see the nations that had become in the past few years part of France's Third Republic empire. "The French colonies are bravely represented here; and the French people look with intense interest on these natives of their colonies living as if at home in this great capital." The Vicomte de Vogüé, a man whose writings about the Arab worlds (*Voyage en Syrie et en Palestine*) had just earned him membership to the elite Académie Française, often rambled in these sections of the fair, passing an hour here and there observing the unlikely cultural encounters. He was charmed to glimpse "an African coastal king nibbling on Guadaloupian sweets at a mulatto's snack stand" or a Vietnamese "Buddhist hobnobbing with a Greek priest."

During another evening at the fair he watched four French female workers (all respectable) enjoying a late dinner when they invited three passing Arabs to join them. The men sat down at the table, declining, however, the wine and pork sausage. Then two black men joined the group and all chatted happily away as best they could, the embodiment of a new polyglot conviviality. De Vogüé could not know it, but he was seeing the future of Paris, a world city to which people of all races and religions would gravitate from every corner of the globe, above all from these new colonies, to settle and live, to seek education and a new life, ultimately creating a twentieth- and twenty-first-century Paris as international as this short-lived exposition.

But while de Vogüé was touched by such surprising mingling he was also concerned that many French, after encountering these new brown, yellow, and black quasi-citizens, were succumbing to unattractive "feelings of pride and domination not unlike that of the old Roman citizen on a day of triumph when he watched passing before him the conquered. . . . [The Frenchman] thinks, 'Here are our slaves!' Maybe this word is not spoken," conceded the count, ". . . but you have only to see the way a fair employee or café boy treats these colored people." Third Republic officials of course justified their foreign adventures and empire building as bringing civilization to the lesser races.

De Vogüé remained very much the skeptic. French officials were deluded if they imagined that their colonial "guests" marveled at "our grandeur, or would be inspired by our ideas. . . . According to those men familiar with that part of Asia, our Annamites [Vietnamese] are so many big children, amused by novelties but blinded by a prejudice like that of the Chinese . . . to see anything favorable [in the West]. As for the Arabs and other Muslims, long experience with these races leaves little doubt about how they perceive: the vision of our world stops at their eyeballs, which is to say, nothing penetrates into their soul; they will return home with a profound contempt for our customs."

Where others saw only a delightful exoticism in these new colonial quasi-citizens, the count expressed a certain prescient trepidation. "All these exotic peoples, we must say, are now to some degree ours; they represent to us heavy obligations or great hopes. . . . Recent history suggests that we are in the process of constructing a colossal empire in these three parts of the globe. . . . Arab France, in north Africa; black France, in the heart of the continent of Africa, and yellow France, in the far reaches of Asia."

With the Exposition in full swing, James Gordon Bennett decided his readers needed guidance to the many eateries around the fairgrounds, and dispatched "The Roving American" to report back to his countrymen. The journalist's wife's friends had insisted that the Austrian restaurant Kuhn served the fair's best food, and so after a long search the couple located Kuhn behind the Folies Parisienne. "The inevitable Tsiganes musicians," he reported, "were dancing about in their blue hussar tunics and scarlet trousers, and scraping away at their violins." Orders for such classic national dishes as Wiener schnitzel or goulash produced blank looks. "Take it all in all the Restaurant Kuhn is not a bad place, but there is nothing Austrian about it except the beer and the name," concluded the *Herald* man. Their check, reprinted in the paper, showed they had eaten and imbibed heartily for the rather hefty sum of twenty-six francs, including a franc to the orchestra. The next evening, "Roving American" visited the fair's Russian restaurant and "found the tables very uncomfortable for a man with long legs . . . severe upon the knee pans and very damaging to one's trousers." That aside, he enjoyed his dinner of cucumber soup, salmon in pastry, and Zrazi croquettes, though he regretted the complete lack of vodka on the menu.

Two evenings later, the food critic and his spouse sauntered into the English restaurant near the luminous fountain. He noticed that the few French present "insisted upon speaking English, while the English and Germans and Americans quite as persistently spoke French." He and his wife had oxtail soup. "The plates were cold and the soup was very watery. Then followed turbot. This was good." His porterhouse steak, however, disappointed, being "pale, and rather tough. The waiter declared that it had been brought from England. If so, it must have been sea sick crossing the Channel. Not only was the steak poor, but the grilled mushrooms were very 'soggy' and 'leathery.' The grilled tomatoes, however, were good." As usual, the check was shown and totaled: a pricey twenty-five francs.

In late June, as *The Herald*'s man was eating his way through the fair's restaurants, the American Society of Civil Engineers, three hundred strong, visited the Exposition. They put aside their envy long enough to march en masse to the Eiffel Tower to pay homage, proudly ascending in the Otis lifts to inspect the tower's every triumphant bolt. Their French engineering brothers hosted a midmorning breakfast at Brébant on the first platform. It was a proud moment for every engineer present, for their profession was literally building the modern world of railroads, skyscrapers, steamships, telephones, telegraphs, and electricity grids. And now here they were convened upon the long-dreamed-of 1,000-foot tower. Minister Whitelaw Reid was among the guests listening to Eiffel's graceful speech, greeted with many toasts, hurrahs, and cheers. The Americans remarked among themselves how much Monsieur Eiffel looked like the deceased American war hero and former president, Ulysses S. Grant.

As noon approached on Monday, July 1, *le tout Paris* was not at the fair or the Eiffel Tower, but crammed anxiously into the Sedelmeyer Gallery on rue de La Rochefoucauld, a steep street in rustic Montmartre. Carriages lined the curbs for blocks all around, and even the most elegant gentlemen and ladies had trouble pushing through to their reserved seats. It was the much-anticipated sale of the art collection of Hyacinth Secrétan, the foppish speculator whose copper corner fortune had enabled him to buy hundreds of works of art, including some very famous paintings.

When the price of copper collapsed, spreading disaster all around, Secrétan had vanished, leaving only his spectacular art collection to make good his considerable debts. As all present knew, either a Frenchman or an American would depart today with the auction's biggest prize: Jean-François Millet's *The Angelus*. The air was electric with the prospect of an imminent cultural combat. This auction was about to reveal to all the world—and especially to the Americans—just how angry the French cultural mandarins had become about American plundering of Gallic treasures.

Aside from the Eiffel Tower, no subject roiled up as much ill will and trouble between the two nations as fine art. When it came to Americans and art, the French harbored mixed feelings. French masters were happy to have young American artists pay to study in their ateliers, and eminent French artists were delighted to sell their canvases to wealthy Americans, jacking up their prices accordingly. Meissonier, Gérôme, Bouguereau, Rosa Bonheur, to name but a few, had become rich through the munificence of American patrons. However, as the ranks of American artists in Paris proliferated and they aspired to exhibit in the yearly Salon, palpable resentment began to arise against foreigners taking up valuable French exhibit space. As one American painter complained, "In France, the American only has a right to learn painting. But he must not paint anything saleable or sell it when painted."

At the Sedelmeyer Gallery, prominent among the wealthy and fashionable crowd was M. Antonin Proust, French minister of fine arts, impeccably dressed, his reddish beard stylishly parted down the middle. The minister was determined to outbid the Americans and retain Millet's masterpiece. A childhood friend and longtime champion of the late Édouard Manet, Proust had been a major power in the organization of the Exposition Universelle. In that role he had suffered no end of complaining from French artists over who had been selected for inclusion in the prestigious official exhibition, how many paintings each could hang, and why this painting or that did not have a better spot. No truer words had been spoken than Proust's rejoinder to it all: "The secret of satisfying everybody has not yet been discovered."

But this morning, he had far more serious matters on his mind, for he had single-handedly raised four hundred thousand francs to secure the Millet, expecting any difference in price to be paid by the Chamber of Deputies to ensure *The Angelus* would hang in the Louvre. In Belle Époque Paris, where no métier was more hallowed than that of the artist, few objects were more venerated (or valuable) than works of art. And when artistic provenance included a dollop of copper corner scandal, all the better.

To the distress of the French, a good one half of those present for the sale were Americans, many of them absurdly wealthy. In recent years the French government had become sufficiently concerned about the art exodus across the Atlantic to dispatch an investigator to the United States. In 1886 he reported back, "I would never have believed, had I not confirmed it myself, that the United States, so young a country, could be so rich in works of painting, especially works of the French school. It is not by the hundreds but by the thousands that one must count them."

Most of those present in the stifling Sedelmeyer Gallery recognized Andrew Carnegie, the Steel King, moving about restlessly, while it was whispered that Monsieur Durand-Ruel was attending on behalf of the Havemeyers of the Sugar Trust, and that Monsieur Bague would bid for the Vanderbilts. Mr. Sutton of the American Art Association sat with the dealer

Monsieur Montagnac, engaged to conduct the AAA's actual bidding, while nearby were buyers from the Corcoran Gallery. All present already knew "the thrilling story of [Mr. Sutton and associates'] late landing at Queenstown, their catching of the Irish mail, their hiring at Chester of a special train for $400, which carried them to London at the rate of sixty-four miles an hour, and then of their further timely advance upon Paris," arriving just in time for this very sale. Even now Mr. Sutton was said to have a train waiting in Gare St.-Lazare to return him to Le Havre so he could catch the steamship home the instant he had bagged *The Angelus.*

The French stared with ill-disguised loathing at the Americans, philistines who presumed to spirit off French patrimony. The Yankees, in contrast, confided one American writer present, experienced "a moment of intense satisfaction . . . to see so young a nation as our own . . . coming breast to breast with old Europe for the acknowledgment and purchase of a work of art."

More and more newly wealthy Americans savored the joys of owning rare, expensive things, and despite the 30 percent tariff imposed on art in recent years, the pace of voracious collecting was escalating. While some of these Yankee art patrons, such as New York financier J. P. Morgan and his uptown neighbors, the Vanderbilts, were by now familiar, others were not as well known to the French—men such as New York architect Stanford White, who had just arrived in Paris intent on snapping up antique furnishings, tapestries, sculptures, and other art to furnish traction millionaire William Whitney's gigantic country villa. American George Lukas, a permanent Paris resident who was very French in his ways (complete with a longtime mistress), did nothing but locate and sell art to rich Americans such as railroad magnate Henry Walters. Painter Mary Cassatt was always urging American millionaires, especially her friend Louisine Havemeyer of Sugar Trust wealth, to buy the work of her Impressionist friends. Claude Monet had started a subscription to purchase Manet's incomparable *L'Olympie*, now hanging in the fair's official French painting pavilion, to guarantee that it stayed in France, preferably in the Louvre. John Singer Sargent had contributed a thousand francs to that fund. Given American rapaciousness, it was not surprising that the French were so adamant that Millet's much-admired *The Angelus*—of all paintings—not disappear across the Atlantic.

At about one o'clock the auction began, personally conducted by

Messieurs Sedelmeyer and Boussod. They worked steadily through the vanished Monsieur Secrétan's watercolors and drawings before bringing on major paintings by Eugène Delacroix and Ernest Meissonier, for which fabulous prices were paid. Then, after a brief pause, a gallery man carried out *The Angelus* and reverently set it on the easel. The picture had a wonderful story behind it. Millet, an artist of the Barbizon school who lived in the country, was walking home one day when he heard the tolling of the local church bells even as he "saw across the wide stretch of autumn fields, against the crimson sky of sunset, two peasants, a man and a woman, stop instantly from their potato digging at the sound of the Angelus and devoutly fall to prayer." Millet rushed to his studio and painted the scene, selling the work to a dealer for $500, who in turn sold it for $10,000.

With the appearance of the coveted painting, Monsieur Proust stood up and strode forward to bid personally against Monsieur Montagnac, who represented Mr. Sutton. The French seemed in agony as the price rapidly soared. When Monsieur Montagnac faltered, an American stood up and said, "If you haven't money enough, I'll stand by you." The French, in a frenzy, made the offer to Monsieur Proust, now ashen and tremulous with emotion. Monsieur Montagnac bid again, and when Monsieur Sedelmeyer crashed the hammer, the French leapt up in an uproar, women breaking their fans in anger. The bidding was reopened and this time Monsieur Proust prevailed, the hammer coming down at 553,000 francs. Monsieur Proust had just paid the highest price on record for a modern painting, $110,000. The French rushed forward and surrounded him like a conquering hero. As calm returned, Monsieur Sedelmeyer asked for the next lot of paintings to be brought out, and the auction continued. Many French in the audience that day and the next observed unhappily how often the American millionaires prevailed, bagging other prized paintings to carry away across the Atlantic.

Like every other person at the Secrétan sale, the *New York Times* reporter knew the final funding of Millet's masterpiece was politically controversial. In a France where conservatives were actively machinating to resurrect the monarchy, the right was as hostile to Millet, an artist they considered a communist, as it was to his painting, which depicted poor peasants. "They thought," said the *Times* man, "the Louvre needed many other painters more than Millet." But the proud Monsieur Proust assumed that his fellow Frenchmen, whatever their political stripe, would not tolerate

Americans making off with such a high-profile Barbizon piece. As soon as the auction ended, he submitted his request to the Chamber of Deputies. For two weeks, as the matter was debated, much was rightly made of the impoverished state of Millet's widow even as his paintings sold for fabulous prices. The days passed, and still the conservative deputies blocked the credit needed to complete *The Angelus* sale, leaving Monsieur Proust to agonize once again over the impending loss of this painting to the Americans.

Commissioner Hawkins watched all this with his usual bilious eye, later expressing his displeasure through the words of the painter Couture, who dismissed Millet thus: "Today we see a canvas upon which is uncouthly painted a rough peasant standing before a log of wood; three months later we see upon another canvas, the same peasant with the same log of wood upon his shoulder; three months after, upon a third canvas, there appears the same log, but this time upon a fire, and our friend, the peasant, as badly painted as in number one, is standing in front of it and looking at it burning, and so ends, in three chapters, Millet's great story of the peasant and the log of wood." To Hawkins, and many others, Millet's work expressed "only the grossest, most unpicturesque, and most uninteresting realism. His subjects, as a rule, were unworthy of a great master; his human types nearly express idiots or monsters, who could not have existed out of asylums, and [their] portrayal . . . neither elevates nor refines."

Like every denizen of the art world, Vincent van Gogh followed the fracas and wrote to Theo: "What a business, that Secrétan sale! I am always pleased that the Millets hold their own. But I should very much like to see more good reproductions of Millet, so as to reach the people.

"His work is sublime, especially considered as a whole, and it will become more and more difficult to get an idea of it when the pictures are dispersed."

By midsummer most of the writers and artists who had denounced the tower in *Le Temps* had expressed their mea culpas, with the notable exception of Guy de Maupassant. In his travel memoir, *La Vie Errante*, the writer claimed, "I left Paris and even France, because the Eiffel Tower just annoyed me too much. Not only did you see it from everywhere; you found it everywhere made out of every known material, displayed in all the shop windows, an unavoidable and horrible nightmare." De Maupassant wondered what posterity would think of his generation "if, in some future riot, we do not unbolt this tall, skinny pyramid of iron ladders, this giant and disgraceful skeleton with a base that seems made to support a formidable monument of Cyclops and which aborts into the thin, ridiculous profile of a factory chimney."

But de Maupassant and his sour opinions were by now very much in the minority. Most days, even during bad weather, eleven thousand or twelve thousand people swarmed about the tower. Eiffel hoped that he and his shareholders would see almost two million persons pay admission, thus recouping the entire cost of the tower by the end of the fair. The Eiffel Tower was proving to be not only a technological milestone, a potent political symbol, and a great popular and artistic success but also a financial triumph.

It was not just the hoi polloi who had become smitten with the tower. Sarah Bernhardt, the most famous woman in Paris, the greatest and most consequential actress of her time, made an ascent. Auguste Bartholdi, sculptor of the Statue of Liberty, would pay a visit, signing Eiffel's elegant *Livre d'Or*, "Homage to M. Eiffel with many memories of the Statue of Liberty whose bones of iron he built." The most chic Parisians and the city's intellectuals all flocked to its restaurants. Even Guy de Maupassant, before he fled, found that he had no choice but to visit the tower if he wished to socialize. "Friends no longer dine at home or accept a dinner invitation at your home," he complained. "When invited, they accept only on condition that it is for a banquet on the Eiffel Tower—they think it gayer that way. As if obeying a general order, they invite you there every day of the week for either lunch or dinner."

On the evening of Tuesday, July 2, the splenetic literary lion Edmond de Goncourt, sixty-seven, dined with his eminent protégé Émile Zola and other writers on the Eiffel Tower. Beginning in 1848, the brothers Edmond and Jules de Goncourt had together published a prodigious number of documentary novels, plays, social histories, and biographies, all dedicated to a certain grim social realism. Independently wealthy, self-conscious aesthetes and snobs, they collected rarified *objets* and experiences.

All the while, looking to posterity, they carefully recorded their impressions and certain minutiae of Parisian literary life in a private diary. In 1870 Edmond even chronicled his brother's slow descent into dementia and death from tertiary syphilis. What little joie de vivre Edmond had ever possessed had long been exhausted by 1889, but he was still a diligent diarist. About the time the fair opened, the ever-dour de Goncourt reported that his dear friend Daudet had passed along this juicy tidbit about a conservative editor: "The madame of a whorehouse told Daudet that Charles Buloz comes regularly to her, has himself surrounded by four or five half-naked women who whirl around him while lifting up their skirts, and that during this spectacle the serious editor of *Revue des Deux Mondes* egotistically masturbates." Too impatient to wait for the judgment of posterity, Edmond had already published excerpts of the early diaries and predictably irritated quite a few of his contemporaries.

After his evening at the Eiffel Tower, de Goncourt wrote: "The ascent on the elevator: the sensation of a vessel putting out to sea, but not dizzying. Up on the platform, a perception, far beyond one's thinking at ground level, of the grandeur, the size, the Babylonian immensity of Paris, a city of blocks of buildings on which the sun was setting, with the hill of Montmartre a picturesque indentation bursting up among the great flat lines of

Entrance to one of the Otis elevators

the horizon and taking on, in the dusk, the appearance of a great ruin that had been illuminated.

"A somewhat dreamy dinner . . . then the very special impression of a walk down, like a head diving into infinity, the impression of a descent on these open ladder rungs into the night, with here and there semblances of plunges into boundless space, where you feel as if you are an ant descending the rigging of a warship on which the ropes are made of iron."

The Paris *Herald*'s "Roving American," himself no aesthete or philosopher, dined three evenings later up on the Eiffel Tower and recorded his impressions. He and his wife enjoyed watching the sunset from the top of the structure and found that "the bracing air up there" stimulated "an excellent appetite." They descended to the first platform to dine at Café Brébant. Too late for a prime spot on the open-air verandah, they were seated at a table inside with "a very fair view." The soup course was a disappointment—watery, lukewarm. The sardines they ordered were undercooked, "and these little fish had a painful expression about their eyes as if they had been suffering slow torture while being cooked. They were quite fresh, however, and they soon disappeared."

While the couple waited at length for their saddle of lamb with asparagus points, they admired "the profusion of pretty women, all in very smart dresses and hats. They were nearly all Parisiennes. . . . There were also several *mères de familles* present with their sons and daughters and provincial cousins." Then there were "the luminous fountains and the fairylike view from our little perch." At one point, the waiters fanned out through the restaurant delivering to all the ladies not the long-awaited food but roses left over from a banquet, an amusingly transparent bid for bigger tips. When eventually the lamb came "it was not bad," though the dessert course of "parfaits au café" was "unevenly frozen." The bill come to thirty-five francs. "Altogether, the Restaurant Brébant, on the Eiffel Tower, is vastly inferior in every way, except altitude, to the Restaurant Brébant at the corner of rue du Faubourg Montmartre and the boulevard. . . . The waiters are inattentive, dilatory, and noisy. The cooking is done by steam . . . [making for] pale, anemic appearance and taste."

This last culinary field report on "the art (not very difficult in Paris) of squandering money on high-priced dinners" provoked a letter two days later from a "Sensible American." The writer proposed to explain to readers of the Paris *Herald* "how to dine comfortably at a moderate outlay." It was true that their party of three always ate a substantial breakfast. Still, when "Sensible" and party needed lunch "about noon in the avenue Rapp just near the main entrance to the Exhibition," they found a small café where they ordered "bread and butter for the party, a glass of lemonade for each and some Swiss cheese. These, with the fruit, gave us an ample lunch for which our entire outlay was 6 francs. . . . Average cost of lunch for each person, 2 fr."

On the fairgrounds, Edyth Kirkwood recommended the Duval restaurants, "where refreshments are well served and cheap," while noting that at noon each day at the fair, "a little cannon from the Tour Eiffel gives the signal for the closing of the galleries, and then follows a very amusing and picturesque phase of French middle-class life. While the rich and well-to-do throng to the restaurants, families and couples in moderate or poor circumstances sit calmly down anywhere, on benches, chairs, or the ground, what does it matter? unpack their baskets of provisions and enjoy their dinner; while those who have come unprovided crowd around the booths, or buy great slices of bread and cheese and smoked sausage from men and women who stand on the outside of the grounds and offer their wares across the fence."

The Fourth of July dawned blue and warm out at the Wild West camp, where everyone was up early to hang French and American flags. Buffalo Bill decorated his tent with the Stars and Stripes and the tricolor, flowers, ferns and portraits of Generals Washington and Lafayette and Presidents Harrison and Carnot. All the Wild West troupers gathered while the Cowboy Band played sprightly versions of "Yankee Doodle" and "Hail, Columbia."

Then Nate Salsbury, ever the well-dressed gentleman amid all the buckskins and beads, stepped forward and signaled that he was ready to read, according to custom, the Declaration of Independence. When Salsbury, who had once strode the theatrical boards, delivered the document's final line—"And for the support of this Declaration, with a firm reliance on the protection of Divine Providence, we mutually pledge to each other our Lives, our Fortunes, and our sacred Honor"—the assembled Americans began to holler and applaud. Buffalo Bill came forward to deliver a few patriotic remarks, punctuated by celebratory gunfire.

With that, Cody, the Salsburys, and a visiting sister hastened to a waiting horse and carriage, for their next patriotic event was in the far reaches of the twelfth arrondissement, in southeast Paris. An hour later, just before 10:00 a.m., they pulled into the tiny rue de Picpus and joined U.S. minister Reid, a contingent of thirty U.S. Marines, and several hundred Americans as they filed into the high-walled cemetery attached to the Convent of the Sacred Heart. The group threaded past the many tombs of guillotined aristocrats to gather round the simple grave of General Lafayette, French hero of the American Revolution. By the time the Americans had bestowed all their bouquets and wreaths, Lafayette's tomb had disappeared under a floral mound. Minister Reid said a few words and placed his wreath, whereupon the general's grandson, Senator Edmond de Lafayette, eloquently thanked the Americans (in English) for honoring his ancestor. The marines concluded by shooting several volleys and mournfully sounding the bugle.

Some hours later, after lunch, Minister Reid and the American colony, now swelled to almost a thousand strong, reassembled by the Seine on the Pont de Grenelle at the Île des Cygnes. As the river shimmered in the summer light and barges passed, President Sadi Carnot and hundreds of uniformed French officials soon joined them, while Major Burke, Chief Rocky Bear, and Buffalo Bill squeezed onto the quay to watch. The Americans resident in Paris were bestowing upon the Third Republic a bronze statue cast from the original model for Bartholdi's statue, Liberty Enlightening the World, one fifth the size of its New York sister. All chose to ignore rude comments by French anarchists that Lady Liberty's statue required further embellishments to show American slums and the evils of child labor in American factories.

As the *New York World* correspondent observed, "Altogether, Paris and America are on exceedingly good terms with one another." After more speechifying (Minister Reid essaying his remarks in French) and music, most of the crowd boarded seven flag-bedecked steamboats and floated pleasantly to the Hôtel de Ville to drink champagne *vin d'honneur* in the ornate *salles*. The Wild West trio departed to attend their own Fourth of July festivities at the camp before the three o'clock show. U.S. minister Whitelaw Reid was delighted to see that the Exposition Universelle was a roaring success, for the fair and its roundelay of fêtes, dinners, and socializing were cementing ever-warmer diplomatic relations between France and America.

As Cody and the others rode their carriage out to Neuilly, they could see the rare sight of the American flag flying atop the Eiffel Tower, where it had been hoisted at 2:00 p.m. and remained till 5:00 p.m. That night a special Fourth of July fireworks display would be held at the Exposition Universelle to honor the American republic. But first, a crush of Yankees jammed the avenue Hoche off the Place de l'Étoile as they turned out for Minister Reid's Fourth of July evening open house and celebration. The Reids had moved into the *hôtel* of the Duc de Grammont, one of the city's legendary private mansions, and the American colony was avid to have a look. Carriages clogged the cobblestone porte cochère entry, while Mrs. Reid, her large diamond necklace glistening on a black-and-white-striped silk gown, greeted the throng. The Hôtel Grammont did not disappoint with its four mirrored Louis XV drawing rooms and a crimson-brocade dining room (seating twenty-four). Unfortunately the rented mansion's "vast collection of Egyptian curiosities," including numerous mummies and basalt statues of Isis and Osiris, had been consigned to storage, leaving only two sphinxes on the marble staircase.

For years, Americans in Paris (or the select who were invited) had celebrated the Fourth of July at Bella Rosa, the magnificent mansion near the Bois de Boulogne belonging to Dr. Thomas Evans, longtime dentist to the nobility of Europe, and one of the American colony's leading lights. A Quaker from Philadelphia, Dr. Evans had arrived in Paris in 1847 at age twenty-four with his wife, Agnes. Within five years, his pain-reducing services had won him appointment as official court dentist to Emperor Louis Napoleon III and his wife, Eugénie, as well as the Prince of Wales, the Russian czars, and many others. He amassed great wealth, which he used to build a palatial marble *hôtel* furnished with carpets from the Turkish sultan, vases from the Russian princes, and many royal bibelots. The graceful mansion was set in a verdant park with fountains, famous rose gardens, an American walnut tree and weeping willow, and several splendid aviaries stocked with rare pheasants, brilliant parrots, canaries, an ostrich, and four American bluebirds.

American diplomats assigned to Paris had long resented Dr. Evans, for not only did he have better access to the nobility of Europe, but no U.S. minister had ever been able to afford to live in comparable splendor or entertain in such lavish style. Moreover, this now-elderly man with his signature muttonchops was something of a royal sycophant and, worse yet, a bore. How many times had those at his dinner table been subjected to the story of how he secretly helped the empress Eugénie escape from Paris across the Channel to England after the fall of the Second Empire? A few years earlier he had even privately published his oft-told tale. The good dentist also loved to recount how, after a special mission to America to see how the Civil War was going, he had sailed back to Paris and convinced his friend the emperor to support President Lincoln. And then there were his two dozen noble honors and medals—French, Dutch, Russian, Prussian—awarded for services dental and diplomatic and prominently displayed in elegant cases. His wife, often bedecked with dazzling diamond necklaces, brooches, and earrings, served as further evidence of his success, for these expensive jewels were bestowed by grateful aristocratic clients and governments. One visiting American diplomat had remarked to his host while the men smoked their cigars, "Well, Doctor, we certainly owe you a debt of gratitude. For us it is a great thing to see a king or prince; but it seems that they all have opened their mouths to you."

In 1875, Dr. Evans had purchased the weekly *American Register*, thus becoming a pivotal voice in the American colony. Not surprisingly, the dentist was an ardent royalist who hoped that the revived French republic would not last. He used his column, "Paris Local," to write admiring tidbits about the remnants of aristocratic society. While James Gordon Bennett loved to attack the other English-language newspaper in Paris, the venerable *Galignani's Messenger*, he did not bother often to acknowledge Evans's *American Register*. Moreover, the columns of the Paris *Herald* somehow never managed to get the doctor's name right, as if he were some visiting fireman not worthy of proper identification. In Bennett's paper, Dr. Thomas Evans was invariably identified as Dr. Theodore Evans.

On this particular Fourth of July, quite a few of the longtime American colony and certainly the whole of the resident U.S. diplomatic corps were delighted to find custom turned on its head. Since the very wealthy new minister Reid had issued an open invitation to *all* Americans to celebrate Independence Day at his new mansion, no longer would Dr. Evans be able to lord it over his fellow countrymen, as Bennett was pleased to point out in his editorial columns: "We offer our hearty congratulations to the United States Minister for the wise step taken in the way of invitations. Instead of making a great stir and commotion by drawing up 'visiting lists' and ruling out Mrs. Flibertygibit, and ruling in Mrs. Humdrum, and causing heart-burnings and tempests in teapots, Mr. Whitelaw Reid simply reverted to the old ways of Washington and Jefferson, and Adams. All Americans were informed they were welcome to the Minister's home. And they went there, and they enjoyed themselves."

The *Chicago Tribune*'s reporter M. E. Sherwood declared the Reids' soirée a great success: "Miss Eames and Miss Marie Decca sang, and everybody came, 'some in rags, and some in tags, and some in velvet gowns.' Ladies in bonnets and gentlemen in dusters elbowed the latest creations of Worth, and the American colony had great pleasure. . . . Champagne flowed in an unceasing stream and a bountiful supper was spread in the grand dining room." A thousand Americans of every station happily inspected the avenue Hoche mansion and one another.

The next day Colonel Cody wrote his favorite sister, Julia, back at Scout's Rest: "Yesterday was a busy day for me. First I went with the American Minister to the tomb of General LaFayette then to the unveiling of Barthold's Statue, then to a reception & dinner we gave in camp—then the afternoon performance—then to the Legation reception—back for the evening show—then into my evening dress and to Minister Reid's reception, turned in at daylight—and today I am off my feed—I am like you I can't stand so much as I used to and I am not all well this summer. Now as we are getting old we must not kick at our breaking down, it can't be helped, but I don't want to break down until I get out of debt and ahead of the hounds far enough to take it easy. Sorry you & Al are not well—but don't worry. Love to you all Brother Will. P.S. About getting ahead and not loosing it, that is a hard thing to calculate on—as I have to take such awful risks in my business—Brother."

The elderly Dr. Evans had enthusiastically embraced one French custom: he had long kept a mistress. One of the more famous of Paris's *grandes horizontales*, Méry Laurent "was tall, with an exquisite tea-rose complexion, blue eyes, and fair hair with hints of red, a laughing beauty with arched eyebrows and a wide-eyed gaze. . . . Her mouth was sensual, her bosom formidable." Dr. Evans, nearing fifty, had been smitten back in the spring of 1872 when Laurent, twenty-three, played a small part in the

Offenbach operetta *Le Roi Carotte*. He wooed her with giant baskets of white roses and champagne dinners. Not long after she became famous for emerging nude from a large silver shell at the Châtelet theater, he installed her in a luxurious apartment at 52 rue de Rome with a monthly allowance of five thousand francs. Every day, Evans strolled over from Bella Rosa for a lunchtime visit. As the years passed, he also provided his mistress with a pleasant little summer villa.

The doctor was a busy man who frequently traveled to attend to his far-flung patients. Given that he also had a wife, Laurent developed her own interests, which included affairs with some of the more artistic men of Paris, who flocked to her Tuesday salon. Until Manet's death in 1883, they had been lovers, and in 1881 he had painted her portrait, titled *Autumn*. Evans had enjoyed meeting Laurent's bohemian friends and inevitably began adding some of their modern art to his large but otherwise conventional collection. The ever-gay Laurent was devoted in her own way to Evans, and said that leaving him "would be a wicked thing to do. I content myself with deceiving him."

After Manet died, Laurent took as her lover Stéphane Mallarmé, the Symbolist poet, even as he was becoming friends with James McNeill Whistler. Soon, whenever the Master was in Paris, Whistler dropped in to Laurent's evening salon. The Butterfly met Dr. Evans and happily fed him publicity items for the *American Register*.

In the wake of the Fourth of July, Minister Reid felt that the warm ceremonies of republican solidarity boded well for his overarching diplomatic mission: to persuade the French government to rescind the ruinous restrictions on the import of American pork. In 1881, the last year for the free flow of pork, U.S. farmers had earned almost $4 million, a figure that plummeted to a meager $5,000 in 1888. Minister Reid's pork problem—what the French would call *l'affaire des petits cochons*—began when the French discovered that the phylloxera pest that had been decimating their wine industry had almost certainly originated in the United States. Claiming to be worried about trichinosis, the French effectively banned pork imports, though some believed it was just a form of revenge.

Two years later, in 1883, the U.S. Congress retaliated with 30 percent U.S. tariffs on French art. French master Jean-Léon Gérôme complained to one of his New York collectors about "the strange, odd idea of likening the products of the mind [art] to sardines in oil and smoked ham. All over the world works of art were duty free. In one country alone were they saddled with excessive tax, and that country was the youngest, the greatest, and the wealthiest of nations." It was Minister Reid's task to quietly untangle this mess.

Just a week earlier, he had written to Secretary of State James G. Blaine, who had heard once again from the aggrieved Chicago Board of Trade about pork. Reid advised that the United States would do best to bide its time until autumn. While President Sadi Carnot's government did favor repealing the pork tariff to make available cheaper food, the Chamber of Deputies remained hostile to the proposal. In any case, the politicians were presently too absorbed by the Exposition, the possible return of Boulanger, and coming elections to take up the issue of pork.

In the meantime, Reid noted, he had learned that a reduction in the U.S. tariff on French art "would materially help in securing the concession we ask, and would besides give great satisfaction throughout France. Conversation with others confirms this opinion. As our own artists generally wish for such a reduction also, this would seem to indicate a practical and easy method of facilitating future negotiations as to the prohibition on pork."

Right after the Fourth of July, the French horsey set, skeptical about the Wild West's bronco-taming act, had issued a challenge to Buffalo Bill. A Monsieur Tailard of the elite Jockey Club had a "fiery untamed steed." During a regular Wild West performance, he proposed, this wild "colt shall be lassoed, saddled and ridden within the time usually given to the bucking show of the set." Colonel Cody was more than amenable, and on July 8, the horse, a fine-looking sixteen-hand black stallion, was delivered to the horse corral next to the arena as Buffalo Bill and the cowboys watched. "I want you to capture him," said Cody to his men, "ride him, and subdue him; but you must be careful and not injure him. It must be done carefully and without any cruelty." Mexican Joe and Jim Kidd vied for the honor, but in a cut of the cards, Jim Kidd won. Word of the challenge had gotten out, and a huge crowd, including much of the Jockey Club in ringside boxes, jammed the stands for the three o'clock show, with much heavy betting involved. When the time came for the bronco act, Buffalo Bill lassoed the wild stallion on his first try and with great trouble got him saddled up.

Jim Kidd sprang into the saddle, and off charged the stallion, bucking furiously. "No other horse has ever pawed so much air under a cowboy," said the *Chicago Tribune*. "Once he tried to jump over the stand. But Kidd kept his seat and presently had the horse under such control that he actually took 'Mother' Whittaker [the Wild West's beloved wardrobe mistress] up behind, and the two rode around the ring as the cowboy band played, 'See the Conquering Hero Comes.' It was the finest specimen of riding ever seen in Paris and the immense audience showed its appreciation of the young man's skill by round after round of applause. . . . It was said one member of the Jockey Club lost 15,000 francs."

Annie Oakley was having a wondrous Parisian summer, full of acclaim and amusements. Coached by Ira Paine, another American sharpshooter performing in Paris, she had mastered amazing new skills. Using a Smith and Wesson revolver, she shot directly through the middle of an ace of spades at ten yards. Then, even more astoundingly, that card was held sideways, and she shot and split it! President Sadi Carnot himself had paid Oakley the highest compliment, telling her, "When you feel like changing your nationality and profession there is a commission awaiting you in the French Army."

On July 12, the monarch of the West African nation of Senegal, Dinah Salifou, a Muslim, came out to Neuilly with his entourage of veiled wives, his twelve-year-old prince, and various officials to see the Wild West. "His Sable Majesty," as the press called him, was a striking figure in his black burnoose richly embroidered with gold. He had an intelligent face with a long sculpted beard, and his high forehead and bald head were emphasized by a distinctive conical high black hat, also covered with gold. King Salifou was riveted by Annie Oakley's unerring blasting of glass balls and all manner of flying objects. After the pioneers' cottage had once again been saved from the attacking Indians in the performance's finale, King Salifou sought out Buffalo Bill in the campground and expressed his admiration for Little Missy's sharpshooting talents.

Then the king asked Cody, "How much do you want for her?"

"Want for her?" responded Cody, nonplussed. "How do you mean?"

"To sell her. I wish to take her back with me. In my country, my people are not safe in many of the small villages. There are man-eating tigers in many districts, and even one of these animals can cause much damage. But with a person of such wonderful skills as she, it would be easy to organize parties with her as the chief huntress; the danger would be soon past. Would you consider a hundred thousand francs sufficient?"

Buffalo Bill's eyes glinted with fun, and he called for Oakley.

"Missy," the colonel said, introducing the king of Senegal and relating his offer.

Annie Oakley with some of the medals she won in sharpshooting contests

Miss Oakley looked wryly at Cody. "But am I for sale, Colonel?"

"Come to think of it, I guess you ain't."

Even as the king raised his price, Cody put an end to the joke and explained that Oakley was no slave, but her own modern woman, a citizen of the United States, and a world-class sharpshooter with a contract.

"When I told him I did not wish to go," said Oakley, "he went down on one knee with a sweeping grace that would have done credit to ye knights of old England, and lifting my hand, raised my fingertips to his lips. He departed with the air of a soldier." The king was learning that republics were more complicated than kingdoms. In truth, the French, who had long had a presence in his nation and now eyed it as a prospective colony, had invited this African monarch to the fair to advance their empire-building designs.

One wonders what emotions Annie Oakley felt over this seemingly amusing encounter with the Senegalese king, for her dark secret was that she *had*, in fact, once actually been enslaved, a terrifying episode that began when she was only ten, an episode revealed to the public only just before her death. Oakley's childhood had started happily enough. Her parents were settlers in Ohio, doing reasonably well, when her father almost froze in a blizzard and then died in 1866. It was hard times thereafter for the widow, left with five daughters and a baby son. Little Annie wanted to help out. "I was eight years old when I took my first shot, and I still consider it one of the best shots I ever made. I saw a squirrel run down over the grass in front of the house, through the orchard and stop on a fence to get a hickory nut." She rushed inside to get a rifle, and got the animal in her sight. "It was a wonderful shot, going right through the head from side to side." She turned out to be an absolute natural with a gun, and her hunting helped the family scrape by.

When Annie was ten her mother remarried, and family friends, the Edingtons, who ran the Darke County poor farm, proposed that Annie come live with them, attend school, and help sew dresses for the orphans. Oakley liked her new "Auntie" but missed the country. "I was deprived of my beloved hunts through the beautiful snow-clad woods." Then a farmer dropped by, a man she later called only the "He-Wolf," hoping Oakley might like to come help his wife with their newborn baby. When he promised that she could hunt, she agreed. "All went well for a month," she would later write. "Then the work began to stack up. I got up at four o'clock in the morning, got breakfast, milked the cows, fed the calves, the pigs, pumped water for the cattle, fed the chickens, rocked the baby to sleep, weeded the garden, picked wild blackberries, got dinner after digging the potatoes for dinner and picking the vegetables—and then could go hunting and trapping." When her mother asked to have her come home, the couple would not let Oakley go but wrote her mother that she was fine and attending school.

"One night I nodded over the big basket of stockings I had to darn. Suddenly the 'She-Wolf' struck me across the ears, pinched my arms and threw me out of doors into the deep snow and locked the door. I had no shoes on and in a few minutes my feet grew numb.

"I was slowly freezing to death. So I got down on my little knees, looked towards God's clear sky and tried to pray. But my lips were frozen stiff and there was no sound."

The "She-Wolf," worried because she heard her husband returning, opened the door and barked at Oakley to come in. "But I could not move, so she yanked me in, pushing me into a chair by the fire. My head sank limp just as the 'He-Wolf' entered and demanded to know what was the matter."

They dragged her to bed, where she spent the night in a delirium, begging again and again to be let in. "They did not bring me a thing to eat or drink until I could crawl downstairs." The "She-Wolf" left Oakley alone for two weeks, but then it was back to grueling amounts of work and chores. "I constantly begged her to send me back to my mother," but they refused. Now eleven, Oakley was effectively their slave. She was not allowed to go home, and when she displeased them, they beat and abused her. For two more years Oakley endured this virtual serfdom.

"One fine spring day the family was gone. I was ironing a large basket of clothes. Suddenly I thought—why not run away?" She was now thirteen years old and no doubt a sad-looking waif. And so she fled.

Very luckily she encountered a kind man at the train station who took her under his wing. She had all of forty-eight cents. He purchased her ticket, made sure she changed trains in the right place, fed her dinner, and then put her on the train that would stop that afternoon near her mother's house. Before debarking, he enlisted another adult to accompany young Oakley, and to make sure she got off at her proper station.

Oakley arrived at the family home only to find that her stepfather had died and her mother had moved back to their old village. The woman who now owned the house insisted that Oakley stay the night, and the next morning after breakfast, Oakley walked ten miles to reach the home of family friends, eluding a frightening tramp on the road. From there, it was another five miles to her mother and safety. Oakley offered no description of her reunion with a mother who had not bothered to find her as year after year passed. But she did describe her return to school: "I was happy for the first time since I left Auntie's."

Six months later, there was a loud banging on the school door, and the "He-Wolf" stormed in. "He took me by the arm, twisting it until I almost fainted with pain, and dragged me through the door." He pulled her up on his wagon and took off, the teacher in hot pursuit.

"I knew he must pass Edington's and I kept figuring out how to escape. I planned to turn a back somersault and leap just as he reached the gate." But Mr. Edington, who knew the "He-Wolf" well, stood in the middle of the road, stopped the horses and acted as if Oakley's captor would naturally be staying for dinner. Her aunt reassured her they would not let the "He-Wolf" take her, and at that, "I had Auntie unbutton my little dress and look at the scars on my back where the 'Wolves' had struck me.

" 'My God, child,' said Auntie, 'six months ago, and your back and poor little shoulders are still green. How did you live through it?'

" 'I do not know,' I told her."

After dinner, the "He-Wolf" said he was taking Oakley home with him, but the men of the household told him to leave, warning him, "You are a lucky man to escape."

For the first time in almost four years, fourteen-year-old Oakley felt safe.

As an adult, Annie Oakley was famously tight with money, a characteristic that was especially notable in the company of the ever-generous, wildly profligate Bill Cody. Oakley knew her reputation, but she preferred to give her money to the young and needy.

By July 16, the sunny summer days had been blown away by heavy winds, followed by day after day of cold, rainy weather. This suited the mood of Minister Antonin Proust, who by now knew there was no hope he would be able to buy *The Angelus* for France. The conservatives in the Chamber of Deputies had permanently tabled a bill to finance the purchase because poor François Millet was too close to republican hearts. Nor in this season, when the Panama Canal collapse had struck so hard, was there any rich, gallant savior to step forward to offer to preserve this French patrimony. After that frenzied moment of triumph in the Sedelmeyer Gallery, Monsieur Proust accordingly had to officially relinquish his prize and watch Mr. Sutton sally off with a picture that should have been enshrined in the Louvre. The situation was not made any less bitter when Monsieur Proust learned that his American nemesis proposed to display *The Angelus* in Paris for two months before shipping it home. The culture minister's only consolation was knowing that the U.S. tariff on fine art would cost the American a painfully large sum.

On Tuesday, July 16, despite the steady drizzle outside, jubilation reigned at 27 avenue de la Bourdonnais, American Exhibition headquarters. An exultant Gen. Rush Hawkins had received good news, which he immediately shared with the Paris *Herald*: The 255 American artists exhibiting at the World's Fair had won an impressive 108 medals. This was a huge relief, after nasty rumors that the juries had seen little to reward on the crowded walls of the second-floor American galleries. "Our countrymen will doubtless be surprised . . . [and] rejoice in the success," opined Hawkins proudly, especially as "this is the first time we have entered the lists to contend with the artists of the world." Three Americans had won the highest award, the coveted medal of honor: painters John Singer Sargent and J. Gari Melchers and sculptor Paul Wayland Bartlett, while another seven artists had won gold medals. Had James McNeill Whistler not defected to the British exhibit, his gold medal for his portrait of Lady Archibald Campbell would have upped the gold medal total to eight.

In London Whistler was especially pleased about his gold medal, for Lady Campbell was an old friend of his and daughter-in-law of the Duke of Argyll. Whistler graciously accepted the many felicitations from French friends Montesquiou and Mallarmé, even though he viewed the honor as inevitable. Of course, his multitude of enemies, carefully cultivated over the years, declared it "a horror" that Whistler had won over more-deserving English artists. Some American critics swooned with admiration, hailing Whistler as "the only and original painter. He has narrative, natural aptitude for the presentation of form, repartee, and originality." At the same time, Whistler was embroiled in a legal fight with London brewer Sir Henry Meux over a portrait of his young wife, Valerie, which Whistler had destroyed after she dared to complain about too many sittings and the portrait's taking too long. Whistler had long since perfected using the modern art of scandal amplified by the newspapers to keep his name on everyone's lips. The notoriety was more than useful in drawing crowds to see his art and in selling it.

Alfred O. Tate, Edison's young private secretary, had remained in London, and after almost two months there had concluded nothing would ever light a fire under the ever-amiable Col. George Gouraud. On July 23, Tate wrote to Samuel Insull, Edison's private secretary, that Gouraud's recent "order" for a thousand phonographs was a ploy. "He might just as well have made the order for 10,000." In truth, Gouraud was actually asking for only

"50 phonographs and supplies—and you can rest assured that he will not ask for a further shipment for several months, if he ever does. . . . The commercial success of the phonograph will never be seriously considered and worked out energetically until it leaves Gouraud's hands."

Insull, who had been Gouraud's secretary for two years before immigrating to the United States in 1881 to work for Edison, was not surprised. "I have always insisted that Mr. Gouraud would never be able to float anything successfully . . . and I want no better justification of my opposition" than Tate's reports. Unfortunately, Gouraud had a contract.

General Hawkins, who had survived many rounds of combat in his Civil War years, felt pleased and grateful to emerge from his own Paris art wars bruised but victorious. First, he had put up with a great deal of complaining from his own artists, followed by considerable carping from American critics. *The Tribune* complained that the U.S. painters failed to convey "a national story, a national landscape and a moral elevation." The French concurred, with one critic writing, "What is wanting in this American Exhibition is native painting on native subjects." Back in 1887, Henry James had summarized the situation neatly: "It sounds like a paradox, but it is a very simple truth, that when today we look for 'American art' we find it mainly in Paris. When we find it out of Paris, we at least find a great deal of Paris in it." While the Americans had held their own at the exhibition, the fact was that the French had simply rewarded their acolytes for sensibly studying and practicing art in Paris.

The irascible General Hawkins took the occasion of the penning of his official Exposition report to skewer such troublesome sorts as Whistler, describing the prize-winning portrait of Lady Campbell as "truly Whistlerian, and in no respect satisfactory. The subject is neither walking nor standing. A rudimentary foot is shown, but it seems to be suspended from something and incapable of bearing weight; it is not an English foot, nor does it even appear to rest on anything. It is only an incorrect suggestion of a foot." To be fair, he did have kinder things to say about another Whistler painting, *The Balcony*, which featured a Japanese-like scene.

Amid all the pleasures and exhilarations of the World's Fair, Eiffel was disturbed by one great disappointment: the final and total collapse of Ferdinand de Lesseps's Panama Canal Company. When the receiver appointed in February 1889 had advised in mid-May that no further work would be reimbursed, Gustave Eiffel had reluctantly instructed his men in Panama to stop work on the locks. Even as the World's Fair persuaded the Western nations not to underestimate the French industrial spirit—"the French capacity for work has not been idle for a single moment"—the canal venture was in its death throes. Throughout France families were financially devastated. In July Eiffel signed a document returning $600,000 and giving over all the equipment and the locks that had been built to the receiver, thus retiring his own contract. He had expected the Panama Canal to be his final great work, another colossal engineering project for the greater glory of France, and one of far greater significance than his *Tour en Fer*. Alas, that was not to be.

Fairgoers near the fountain on the Champ de Mars,
with the Central Dome in the background

CHAPTER EIGHT

The Monarchs of the World
Ascend the Republican Tower

At 8:00 a.m. on Friday, August 2, all those who worked at the Eiffel Tower were in a state of intense anticipation: When would Nasir al-Din, His Majesty the Shah of Persia, the King of Kings, arrive to ascend the tower? The *Figaro* reporters, the ladies selling trinkets and cigars, the waiters, the elevator men—all attired in their Sunday best and bedecked with nosegays and medals—crowded the platform railings to watch the Pont d'Iéna for a glimpse of the imperial landau and its honor guard of dragoons. After a fortnight of wintry rain, a few days earlier the sun had mercifully come out, and it was the clearest of summer mornings.

By eleven o'clock the men of *Le Figaro*, facing their deadline, called the tower's office, asking plaintively, "Is he coming?" Down below at the fairgrounds, they spied only the usual crowds and a bobbing sea of women's colored parasols unfurled to protect fair skins. By noon a pall of disappointment had settled over the tower: His Majesty the Shah, despite official advance notice, was not coming.

Two days previous, in midafternoon, the sixty-year-old Shah, whose royal line descended from Darius the Great, had made his first informal visit to the Exposition. Though short of stature, he was a striking personage with his dark mustachios, tall astrakhan fez, and colorful uniform resplendent with very large precious stones. "His Majesty," reported the Paris *Herald*, "went immediately to the Eiffel Tower, but after mounting a few of the steps leading to the lifts, renounced any intention he might have had of ascending."

The Shah quickly recovered his sangfroid and pressed on to the fair's other seductions. On two earlier state visits, the Shah's Oriental extravagance had become legend, and now as he strolled through the fair, he more than gladdened the hearts of the vendors. He gravitated toward an Antwerp diamond-cutting exhibit, where he added to his collection of royal jewels by purchasing a large black diamond for 32,000 francs ($6,400). Then "all along his passage the Shah made numerous purchases at different stalls he passed, greatly to the satisfaction of the stall keepers."

His first visit to the fair concluded, the Shah's cavalcade of carriages, led by galloping dragoons, crossed the Seine on the Pont d'Alma, heading to 43 rue Copernic, a palatial mansion in a large walled park. Owned by the French republic, the mansion had been freshly painted, gilded, and opulently furnished with antiques from the reigns of Louis XV and Louis XVI. The Shah occupied the entire second floor, and from the private Italian balcony off his bedroom he could see the very Eiffel Tower he had thus far declined to ascend.

At this most democratic and republican of World's Fairs, the French government relished the visit of every single royal, as did Gustave Eiffel. Certainly, high above Paris on his tower, Eiffel found no set of *ascensionnistes* so politically gratifying as the foreign nobility. First had come the Prince and Princess of Wales, flouting Queen Victoria's express wish that her government boycott the fair. In ensuing weeks he had had the pleasure of welcoming to his republican tower the former queen Isabella II of Spain, whose misrule had caused her to be exiled in 1868, followed shortly by her abdication. Now a longtime resident of Paris, she was a notorious libertine. In the course of the summer, other royals also ascended: the Duke of Edinburgh, an admiral in the British navy; the Russian czar-to-be Nicholas II; and Tewfik Pasha, the Khedive of Egypt. On July 22, Prince Kitiyahara, heir apparent to the throne of Siam, and his younger brothers, Pravita Chira and Rabi, had been up, squired by members of the Siamese Legation. The very next day King George of Greece had visited, ignoring the heavy rainsquall impeding the view. As his queen had been a czarist princess, he elected to dine at the Russian restaurant.

Eiffel's most exotic royal visitor had been the Muslim king of Senegal, Dinah Salifou, who attended with his entourage and a four-man orchestra providing background music with stringed instruments and xylophone. On the last day in July, Eiffel scored a patriotic coup, for with him atop the tower was none other than the German ambassador, whose government and private enterprises had been ostentatiously boycotting the fair.

On the very day that the Shah bolted, King Salifou ascended the tower with his queen and their entourage for their *second* visit. On that occasion, the king and queen brought along eight young princes—all speaking good French, noted *Le Figaro de la Tour*—who had been entrusted to the Senegalese king for the journey to France. His own son, Prince Ibrahim, would soon travel to Algiers to attend lycée there. Once again the king's musicians played their instruments up at the tower's summit as *Le Figaro* went to press.

In the wake of so many bruited royal visits, the Persian Shah's failure to ascend had been duly noted and ridiculed. It seemed the King of Kings had been brooding over his embarrassing departure from the Eiffel Tower and subsequent nonappearance. For on Saturday, August 3, around midday, a *New York Times* reporter strolling the tower's first platform stopped in his circuit, unable to believe his eyes—could this be the Persian king ascending the staircase, dressed in a blue Turkish-style tunic with gold braid epaulettes and sky blue trousers? "To my astonishment," he wrote, "and the utter stupefaction of the bewildered authorities, up climbed the Shah. He had been trying to screw up his courage ever since his arrival, but had never gotten above the third step, and there he was, all by himself, far in advance of his frightened suite and looking like a very brilliant, anxious fish, suddenly landed from deep water on high ground. Such a funny scene of confusion I never saw."

The *Figaro* reporter was directly behind His Majesty on the stairs. A tower official had called excitedly up to the tiny newsroom to say that the Shah's imperial landau had halted unexpectedly at the foot of the tower and that the Shah had emerged and announced his intention to ascend. *Figaro*'s Monsieur St.-Jacques rushed down on the Otis elevator, and indeed, there was Nasir al-Din, walking up the western staircase with two fair officials in his wake. "The king climbed slowly, stopping a few minutes at each landing, admiring the view that is always so fine. After walking around the first platform's exterior gallery . . . the Shah of Persia leaned on the balcony and spent a long time admiring the structure's proportions, conversing animatedly with Monsieurs Berger and Ansaloni. A large crowd surrounded him. Servants from the Russian Restaurant offered flowers to the monarch."

The Paris that the Shah gazed out over, on this, his third visit to the city, was noticeably more prosperous and democratic than during his earlier stays. The self-made man had come to the fore, and new industrial fortunes such as Gustave Eiffel's had upended the established class-based nobility and social order. Paris, with all its opportunities, culture, and freedom had become a great magnet for the ambitious, much to the outrage of the old guard. The aged Edmond de Goncourt lamented, "The truth is that Paris is no longer Paris; it is a kind of free city in which all the thieves of the earth who have made their fortunes in business come to eat badly and sleep with the flesh of someone who calls herself a Parisienne." Of course, the republicans saw the changes very differently.

The *Times* man soon learned that the Shah was supposed to be at an official function across the Seine at the Trocadéro, where "everyone was waiting for him in state and expectation." The French republican government, determined to show that democrats were as capable as royalists of proper ceremony, had heaped all possible formal pomp, protocol, and receptions upon the Persian Shah, their first official royal state visitor to the fair. But now here he was wandering about like any tourist. Utterly unprepared for Nasir al-Din, the flustered Eiffel Tower officials politely tried to shoo the hoi polloi off the first platform.

"But," noted the *Times* man, "they could not be thrown over the railing and it takes time to get down the stairs, so a good many staid [*sic*]." As for the Shah, "He looked exactly like a schoolboy caught in mischief, and expecting a parental earthquake to swallow him up." A royal luncheon was quickly organized at Café Brébant. Monsieur St.-Jacques of the tower *Figaro* had no choice but to return to his office on the platform above and compose a quick story, for his paper was already behind deadline. But the *Times* man happily lingered, waiting to see the next installment in this spur-of-the-moment royal appearance.

Having cooled his heels for quite some time, the *Times* reporter was pleased to see his royal Persian quarry finally exiting the Café Brébant. What would happen next? "The Shah walked bravely to the elevator to rise to the second platform. He actually got inside the square box." Apparently Monsieur Berger had persuaded the Shah to tour the rest of the tower. But then, apparently, the Shah reconsidered, once again reluctant to entrust his life to these machines. "[He] looked imploringly round, and made a bee line for the stairs, disappearing downward and onward, as fast as his legs could carry him, and unassisted by any native dignity or borrowed decorum. His suite followed, forgetting the elevator's rapidity, and when the distinguished crowd reached the Shah, he was as unconcerned and composed once more as if nothing extraordinary had happened." And thus ended the Shah's extempore visit to the Eiffel Tower, leaving in his wake many disappointed salespeople, for the Persian monarch had purchased but two dozen tiny towers and a walking stick with a tower handle before disappearing swiftly down the staircase.

It was surprising that the Shah had balked at riding the Eiffel Tower elevators, because in his own nation he had been an apostle of modernity. After visiting France in both 1867 and 1873, he had subsequently introduced up-to-date postal and banking systems, trains, and newspapers. Unfortunately, he "lacked application and tenacity of purpose where reform, social justice, and good government were concerned. His absorbing passions were eating, drinking, sex, hunting, riding, and money." And also, oddly, photography, a fascination that dated back to boyhood. In 1858, Nasir al-Din had invited French photographer Francis Carlhian to set up a studio in the Tehran palace, and royal life there was regularly photographed and memorialized in albums filled with pictures of his vast harem and his many children. The Shah ordered provincial governors to send in photos documenting their official reports, while foreign archeologists maintained similar records.

By now it had become de rigueur for every celebrity and royal visiting the Paris World's Fair also to make the pilgrimage to see Buffalo Bill's Wild West show. When word came that Nasir al-Din would attend, the mayor of Neuilly, Gen. Henrion Berthier, implored Nate Salsbury to allow him, the mayor, to receive the Shah when he arrived at the campground. The Wild West camp was in a great lather preparing the grounds and making the loge of honor suitably sumptuous for this exotic potentate. Major Burke and Nate Salsbury made certain that luxurious chairs had been arranged just so, abundant flowers and greenery properly arrayed, and an elegant refreshment table made ready with iced drinks and plates of fruit. The flags of Persia, France, and the United States were draped over the box.

Salsbury was happy to let the mayor of Neuilly do the honors for the Shah. "I readily assented," he said, "and in return he said he would take much pleasure in presenting Cody and myself to the Shah." As the momentous hour approached that hot summer afternoon, "Cody got into his buckskins and I pushed myself into a spike-tailed coat, and soon the mayor appeared. Covered with decorations, spattered with medals and resplendent in the uniform of a Major General of the French Army, [the Mayor of Neuilly] was calculated to make the most extravagant picture of Solomon look like a spoiled deuce in a new pack."

Cody, Salsbury, and the mayor waited nervously in the rising heat, when "the equerries of the Republic dashed into the grounds followed by a state carriage in which was seated the most unimpressive man I ever saw," recounted Salsbury. "The postilions stopped the horses, the footmen flung the carriage doors open, and the Shah descended to the ground, where he was met by the Mayor, who addressed him. . . . The Shah [wearing a gigantic diamond] never stopped to hear the finish of the speech but waved him away with petulant disdain and passed into the grand stand. . . . The Mayor, strutting and fuming, strode away."

The whole Wild West camp had gone all out for the Shah, starting with the boss. "Cody had on all his war paint," reported the Paris *Herald* with bemusement. "Soft black leather boots covered three-fourths of his legs, the spurs clanking at the feet. Over a shirt of crimson satin, heavy with embroidered flowers, he wore a buckskin jacket covered with Indian bead work, and fringed with thongs of deerskin. Then on his breast were medals, badges, and ribbons *ad libitum*. Taking him all in all, costume, hair, figure, the Colonel looked every inch the genuine Buffalo Bill and the Shah was duly impressed."

In the stands "the silks and ribbons flashed bright from hundreds of summer gowns worn by bright eyed Parisiennes, bearers of bright hued parasols." The lemonade vendors were doing a brisk trade as the sold-out crowd craned for a glimpse of the Shah as three o'clock came and went. When the Persian monarch walked in by the side entrance at three thirty, a roar went up and the crowd rose in a standing ovation. Escorted by many French ministers, Nasir al-Din stepped into the box of honor. Some of the city's most famous courtesans had secured ringside boxes where they could not be missed by His Majesty, and fanned themselves coquettishly and

smiled alluringly at the famous sovereign. *Le Gil Blas* sniffed that the courtesans' goal was "obvious. . . . And we can safely say it was a sheer waste of
time, for the Shah did not pay an iota of attention to these mice."

These ladies of the demimonde were certainly unaware that the Shah,
unwilling to bring along any of his veiled harem on his trip abroad, had
ordered his ambassador to Istanbul to buy two Circassian concubines,
dress them as men, and send them to Paris for his enjoyment during his
sojourn at the fair. The French *cocottes* might also have reconsidered their
pursuit of the Shah if they'd known the fate of some of their Persian sisters.
The Shah, incensed to learn that Persian women in Tehran were consorting
with foreigners, had issued this order: "When you learn that a woman has
relations with the Westerners, and when she leaves the house of a Westerner, have her seized the next day under some other pretext, order her to
be thrown into a sack. . . . Two or three of them should be strangled and
killed right in the sacks; others are to be severely punished, fined, and banished from the city once and for all."

Once the crowd had settled down, the Cowboy Band struck up the
Persian national anthem, followed by those of the United States and France.
Out came Richmond the orator, and in moments the cowboys and Indians
were racing by at terrifying speeds. All eyes remained upon the Shah, who
proved to be a lively spectator. Again, the Paris *Herald*: "[The Shah watched
the show] with an intense, almost childish, interest." He beamed with
smiles "and clapped his hands heartily enough to split his immaculate
white gloves." Like any other member of the audience, he was astonished
when Annie Oakley performed her amazing new stunt of shooting a hole
through the ace of spades at ten yards and then splitting the card sideways.
All the while the Shah was sipping glasses of ice water and nibbling fruit.

The *Herald* reporter, having seen all the Wild West acts many times by
now, directed his attention completely to the guest of honor: "He must be
a very nervous man . . . for he was hardly still for two consecutive moments. He was for ever crossing and recrossing his legs, tapping his patent
leather boots—very small, by the way—against the railing, rubbing his august thumbs together like a nutmeg grater, or pulling at his short black
moustache. His excitement reached a climax when the bucking horses appeared, and if they had kept it up much longer, he would probably have
decorated some of the riders with the order of the Persian Sun, Moon or

Stars." A French reporter, meanwhile, noted the Shah's wild laughter over the bronco riding.

After the show, American minister Whitelaw Reid, along with visiting presidential son Russell Harrison, came forward to have a few words with the potentate. At a dinner the previous night, hosted by carriage magnate P. E. Studebaker at the Hôtel Meurice, Reid had "made an amusing speech . . . [saying] how busy he was . . . with wandering Americans whose curiosity prompted them to pry into the Sewers, Catacombs and all sorts of queer places. He also described his sensations yesterday at finding himself, for the first time in his life, clad in evening dress in broad daylight. As he stood before the Shah among some eighty other Ambassadors, he had been struck by the modesty of his plain black attire compared with the rainbow-like costumes of his colleagues. He had consoled himself, however, by reflecting that in many cases those Governments which put the most gold on their uniforms have the least of it in their treasuries. Mr. Russell Harrison made a speech in which he expatiated on the 'red hot' time he was having in Paris, where he had come to enjoy 'perfect rest.'"

As the Shah of Shahs, Nasir al-Din, departed his box, the audience in the Wild West grandstands again rose up in a roar of approval. The Shah followed custom and set off to stroll the Wild West campground. Escorted by Buffalo Bill, he inspected the tents and teepees. "One little Indian boy about five years old seemed to strike his fancy. His name is Billy Irving, and he stood at dress parade as the monarch passed. Billy had nothing much on, except paint, but he had plenty of that, and most artistically applied. His face was yellow, his body striped, his knees red and the rest of him green. The Shah 'took him in' silently for a minute and then shook his head and passed on. One of these days he may take it into his head to buy Billy, and make him Grand Visier." At five thirty the Shah had to depart, but before entering the imperial landau, he upheld his reputation for munificence by bestowing a large sum upon all the company. A baby buffalo born that day, the first such in Europe, was named Shah in His Majesty's honor. The King of Kings was also rumored to have presented Cody with a large diamond star pin.

As the summer waned Paul Gauguin and a new disciple, painter Paul Sérusier, had retreated from what they saw as the cloying tourism of

Wild West Indians—mainly Sioux—pose at the Neuilly camp.

Pont-Aven to the tiny, bleak Atlantic Coast farm village of Le Pouldu. Many locals collected seaweed for iodine, hard but picturesque work that Gauguin captured in his paintings. By August, Sérusier had departed for military service, and Dutch painter Jacob Meyer de Haan, at the urging of Theo van Gogh, had joined Gauguin. Gauguin and his dealer had largely put behind them their differences over the Volpini show still hanging at the Exposition. The artist had acquired numerous souvenirs from the Paris fair, but his most prized object was a piece of plaster Khmer sculpture.

With his love of the exotic, Gauguin had been thrilled to find at the fair a Khmer temple compound dominated by a towering life-size plaster replica of three ancient Angkor Wat stupas, all covered with fantastic statuary of gods and goddesses in sinuous poses, with many more statues displayed around the grounds. Gauguin made numerous sketches of these deities, and when one day he spied a part of a statue that had broken off and fallen to the ground, he took it and secreted it in his clothes.

On the Esplanade des Invalides, the Paris Exposition also hosted a genuine Buddhist temple, known as the Great Tranquility, constructed with massive bronze-like lim wood columns from the royal forests of Thanh-Hóa. Fifteen gilded wooden Buddhas were arrayed upon altars in the temple's serene interior, its air sweet with incense. This temple was not intended for tourists, but for the two hundred North Vietnamese who had come to Paris to work in the fair. Nine bonzes, or priests, oversaw the temporary pagoda. "Their religious services consisted, apparently," said one writer, "in presenting before the fifteen idols in gilded wood, ranged in their hieratic rank on the five degrees of the high altar, flowers, fruits, and rice cakes, and then, squatting in a semi-circle facing their gods, abandoning themselves to the chanting of interminable psalms, accented, from time to time, by the striking together of bronze gongs and wooden plates."

In early July, Gauguin had written to Theo, who had just sold one of his Martinique paintings, *Négresses*: "Thank you for your kind letter. Please find enclosed with mine the receipt for 225 francs. Although it is cheap, you did *well* to strike a bargain at that price with Lerolle, an artist." Gauguin could not resist adding a few words about his show at Volpini's Café des Beaux-Arts. "Do you think this exhibition is of little use to me? On the surface yes! In reality, *no*. Seeing that my real purpose is to demonstrate to Pissarro etc. that I can function without them, that all their talk about artistic *fraternity* is not reflected in their actions. . . . The thing that pleases me most in your letter (is your brother's good health). Keep the picture available for me! And when you judge it's the right time for me to write to him *write to me and send his address.*"

Vincent van Gogh was still at the sanitarium in St.-Rémy. While he felt he was in good medical hands there with Dr. Peyron, the nuns were another matter. "What annoys me is constantly seeing these good women who believe in the Virgin of Lourdes, and make up things like that: and to think I am a prisoner under an administration of that sort." While Vincent had been painting at a great pace, he still found the religious atmosphere oppressive. "I am astonished that with the modern ideas that I have," he explained in a letter to Theo, "and being so ardent an admirer of Zola and de Goncourt and caring for things of art as I do, that I have attacks such as a superstitious man might have and that I get perverted and frightened ideas about religion such as never came into my head in the North." He had been doing well until mid-July, when he was stricken with another attack and, by early August, was so unwell that he had stopped painting.

The major news in the van Gogh family was not Vincent's relapse into illness and melancholy, however, but Theo and Jo's announcement that they were expecting a baby early in 1890. Jo wrote to Vincent and admitted that she had not been happy to find herself pregnant. "When I think how neither Theo nor I are in very good health, I am greatly afraid that we are going to have a weak child." Theo wrote his brother, "I look like a corpse."

After so much success and adulation Annie Oakley was thoroughly vexed to find herself—of all things—embroiled in a French lawsuit. Two years earlier, in 1887, she had signed a contract to come over from London for "a five week Paris engagement. I was to appear in November. But an hour after the contract was mailed my doctor told me I must take a rest. I immediately canceled the contract by enclosing two certificates signed by the best doctors in London and then I sailed for New York." Those French theater managers had joined their countrymen in the Wild West grandstands, observed Annie Oakley's popularity, and had come away feeling cheated long after the fact. They "waited for three weeks after our opening in Paris to see how I went. My contract with them had called for $3000. They then entered suit and received a verdict for $2000 damage on the grounds that my performance with the Wild West would take all novelty from any shooting act they might thereafter engage. That showed French justice for shooting too well! I appealed and the case hung. All in all, it finally cost me $1500, all because I was too good a shot!"

Oakley's legal predicament was nothing compared to that suddenly confronting the Sioux Indians. In recent weeks U.S. minister Whitelaw Reid had come repeatedly to the Wild West camp at the behest of Secretary of State James G. Blaine, who had instructed Reid to secure signatures from the Sioux on a new U.S. treaty that would take half of their Dakota reservation (eleven million acres) near the gold-rich Black Hills, reluctantly ceded in 1877. As Reid explained repeatedly to the impassive Indian chiefs, the federal government was making an offer of $14 million for this huge territory—an offer, it was clear, that could not be refused. The Paris

Sioux, who were illiterate, had no way of knowing how their leaders at home were responding to this latest land grab, and were therefore unwilling to be party to any such agreement.

Back in the United States, a *New York Herald* reporter out on the Dakota reservation wrote, "The Indians are very bitter in spirit. Since they first ceded land to white men in the Big Sioux Valley, about 1851, they have seen the white race gradually elbow them out of their country. They lost the Black Hills in 1877 and now they have yielded one-half of their whole possessions. The great chiefs admit that they simply bow to a superior force. If they could fight they probably would. Sitting Bull, that malignant and restless old politician, is outvoted. To a *Herald* correspondent he expressed his feelings tersely, 'Don't talk to me about Indians. . . . Those still wearing the clothes of warriors are only squaws.'"

The United States government and the Bureau of Indian Affairs wanted only for the Indians to forsake their nomadic, warlike ways, move aside for whites, and settle down quietly to farming. Buffalo Bill knew full well that the bureaucrats disapproved of the Wild West show for its showcasing Indians as warriors, and he did his best not to provoke the government agency. Even as Cody was swanning about at Parisian parties and receptions, he "told his Indians that they must not go out at night or go with the gay frivolous young women who see Paris by gaslight." Various chiefs were entrusted with enforcing these rules. "'When I tried to do so,' said No Neck, 'the braves had no ears and paid no attention.'" Some paid for their dissipations with "various forms of debility which are the inevitable results of fashionable life." Chief Rocky Bear became a "rake himself doing considerable mashing among the continental belles."

Not long after the Shah of Persia's visit to the Wild West show, the legendary actress Lillie Langtry, thirty-six, made her pilgrimage. She had first captured attention at twenty-three as the rich, violet-eyed society beauty who captivated the ever-randy "Bertie," Prince of Wales, serving as his very public mistress for several years. Later she overcame divorce and hard times by becoming a star of the stage. Now an American citizen of just two years' duration, Miss Langtry rode in the famous Deadwood Stage with numerous other ladies. In this "bouquet of beauty," swooned one reporter, "the center flower [was] Mrs. 'Lillie' Langtry." She was in town, among other things, to be fitted at the House of Worth for the wardrobe for her next play.

Presidential son Russell Harrison had recently been similarly fêted, sitting atop the careening coach and waving his silk top hat to the cheering grandstands. Harrison, a typical example of the amiable but feckless son of an eminent family, first came to public notice as a young man when assigned the unfortunate job of telling the press that the stolen corpse of his grandfather (also the son of a president, William Henry Harrison) had been found at Ohio Medical College, where the corpse was hanging by the neck, waiting to be dissected. Subsequently, young Russell had moved to Montana to seek his fortune, but various mining and cattle ventures had gone disastrously wrong. His father, Indianapolis lawyer Benjamin Harrison, repeatedly bailed his son out. In the 1888 election, Russell, forty-five, had worked to elect his father, yet just before leaving for Paris, Russell had once again been making unwelcome headlines, this time for a convoluted libel case brought by the governor of Montana involving disappearing diamonds and a politician's wife.

Colonel Cody, no stranger to the White House, treated the presidential son to a Wild West breakfast. As ever *The Herald*'s man was there: "Such a breakfast had the gallant Colonel prepared for his visitors as they had not eaten for many a day. Baked beans, with the flavor of savory pork, corn bread, custard pie and ice cream. Where all these wonderful things came from was a mystery, but there they were, and very good they were. Nor was the menu limited to purely American dishes, but various products of Parisian culinary skill were pleasingly blended therein. The collation was served up in one of the luxurious tents, which was fitted up for the occasion with flowers, flags and all sorts of trophies from the Wild West." Major Burke and Nate Salsbury were present, along with numerous American journalists and other visiting dignitaries. Many toasts were drunk. "Mr. Harrison himself is a genuine Westerner. Consequently he enjoyed to the utmost all the stories of life on the plains, which grew more and more thrilling as the repast advanced."

Unlike social lion Buffalo Bill, who was the public ambassador and face of the Wild West show, Annie Oakley and her husband, Frank Butler, preferred to spend their free time at private shooting clubs or in high-stakes shooting matches. In Paris, Oakley was invited to join the elite club Le

Cercle des Patineurs. "Thereafter Mr. B and I often spent a pleasant afternoon after the performance at the club, meeting many charming people and carrying away beautiful bouquets of tea roses grown in the club rose gardens.

"Mr. B and I arrived at the club rather early one morning and found two strangers shooting. There was no one to present us, but the taller stranger asked Mr. B if he would join them. Mr. B answered that the gun belonged to the lady. Then they bowed and asked if I cared to shoot. Mr. B said that he would go to the pool, so we shot for an hour and Mr. B's pockets were some puffed out when the secretary arrived and said, 'I see you have met the Grand Duke.'

"Then I was presented to the Grand Duke Michaelvitch of Russia with whom I had been shooting for the last hour."

During breaks in the Wild West schedule, Annie Oakley also relished special shooting holidays on great estates. When she had been in England, she wrote, "there were 12 days spent in roaming over their 5000 acres, shooting partridges, pheasants and black cock, the latter being rather scarce and the mountain climbing hard. The lodges were furnished comfy on the shooting estate, and after a 12- or 15-mile walk each day, there was a hot bath, a delicious dinner, then gathering around the open fire, in easy chairs to talk over the day's sport and bygone days, then the soft bed at 9:30 and out at the first streak of dawn."

By late summer the American artists of Paris were still venting their ire at Gen. Rush Hawkins in the pages of the Paris *Herald*. On August 5, a letter writer weighed in with the following revelations:

1. The American jury for admission of works of sculpture in Paris was composed of two sculptors, Messrs. Kitson and Bartlett, to whom was added, at their own request, Mr. Harrison, a painter, already one of the jury on paintings.
2. This [sculpture] jury originally admitted works by Messrs. Kitson and Bartlett, and by a pupil of the former also a bust of Mr. Adams. . . . Subsequently, however, on a revision, they consented to allow three or four other [sculptural] works to be placed, not within, but outside the American galleries.

3. The same Mr. Bartlett, of the American Jury of Admission, became a
supplementary member of the international jury. . . . It is hardly to be
wondered at that the only medal of honor to any American sculptor
was awarded to Mr. Bartlett.

As if all these conflicts of interest were not galling enough, Commissioner of Fine Arts Hawkins, the letter writer continued, "refused to admit
anything from the Salon, even the only work of an American sculptor that
had received a recompense [prize] this year. This statue, a 'Diana,' by Mr.
MacMonnies, was, however, finally by the act of Commissioner-General
Franklin, placed in the Exhibition apart from the American galleries, and
maintained for days without indication to what nation it belonged. . . .
Had Commissioner Hawkins promptly admitted this work . . . it would
have enabled Mr. Bartlett, as member of the jury which adjudicated to himself the medal of honor, to feel that he had at least one competitor."

When the artists of all nationalities were not squabbling about whose
work deserved to be displayed or to win honors at the Universal Exposition, many were actually engaged in painting and sketching its astonishing
sights. Paul Signac, an architecture student who became an artist and fol-
lower of the pointillist Seurat, was the first, painting the Eiffel Tower when
it was still half-finished. Henri Rousseau, a self-taught naïve artist and employee of the Paris Customs Office who was known as Le Douanier, painted
a charming self-portrait with the new tower in the background, French flag
flying at its pinnacle. Young Henri Rivière, an artist who worked at the
avant-garde Chat Noir cabaret in Montmartre, helping with its weekly
journal and also putting on shadow puppet shows, spent hours making
sketches around the tower and its environs. Inspired by Japanese prints,
he depicted the workers erecting the tower in all the seasons, as well as the
under-construction and finished edifice from many different vantage
points. A series he titled *Thirty-six Views of the Eiffel Tower* evolved through
sketches, colored woodblocks, and finally colored lithographs into a lovely
homage to Japanese print master Hokusai's *Thirty-six Views of Mount Fuji*.

After the Eiffel Tower, the Exposition subject that most attracted French
artists was the Javanese dancing girls. Camille Pissarro described them
as "very picturesquely costumed . . . yet bizarre in their gilt head-dresses
decorated with black feathers." Gauguin, Rodin, and Toulouse-Lautrec

all made sketches or paintings of them, as did American John Singer
Sargent.

Despite James Gordon Bennett's early insistence that his Paris *Herald* was
never intended to make money, it flourished during the Exposition, turning a tidy profit. Moreover, his cable company was reaping extra income
from all the American journalists reporting back to their papers, not to
mention all the Americans needing to be in touch with home. When Bennett first began running his New York paper from Paris, cable rates had been
reasonable. Imagine, then, his ire when in 1881 his longtime nemesis Jay
Gould seized control of the transatlantic cable and began jacking up rates.

Deliverance arrived in the person of Comstock Lode millionaire John
W. Mackay, who also resented Gould's extortionate charges. A resident of
California, Mackay depended on the cable to maintain uxorial contact
with the flamboyant Mrs. Mackay (late of the Virginia City silver mining
camp), who preferred life in Paris and London. In late 1883, Mackay and
Bennett launched their own cable company. Jay Gould used every means
to derail the new venture before admitting defeat in 1885, complaining,
"There's no beating John Mackay. If he needs another million or two he
goes to his silver mine and digs it up."

The success of the cable enterprise came at a convenient time, because
by 1889 James Gordon Bennett was living a wildly extravagant life. In addition to his two sumptuous apartments on the Champs-Élysées, *The Herald*'s publisher was the proud owner of a bosky country estate out in
Versailles of a Louis XIV provenance, well situated for coaching and hunting parties. On summer evenings there Bennett entertained impecunious
barons and countesses, the ragtag European nobility that he, like so many
rich Americans, found irresistible. The aristocrats, in turn, were more than
happy to dine and drink al fresco at Versailles under ancient oak trees bedecked with glowing lanterns and multiple hanging centigrade thermometers. Like the owls, the thermometers were ubiquitous in the many Bennett
abodes, allowing the Commodore to monitor the temperature and be reminded of his mission to convert the English-speaking world to centigrade.

Anxious *Herald* correspondents summoned from New York to see Bennett in Paris not infrequently found themselves directed to yet another

Bennett domicile, this one in the Riviera village of Beaulieu-sur-Mer between Nice and Monaco. Bennett's favorite home was a magnificent sun-washed villa famous for its elaborate rose gardens. (Few ever saw his Scottish Highland castle, a place he himself rarely set foot in from one year to the next. It served primarily as the all-important source for the Bennett table's grouse and, above all, his beloved tiny plovers' eggs.)

The capricious Commodore, if in the best of spirits, might bestow upon his visiting New York employee a generous raise or elevation to a plum job. As a leader, Bennett was a terrifying figure, mercurial, haughty, ruling his "news empire with an iron hand. Every man who worked for *The Herald*, no matter how important or lowly his job, had to please Bennett, who was as changeable as a chameleon, domineering, hypersensitive and full of whims." It was just as likely that the anxious reporters might arrive to find their capricious boss (and soon themselves) aboard his ocean-going steam yacht, the gleaming white 167-foot *Namouna*, complete with its own Alderney cow aboard.

Reporters and editors had all reason to feel anxious about precipitous firings. One day, when Bennett summoned a particular reporter to Paris, the New York editors balked, wiring back that right then the man was "indispensable." Who else on the staff, Bennett wondered via cable, was indispensable? A dozen names were sent. Back came the order that every one of them be fired. Said Bennett, "I will have no indispensable men in my employ."

Bennett also maintained another three homes in the United States, though he had not lived there for a dozen years: a mansion on Fifth Avenue, his late father's rustic estate up in Washington Heights, and a "cottage" in Newport. Each was fully staffed, ready to serve Bennett should he stride in the front door unannounced—the wine cellars were kept stocked, fires roared in the grates, and sheets were turned down nightly. In truth, Bennett could long since have returned to live and work in Gotham. "A wealthy bachelor and a powerful editor is always forgiven and always welcome," one contemporary noted with vexation; "this is an axiom which Mr. Bennett has learned too well and upon which he often trespasses too far. But just as everyone is blaming him for some social error, he gives $100,000 to the starving poor of Ireland or cables $10,000 to the Actors'

Fund." All in all, like many expatriates, Bennett lived in beautiful Paris out of preference.

On Friday, August 9, about a week after the Shah's visit to the Wild West show, Major Burke once again gathered together forty of the Indians and set off downtown in the large brakes. By 9:00 a.m., they had ridden the elevators to the top of the Eiffel Tower, where they caused a sensation. "With their large dark coats thrown over their shoulders, their big sheepskins dyed in bright colors," reported *Le Figaro de la Tour*, "and their long hair ornamented with feathers and their tattoos, they have a striking and original beauty." The Indians "admired the panorama of Paris and its suburbs with great exclamations of surprise and great gesturings." Most of the 12,237 Eiffel *ascensionnistes* that day visited only as far as the second platform. The Indians were among the 3,527 who pressed on all the way to the top.

When the Wild West group came down to the second platform, the Indians and Major Burke squeezed into *Le Figaro*'s little newsroom while "all around, the many other visitors pressed in to see them, filled with enthusiasm." Because the Indians wanted their names to appear in that day's newspaper but could not write, Major Burke had them line up behind him and helped each one in turn make an X, after which Major Burke wrote the man's name. *Le Figaro de la Tour* duly printed each one: Red Shirt, Agulalla Chief, Feather-Man, Black-Heart, Long Crane, Billy Peno, Ju Bisnett, Kills Enemy No. 2, Little Bear, Yellow Horse, Little Iron, One Side, Left Hand, Dog Ghost, Wooden Face, Black Fox, Big Chief, Kills Enemy Quick, Fast Hawk, Standing Bear, Goes Flying, Two Eagle, Little-Chief, Stands Still, Prairie Chicken, Runs on Edge, No Neck Chief, Charging Crow, Bear Pipe, Medicine Horse, Short Bear, Blue Shield, Black Hawk, Swift Bear, Short Man, Brave Bear, Jule Keen, Billy Langdon. The final name was Raphaël Weill, Major Burke's interpreter.

"Paris is again Paris, the gay, glad city of old," enthused American writer Edyth Kirkwood in her report on the World's Fair. "High and low, rich and poor, are, for once, of one mind. Merriment, joy, feasting succeed in a giddy whirl. . . . No more politics. Who cares for M. Ferry or General Boulanger? Hurrah! For the Eiffel Tower! Which edifice is, indeed, the present

"Meet me under the Eiffel Tower!"

point of interest for the whole world. Even the Chinese, who are not easy to astonish, gaze with awe and admiration at 'the big pagoda.' . . . 'Meet me under the Tour Eiffel!' is the general cry for a rendezvous." Miss Kirkwood and her friend, in their summer hats and light gowns, promenaded on the first platform, with its restaurants and "twelve little shops or counters for the sale of photographs, guides, cigars, etc.," and enjoyed the clear, wide view.

They decided—"I should say rashly"—to ascend to the second platform via the spiral staircase. "Woe are we! Once started there is no returning. That is against the rule. You may find yourself dying from fright, *n'importe*, on you must go, as there are stairs for people to go up, and others for them to come down. After going many times round and round on a shaking little iron spiral two feet or very little wider, and very steep, Agatha says, positively, that she has had enough of it, and really must go back, and be pretty quick about it, too. I agree with rapture. We turn, but are met by a line of ascending men who greet us with assurances that it's not permissible to go down, and insist firmly that we must proceed. They warn us that we may only be sent back from the foot of the stairs and it will save fatigue to go on.

"We yield and so march up, up, up to the weary top, wrathfully thinking unpleasant things about M. Eiffel for not making his little stairs wide enough to allow people to change their minds. In desperation I look up to see how much further it is to the top, and am seized with a dizziness that makes me long to sit down and remain where I am indefinitely. But the multitude behind push us on, and on we have to go.... At last we arrive, very warm and pink, and out of breath, still possessed by the delusion that we are on the main-mast of a ship, and if we don't mind our steps we shall fall into the sea." Having reached the second platform, Miss Kirkwood saw no great advantage to its superior height. "Altogether it is a wonderful thing this tower; but I like it best from below, especially on the gala nights, when it rivals the luminous fountains with the splendour of its red fires."

The artist Henri Rousseau was so taken with the Eiffel Tower that he not only painted it into the backdrop of his self-portrait but wrote a three-act vaudeville show titled *Une Visite à l'Exposition 1889,* about a family of French country bumpkins (speaking thick patois), which included their encounter with the Eiffel Tower and other marvels of the fair. Mariette, one of his characters, exclaimed upon seeing the tower: "Ah, Saint Virgin Mary, how beautiful it is, how beautiful it is, and how big that huge ladder is, bigger than the bell tower of our church." They wondered how they could possibly go to the top where the French flag was flying. A gendarme directed them, but then Rousseau said only in his play directions: "They ascend the tower, and then continue their visit, heading towards the Trocadéro."

During these warm August Sundays, those Parisian families who were not sampling the delights of the Exposition Universelle could be found enjoying the countryside along the Seine out in "Neuilly, the Isle of La Grande Jatte, Bougival, Argenteuil, Charenton or along the Marne. It was there by preference that they would spend their Sundays fishing, picnicking *en famille*, dancing in *guinguettes* among the trees and eating the delicious little fried fish from the river. There were fairs and sideshows in the Parc de Vincennes."

On August 10, the Shah of Persia departed Paris in a final blaze of pomp. Edmond de Goncourt, ever the faithful diarist, recorded a few evenings later how much this Eastern potentate had irritated de Goncourt's old friend Princess Mathilde, the niece of Napoleon I, when he graced her with a call. "Before the Persian shah's visit, the Princess received a message instructing her to prepare: 'A glass of iced water, cakes, and a night commode.' She placed the commode chair in a corner of the library, and Primola [her nephew] chose this place for taking a [surreptitious] snapshot of the Shah; unfortunately, the Shah wanted the commode chair placed like a throne, in the middle of the room, and Primola was thwarted. 'A swine,' exclaimed the Princess, 'a swine!'"

Later that evening de Goncourt and friends went out with the Shah's physician of thirty years, a man named Tholozan, who indiscreetly revealed the Shah's disdain for European nobility. He also regaled his hosts with bloodcurdling accounts of palace life. "He told us," wrote de Goncourt, "that a few years back, [when] the [Persian] minister of Police had committed various abuses of his office, the Shah had the whim to have him whipped in front of him; and when he found the minister screaming too loudly, [the Shah] asked for a lovely, a very lovely cord, and proceeded very calmly to have him strangled."

Thomas Edison poses with Monsieur Salles atop the Eiffel Tower.

CHAPTER NINE

In Which Thomas Edison Hails the Eiffel Tower and Becomes an Italian Count

On Sunday, August 11, at 6:00 a.m. *La Bourgogne* was steaming through the morning sea mists toward Le Havre, bringing to France and the World's Fair a new, modern kind of royalty: the great American inventor Thomas Edison. At the urging of his wife, Mina, Edison and a small entourage had joined the flood tide of Americans come to see the marvels of the Paris Exposition. On the upper deck of the sleek black steamship with smoke plumes trailing from its two dark funnels, the Wizard of Menlo Park stood waving his white handkerchief. Edison had spotted racing toward him a fast tender carrying his electric company's European executives and a small herd of reporters.

Soon enough, the latter were clambering up the steamship's ladder and had gathered in the first-class salon, where Edison announced, "I have come to Europe not for business, but for rest and recreation. Like everyone else I've come to see the Eiffel Tower." His decision to attend the World's Fair was a complete surprise to all those outside his inner circle, for he had given no public inkling of his plans.

The French were rhapsodic, for they revered "Le Grand Edison" and viewed his unexpected first-ever visit to Paris as a wondrous endorsement of their fair and nation. "The famous inventor Edison has come from America to study Paris and the Exposition," reported *Le Journal Illustré*. "He speaks only English, but he may use his time here to learn a bit of our language. . . . With his long redingote, he seems like a clergyman and appears to everyone to be simple and affable." "The French public," noted one American somewhat tongue in cheek, "considers Edison is the sole inventor of the telegraph, telephone, electric light, and even electricity itself, if not the solar system as well." Edison, a stocky man of forty-two whose hair had gone gray, was on the whole plainspoken, folksy, and genial, and so was thoroughly bemused (and pleased) by the enthusiastic welcome on this, his first trip to the Continent.

Alfred O. Tate, having quietly made all of Edison's Paris arrangements, expected to be on that fast boat greeting him. Instead, the Channel ferry had been late, and Tate's train steamed into Le Havre just in time for him to spot his boss "strolling down the long platform of the railroad station with a box of cigars under his arm and behind, hurrying to overtake him, a little uniformed Customs official." Edison was getting an earful in French about the duty due on American cigars when Tate caught up with him and intervened, explaining to the Customs official that this was *"Monsieur A-de-sohn! Comprenenez? Monsieur A-de-sohn!"* Tate shook Edison's hand as the Customs officer regarded the inventor with awe. Explained Tate to his boss, "Tobacco over here is a government monopoly. Shake hands with him and that'll pay the duty."

Ever good-natured, Edison did just that. The Customs officer took the famous hand, made a "deep, reverential bow and then," recalled Tate, "as we proceeded to the train compartment where the rest of our party awaited us, he followed, walking on tiptoe and breathing, 'Ah-a-a, M'sieu A-de-sohn,' until we disappeared."

The unheralded arrival of the world's greatest inventor in Paris was a huge triumph in a summer of triumphs for the city. Tate had arranged for the Edisons to stay in a luxurious suite of rooms at the Hôtel du Rhin on the south side of the Place Vendôme, one of the city's seventeenth-century architectural gems. Stately identical cream-colored mansions with Corinthian columns, mansard roofs, and sidewalk-level arcades enclosed the cobblestoned square, which had at its center a bronze spiral obelisk topped by a statue of Napoleon dressed as a Roman emperor. The Ministry of Justice had long occupied two of the buildings. Three blocks south was the Jardin des Tuileries, immediately north the rue de la Paix, with its crowded shopping streets devoted to such denizens of fashion and luxe as the House of Worth, the great Paris couturier, exclusive milliners, tiny parfumeries, and glittering jewelry shops.

In the Edisons' suite at the Hôtel du Rhin, all was bustle amid the gilded furniture, velvet curtains, and lace hangings, as the bellboy knocked yet again to deliver another basket of rare flowers. Outside in the Place Vendôme, a permanent crowd gathered hoping for a glimpse of the renowned inventor. Elsewhere in Paris, French powerbrokers were frantically organizing banquets and soirées to honor this most famous of Americans. On Monday evening, the day after his arrival, Edison held court for a mob of journalists in his chandeliered salon. The predictable first question: "How do you like Paris?" Edison, attired in his somewhat rumpled dark suit, leaned against the marble mantel with its tall silvered mirror, puffing away on his cigar: "I think Paris is *immense*, at least what I have seen of it. . . . The boys propose to show me some of the sights this evening." That afternoon, he and his entourage had made their first visit to the World's Fair, braving the huge throngs and heat: "It is simply overwhelming, and the Eiffel Tower surpasses anything I had imagined."

But what Edison most enjoyed talking about were his ideas and inventions. "When I was on shipboard coming over I used to sit on deck by the hour and watch the waves. It made me positively savage to think of all that power going to waste. But we'll chain it up one of these days along with Niagara Falls and the winds. That will be the electric millennium." What else had he been up to? "I am and have been at work at an invention which will enable a man in Wall Street not only to telephone a friend near Central Park, say, but to actually see that friend while speaking to him. That would be a practical and useful invention and I see no reason why it may not soon become a reality."

A master of the nascent art of PR and a veteran proselytizer for the wonders of modern technology, Thomas Edison had not, in truth, come across the Atlantic to the Paris World's Fair simply to sightsee and relax. Certainly, he had planned to visit the Eiffel Tower, inspect his company's wildly popular exhibit, study the fair's vast technical offerings, meet eminent Gallic men of science and engineering, and see firsthand some of his own Société Industrielle Edison's hundreds of electric light installations. But always, at every step of the way, he would be advancing the Edison companies.

A shrewd and brilliant promoter, Edison had brought along dozens of phonographs, as well as hundreds of wax cylinders, which he intended to deposit strategically about town, where journalists who had gathered from all over the globe to cover the fair would write about him and his products.

Among Edison's small entourage was Francis Upton, president of the Electric Light Company, who was combining business with romance, for he was honeymooning with his new bride, Margaret. Edison's English partner in the phonograph, Col. George Gouraud, was also on hand, ostensibly to make himself useful. Unfortunately, Edison already knew from his young private secretary, Alfred O. Tate (fresh from several frustrating months in England), that Gouraud, lacking capital and organization, was now a hindrance in their pursuit of rapid commercialization of the phonograph.

For the French republicans, Edison was the embodiment of all they held dear: the hardworking self-made modern citizen. Paris shop windows were filled with framed photos of the inventor, still boyish looking despite his thatch of gray hair. Crowds surrounded him wherever he went. Edison, always good-natured about his enormous fame, did not hesitate to exploit it. Alfred O. Tate had deliberately set himself up around the corner from the Hôtel du Rhin. "This was done to divert from Edison the procession of visitors of various kinds who might wish to see him, all of whom, inquiring at his hotel, were directed to me at the Hôtel Castiglione. And they came in droves, mostly aspiring young inventors seeking advice or endorsement of their inventions. Many carried models in their arms, and usually these were flying machines. Indeed, it seemed to me from the numbers of models left with the concierge, delivered by mail and by express, that half the population of France must have been engaged in attempts to solve this problem."

Aerial navigation fascinated Edison, too, and despite "some hard work" on the subject, he had "met with great discouragement—great discouragement . . . [However,] these fellows fussing around with gas bags are wasting their time. The thing can't be done on those lines. You've got to have a machine heavier than the air and then find something to lift it with. That's the trouble, though, to find the 'something.' I may find it one of these days. Who knows?"

Like Edison's wife, Mina, Tate found the tremendous hullabaloo surrounding Edison's visit a bit overwhelming. "The strenuous work which I had to perform in attending to a heavy mail with the aid of two stenographers, one French and the other English, the reception of visitors, and attendance at the various functions organized in Edison's behalf, left me little time for rest." But when there was time, Parisian nightlife beckoned. Tate's friend Dickie, who had come months earlier to help William Hammer set up Edison's World's Fair exhibit, had become quite a regular in the Latin Quarter. On one of Tate's rare free nights, Dickie invited him to a students' *bal masque*. "When we reached the place," wrote Tate, "the dancing had been in full swing for an hour or more, and as we were standing at the periphery of the whirling circle trying to identify our host amidst a confusion of kaleidoscopic colors, a tall young lady in mask and domino detached herself from her dancing partner and stood for a second in front of us.

"Then there were two swift flashes disclosing a profusion of flounced white lace lingerie and our hats soared aloft in the general direction of the chandeliers. We never saw them again. . . . [And so Tate experienced the infamous can-can.] Well, legs were a treat to us and we glimpsed many of them that evening and enjoyed it hugely."

On Thomas Edison's third day in France, the morning dawned crisp, cool, and clear, ideal weather for the day's signal event: a visit to the Eiffel Tower. By 9:00 a.m., Edison (bearing a gift phonograph), his wife, and her sisters had crossed the Seine, where gaily decorated *bateaux-mouches* ferried visitors to and from the fair, and assembled at the foot of the tower. As they marveled at the sheer enormity of the structure soaring above them, Monsieur Salles, Gustave Eiffel's son-in-law, greeted them. Eiffel himself– unaware of Edison's imminent arrival–had departed several days earlier to take the waters in Évian, near Switzerland. Russell Harrison, who spoke French, had joined Edison's entourage, as had many Edison executives and several journalists. "An elevator was reserved for us," Margaret Upton wrote her mother of their visit, "and soon we were on the biggest landing stage [second platform]. Here Mr. Eiffel's sister, a maiden lady, introduced herself, a typical autocratic French woman of fifty or more years. She was accompanied by an attendant in livery with immense silver buttons with Mr. Eiffel's monogram."

Edison and his party rode the elevator halfway up, changed cars, and then continued to the tower's summit. As they debarked and exclaimed over the panorama of Paris unfolding all around, they were startled to hear loud ululating howls. What strange phenomenon was this so high above

Paris? American Indians! Chief Rocky Bear and several dozen Sioux, big strapping fellows attired in buckskins, their long hair beaded and feathered, were whooping and crying, with Major Burke in attendance and beaming. The Indians, like everyone else in Paris, were thrilled to meet their famous compatriot. Had they not just listened and spoken into his miraculous talking phonograph in an earlier visit to the fair?

The Indians "saluted him in their own way," *Le Figaro* reported: "unleashing all together a gutteral cry while slapping their cheeks with their hands, which means in their language, Long Live Edison! They made the same salute in honor of Mr. Harrison, son of the president of the United States, and for M. Salles, M. Eiffel's son-in-law, to the delight of all people present." "Mr. Edison was not quite prepared for this reception," said *The Herald's* man covering Edison's day. Ever jocular, Edison regained his self-possession enough to ask the Indians what had become of Sitting Bull.

After a tour of this top platform, Monsieur Salles ushered his American guests up the tiny staircase into Eiffel's private apartment and aerie with its comfortable plush sofas and chairs with fringe, paintings and sculptures, and carved wooden sidepieces. There a host of French luminaries—politicians, businessmen, musicians, and editors—waited eagerly to meet Edison. Margaret Upton wrote to her mother, "We were invited, after gazing a long time at the magnificent view, into Mr. Eiffel's private salon up there and served the very daintiest luncheon you ever saw of chicken and truffle sandwiches not an eighth of an inch thick, cakes, and bon-bons, and the finest of wines which Mademoiselle Eiffel herself poured to the guests.

"We listened to some lovely music by three of the finest musicians in Paris—a flutist, violinist, and singer. A phonograph had been carried up there and these musicians performed in front of it—the sound was registered—and then all the guests had the pleasure of hearing it repeated as often as they chose. As there were numerous tubes attached to the instrument several could listen at once. It was a most delightful affair. . . . Everyone pays homage to Edison. The day he arrived the papers all had long articles calling him His Majesty Edison, Edison the Great, Vive l'Edison." After the musicale ended, Monsieur Salle invited the whole party to dine at Café Brébant.

Not surprisingly, Edison was eager to see *Le Figaro's* newsroom in the sky. Monsieur St.-Jacques was more than happy to help the always-hands-on

Edison operate their printing press, which produced a few numbers of a Farsi-French edition of the paper created for the Shah of Persia. The editor presented a souvenir copy to Mina Edison, and then the whole party signed the paper's visitor register, their names appearing not far down from those of Major Burke and the Wild West Indians. The Edison party's visit to the second platform complete, they descended to the savory smells and lunchtime clatter of Brébant. Margaret Upton was pleased to be seated in the place of honor next to Edison. "Toasts of all kinds were given and a most delightful affair it was. At the end each lady was presented with a beautiful rose. I forgot to mention that Mademoiselle Eiffel presented each lady with a gold bronze medal of the tower in a little leather case as a souvenir."

On Friday morning, August 16, just days after Edison's first visit to the Eiffel Tower, Major Burke was up atop the tower again, this time with Annie Oakley, various Wild West managers and staff, and a few Mexican cowboys. Oakley had finally found time between Wild West shows and private matches at French shooting clubs to make her own ascent. True to her reputation for being tight with money, rather than purchasing postcards of the Eiffel Tower to send to all her myriad friends and relations back home, she bought just one, affixed a stamp, and sent it to *American Field*. Wrote the magazine's editors, "Miss Annie Oakley has probably taken the longest sight of any in her life as under date of August 16, top of 'Tour Eiffel, Exposition Universelle, Paris,' she sends greetings to American shooters."

Annie Oakley knew people viewed her as cheap, and very late in life, she wrote, "If I spend one dollar foolishly I see tear-stained faces of little children beaten as I was. . . . I've made a good deal of money in my time but I never believe in wasting a dollar of it . . . it is not right to squander that money in selfish, extravagant living. . . . [I] must try to do good with it. I have never had any children of my own but I have brought up eighteen of them and last fall I started on the nineteenth. I do not adopt them legally but help them out with money as it is needed."

On the same morning that Annie Oakley visited the Eiffel Tower, the well-known English journalist Robert Sherard navigated the ever-present crowd to enter the Hôtel du Rhin, where he asked for Edison's suite. Sherard, twenty-eight, was the great-grandson of the poet Wordsworth and had been making his own way as a writer ever since his father disinherited him a decade earlier, forcing him to leave Oxford. Edison had granted Sherard an interview, writing in a note: "All right, Friday about 11 in morning. I'll be sane by that time. My intellect is now making 275 revolutions a minute." The journalist entered the inventor's front salon, which was headily perfumed by all the flowers, joined now by piles of visiting cards and numerous framed signed photographs of prominent French officials. Sherard found Edison "standing by the mantelpiece listening to an excitable little man who was dressed in the height of fashion and who was waving a box in his hand which looked like a jewel-case. . . . He was most verbose and gesticulative." Edison was smiling sweetly in response.

Colonel Gouraud pulled Sherard aside and explained that the foreigner was Cavaliere Copello, dispatched "on a special mission from the King of Italy." His Highness had been so dazzled by Edison's gift of a phonograph that he was (via the Cavaliere) conferring the title of count upon the American inventor. When Edison, who had been partially deaf since his teens, grasped the cavaliere's message, he gave a hearty laugh.

Sherard was up next, and Edison, who had spent the early part of the morning touring the fair, was feeling loquacious: "The Exhibition is immense. . . . So far, however, I have seen very little of it. Still, this morning I saw a tool which will save me six thousand dollars a year. It is a chisel worked by hydraulic pressure. I just saw it as I was passing by—just a glance. I shall order some and send them out; they will enable us to reduce our labor by eighteen hands."

Edison, a man so absorbed with his work he rarely came home for dinner, had evidently been chafing at what he had observed in the past week of the leisurely French way of life: the long meals, the strolling and ambling flâneurs, the crowded cafés where men and women sipped coffees or enjoyed an ice cream. And so when Sherard inquired just what Edison thought of the fabled city of Paris, Edison could not hold back. "What has struck me so far chiefly is the absolute laziness of the people over here. When do these people work? What do they work at? I have not seen a cartload of goods in the streets since I came to Paris. People here seem to have established an elaborate system of loafing. These engineers who come to see me, fashionably dressed, with walking sticks in their hands, when do they do their work? I can't understand it at all." What made it especially mystifying was that France was the world's fourth most important industrial nation, with America just ahead, in third place. Edison himself had confirmed the industrial stature of France by attending its World's Fair.

About now, Mina Edison (Countess Edison, if she cared to be) emerged into the salon. Daughter of an inventor and manufacturer herself, she was an elegant dark-eyed beauty with high cheekbones, creamy skin, lustrous brown hair piled high, and an hourglass figure. She greeted all those present and invited them to lunch: Copello, Gouraud, Sherard, and a French writer, Émile Durer, who was working on a long article about Edison. Of course, what better spot than the Café Brébant on the Eiffel Tower? And so, off they went in a horse-drawn carriage, joining the multitudes always streaming toward the fair.

From the tower's first floor, the Champ de Mars took on the appearance of a giant picnic grounds, for every day promptly at noon, one of the little Eiffel Tower cannons gave a great BOOM! to announce the commencement of the sacred hour of the midday meal.

"My *déjeuner* with Edison on the first floor of the Eiffel Tower," wrote Sherard, "was one of the most pleasant meals it has ever fallen to my lot to share. I sat next to the great man, and we talked together all the time. 'When we were on board ship,' he said, as we sat down, 'they put rolls and coffee on the table for breakfast. I thought that was a very poor breakfast for a man to do work upon. . . . I would like one American meal for a change—plenty of pie.' He then smashed his *petit pain* with his fist. There were some shrimps among the *hors d'oeuvres*, and he looked at them in a surprised fashion. He had never seen shrimps before. 'Do they grow any larger?' he asked me. I suppose that he imagined they were the young of lobsters . . . he said, 'Well, they give a great deal of trouble for very small results.'

"We talked of many things," Sherard continued. "Over the *soles frites* somebody asked him if it were true that he had been experimenting in photography in colours. He said, 'No, that is not true. That sort of thing is sentimental. I do not go in for sentiment. [Andrew] Carnegie does. Poor Carnegie has turned sentimental. When I last saw him I wanted to talk to him about his ironworks. That is what interests me—immense factories going day and night, with the roar of the furnaces and the crashing of the hammers; acres and acres of activity—man's fight with the metal. But Carnegie wouldn't talk about it. He said, "All that is brutal." He is now interested in, and will only talk about, French art and amateur photography.'"

And what of this very Eiffel Tower? "The work of a bridge builder," sniffed one guest.

"'No. It is a great idea,' said Edison. 'The Tower is a great idea. The glory of Eiffel is in the magnitude of the conception and the nerve in the execution. That admitted, and the money found, the rest is, if you like, mere bridge building. I like the French. They have big conceptions. The English ought to take a leaf out of their books. What Englishman would have had this idea? What Englishman could have conceived the Statue of Liberty?'

"'Will you beat the tower in New York?' asked Sherard.

"'We'll build one of 2,000 feet,' said Edison. 'We'll go Eiffel 100 per cent better, without discount.'"

With gravest ceremony, the sommelier stepped forward, cradling in a white napkin a bottle of Clos Vougeot, one of Burgundy's legendary red wines. Edison watched with amusement as the sommelier reverentially poured a half glass and then waited as the ruby red vintage was tasted and approved. Edison said, "There is a great deal of humbug about wine . . . and about cigars. Men go by cost. The real connoisseurs are few. At home, for fun, I keep a lot of wretched cigars made up on purpose in elegant wrappers, some with hairs in them, some with cottonwool plugged into the middle. I give these to the critical smokers—the connoisseurs, as they call themselves—and I tell them that they cost me 35 cents apiece. You should hear them praise them."

Sherard found that "Brébant's _déjeuner_ was _recherché_ in the extreme; but Edison barely touched anything. 'A pound of food a day,' he told me 'is what I need when I am working, and at present I am not working.' And just then as a fresh course was brought in, Edison took advantage of the café's open door and slipped out.

"A minute or two later," wrote Sherard, "I found a pretext for following. . . . Edison was leaning over the railing, gazing down at the people hundreds of feet below. He told me that he was calculating the vibration or swaying of the tower. . . . 'Say Sherard,' said Edison, 'don't let them know in New York about that tomfoolery about the count and countess. They would never stop laughing at me.'" It was too late. Sherard confessed he had already cabled the story from the hotel before coming to lunch. Edison laughed, envisioning the newspapers "getting pictures out of me represented as an Italian organ-grinder with a crown on my head, and perhaps Gouraud as the monkey." Now it was time to return to the restaurant for iced champagne and heartfelt toasts. Only when the coffee and cigars appeared did Edison perk up. "'Mr. Edison is beginning to breakfast now,' said Colonel Gouraud.

"'Yes,' said Edison, taking an Havannah, 'my breakfast begins with this.' Then, speaking of his habit of smoking, he added, 'I don't find smoking harms me in the least. I smoke twenty cigars a day, and the more I work the more I smoke.'

"His wife remarked, 'Mr. Edison has an iron constitution, and does everything that is contrary to the laws of health; yet he is never ill.'"

From the day the fair had opened, Whistler's friends had been pressing him to come over to Paris with his new wife, Trixie. Back in May, John Singer Sargent had written, "They are all clamoring for you in Paris. Shan't we see you there soon?" In late June, poet Stéphane Mallarmé wrote posing the same question, and Whistler reassured him, "I would very much like to be with you all in Paris—besides you will see us soon!" Yet mid-August found the Whistlers still ensconced in London.

"The Master," as Whistler liked to style himself, had agreed to let a London-based *Herald* reporter named Sheridan Ford assemble the clippings and correspondence regarding Whistler's many artistic tiffs, feuds, and bons mots into an amusing little book, which was now at the printer's and ready to be published. But on August 18, the ever-fickle Whistler, annoyed at Ford's pressing for the final go-ahead, changed his mind. In a letter to Ford, he said, "I fear that I have an inherent objection to being at all hurried about any thing, [but] do let me recognize slightly the time & care you have taken to give the collection the shape it already has—I enclose therefore a cheque for ten guineas." He thus dismissed as mere bagatelles Ford's coming up with the clever book idea and title, *The Gentle Art of Making Enemies*, as well as the writer's many hours of work. Apparently Trixie had sensed a lucrative enterprise in the project and had urged Whistler to cut Ford loose and reap all the profits himself.

In Paris, Lady Campbell, the subject of Whistler's prize-winning Exhibition oil portrait, was among the many people hoping the Whistlers would arrive soon. Lady Campbell had had her differences with the painter while sitting for him, but her easygoing nature had prevailed. On August 18, she wrote to Trixie: "But Paris is so lovely. The weather so perfect, with a brilliant sun & a fresh breeze, that I should feel positively selfish if I did not do my best to persuade you & the Master to give up this tarrying by the grey & foggy banks of the Thames, & come over here to all this dainty brightness. . . . [T]he trees are one mass of refreshing shade, the Eiffel Tower is a thing of beauty & grace—surely you will not resist such a list of attractions, but will pack up your traps at once." But even with so gracious an invitation, the Whistlers declined to appear.

Thomas Edison had certainly displaced Buffalo Bill as the most talked about American in Paris. If the World's Fair had become a showcase for the triumph of technology, a new modern way of life, and republican democracy, Edison was happy to do his part to burnish that image, presenting himself and his latest products as embodiments of all those virtues. The American press obliged by exulting over Edison's Parisian triumphs, boasting that no Old World eminence at the fair had received "a more enthusiastic welcome than this master mechanic. Even royalty has joined in this democratic greeting to an untitled and unostentatious man of genius. The English Queen has honored him by sending a message of congratulations breathed from her own lips into one of his phonographs."

Colonel Cody's Wild West show continued its successful run, having become such a beloved fixture that the clowns at the Cirque d'Été had worked up a parody called *Kachalo-Ball*. The real Wild West Indians instantly gave it cachet by attending the show in groups each night, cheering wildly as the French clowns satirized their riding and their wars and attacks. When the clowns took to dancing their version of Sioux war dances, the visiting Native Americans laughed so hard they had tears running down their faces.

After three months of rapturously received performances, Buffalo Bill's fame had risen to unprecedented heights in Europe. The wife of a London embassy attaché discovered just how famous one evening when "seated at a banquet next to the Belgian Consul. Early in the course of the conversation he asked:

"'Madame, you haf undoubted been to see ze gr-rand Bouf-falo Beel?'

"Puzzled by the apparently unfamiliar name, I asked: 'Pardon me, but whom did you say?'

"'Vy, Bouf-falo Beel, ze famous Bouf-falo Beel, zat gr-reat countryman of yours. You must know him.'

"After a moment's thought, I recognized the well-known showman's name in its disguise. I comprehended that the good Belgian thought him to be one of America's most eminent names, to be mentioned in the same breath with Washington and Lincoln."

Perhaps the Belgian consul had attended too closely to the booklet for sale at the Wild West show, which certainly did imply that Colonel Cody had almost single-handedly conquered the West, thus becoming a major historical personage.

The New York Sun reported that "Edison has had a reception in Paris such as no American or foreigner has ever received" when at the Élysée Palace President Sadi Carnot welcomed the inventor with full pomp. Edison had not attended the 1878 Paris World's Fair, but his exhibit that year featuring the original primitive phonograph had garnered him induction as a chevalier in France's Legion of Honor, which entitled him to wear a red ribbon on his lapel. Now, in a formal ceremony, President Carnot elevated Edison to an officer in the Legion, which meant that, like Eiffel, he could wear the coveted red rosette in his buttonhole.

Prime Minister Tirard and the City of Paris, the Academy of Sciences, and the Paris Telephone Company each organized on the spur of the moment elaborate formal banquets to honor this American inventor. Edison was more than happy to oblige, for he viewed these eight-course gastronomic evenings as perfect opportunities to promote the new Edison phonograph before influential audiences. And so each banquet invariably featured a demonstration of the miracle of the improved phonograph.

"Dinners, dinners, dinners," Edison would say later, "but in spite of them all they did not get me to speak." Instead, Minister Reid, who spoke decent French, often undertook that honor. "Like every American abroad

who finds himself in an embarrassing situation," said Reid at one such banquet, "Mr. Edison calls upon his Minister to get him out of it. Well, I have
come to his relief, and I find that all he wants is that I should speak for
him. Now, Mr. Edison can speak for himself if he chooses—indeed, so fond
is he of the sound of his own voice that he has spent months upon months
devising a mechanical method of making it immortal. Besides, the man
who has turned electricity into a domestic servant, carried the human
voice hundreds of miles, and so vitalized it that it can be heard for hundreds of years, has no need of either speaking for himself or having others
speak for him. His works speak for him." Reid reminded the French that
America's first minister to France, Benjamin Franklin, had been another
giant in the field of electricity.

While U.S. minister Reid's "duties" with respect to Edison were enjoyable and easily discharged, other official matters continued to prove
more frustrating. He had still failed to obtain satisfaction in the matter of
the young American women briefly arrested and jailed in early May over
the disputed dressmaker's bill. Early in August he had sent a coded telegram to Secretary of State James G. Blaine explaining that the offending
"police agents at Mentone cannot be dismissed because not Government
officers, only municipal agents. . . . Minister of Justice, while ready to
rebuke, flatly refuses to dismiss for an offense which he says was not
wanton but only a mistake and for which he apologized at once the next
day." Moreover, the French had dredged up some comparable incident in
Philadelphia concerning a French citizen in which they had received no
satisfaction.

And then there was the matter of the Sioux Indian treaty. U.S. minister
Reid had failed thus far to persuade the Wild West's Sioux to sign the federal agreement selling almost half their lands. Having gotten nowhere on
his visits out to the Wild West camp, the minister had deputized Cody,
Salsbury, and Major Burke to exert their influence, but on August 15,
Burke wrote Reid, "I have repeatedly read the bill regarding the opening
up of the Dakota Sioux Reservation lands and explained carefully its various features. . . . [The Sioux] declined to sign it saying they were willing to
abide by what ever decision the Indians at home made. . . . As they said,
'We have to go home again and years from now we don't want them to say

we did what our people would be sorry for.'" Major Burke returned the unsigned treaty documents to the Legation.

The next day, at Minister Reid's behest, Major Burke brought the Indians into Paris to see Reid. Once again, Reid addressed the Indians, as he reported to the secretary of state: "I stated what was expected of them, explaining that the Government desired nothing contrary to their interest or inconsistent with their welfare. They withdrew without expressing any opinion and finally declared that they would take no action in the matter. They said they did not entertain any doubt that the intentions of the Government were just and fair, but that being only a few over here and without any means of communicating with their tribe, they preferred not to act independently on a subject which the great majority of their tribe at home understood better." Admitting defeat, Reid entrusted the unsigned papers to the diplomatic pouch and sent them back to Washington.

Alfred Tate had heard the first *"Vive A-de-sohn!"* from the French Customs official back in Le Havre. Now Tate observed in wonder as this cry became the background chorus to Edison's visits whenever he ventured out in public. All those framed photos in shop windows and the reams of newspaper and magazine stories had made Edison's a familiar face, and as his carriage rolled by, Parisians saluted his genius. "It came from a multitude of throats; from groups of sightseers on their way to feast their eyes on the glittering baubles in the jewelers' windows of the Rue de la Paix . . . from the drivers and occupants of the swift little one-horse carriages that endangered the lives of all pedestrians; from the pretty mouths of petite midinettes hurrying with their bandboxes to some rendezvous with Fashion, from strollers along the tree-lined boulevards and loungers at the tables of the wayside cafés. . . . [From all] came this ringing salutation, *'Vive A-de-sohn!'*"

One night early in their visit, the Edison party arrived at the gilded Paris Grand Opera House during the first act. Commissioned by Napoleon III, this magnificent neo-Baroque confection bedecked with sculptures was one of the first places in France to be lighted by Edison incandescent lamps. "The managers took great pleasure," said Edison, "in showing me through the labyrinth containing the wiring, dynamos, etc." After their electrical tour, the Edison party slipped into the French president's private loge, festooned with garlands of roses and decorated with French and American flags and potted ferns and palms. As soon as the curtain came down, wrote Margaret Upton, "the grand orchestra played The Star-Spangled Banner and everyone in the house rose, and turned around to face our box." The bejeweled crowd began to applaud and yell out, "*Vive l'Edison! Vive l'Edison!*" "Edison rose first and bowed in acknowledgement," wrote Margaret, "then we all rose and bowed—then every body turned their glasses on us and stared to their heart's content. After that the opera went on. The manager came to the box and offered Edison the use of his own box at any time."

About an hour later, Edison said, again "the manager came around and asked me to go underneath the stage, as they were putting on a ballet of 300 girls, the finest ballet in Europe. It seems there is a little hole on the stage with a hood over it, in which the prompter sits when opera is given. In this instance it was not occupied, and I was given the position in the prompter's seat, and saw the whole ballet at great range." Prince Roland Bonaparte had personally invited Edison and Francis Upton to his mansion at 22 cours la Reine later that night for a soirée for the Congress of Criminal Anthropology, which Margaret Upton reported was a "gorgeous affair" for men only.

The French admired Edison's lovely and fashionable wife, Mina, but she was already deeply homesick for their fifteen-month-old daughter, Madeleine, who was staying with Mina's mother and had just learned to walk and talk. "It must be cute to see baby running about," Mina wrote her; "I suppose she will be quite changed when I get home. . . . Has she been getting any more teeth and does she say any more words? I am getting hungry to see her." While Edison was used to his fame and turned it to his own purposes, his young wife found it stifling. "It is terrible to try to do anything here," she wrote, "everything is so crowded and everybody is on the make. It seems impossible to go anywhere with Mr. Edison. We never get out as somebody is after him all the time. Although we have been to a great many entertainments."

Even Edison, as he admitted to Robert Sherard, was astounded by the sheer number of people wanting a piece of his time or money. He was also dismayed at "the enormous number of cranks and crooks that there are here. You would be surprised to read some of the letters which I receive by the hundreds. I have given up looking at them at all. Some of these letters contained the strangest offers that you could imagine. Many were from inventors, who begged me to come to their places to give the last touches to some lunatical invention of theirs. There was one man who wrote several times. He had invented an electrical toothbrush or some such nonsense. But the bulk of them wanted assistance in another way. I have had hundreds of applications for loans. . . . It would have required an enormous fortune."

Mina Edison's discomfort in Paris was not eased by the presence of her two sisters, for they had been feuding with Edison's sixteen-year-old daughter, Marion, known as Dot. After her mother's death, Dot had become Edison's frequent companion and she was not pleased to find this role usurped by her young stepmother. Allowed to sail to Europe earlier in the summer with Mina's sisters, Dot had turned sulky and troublesome before the ocean liner even reached the Continent. And once on the Grand Tour, she did not get any easier. "She doesn't give a snap for really seeing things," complained Mina's sister Mary Miller. "I think you ought to know how she is spending her money [in Paris]. When she came she was to get one dress for the summer. . . . Well, she got a dress but such a dress. It is heliotrope with deep hand embroidery around the bottom. . . . It is very pretty."

But Dot had decided the garment didn't suit and thus ordered another with large white stripes that she then ruled "hideous." Miss Edison had then ordered yet a *third* gown from the dressmaker that she then also rejected. "Then her hats—three great immense hats," all of which she also did not like, or so she said to Mary Miller, whom she also declared she did not like. Mary had gone to a spa to recover, while Dot stayed in Paris with a chaperone and refused to study French.

Edison, when not attending banquets or promoting the phonograph and other business matters, acquiesced to some sightseeing with his wife and their friends. They toured the French painting galleries at the Exposition, and later took in the many treasures at the Louvre. Not surprisingly, Edison had opinions on them all. The French paintings displayed at the World's Fair? "Oh, yes," he told Sherard, "they are grand art. I like modern pictures as much as I dislike the antique stuff. I think nothing of the pictures in the Louvre. I have no use for old things; they are wretched old things. Now the pictures at the Exhibition are all as new and modern as they can be; they are good." As for his fellow American millionaires snapping up old European paintings, Edison was dismissive: "To my mind the Old Masters are not art, their value is in their scarcity and in the vanity of men with lots of money."

Edison made numerous sorties to sample the fair's smorgasbord of human achievement. At "the exhibit of the Kimberley diamond mines," he said, "they kindly permitted me to take diamonds from some of the blue earth which they were washing by machinery to exhibit the mine operations. I found several beautiful diamonds, but they seemed a little light to me when I was picking them out. They were diamonds for exhibition purposes—probably glass." When strolling through an art gallery, Edison and Mina spotted A. A. Anderson's *The Morning After the Ball,* an oil in pale blues and pinks of a young woman in a negligée sitting up in a frilly bed reading a newspaper account of her debut. It had won a prize in the Salon, and sold endless copies as a popular lithograph. The Edisons arranged to buy it and would hang it in a place of pride at their Llewellyn Park mansion, Glenmont. Edison was especially fond of sculpture and he wandered contentedly through those galleries. It was in the Italian section of the fair's fine arts department that he spotted another piece of art he simply had to possess: a two-foot-tall white marble sculpture of a lithe nude winged sprite holding aloft a working lightbulb. Edison paid $1,700 for *The Genius of Electricity,* sculpted by A. Bordiga. It would sit atop the desk in his West Orange laboratory study for years, a happy souvenir.

A. A. Anderson, painter of *After the Ball,* was one of the Paris expatriates, a formidable businessman who had changed careers to become an artist. He had spent a decade in Paris painting, and had made a success of that as well. Concerned about the naïve young Americans coming to France to study art, Anderson had organized and underwritten the American Art Association of Paris, establishing it in a spacious leased mansion surrounded by a large walled flower garden on the boulevard Montparnasse. He wrote, "We had a good library, a reception room, a dining room where a student could get a meal for one franc, and a garden where we could recreate and could sketch and paint. There were frequent social occasions, receptions, lectures, and dances."

Interior of the Galerie des Machines

Anderson proposed to Edison that while the inventor was in Paris Anderson paint his portrait. "To avoid the crowd and find quiet, he visited my studio frequently," wrote Anderson. "I have never had a more interesting sitter. Like most great men, he was exceedingly modest, as ingenuous as a boy, and revealed a decided fund of humor. I painted him listening to his first perfected phonograph." Anderson joined Edison's entourage at times, serving as an interpreter. "One day he remarked to me, with a twinkle in his eye, 'Anderson, I am never so happy as when I sit down to a ten-course dinner between two Frenchmen who cannot speak a word of English.'"

For Edison, Eiffel's Tower remained the highlight of Paris and the fair. "I must say that the Eiffel Tower is grand," he said, "and after that, what impresses me most is the machinery hall." But Edison felt solidarity with all the other footsore fairgoers, complaining that the gigantic Galerie des

Machines with its sixteen thousand machines was "a sadly tiring place . . . altogether too big, miles and miles too much of it. I have a headache when I even think of it. I can't say I have seen a quarter of what there is to be seen in it and I don't suppose I ever shall. So far as I have noticed I have not been struck by any novelty on a large scale. There are plenty of improvements in small things." Edison was equally dispirited by the official American exhibit, observing, "It represents nothing. It represents American industry just as much as that cab-horse outside represents the animal kingdom. It is a one-horse concern altogether. . . . That's exactly how I feel about it, and so, I must say, does every American I meet in Paris."

As for the French inventors, Edison was likewise unimpressed: "Oh, they don't have inventors, in our American sense of the word, in Paris at all. They haven't any professional inventors here, as we have on the other side; that is to say, men who will go into a factory, sit down and solve any problem that may be put before them. That is a profession which they seem to know nothing about over here. In America we have hundreds of such men." Of course, Gustave Eiffel and other masters of French industrialism might have begged to differ.

In the waning days of summer, James Gordon Bennett made his semiannual trip to New York City. Bennett sensibly kept his homecomings to Gotham as secret as possible, and not just so he could surprise his unwary staff. His stealth served a very specific purpose. "The fact is this," New York's sheriff Grant had explained to a rival paper, "Bennett [as publisher of *The New York Herald*] is the defendant in a large number of civil suits ranging from $1,000 to $25,000. Some of the suits were instituted several years ago. He deems the suits unjust and won't pay. We have been trying to serve him with the summonses ever since, but it seems impossible to catch him. . . . The law says if a man remains away from a place more than six months he thereby loses his legal residence, and then if a suit for money is pending against him . . . an attachment can be taken out" on his property. Bennett had no intention of letting any enemy of his get hold of his Fifth Avenue mansion or his Washington Heights estate. And so each winter and summer he would sail stealthily to Manhattan—either on his own yacht, *Namouna*, or on a steamship using an alias for the passenger list.

Always deeply suspicious, Bennett delighted in appearing in his New York newsroom with "what one of his editorial writers called a 'terrifying suddenness,' [whereupon] shock waves of hirings, firings, promotions and demotions, accusations and recriminations would hit the place like a man-made earthquake." Naturally, the newspaper staff dreaded these unannounced visits by their fearsome boss, and sometimes, if their luck held, *The Herald*'s maritime reporter garnered advance word that Bennett's yacht had been sighted arriving in New York Harbor. The city desk went into high alert, and after "the usual panicky reaction, reporters were rounded up from Park Row saloons, bullied into sobriety, ordered to shave and put on clean collars. All through the building, in fact, the Commodore's satraps were frantically tidying up for his inspection." After making his appearance at *The Herald*, Bennett then eluded the sheriff (once again) and sailed quietly home to France. As the patient sheriff said, "This last trip he got ahead of us, but he will be back again in six months time, and then we will have more fun with each other."

Bennett returned to Paris in sufficient time to observe the continued lionizing of Thomas Edison at numerous lunches and dinners. As a matter of principle, he himself avoided such functions, not wishing to be influenced by friendships with the powerful or buttonholed by editorial favor seekers.

On the wet Monday night of August 26, *Le Figaro* hosted the most glittering of the many soirées to honor Edison. Alfred Tate accompanied his boss to "this most spectacular tribute," and the two stepped in from the rain at half past ten to find the *Figaro* office-mansion ablaze with electric lights and bedecked with the Stars and Stripes. Edison and Tate passed through the paper's little greenhouse fernery, charming with perfumed flowers and colored fountains, and then entered the *salle*, where they were greeted by editor Francis Magnard, the nation's leading political writer, and his staff. Minister Whitelaw Reid arrived moments later, whereupon he and Edison were seated in two velvet armchairs by the stage. A large portrait of Edison inscribed SA MAJESTÉ EDISON faced the arms of the United States. Other luminaries were not far behind.

First came the Bey of Tunis, His Highness Tieb, with his suite, all in picturesque costumes. "Then, blazing in diamonds and gold lace, two popular idols came swaggering in," Tate wrote, "the famous toreadors Garcia and Valentin, followed by the no less idolized figure of Buffalo Bill, also glittering in his well-known costume of white and gold, topped by his ten-gallon hat, which he removed with a sweep that comprehended the whole audience." In Cody's wake came the composer Jules Massenet and Prince Roland Bonaparte, who in turn "were trailed by a procession of Foreign Ministers, French generals, and various exponents of Art and Literature, marching to the weird strains of an overture by a company of Roumanian musicians."

Once the guests were seated, the renowned actor Jean Mounet-Sully declaimed, followed by sopranos singing light chansons. *Le Figaro* had engaged no less a giant of the French theater than the beloved star of the Comédie Française, Coquelin the Younger, who "mounted the stage and in the role of a penniless inventor delivered a monologue that evoked uproarious laughter. He produced an instrument which he called the 'Perfected Telephone' and which would translate French into English or vice versa. With his lips to the mouthpiece he said: *'Edison est un roi de la république intellectuelle. L'humanité lui est reconnaissante.'* And then turning the instrument around there appeared on its reverse side the translation of this tribute into English in large printed letters: EDISON IS A KING OF THE REPUBLIC OF THE MIND. MANKIND IS GRATEFUL TO HIM.

"'And you can't invent an instrument that will do that, Mr. Edison, can you, my illustrious confrere?' asked this inimitable comedian, as with an assumed air of superiority and triumph he vanished through the wings of the stage."

The comedian was followed by more singers and dancers, including the Exposition's exotic Javanese troupe. As ever, Edison saw to it that the phonograph was center stage. Reported *The Herald*'s man: "It reproduced speeches made by the *Figaro* staff to Mr. Edison and Mr. Edison's reply. The phonograph also reproduced the 'Telephone March' that was played recently at a banquet." The evening continued merrily on until 2:00 a.m.; "everybody was sipping champagne and nibbling away at *pâtés* or sandwiches." Many guests did not leave until dawn.

Later that same morning, the Edison party reassembled to journey out for a very different homage American-style: a late-morning "grub steak" breakfast at Buffalo Bill's Neuilly camp, capped by the three o'clock performance of the Wild West show. Days of heavy rain had given way that Tuesday morning to a sparkling blue sky. Edison and his entourage, Minister and Mrs. Reid, a clutch of American millionaires and theatrical personalities, many distinguished French guests, the usual favored journalists, and all the Wild West higher-ups walked through puddles past the teepees and tents to a luxurious sprawling dining tent decorated with French and American flags, flowers, and potted palms. Cody, flanked by Reid and Edison, presided at the head of the flower-strewn table. The Cowboy Band played airy tunes to aid digestion. The eighteen-course meal was strictly American, and included (to Edison's utter delight) two kinds of much-missed pie. The menu:

Clam Chowder

Soles

Quail on toast

Sweetbreads

Pork and Boston baked beans

Grub steak with mushrooms

Chicken, Maryland style

Green corn

Hominy

Baked potatoes

Blanc Mange

Jelly

Pumpkin pie

Apple pie

Watermelon

Pears, peaches, grapes

Nuts

Pop-corn—Peanuts

Coffee

Corn bread—Biscuits

This daunting feast was followed by the inevitable few words from Minister Reid, followed by Nate Salsbury, a famous wit who no doubt revealed how he and Cody had *not* been formally introduced to the Shah of Persia

Buffalo Bill *(fourth from left in suit, holding cane)* poses with the Deadwood Stage and various Wild West performers. Major Burke is behind Cody, on the front coach step.

just a few weeks earlier, and who "kept the company in roars of laughter until it was time to adjourn to the performance."

That afternoon, as Buffalo Bill and the painted Indians galloped forth and the show opened, the crowd spied Edison, and as at the Paris Opéra, they leapt to their feet roaring *"Vive Edison! Vive Edison!"* As was now the custom, when the battered Deadwood Stage lumbered into the arena, the show's guests of honor were invited to climb in for the fun. Edison declined, instead urging William Hammer to join Chauncey Depew and actress Ada Rehan inside. Young Alfred Tate chose, he recounted, "with special permission, a seat on the roof at the rear of the coach beside the hardy plainsman clad in buckskins and armed with a rifle, who formed the rearguard of the perilous expedition. I never had enjoyed the horrors of an Indian raid outside the pages of certain proscribed yellow-backed literature and did not want to miss anything.

"As we rounded the extreme end of the enclosure we were greeted with a series of savage yells and then a swarm of mounted Indians began to pursue us to the accompaniment of blasting volleys of rifle fire. As these raiders came closer and began to shoot from all sides, I began to speculate uncomfortably on the possibility of one of those savages having inadvertently, or otherwise, slipped a ball cartridge in his rifle, when I was restored to reality by the buckskinned scout at my side holding his fire long enough to lean over and shout at me above the din of battle, 'You'd better pull yer legs up. Ye might git them pants o' yours dirtied!'" And then! On cue, here came Buffalo Bill and his men to the rescue. The audience cheered lustily as the two most famous Americans in Paris, both notable for their easygoing modesty and humor, occupied the same arena. Reported *The Herald*'s man, "At the end of the performance, the whole house rose and gave one loud shout of '*Vive Edison.*' Crowds waited long round Buffalo Bill's tent to catch a glimpse of the celebrated inventor."

After the show, the Edisons toured the camp, followed by a large crowd of enthralled French. When they came to her tent, Annie Oakley inquired if Edison might invent an electric gun, one that would dispense with gunpowder? "I have not come to that yet," he replied, "but it may come." Then Oakley produced her autograph album. While in London, she had collected the signatures of every member of the Chinese and Japanese embassies, as well as that of the Duchess of Cumberland. Mark Twain had signed on one page, "You can do everything that can be done in the shooting line and then some." And the ever-gallant Cody had written, "To the loveliest and truest little woman, both in heart and aim in all the world." Edison added his signature, not far from that of Salifou, king of Senegal.

While Thomas Edison and Buffalo Bill were savoring triumphs, Paul Gauguin was lamenting his failure to make *any* impression at all during the fair. Despite the thousands of visitors who supped at Volpini's Café des Beaux-Arts these many summer months, not a single painting of Gauguin's had been sold. "Nothing either in the daily papers or in the so-called art periodicals. Isn't that fine?" bemoaned Gauguin. In September he returned again to Pont-Aven from Le Pouldu, for he could live now more cheaply there while he tried to secure a colonial job in the tropics.

On September 1, Gauguin wrote two letters. The first was to Theo van

Gogh, revealing his impoverished state and wondering, "Is Manet [brother of the dead artist] in Paris at this moment? I want to write him to ask him if he could speak to [Minister of Culture] Antonin Proust about a government job for me in Tonkin? These are jobs one can get through patronage." The second letter was to his old friend Schuff to complain that all their efforts and excitement in mounting their show at Volpini's café at the World's Fair had come to naught. "And this exposition! Look at it. Guillaumin wrote me that no one has paid any attention. . . . No real news from here. I do no real work. The struggle in Pont-Aven is finished; everyone is gone." Later, he confessed, "I have been in a horrible state of depression," idling away his days in Brittany shooting arrows in the sand like the Wild West show Indians.

At the St.-Rémy asylum, Vincent van Gogh had endured a wrenching summer, suffering more of his attacks. By August he was painting feverishly again, and in early September he wrote Theo: "I am working like one actually possessed. . . . And I think that this will help cure me. . . . [M]y distressing illness makes me work with a dumb fury—very slowly—but from morning til night without slackening—and—the secret is probably this—work long and slowly. How can I tell, but I think I have one or two canvases going that are not so bad, first the reaper in the yellow wheat and the portrait against a light background. . . . I will go on working very hard and then we shall see if the attack returns about Christmas, and that over, I can see nothing to stop my telling the management here to go to blazes, and returning to the North for a longer or shorter time. . . . It is six weeks since I put a foot outside, even in the garden; next week, however, when I have finished the canvases I'm on, I'm going to try."

Theo, who was deeply impressed with his brother's recent work, sought to cheer him by praising the two paintings—*The Irises* and *Starry Night*—that Theo had submitted to the open-to-all Paris exhibition of Artistes Indépendants. Theo wasn't happy with the way the first painting had been hung, but *Starry Night* "makes an extremely good showing." Far more exciting, the avant-garde Vingtistes had invited Vincent to show at their annual Brussels exhibit, which was quite an honor. And artist and writer Joseph Isäacson had singled Vincent out for highest praise in an article: "Who is it who interprets for us, through form and color, that greatness of life, that power of life, of which the 19th century is increasingly aware? I know of one, a solitary pioneer; he struggles alone in the deep night, and his name, Vincent, is destined to go down in the succeeding generations. There will be more to say in time about this remarkable hero—a Dutchman."

Among Edison's excursions outside Paris was one to the southwest suburb of Meudon, to spend a day with Pierre-Jules-César Janssen, a venerable physicist and astronomer renowned for his devotion to documenting solar eclipses. In 1870 Janssen had made a daring balloon escape from Paris, besieged by the Prussians, so he could travel to Oran, Algeria, in time for an important eclipse. (Nature being indifferent to human ambition, it was, of course, too cloudy in Oran to view the event.) In 1876 the government had given Janssen an old palace in Meudon, where he ran the National Observatory. As Edison related, "He occupied three rooms, and there were 300. He had the grand dining-room for his laboratory. He showed me a gyroscope he had got up which made the incredible number of 4000 revolutions in a second. A modification of this was afterward used on the French Atlantic lines for making an artificial horizon to take observations for position at sea." Janssen had advanced his studies of the sun and endeared himself to Gustave Eiffel by using the Eiffel Tower "with its powerful electric lamp . . . to prove that the oxygen rays of the solar spectrum are purely terrestrial."

Another day, Sir John Pender, whom Edison described as "the master of the cable system of the world at that time" came round to the Hôtel du Rhin to meet the great inventor. This was the same Pender who only four years earlier had threatened legal action against Edison over telegraph patents. But all that was in the past, and the two men sallied forth to enjoy some fresh air. "I think [Pender] must have lived among a lot of people who were very solemn," said Edison, "because I went out riding with him in the Bois de Boulogne and started in to tell him American stories. Although he was a Scotsman he laughed immoderately. He had the faculty of understanding and quickly seeing the point of the stories; and for three days after I could not get rid of him. Finally I made him a promise that I would go to his country house at Foot's Cray, near London."

After his visits to the Eiffel Tower, Edison most enjoyed the time he spent with Louis Pasteur, another genius with a bent for the practical. Edison had invented revolutionary technologies and devised entire new corporate models to capitalize them. Pasteur, sixty-seven, was a brilliant chemist and researcher who had used his revolutionary germ theory to create pasteurization, save the French silkworm industry, and develop vaccines for anthrax and chicken cholera. And now he had also created a new kind of medical enterprise: a private institute with applied scientific medical research, a clinic to treat rabies, and a school to train young scientists and doctors in laboratory work. Pasteur had personally led the fund-raising, and the previous November the Pasteur Institute had opened in two handsome Louis XIII–style brick-and-stone buildings in the Paris suburb of Vaugirard.

Though Pasteur had many great accomplishments, it was rabies that had catapulted him to worldwide fame. In the mid-1880s he had already successfully treated forty rabid dogs, but he felt far from ready to apply his experimental results to humans. Then, on July 6, 1886, a mother had appeared at his small Paris laboratory pleading for help for her young son, who had been savagely attacked two days earlier by a rabid dog. Pasteur reluctantly agreed, and the boy—otherwise doomed—recovered and lived. A few months later, a young shepherd bitten by a mad dog sought the same treatment and also survived in fine health. This second cure set off a storm of acclaim for Pasteur, who found his laboratory overwhelmed with rabies victims from near and far. As the cures mounted, the newspaper coverage of these miraculous medical feats turned Pasteur into a hero and legend. He then parlayed his unsought fame into the new institute, where he could finally pursue science under ideal conditions, train new researchers, and provide proper facilities for the steady stream of desperate rabies victims.

As Edison later told a colleague, "Pasteur invited me to come down to the institute, and I went and had quite a chat with him. I saw a large number of persons being inoculated, and also the whole modus operandi, which was very interesting. I saw one beautiful boy about ten, the son of an English lord. His father was with him. He had been bitten in the face, and was taking the treatment. I said to Pasteur, 'Will he live?' 'No,' he said, 'the boy will be dead in six days. He was bitten too near the top of the spinal column, and came too late!'" The Paris *Herald* reported that during that month of August, 145 people came to the Pasteur Institute to be treated for rabies, 136 being bitten by dogs, eight by mad cats, and one by a rabid donkey. The little English boy was mentioned as the only death recorded that month.

Pasteur himself was not in good health, having suffered numerous small strokes that left him with a limp and diminished speaking ability. While the two great men, Pasteur and Edison, had much in common, when it came to commercial gain, they parted ways. Edison viewed profits and large sums of money as absolutely essential to underwrite his "invention factory," while Pasteur believed that such pecuniary pursuits "would complicate his life and risk paralyzing his inventive faculties." But Pasteur certainly appreciated the importance of private funding in establishing an institute that would carry on his work.

Thomas Edison's only real complaint during this delightful roundelay of honors, sightseeing, and hobnobbing with fascinating personages was the surfeit of rich food. Sherard, the British journalist, had taken to dropping in at the Hôtel du Rhin from time to time to chat, and one morning he found Edison looking quite pale. Edison explained, "At first it was my head that worried me in Paris. I was quite dazed; but now the worry is lower down—the effect of all these dinners. Another banquet, or whatever you call it, last night upset me dreadfully. And," he added with a groan, "I have a whole lot more banquets to attend before I leave for Berlin."

It was just such an event in his final week in Paris that enabled Thomas Edison to finally meet Gustave Eiffel, creator of the tower he so admired. On September 7, Prime Minister Tirard held another banquet to honor Edison and he had invited Eiffel, who had finally returned from the spa in Évian. Edison, always forthright and full of opinions, later said to Sherard, "I think Eiffel is the nicest fellow I have met since I came to France. He is so simple and modest." Despite Eiffel's having just taken the waters, Edison confided, "he is not looking well. I dare say that his work and all the worries attending it have worn him out. I was sorry to see him looking so bad, for he is a splendid fellow." Like everyone else of importance in Paris, Eiffel wanted to celebrate Edison, who was genuinely delighted with this latest invitation. Edison told Sherard, "He is going to give a lunch in my honour on the very top of the Tower before I go to Germany."

Thomas Edison, Buffalo Bill, and Gustave Eiffel were three celebrities who had taken advantage of the World's Fair to burnish their glory, but even average citizens were determined to use it to achieve momentary fame. There were all manner of attention-getting gimmicks: On a bet, two handsome young men, dressed in matching striped sailor shirts, took turns pushing each other in a wheelbarrow the 750 miles from the city of Vienna to Paris in thirty days. Even more astonishing was a Russian dragoon, Lieutenant Michel Assiev, who rode 1,600 miles on his two horses, Diana and Vlaga, from his garrison in Poltava in the Ukraine to Paris, also in thirty days.

The champagne maker Monsieur Mercier of Épernay (capital of the Champagne district) commissioned the construction of Le Tonneau Monstre, the world's largest oaken wine cask, which boasted a gilded, carved head and held enough wine to fill two hundred thousand bottles. Carting it to the fair required ten pair of oxen laboriously hauling it along a ninety-mile route, and it quickly became one of the astonishing sights at the Palace of Food Products on the Quai d'Orsay. Parisian jeweler Martin Posno devised a far more glamorous attraction: a three-foot-tall diamond-encrusted Eiffel Tower sparkling with forty thousand precious stones. Crowds mobbed the Galerie Georges Petit on rue de Sèze to see this miniature *Tour en diamants* dazzling under brilliant electric spotlights. Its price? Almost half a million dollars.

On the morning of Monday, September 9, the Eiffel Tower's *Le Figaro* staff was charmed to encounter Armand-Sylvain Dorgnon, a baker and one-time shepherd from Les Landes, a remote region where all the shepherds used stilts to get quickly about and tend far-flung herds. Dorgnon had already caused a sensation stalking about the Exhibition on his towering wooden legs, and was now determined to make his mark at the Eiffel Tower, ascending on stilts up the stairs all the way to the second floor. "In our little pavilion," wrote *Le Figaro*, "he mounted his stilts. . . . Dressed in traditional sheepskin, he walked gravely about our print shop and around the [second] platform, to the great astonishment of the onlookers, who tried to understand why, 115 meters up, one would need to wear stilts."

"Our man was a huge success." Dorgnon consequently offered his services to any interested theater.

The great tightrope walker Blondin, who thirty years earlier had stunned Americans by crossing the chasm of Niagara Falls with his manager on his back, had accepted a £4,000 wager "to walk on a cable stretched from the Eiffel Tower to the dome of the main exhibition building in less than five minutes." Sadly, this thrilling prospect came to naught.

On the same morning that Dorgnon was ascending the lower reaches of the Eiffel Tower steps on his stilts, atop the tower's third-floor pinnacle a new telegraph office was opening; its eight employees would soon find themselves besieged. Of course, the first telegram was sent to Monsieur Eiffel, while the second was the work of London *Times* Paris correspondent Monsieur de Blowitz, a man with an uncanny knack for being in the right place at the right time. Just the day before, the staff of *Le Figaro* had inaugurated yet another diversion: throwing little balloons to the wind off their second-floor pavilion with postcards attached requesting those who found the balloons to be in touch.

Had the stilt-walking baker come to the tower but a day later, he might well have crossed paths with Thomas Edison. On the morning of Tuesday, September 10, the weather was cool and breezy, and larger-than-usual crowds lined up at the foot of the Eiffel Tower. By noon Gustave Eiffel, who had welcomed princes and politicians of every rank to his creation, was waiting expectantly for the man he viewed as his most important visitor yet, the great American inventor. Edison, attired in a dark Prince Albert–vested suit, overcoat, and black derby, was maneuvering Mina and Dot

The Eiffel Tower and the 1889 World's Fair grounds

through the throngs of eager tourists and toward the reserved elevator. The Edisons stepped out onto the tower's first platform and into the now-familiar Café Brébant, where Eiffel, president of the French Society of Civil Engineers, had gathered threescore eminent colleagues for a formal lunch to honor the American inventor. Eiffel's older sister was also a guest, as was his daughter, Claire, and her husband, Adolphe Salles.

After introductions were made, the engineers and ladies settled in for a pleasant meal. The golden afternoon and multiple courses glided past, desserts were cleared away, and Eiffel rose to offer a heartfelt toast on behalf of his fellow French engineers. Addressing Edison as "Our dear and illustrious master," he expressed the veneration he felt for one who personified "in everyone's eyes modern progress. . . . Today all of us here are engineers who represent private initiative and applied individual effort, whether for industry or great public works. Among us are many who are devoted to the beautiful branch of the art of electricity for which you have made so many discoveries. We feel very sincere admiration for you."

With this, Eiffel held aloft his glass of champagne. "I drink, dear and illustrious master, to your precious health and the continuation of your beautiful work, work so important to the progress of human science." And so Thomas Edison, who was quite deaf and spoke no French, and Gustave Eiffel, who spoke but little English, celebrated their meeting in best French fashion by drinking champagne upon the world's tallest structure. Eiffel continued: "Since the intimacy of this event allows Madame and Mademoiselle Edison to be at our table, let me also make two toasts to those who are precious to you."

As the convivial luncheon wound down and the gilded domes and church spires of Paris glowed in the afternoon light, Eiffel invited the Edisons and the other guests to ascend to his private apartment for coffee and aperitifs. At that moment Eiffel spied at a nearby table composer Charles Gounod, one of the artists who had infamously signed the *Le Temps* diatribe against the tower, and he now graciously included him in his invitation. Soon the engineers were admiring the view from the third platform. Edison posed for a photograph with Monsieur Salles, which was quickly printed so he could autograph it "To my good friend."

The Edisons now made their second visit to Eiffel's private aerie. "Seventy-five of us did not fill the room," Edison later said. The guests settled in on the dark velvet settees trimmed in fringe. The walls, a warm yellow, were already covered with framed artistic mementos: photographs, drawings, paintings. "Eiffel has a piano there," said Edison. "Gounod, the composer of 'Faust,' played and sang, and he did it splendidly, too, despite his more than eighty years." High above Paris, Gounod's music wafted forth as the guests smoked cigars, drank brandy, talked, and even sang, a magical late-summer interlude. Working quietly in the background was American artist A. A. Anderson, best known for his oil portraits, but invited by Eiffel to try to capture Edison's likeness as best he could in a sculpted bust that would commemorate this occasion of genius honoring genius.

Eiffel asked Edison to inscribe his *Livre d'Or*, and Edison noted the date and wrote in his careful script: "To M. Eiffel the Engineer, the brave builder of so gigantic and original a specimen of modern Engineering, from one who has the greatest respect and admiration for all Engineers including the Great Engineer, the Bon Dieu."

Gustave Eiffel had created for his sister some large souvenir fans (decorated, of course, with images of the Eiffel Tower) for such occasions. On one fold, Eiffel had written, proud Frenchman that he was, "The French flag is the only one to have a staff a thousand feet tall." Next to that, Gounod graciously conceded, "The man who could put an army of workers a thousand feet in the air deserves at least a pyramid," as well as the notes for a tune to sing these words. Perhaps this was a "capitulation" fan, for it also held the signature of another converted Eiffel critic, France's most acclaimed painter, the very rich Ernest Meissonier, seventy-six. He had inscribed these admiring *mots* for Eiffel: "an engineer who speaks like an artist." Edison now added his own praise to one of the folds: "The Eiffel Tower is one of the gravest things done in modern engineering."

Edison had enjoyed himself immensely, but inhibited by his deafness and lack of French, he had done so very quietly—so much so that when Sherard later mentioned to Gustave Eiffel how much Edison had admired Eiffel and his daring tower, the French engineer said, "I am glad to hear it for when Edison lunched with me . . . he hardly spoke, and I must say I should have liked to hear his opinion." Sherard then relayed all of Edison's many compliments about Eiffel—what a splendid fellow he was and how Eiffel's one-thousand-foot tower was one of the boldest of engineering ideas and feats. Eiffel replied, "If Monsieur Edison had said that to me, I should respectfully have pointed out to him that the Forth Bridge is a much greater conception, and that it needed very much more nerve in its execution than my tower. But, all the same, I am much pleased to hear that Edison thought so highly of my experiment."

Sherard could not resist quoting Edison's further remarks: "But he added that New York was going to build a tower of two thousand feet in height. 'We'll go Eiffel 100 per cent better, without discount.'

"*'Eh, bien!'* said Eiffel very quietly; *"nous verrons cela.'*" (We'll see about that.)

Edison had scarcely returned to the Hôtel du Rhin from his wonderful afternoon with Eiffel when he had to change into formal evening wear for yet another banquet. The next morning he, Mina, Dot, and aide William Hammer were off to Berlin, so the Paris City Council had planned one final dinner to honor Le Grand Edison. The venue was fitting: the palatial, gilded Hôtel de Ville, illuminated inside and out by the radiant electrical handiwork of Edison's French subsidiary.

At 8:00 p.m. Edison, accompanied by the artist A. A. Anderson, entered the dazzling rooms lit by incandescent lights arrayed in Baccarat chandeliers. As the band struck up the American national anthem, President Carnot and a phalanx of now-familiar city officials escorted Edison to the table of honor. A quick glance at the handwritten menu must have given Edison serious pause. Tonight's gala eclipsed all the eight-course banquets to date: This was to be an eighteen-course gastronomic extravaganza, all to be consumed with some of France's most legendary wines.

To the accompaniment of the music of Bizet and Massenet, the guests—largely engineers and architects—settled in to serious gustatory business: First a simple potage, followed by dainty Normandy meat pastries and little amuse-bouches, accompanied by a glass of Xérès 1865. Palates whetted, the guests next savored glazed trout *à l'américaine*, washed down with velvety Pomerol *en carafes*, followed by a quarter haunch of veal moscovite, enjoyed with the white Château d'Yquem Sauternes (Lur-Saluces), which had been Thomas Jefferson's favorite white French wine. Then it was on to hen fatted with truffles and foie gras, quail cutlets sauced with Xérès, a small salad, and a gastronomic pause with a light mousse Armagnac. As it was game season, a dish of young pheasant and partridge with truffles appeared, matched with a glass of Château Margaux 1875. Then, to lighten the menu after the many meat courses, an aspic of crayfish tails Villeroy, counter-pointed by artichoke hearts Venetian-style and asparagus points *à la fran-çaise.*

A collective feeling of satiety and bonhomie filled the banquet hall. Now it was time for the sweets, paired with the dessert wine, an 1874 Musigny. First, the refreshing *glace havanaise.* Next came the waiters with the Bombe Nesselrode, a rich confection of Kirsch-flavored chestnut purée encased in vanilla ice cream. A few delicate *gâteaux Valasien et Breton* were also served, followed by a selection of fruits and cheeses. President Carnot arose to offer the first of many toasts, all drunk with Veuve Clicquot. The mayor followed, pronouncing: "Paris, in the Hotel de Ville, has given many notable banquets to emperors, kings, and other royalty, but this is the first time we have ever given a dinner to an inventor. However, in giv-ing a banquet to Mr. Edison, we are giving it to a prince, as he is the prince of all inventors."

By now the waiters were offering liqueurs and cups of strong coffee, concluding a two-hour homage to Edison and French gastronomy. At ten o'clock the entire company of politicians, engineers, and architects rose and made their way into the interior of the Hôtel de Ville for a tour of the Edison Electric Works with the master himself. Many of the guests were introduced to Edison, as was the building's chief electrician. Edison happily shook this fellow's hand, endearing himself one more time to the French republicans. At ten thirty the banquet ended, with the guests re-portedly "enchanted by Edison's good humor and affability, and leaving with excellent memories of the fête honoring this man of genius, who is at the same time a worker, truly the son of his works."

As Edison and his small party departed Paris for Berlin, the inventor fur-ther enchanted the French by announcing a gift of ten thousand francs ($2,000) to benefit the poor of Paris. *Le Figaro* quoted Edison as saying that this was but "a feeble mark of his gratitude to all who have contributed to make his stay in Paris a period of his life he will ever love to recall." During the next two weeks, Edison enjoyed a triumphant tour through Germany and then took the ferry to England, where he kept his promise to stay with Sir John Pender at his Foot's Cray estate in southeast London. On the night of September 26, Thomas and Mina Edison slipped quietly back across the

Channel, headed once more for Paris and a final night at the Hôtel du Rhin. Shortly after arriving in his suite, Edison received a note from Minister Reid inviting him to come by that evening to the avenue Hoche, with the cryptic message, "I've got something for you."

William Hammer, who had accompanied the Edisons on their travels, speculated that it was some further honor, and Edison invited him along. Hammer left to get changed into evening clothes and returned with a horse cab to take Edison to Reid's mansion. There in the sumptuous salon they found many guests who had just finished dinner and were now enjoying cigars, including the recently arrived Charles Dana, editor of *The New York Sun*.

Minister Reid rose and with a knowing smile greeted Edison and Hammer. President Sadi Carnot, he told them, had sent over to the U.S. Legation a gift for the American inventor. He disappeared into another room, returning with a large plush case, which he handed to Edison, who put it under his arm and bowed in thanks. "Hold on there," said Reid, "let's see what you've got." Edison reluctantly opened the box to reveal a broad red sash and a handsome medal. The French had elevated Edison to the highest possible rank for a foreigner in its Legion of Honor: commander. "Every man in the company certainly felt moved by a deep enthusiasm," reported *The New York Tribune*, "and when Mr. Reid delivered to Mr. Edison the official diploma and letter and hung the [red sash with the gold cross] around his neck, this feeling found expression in some of the most fervent applause that ever was uttered. [Edison] blushed like a girl, and, after looking at us in pleased confusion, said, very simply, 'I never in the world can wear it.' A man of such fine and beneficent genius needs no decorations; but he deserves them all."

Edison could not linger, for he had to depart early the next day. He and Hammer said their farewells and returned out into the cool of the night for Edison's last ride through the nocturnal streets of Paris, where across the river the Eiffel Tower was ablaze with colored lights. The Place Vendôme was quiet but for the clopping of passing carriages. Hammer came in to say good-bye to Mrs. Edison, and watched with great amusement as his famous boss proudly proffered the plush box to Mina. She eagerly opened it, held up the red sash and medal, and began to dance around the opulent salon in glee. She then took the sash and hung it around her husband's neck, arranging the medal just so. It was the final, fitting touch to their Paris so-journ.

The next morning Edison and Mina were up early to catch the boat train to Le Havre, where they set sail that afternoon for New York on a French ocean liner named (fittingly) *La Champagne*.

Rosa Bonheur poses with Rocky Bear, William Cody, her art dealers, Red Shirt, and an unknown man.

CHAPTER TEN

Rosa Bonheur Meets Buffalo Bill

On Thursday, September 5, a cold day with hints of autumn, Buffalo Bill entertained yet another personage of great renown: the celebrated French artist Rosa Bonheur, a short, stout woman of sixty-seven whose blunt-cut white hair framed a strong square jaw. Bonheur drove into the Wild West camp in a carriage with her American art dealer, Mr. Knoedler, and her French dealer, Benjamin Tedesco, *fils*. Wearing a dark fur-trimmed coat over her voluminous skirt, her tiny feet in smart boots, Bonheur looked about in wonder at the grazing buffalo; at the tents and teepees, some with small campfires burning; and at the Indians ambling about. Bonheur had been in mourning since her companion Nathalie Micas had died earlier in the year, and thought a visit to this strange encampment might leaven her sorrows.

Buffalo Bill, who had been expecting his illustrious guest, escorted her and the dealers over the grounds, while Bonheur silently absorbed the startling sights. Ever the genial host, Cody invited the party to join him in his tent for an *intime* lunch with Red Shirt and Rocky Bear. As the meal ended, someone commented on how little Bonheur had eaten. "'Why do you want me to eat?' she asked. 'I do that every day, don't I? But it's not every day that I've got two such interesting beings right in front of my face.'" Afterward, a photograph was taken to preserve what became for Bonheur "a memory I really relish."

For years, Rosa Bonheur had been as famous for her unorthodox attire as for her paintings of powerful draught animals and noble creatures, for she dressed *en pantalon*. Back in the 1850s, she had become one of the few women in France possessing an official cross-dressing permit (renewed every six months) that allowed her to wear pants, as long as she did not do so at shows, balls, and certain other public meeting places. She had argued that such attire was necessary as a disguise, because no respectable woman could venture alone to the horse and cattle fairs and slaughterhouses where she needed to sketch and paint. Those youthful forays were over, but at home she still wore a more elegant version of those early outfits—loose velvet trousers, an embroidered peasant smock with amethyst buttons on the collar, and leather boots. Knowing that her occasional visitors would find shocking the sight of a woman in pants, the artist always kept a skirt nearby for quick changes. Rosa Bonheur had also been the first Frenchwoman to be made a chevalier in the Legion of Honor back in 1865, her red ribbon presented personally by Empress Eugénie.

In 1887 Cornelius Vanderbilt had bought her 1853 Salon painting *The Horse Fair* for the fabulous sum of $55,500 and presented it to New York's Metropolitan Museum of Art. Long before that, the popularity of Bonheur's *animalier* art in the United States and England had made her very rich. In 1860 she had purchased the picturesque Château de By, on the edge of the Fontainebleau Forest, where she had thereafter lived and worked in relative seclusion with Micas, her companion since childhood. There they maintained a menagerie that included dogs, horses, cows, sheep, chamois, an eagle, a tame stag with six-point antlers, and a pet lioness named Fathma.

On the day of her first visit to the Wild West, Rosa Bonheur not only began a friendship with Buffalo Bill but also assumed the unlikely role of artist-in-residence at the camp. Many mornings that September she would arrive in her carriage and stroll about until she found an Indian scene that caught her eye. "Observing them at close range really refreshed my sad old mind," Bonheur would later say. "I was free to work among the redskins, drawing and painting them with their horses, weapons, camps, and animals. . . . Buffalo Bill was extremely good to me. He was nice as could be about letting me work among his redskins every day."

Bonheur rarely asked people to visit her château, but "in order to repay some of his kindness, I invited Buffalo Bill to By and loved showing him my studio and animals." On Tuesday morning, September 24, Cody arrived in his carriage wearing his signature scout hat. At Bonheur's high iron postern gate he tugged the bell, setting off "the barking of numerous dogs, the hounds and bassets in chorus, the grand Saint Bernard in slow measure, like the bass drum in an orchestra." Somewhere a parrot awakened and began to squawk. Rosa Bonheur appeared and welcomed Buffalo Bill to her fiefdom. Next to the main brick house with its mansard roof, a quaint carriage house served as a studio, with "a huge chimney at one end, the supports of which are life-sized dogs. . . . The room is decorated with stuffed heads of animals of various kinds—boars, bears, wolves, and oxen; and birds perch in every convenient place."

Over the years, Rosa Bonheur had repeatedly enlarged her country domain, purchasing surrounding lands whenever she could. "Behind the house," said one visitor from this era, "is a large park divided from the forest by a high wall, a lawn and flower beds are out near the buildings, and on the lawn, in pleasant weather, graze a magnificent bull and cow, which are kept as models. . . . At the end of one of the linden avenues is a splendid bronze, by Isadore Bonheur [Rosa's brother], of a Gaul attacking a lion." Across the road was a large meadow bright with autumn wildflowers, where Bonheur kept her horses. She walked over with Buffalo Bill to show him a pair of mustangs, including one named Apache that was too wild to be tamed. Both of the horses, she told him, had been sent as gifts by admirers from the American West. If his cowboys could catch Apache and the other mustang, named Claire de Lune, they were his to keep. Cody gladly accepted the offer.

"Because of his frequent shows," said Bonheur, "he didn't have time to sample my fare. So I took him to lunch at the Hôtel de France in Fontainebleau." But first she brought him to see the old château at Fontainebleau, and as they strolled about, Bonheur told Cody "more interesting things of French kings and queens, prisoner Popes, and great personages generally than he had ever heard before." Before Cody returned to Neuilly for that day's first Wild West show, he promised that two cowboys would come out early the next week to round up the pair of mustangs and take them away.

Imagine Rosa Bonheur's embarrassment when three days later among her mail she found a note from John Arbuckle, president of Wyoming's Post Percheron Company—the very admirer who had sent her Apache. Bonheur learned that he was in Paris for the World's Fair and hoped to come out to visit Apache in his French home. She quickly wrote back on her black-bordered stationery, saying she would be delighted to see him, but "I hope you will not be cross that I have just given two of my mustangs to Colonel Cody. Yours was so wild! I had no use for him any more. Two cowboys are supposed to come lasso them on Monday. I dare not invite you for lunch because I lead a very simple life, but if you like fresh eggs, I would be very happy to entertain you as best I can. I must ask you to give me some forewarning if you accept. Of course, my invitation includes your gracious translator."

On Monday, the two cowboys showed up as promised, and Bonheur and a crowd of locals lined the meadow fence to watch the show. The first cowboy lassoed the mustang on his second attempt. The horse bucked and fell to the ground. In a flash, the cowboy had Apache's four legs pinned and tied, even as he gently slipped on a noseband halter. Speaking softly to the struggling horse, the cowboy eased on a blanket and then a saddle, undid the mustang's legs, and mounted it. Apache, bucking madly, immediately took off.

The French expected the cowboy to be thrown as the horse flung itself ferociously about the meadow. Instead, with a serene air, he rode Apache round and round until slowly the mustang calmed. After a bit, the cowboy dismounted and tied Apache to a fence pole. The second cowboy reprised this startling feat with the other horse, and to the amazement of the onlookers, the two Americans were soon riding the animals down the country road to the Fontainebleau train station and into a railroad stable car. Before the train departed, Rosa Bonheur, no less astonished than her neighbors, congratulated the cowboys on their prowess.

At the World's Fair that very same Monday, September 30, the journalists and typesetters of *Le Figaro de la Tour* were assembling their final issue. On this day the royal tourists scaling the tower's heights were, reported *Le Figaro de la Tour*, the grandsons of Said Pasha, the former viceroy of Egypt: "The princes Saïd and Omar Toussoun are very amiable young people, with open and sympathetic faces; they speak and write French perfectly. Many members of their royal household were with them, as well as some friends. They signed their names in our register in Arabic and French."

Ineluctably, the Paris World's Fair was coming to an end. "Tomorrow begins the last month of the Exposition," editor Émile Barr wrote in his farewell column in *Le Figaro de la Tour.* "The days will become much shorter, the mornings above all, while the evenings will be much cooler; soon enough the foreigners will be thinking of leaving us. . . . It seems to us, also, that our task is largely complete. . . . The exhibitors have received their prizes, and think of little but departure. . . . Our little newspaper will appear no more; but our pavilion remains open to friends and all visitors to the tower.

"Friends will find there, as in the past, shelter when it rains . . . and a register ready for their signatures; the *ascensionnistes* can still receive a certificate of ascension."

Those who had yet to pay a visit to the Exposition Universelle now began converging in large numbers on Paris, determined to see and experience all they had read about, and on Sunday, October 6, such huge crowds flowed happily through the gates that by the end of the day, a new record had been set for attendance: 307,000 paid admissions.

One of those latecomers to the fair was Art Young, a twenty-three-year-old budding American artist, who rhapsodized: "Paris was like some lovely young hostess with arms outstretched that September afternoon as Clarence Webster and I strolled along the boulevards. . . . [We] crossed the bridges over the Seine with its gay Exposition-bound boats, and revelled in the sound of the animate voices all around us, the musical cries, the bright faces, and the cracking of cabmen's whips—a continual cracking above all other sounds. For months I had been hungering for all this, but my visions had never come near the reality." Young had dressed to make a jaunty impression, in a flat-top black derby, cutaway coat with tails, flared trousers, cream-colored Windsor tie, winged collar, and cane.

He drank it all in: "Clear skies and a fresh breeze, and Chicago and New York far behind. Exquisite women passed in magnificent carriages, and on the wide walks were men of leisure topped by silk hats; trim nursemaids with their convoys of children; artists and their girls, known as *grisettes*, whom my dictionary describes as having 'lively and free manners but not necessarily of immoral character.' Spreading green trees, statues of historic figures at every turn, fountains pouring forth sun-drenched water. And in the distance, dominating the whole scene, the black outline of the Eiffel Tower."

The tower had continued to endear itself to even the most snobbish of

Parisians, stirring upwellings of poetry and patriotism. Rastignac, the premier columnist of *L'Illustration*, who had been so dismissive early on, confessed that the tower had become a touchstone. Through the September fogs, wrote this elegant scribe, he looked expectantly for its lighted crown, twinkling on each night at dusk, dominating the landscape, visible from everywhere. "It has become the true crown of Paris, and for five long months already it has shone, shone, shone, seen by all, attracting so many people, like a lighthouse . . . one could say that this little luminous crown is the ray that shines above all else, at this moment, illuminating up there something which we dearly love, a flag that appears little seen from below, but is huge up close, waving in the wind, the beautiful French *tricoleur*."

On Saturday, October 5, John Arbuckle headed out to Fontainebleau and Château de By to visit Rosa Bonheur, accompanied by American portrait painter Anna Klumpke. Klumpke, who came to interpret for them, wrote: "Just as our driver was about to get down and ring the bell, the iron gates swung wide open. On the steps of the house, we saw a short little person dressed like a peasant in trousers and smock and holding a black and white dog. After directing the carriage to pull up at the porch, he stretched out his hands in the friendliest welcome. It was Rosa Bonheur. . . . Her bizarre getup only half surprised me. For a long time I had known that she was in the habit of wearing men's clothes." They sat down—not to eggs, but to a very light and delicate lunch.

Rosa Bonheur apologized for having given away Arbuckle's gift mustang, Apache, explaining, "The animal was so skittish that I could never get near him. As soon as we'd open the stable door in the morning, he'd gallop off into the meadow. Come evening, only hunger made him return to his trough and rack, which we kept full. . . . This wild horse stayed so thoroughly wild that, during the two years that this little game lasted, I was barely able to dash off a few sketches."

Arbuckle was pleased that his horse had been impossible to tame, and remarked, "She wanted a wild horse, and this time she really got one."

"It was, in fact, just what I wanted," Bonheur agreed, "but I had to give up on him, and I thought I was doing the right thing by turning him over to Buffalo Bill, as I wrote you. His cowboys came for the horse just a few days ago. Those fellows really know how to handle ornery beasts without hurting them. It's a real pleasure to watch them work. After one of them lassoed your little horse, he calmed him down so well that he was able to go up and stroke his head. That's a task that I never could have given to a French groom."

When they'd finished lunch with a plate of local white Thomery grapes, Bonheur invited her guests to see the studio. She complimented Klumpke on one of her portraits shown in the last Salon, adding, "I admire American ideas about educating women. Over there you don't have the silly notion that marriage is the one and only fate for girls. I am absolutely scandalized by the way women are hobbled in Europe. It's only because of my God-given talent that I could break free."

At the studio door, Bonheur took out a small key and unlocked it. "Come in to my sanctuary." Klumpke noticed a huge unfinished horse painting, which Bonheur explained: "I'm showing how they still thresh wheat in certain parts of southern France. Treading back and forth, these nine horses crush the husks with their hooves and squeeze out the kernels that are gathered up later on. I've been working on it for years now. I'd like this painting to be my masterpiece, but there's still so much to do that I wonder if I'll ever get it done. Since my dear friend died, I often lose heart." Klumpke took in the rest of the studio, noticing tables and chairs covered by papers and books by Dumas and Zola, stuffed animal heads hung all about. What surprised her was the lack of art.

Bonheur laughed, saying, "It's your compatriots' fault if there aren't any paintings on the walls. They lay siege to my dealers, who carry off my paintings when they're scarcely finished. That doesn't stop me from sometimes making them wait for years. You Americans always go full blast, which has its drawbacks for art." They talked a bit about photography versus painting, and Arbuckle offered to send her "a unique collection of cowboy photographs."

Bonheur accepted happily, but then added, "Only if you'll take a study I drew of your horse. I feel a bit ashamed that I can't show you the real thing."

On Sunday, October 6, across the Atlantic Ocean, *La Champagne* was steaming into New York Harbor, carrying Thomas Edison home. As the ocean liner approached quarantine, a steam yacht with a band playing drew near. On board, Thomas Insull, Charles Batchelor, and other Edison officers were all waving and cheering as they welcomed home their chief. Spotting Edison and Mina up on the crowded deck, they began yelling, "Count and Countess Edison!!" Once the towering liner docked, Edison and Mina boarded the yacht, leaving their baggage to be handled by aides. Young Insull pulled out a tape measure and proposed to determine if Edison's head had swelled as a result of so much praise and attention. Edison remarked that any changes in his physical condition lay elsewhere. "Eight days on the ocean liner have failed to repair the damage to my digestion by a series of French dinners," he said. "I have returned a perfect wreck."

By midday, the Edisons were home at their Glenmont estate in Llewellyn Park, New Jersey, where Mina was gratefully reunited with their young daughter. Dot had stayed on in Europe, but her pretty French tutor had inveigled Mina into letting her come with them to America. (Apparently, *mademoiselle* hoped to land a rich husband while helping Mina learn French.) Thomas Edison, ever the master of PR, held court for the big-city press that first evening home. Happily ensconced in his library and smoking one of his beloved cigars, he held forth, telling *The World*'s reporter, "I went over to see the Exposition. It was a big show. Couldn't begin to see all of it. Acre after acre of things to look at." As for the official U.S. presence: "Very poor. Even the little South American republics beat us hollow."

Edison recounted proudly his many honors, including his elevation to a commander of the Legion of Honor, "the highest rank in the order they confer on foreigners." Still, he reassured *The New York Times*, "I am just as much of an American as ever; I wear the same sized hat now that I did when I left home. They tried their best to spoil me, but my head is not a jot larger than it was, and this week you will see me back in harness as before."

Once again, Edison sang the praises of the tower: "The Eiffel Tower is a wonderful thing. I was given a dinner by the French Society of Civil Engineers on the first landing. M. Eiffel was there, too." Edison could not refrain from mentioning that it took American know-how to design and manufacture the elevators that rose up the tower's curved legs, and he spoke bullishly of the prospects for America's own centennial World's Fair of 1892, and New York City as the natural spot for it. Of course, the Americans would build a tower 1,500 or 2,000 feet tall to outshine Eiffel's creation. "Edison," reported *The Times*, "says the building of one twice as large for the World's Fair [here] is not an engineering problem. He heard in Paris that M. Eiffel was coming to New York to consult with capitalists."

Meanwhile, James McNeill Whistler and Trixie had finally bestirred themselves and departed London. They had journeyed, however, not to Paris and the World's Fair but to Amsterdam, where the Master had a few pieces showing in the Dutch Salon. Like many other artists that late September, he traveled out to sketch the picturesque fishing villages of the Zuyder-Zee district on the North Sea. *The Herald*'s correspondent dropped in to see the couple one rainy afternoon at the Hotel Suisse, where they chatted over wine and walnuts. The journalist was delighted to discover the ever-pugnacious Whistler reviving his feud with Gen. Rush Hawkins, purportedly to explain *why* he and his art had defected to the British. "I did not mind the fact that my sketches were criticized," Whistler insisted, "but it was the discourteous manner in which it was done. If the request had been made to me in proper language . . . I would have given them the privilege of placing [my art] in the American exhibits. I have not yet seen the Exhibition, but I shall go from here to Paris in a short time."

General Hawkins, who had spent the summer being abused by one aggrieved artist after another, had had enough, and the next day in *The Herald* struck back: "I have never in my life written a line to Mr. Whistler. What he did receive was a circular with my name printed at the bottom. . . . It is a little singular that among about one hundred and fifty artists who received this circular, Mr. Whistler should have been the only one to discover its latent discourtesy. . . . Had Mr. Whistler been the possessor of a more even temper and a little more commonsense, he would have had five or six of his works on the line in the American department, and nearly twice as many on exhibition than is actually the case. Really, I fail to see what he gained."

Various artists seized the occasion to hurl a few more of their own brickbats at Hawkins, a Republican appointee. Wrote "Refusé" to *The Herald*: "We can endure the G.A.R. in politics, but spare us, good Lord, their interference in art." One of the lady art scribes who had tangled with Hawkins early on coauthored a long epistle with a male colleague that revisited all of the general's sins. The next morning on *The Herald*'s front page, Hawkins gave as good as he got, even as he insisted, "I never allow myself to be drawn into mud-slinging contests." He dismissed the two "prying scribblers . . . [as] fair samples of multitudes of others who have for weeks past found pleasure in attacking me. And why? Simply because I refused in every case to reverse the decisions of the American Art Jury. . . . There are two sides to this story, and so far, only one has been told—the story of the sour grapes contingent."

Of course, Whistler *would* have the last word and from Amsterdam wrote, "It is a sad shock to me to find that the Good General speaks of me without affection. . . . Here I would point out again, hoping to be clearly understood, that had the methods employed in the American camp, been more civil, if less military, all further difficulties might have been avoided." Nor could "Refusé" resist a final retort: "The truth is, and always has been, that whatever military proclivities our Commissioner may have, he knows no more about art than the fly that crawls wearily over some of the panoramas in our department."

Out at the Wild West camp in Neuilly, in contrast, all was good cheer, for on Saturday, September 28, Chief Red Shirt's wife had been delivered of a healthy boy, "the first papoose which had kicked up its little heels under the shadow of the Eiffel Tower." Moreover, as *The Herald* reported, when the Wild West folk had learned of the impending birth, "bets were at once started among the cowboys and the rest of the crowd as to the sex of the newcomer. For some occult reason the prevailing opinion was that it would be a *demoiselle*, but Red Shirt . . . swore that it would be a *garçon*. Better still, he backed up his opinion with abundant gold. . . . Consequently, when the die was cast yesterday and it turned up a boy, Red Shirt first danced a complicated mazurka and then collected his bets." The French papers marveled that two hours after the baby was born, Madame Red Shirt was up and tending to her wigwam household.

Soon thereafter, to the mystification of the Americans, French newlyweds began showing up at Wild West shows straight from their nuptials, brides and grooms arrayed in full wedding finery, the young women's gowns bursts of white in the grandstands filled with the dark autumn fashions. After the show, the couples strolled about the Wild West grounds looking for Baby Red Shirt. The camp learned that the French were hewing to a purported American custom that promised many offspring to anyone who held an Indian baby on the day of his or her wedding.

Washingtonian Pattie Miller Stocking, a latecomer to the fair, admitted: "We had never cared to see Buffalo Bill at home, but since he is the fashion abroad, why not go and rejoice over him? To be sure, the Indians seemed a little tame to us . . . but it seemed to give foreigners an immense opinion of us as a people in our uncivilized condition. However, the riding and shooting is something to be proud of. . . . We were a little ashamed of the 2-year-old peanuts they handed around during the performance. They were almost as bad as the French of the peanut boy who sold them."

Rosa Bonheur attended the show numerous times, and by late September had become a fixture at the camp, arriving most mornings and then settling in on her canvas stool with her tripod easel and art supplies to sketch and paint. Among other projects, she completed a small equestrian portrait of Buffalo Bill cantering along on his beloved white horse, Tucker, the steed's full, long tail swishing behind. Bonheur's Cody was an idealized, younger man, western virility incarnate, his goatee and long tresses free of gray, his figure notably trimmer in tawny fringed deerskin jacket, thigh-high black leather boots, his scout's eye taking in some distant point. As soon as the painting was done and dry, Cody shipped it home to his Scout's Rest Ranch in North Platte, where it took pride of place. In gratitude, Cody presented Bonheur with "a splendid trotter, very free and very gentle. I take great care of him."

But Bonheur's greatest fascination was with the Indians. Her frequent sojourns at the camp "gave me time to study their tents; I watched everything they did, and talked as best I could with the warriors, squaws and children. I drew studies of their buffaloes, horses and weapons, all tremendously interesting." To help her master the intricacies of the Sioux costumes, Mr. Knoedler gave Bonheur a chief's suit of beaded buckskin and leggings, a silver conch belt, moccasins, and a bow and arrow that she displayed in her studio. Bonheur had, she said, "a real passion for this unfortunate race, and it's utterly deplorable that they're doomed to extinction by the white usurpers."

Chiefs Red Shirt and handsome young Rocky Bear posed for Bonheur, who painted a double portrait of the two men, solemn in fringed, beaded buckskins riding bareback through a scrubby countryside. "It's unbelievable how I get the old fire back," Bonheur enthused to Anna Klumpke, with whom she had become close, "when my pencil brings to life those thrilling [Indian] scenes from Fenimore Cooper." Other Wild West Indians also posed, and over the next several years Bonheur's many sketches served as inspiration for seventeen paintings. A half-dozen were portraits of Indian chiefs and braves riding or hunting, while another six captured

Rosa Bonheur at her easel, painting Buffalo Bill

buffalo stampeding across the prairie, some wild-eyed as they escaped prairie fires, while others were pursued by Indian hunters on bareback. The remaining paintings depicted the more domestic side of Indian life with families outside their teepees, or horses, often wild mustangs, or cowboys on horseback.

It was while he was posing for Rosa Bonheur that Rocky Bear discovered Albert Bierstadt's *The Last of the Buffalo*. This panoramic (six-by-ten-foot) painting, set on the Wyoming prairie, had captured for the Sioux chief as nothing else had the tragedy of the Plains Indian. On certain mornings in late September and early October, Rocky Bear could be found at the Boussod and Valadon Gallery studying Bierstadt's dramatic scene of an Indian buffalo hunt unfolding on the golden prairie, the Wind River Mountains violet-hued on the horizon. A *New York Times* reporter happened by as Rocky Bear, accompanied this time by numerous other Sioux, lamented how the Indians had taken "the hand of the white man and his whisky and sold their plains, where the buffalo was wont to run wild as in this splendid picture." The Indians spent a silent half hour contemplating the poignant work Bierstadt had painted specially for the Paris show.

Bierstadt's picture was an uncomfortable reminder that in the course of a century white men with guns had slaughtered almost sixty million of the great beasts, wiping out the vast herds that had once darkened the plains. Now a few hundred buffalo survived in pockets here or there—including the eighteen Cody had brought to Paris. The American jury, however, had rejected Bierstadt's entry, the only submission of the venerable Hudson River School artist, leading *Art Amateur*'s critic to wonder how it had ruled that "Mr. Bierstadt, a veteran of established reputation, cannot paint well enough to earn a place even in such a miscellaneous collection of pictures as has been sent over to represent the United States"—especially when his was a uniquely American subject certain to be "highly interesting to the foreign visitors to this Exposition."

Of course, in his hunting years, Bill Cody himself had reportedly slaughtered as many as ten thousand of the beasts that gave him his famous nickname. Ironically, the success of his Wild West show would so glamorize all things western—including the buffalo—that millions of urban

Americans would come to support laws saving the few bison remaining, enabling the herds to slowly climb back from near extinction.

Down in St.-Rémy, Vincent van Gogh had grown much better and had begun corresponding again with Paul Gauguin after their violent parting the previous winter. In mid-October, Gauguin had written Vincent from Le Pouldu to report, "Among other things, a fairly big project that de Haan and I have jointly undertaken: decorating the inn where we take our meals. We're beginning with one wall and we'll finish by doing all four, including the stained glass window. We're learning a great deal, so it's a useful thing to do." Gauguin was noticeably upbeat, for after a fallow period, he was working not only on the wall mural but also on a painting of the local Breton women gathering seaweed on the beach.

Vincent himself had never been so productive, deeply inspired by the local landscape. As he wrote to Theo, "From time to time there are moments when nature is superb, autumn effects glorious in color, green skies contrasting with foliage in yellows, oranges, greens, earth in all the violets, heat-withered grass. . . . And skies—like our skies in the North, but the colors of the sunrises and sunsets more varied and clearer." Theo, who was receiving a steady supply of new canvases from Vincent to show, congratulated his brother for his success in capturing the Provençal world: "I like the wheat field and the mountains enormously; they are very beautiful in design. In the wheat field there is that unshakable something which nature has, even in her fiercest aspects. The orchard too is extremely fine."

Perhaps because Vincent felt that he had by now mastered the local countryside, he was beginning to think about a change of scene—moving north to Auvers, where he had the prospect of boarding with a Dr. Gachet. "The main thing," he wrote Theo, "is to know the doctor, so that in case of an attack I do not fall into the hands of the police and get carried off to an asylum by force." Vincent, as always, sent kindest regards to his sister-in-law, Jo, whose pregnancy was now well advanced.

At the U.S. Legation in Paris, Minister Whitelaw Reid was pleased to note that the French republican government had trounced its political foes in the late-September elections. As he had advised Secretary of State James

Blaine back in June, this would be an opportune time to press forward on the pork question. On October 16, Reid accordingly invited Monsieur Spuller to join him for a thorough tour and inspection of the full array of American pork products on exhibit at the World's Fair, recently awarded the fair's "highest prize." Reid presumed that the French would thus see for themselves "the perfect healthfulness of the meat."

Monsieur Spuller proved very friendly, reported Reid to Blaine, and "had no objection to re-opening the question of admitting American salted meat in France, and he would like to settle it to our satisfaction." Though Spuller was a free trader, the recent elections had not really changed matters: "The tendency of the new Chamber seemed to be strongly in the opposite direction," despite the fact that French republican politicians ought to have favored "cheap food" for their constituents. And there remained, of course, the problem of America's 30 percent tariff on French art.

Throughout the summer, Cody had endeared himself to one and all with his many acts of generosity. It had long been his custom to set aside blocks of free seats for the less fortunate, especially the young. In New York, newsboys got free admissions to the show; in Paris, it was one hundred orphans from the Auteuil orphanage, or a group of apprentices, or young soldiers. While Major Burke wrung all possible publicity from such beneficence, it was genuinely true to Cody's character.

Annie Oakley told of the time the Wild West show was playing New York's Madison Square Garden. "Business had been bad for several weeks, and a more worldly man would have been worried ill. . . . The show had just finished and as was our custom we were leaving by the stage door to get a little supper at a nearby restaurant. There were three of us, my husband, Buffalo Bill, and myself. Gathered at the door were twenty or thirty of the most tatterdemalion and hopelessly mendicant down and outs I ever saw anywhere—the riff of a continent. It was snowing and everyone else was rushing for shelter. But Cody stopped and made the habitual movement into his pockets for the money. It wasn't there." Oakley and her husband between them scraped together twenty-five dollars—a large sum—and gave it to him. "With that he turned and said in the most cheerful and wholehearted manner: 'Here boys, here's a dollar apiece. Go get a square meal and a bunk. It's too rough for a fellow to cruise around out here in the blizzard this night.'

"There were twenty-three of them, which left us just enough for a frugal fare. Of course he paid it all back in the morning."

That fall Oakley and Frank Butler mourned the sudden death of their friend and fellow marksman Ira Paine, who had been in Paris dazzling audiences at the Folies Bergère. As Butler had written on September 10 to the shooting community about Ira Paine: "A few days ago he spent the day in my company and talked cheerfully with Miss Oakley of things past. Two days ago, after his regular performance, he was taken with cramps, but gave another entertainment the next evening. Last night, he was unable to appear and this morning died. . . . He was a great favorite here. It was his eighth engagement in Paris. He left a reputation that no one in his line will ever eclipse. . . . May he rest in peace."

With the World's Fair winding down, Buffalo Bill graciously allowed three hundred Scots to hold their Highland Games in the Wild West arena on the Thursday and Friday afternoons of October 17 and 18. Promptly at 3:00 p.m., the bagpipers in tartans and kilts strode in, ignoring the wet weather. The Sioux Indians, in full show paint, filled the covered upper tiers of the bleachers and smoked cigarettes and applauded heartily as eleven brawny Scottish chiefs vied with one another in "tossing the caber," a giant log-throwing contest. There followed footraces, the Highland fling, wrestling, and the famous Highland dance known as Seann Triubhse.

Rastignac of *L'Illustration*, ambling like a true flâneur through the Exposition Universelle, lamented its inevitable end and the imminent departure of the Algerians, the Congolese, and the Annamites, all mainstays of the colonial exhibits on the esplanade. "In the front of the Tonkin village, leaning against the bamboo fence," he wrote, "an Annamite worker spoke of his joy at returning home, to the shop in Hanoi where he makes and sells his paper lanterns shaped like fantastic creatures. Forty-five days on the sea, a bad sea. 'At Colombo, sadly, in coming,' said the worker, 'an Annamite died . . . bad, bad, the sea.' But, at the end of the voyage there is his country, a poor straw hut perhaps, but still the hearth of his father. This boy is 19. His parents await him. There have been too many days when he has seen nothing but the wan faces of Parisians—some bored, some gawking, others curious, and some just plain boorish. He longs to behold the wrinkled faces of his elders."

The myriad fair exhibitors had waited expectantly for the awarding of prizes for various bests of the fair in a variety of categories, and so it was inevitable that when on September 29 the Exhibition Jury had published its list of 33,000 winners in every possible category, those passed over felt slighted. A reporter for the weekly *American Register* strolling the fair aisles was amused to discover that some "have given vent to their disappointment by placing placards on their stalls worded in more or less bitter language; several others by displaying their goods upside down, etc. The administrators, however, will not tolerate these proceedings and threaten with legal measures any exhibitors not complying."

The Parisians now found every excuse possible to attend the soon-to-close Exposition Universelle. Litterateur Edmond de Goncourt, having returned from vacation, now began regular forays to see the fair's more esoteric exhibits. On Friday, October 11, toward dusk, he paid a visit to the Forestry Pavilion, where the fading light had an enchanting effect: "For me, it was truly like entering into a magic palace, built by woodland fairies, its towering columns fashioned from the mammoth trunks of ancient trees, each of the most subtle colors of the wings of night-flying moths. I could not tear my eyes away from the huge mottled birch tree, with its whitish spots, or the wild cherry, trimmed with ribbons of knots, reminiscent of an intricate armoire designed by Labelle, and then there was the towering beech tree pillar, speckled, flecked, as if lime had been blotted on something glossy, creating such beautiful grays, or the noble giant spruce, with its bark seemingly sculpted all over with little round leaflets, or the old gray poplar with its beautiful greenish tone, the very shade you find in the amorous drawings of the seventeenth century."

As the October days ticked by and the end of the wonderful fair loomed, a campaign arose for it to remain open a bit longer. Finally, on October 12, the fair commissioners capitulated, agreeing to extend the fair an extra week, which would round out its duration to exactly six months. "We have the Exposition till November 6!" exulted Rastignac. "It's the big news of the week. Six extra days of this fairyland. And an All Saints' Day that will be a fair day."

On his next foray de Goncourt wandered the realms of Asia. "Cambodian antiquities. These monsters with bird beaks who have the quality of coming from the Plesiosauric age, these sphinxes in the form of dog-headed gods, these elephants like odd snails, these griffons that look like the ferocious flourishes of a calligraphy gone wild. . . . This whole world of stone has a hallucinatory quality that isolates you for a moment from your time and your humanity." The next Saturday, de Goncourt was visiting the Pavilion of the Equator when he encountered "A head the size of a large nut, which still had its hair, and of which one read: *Real head of an adult Indian,* shrunken by a process known only to certain tribes." Once back out in the walkways of the fair, de Goncourt recoiled in horror from the surging crush of people. The weekend crowds were surpassing 350,000 a day! A fair whose managers had hoped for attendance of twenty million now expected more than thirty million.

Those who came at the fair's end did miss one of its most exotic sights: the Javanese dancers. On Tuesday, October 22, reported the weekly *American Register,* "The Javanese kampong broke up and its inmates left on Wednesday for Marseilles on their homeward voyage. They were given a farewell banquet on Tuesday night and a bronze commemorative medal presented to each of the natives by the Exhibition authorities."

Like many locals, de Goncourt returned to the fair every few days, wandering the Forest Pavilion again to rhapsodize over the rare trees, to marvel at the "strange plants of Mexico," and to complain about the Annamite theater he attended: "I find no other description than this: the howling of cats in heat at the middle of musical alarm bells." He was also displeased and puzzled that the fair's cafés were busily dismantling themselves even as huge crowds sought sustenance. "They are starting to look like those makeshift sheds for eating and drinking that were improvised in the early days of [gold rush] California."

American writer Henry James was among the late arrivals. "I relented in regard to the exhibition," he wrote his brother William, "and came over [from London] in time for the last fortnight of it. It was despoiled of its freshness and invaded by hordes of furious Franks and fiery Huns—but it was a great impression and I'm glad I sacrificed to it. . . . I shall have been much refreshed by my stay here, and have taken aboard some light and heat for the black London winter."

As for Mr. and Mrs. James McNeill Whistler, ever fashionably contrary, still they tarried in Amsterdam.

In these final days of the fair, the erudite and well-traveled Vicomte Eugène-Melchior, Vicomte de Vogüé, came to see its ultimate value as providing a glimpse of a new modern world: "In this monumental chaos which has arisen in the Champ de Mars, in these edifices of iron and of decorated tile, in the machinery which obeys a new dynamic power, in these encampments of men of every race, and above all, in the new ways of thinking which suggest new ways of living, are to be seen the lineaments of a civilization which is as yet only outlined, the promise of the world which will be tomorrow."

In fact, de Vogüé, fascinated as he was by the mingling of so many peoples and cultures, gravitated to an exhibit featuring a huge rotating globe: "Here all is truth: the form, the motion of the globe, the immensity of its oceans, the red lines of great voyages, and the discoveries of cities and countries. . . . We will go up in the elevator. It leaves us at the North Pole. With its diameter of about forty feet the Earth presents a really imposing appearance. . . . A spiral staircase leads to the opposite pole, and as we slowly descend it, colored wires permit us to trace on the revolving globe the lines of navigation, of railroads, of telegraphs, and the wanderings of famous explorers. Clusters of nails mark the principal veins and mines of metals—the color and material of the nails indicating the kind of metal. When I expressed my surprise that the great mountain chains were not brought out in stronger relief, it was replied to me that to keep the proportion exact the highest peak of the Himalayas required only an elevation of about one-fortieth of a foot. This must be very humiliating to the Alps and Pyrenees.

"Along the adjacent walls a succession of placards gives in large figures the statistics of the different countries of the world. I learned that China has about seven miles of railroad and the American Union about 140,000, and I understood without any other comment the actual march of civilization around the globe. . . . Another table recalled to me that there are nearly five hundred millions of Buddhists in the world, one-third of humanity; that increased my consideration for the bronze Buddha which smiles in the vestibule of the Palace of Liberal Arts.

"Let no one exclaim over my weakness for this great plaything. By very puerile means, I grant, it suggests grave thought, rectified errors, and establishes knowledge."

Meanwhile, in London and America, discussions continued regarding ways to surpass the achievement of the Eiffel Tower. Sir Edward Watkin announced the purchase of a site and prizes for the best design for a permanent tower: "The designs must show a tower 1,200 feet high, which is 200 feet higher than the Eiffel Tower. . . . [I]t will be useful for astronomy and meteorology . . . and how pleasant to lunch to-day under the clear blue sky, far above the fog."

In the United States, where the wrangling had begun over which city would win the planned 1892 World's Fair, the *Chicago Tribune* envisioned a 1,600-foot-tall tower "which will cause the Eiffel Tower to hide its diminished head." Inside the 400-foot-wide structure two spiral roadways would circle gradually heavenward to the 225-foot-wide top, one conveying horse-drawn carriages, the other propelled cars. But perhaps the oddest of the various towers proposed to out-Eiffel Eiffel was a gigantic swinging structure. Though not much taller than the Eiffel Tower, it would move in a complete upright semicircle, providing a "thrilling aerial flight" to the one thousand persons in a large car. When vertical, it could stop for however long people wished to enjoy the view. "To put the comparison in a nutshell, this Powers Tower will carry people to a greater height than the Eiffel Tower and give them, in addition, an aerial ride which almost takes one's breath away merely to think of. . . . The swinging tower will also serve the additional purpose of transporting people from one part of the fair grounds to another." As Eiffel once memorably observed, *"On verra."*

November rolled in, wet, raw, and cold, but still the crowds swarmed the Paris fair. The final Sunday of the Exposition, torrents of rain pummeled the sightseers and the somewhat bedraggled grounds, which were full of gaps from all the departed exhibitors. "The rush for the Decauville trains on Sunday was so great," reported the Paris *Herald*, "that several people, in their anxiety to obtain seats, were pushed on to the line. One young lady was knocked down just in front of an approaching train, and being unable to get up in time to save herself, was crushed to death by the engine."

Still, neither the foul weather nor the absent exhibits, nor the dismantled cafés nor the tragédy involving the visitor could dampen the holiday atmosphere. "The [fair] grounds, when not presenting the appearance of a collection of small lakes, offered a capital imitation of dark pea soup, yet the good tempered Parisians and Parisiennes plodded through it all and returned to their homes with not only the satisfaction of having a last look at the great World's Show, but with very substantial samples of the Champ de Mars upon their clothes and themselves."

On Monday, November 4, Vicomte de Vogüé and his Russian wife ascended the Eiffel Tower to spend some pleasant hours with Gustave Eiffel in his civilized aerie. Below they saw only gray rain clouds. Before descending, this scholarly former diplomat signed the *Livre d'Or*: "With a last thank-you to my friend Eiffel, who has simply made a great thing." A week before, Eiffel had entertained Wladimir, the Grand Duke of Russia, at a champagne lunch. When they noticed a workman place a ladder at the flagstaff overhead, Eiffel climbed up it to best his own previous record—reaching a new height of 302 meters.

Tuesday, November 5, the Exhibition's second-to-last day, dawned rainy, wet, and miserable, with clouds blotting out the top of the Eiffel Tower. Still, "crowds of people anxious to have a last look flocked to the Champ de Mars.... In the morning, the proportion of better class visitors was comparatively large, but in the afternoon the 'people' predominated. The rain fell heavily and rendered circulation anything but agreeable.

"There was, however, considerable gaiety. Many of the principal exhibitors had invited their friends both in and outside the show to call and have a farewell glance at the marvels now so soon to be distributed to the four corners of the globe.

"The English and Americans were especially busy in this direction, and leave taking and feasting seemed to be the principal occupation of the day.... The brasseries along the terraces were crowded from noon. The strange orchestras with their strangely costumed performers performed with a vigor that indicated that they were none the worse for their six months' labor, but by a singular coincidence they one and all seemed to find it necessary to remind visitors that the entertainment was about to close. A large trade was done in 'tombola' [lottery] tickets, which were offered freely all over the grounds."

The nocturnal Eiffel Tower ablaze with light

On Wednesday, November 6, the rain cleared for the Exposition's last day. Festive crowds poured in for a final visit and that night's closing ceremonies. "What a crush there was! Everybody was there with his wife and family, and everybody was happy . . . and all enjoyed themselves in true, peaceful Parisian fashion. There was no drunkenness and no brawling." When evening descended, a brilliant full moon rose high in the sky, and the mood was magical. "The big Eiffel Tower and all the big domes and all the little towers and the little domes drew themselves to their full height . . . turning on all their gas power, candle power and electric light power, seeming to say to the little world beneath:—'Now take a good, long look at us for you'll never see us again.'"

At nine o'clock, all eyes turned to the Eiffel Tower, where thousands of fireworks transformed the world's largest structure into "a glowing mass of red fire. . . . [At the tower's base,] the fountains shot up their jets of liquid fire in green and violet and red; thousands of Chinese lanterns hung in festoons and clusters from trees and bushes; a solid army of men and women, with here and there a bright eyed, happy child, swayed to and fro, laughing, chatting, and revelling in the beauties around them; in the distance stretched the river, its banks outlined in rows of light, and from the opposite bank the Palace of the Trocadero, with its curving wings, shone like a palace of diamonds. Meanwhile, the full moon, sailing along in a clear sky, did its part in the general illumination."

High up on the *Tour en Fer*, Gustave Eiffel had gathered fifty friends at his apartment to mark this last evening of the great Paris World's Fair of 1889. William Hammer had arrived with a gift—a wax cylinder from Thomas Edison. Eiffel opened his Edison phonograph and installed it, and the sounds of opera flowed forth, lovely, evocative. And then, the voice of Thomas Edison himself, thanking Eiffel for his time on his tower. Hammer had also brought along an empty cylinder, and set it up to record this final evening of the fair. As Eiffel hosted his valedictory party, the tower began to fizz and pop with red fireworks. Gustave Eiffel had tasted success as sweet as comes to few men, and was savoring it thoroughly.

The neophyte American art student Art Young was down below in the happy crowd, where he had decided to spend the evening capturing in quick drawings those final fair hours. "It was a curious experience, watching the spirit of antic play shown by visitors from many lands," he would write later. "There was something both joyous and sad about that farewell to a world event. I looked back into the grounds as two *gendarmes* politely but firmly closed the main gates—the walks were cluttered with newspapers, candy boxes, and other litter. Ahead of me were students, arms over shoulders, dancing in single file across the nearest bridge over the Seine. Behind them some peasants singing. And an old man in high hat and shawl, moving along with spry step."

And so, the great Exposition Universelle of 1889 ended, a phenomenal achievement. The French could not help but glory in their triumph: An unprecedented number of visitors—French and foreign—had "shed over Paris a shower of gold," observed *The American Register*, putting "Frenchmen themselves into an amiable mood." All the prophesies of failure and warnings of certain violence had come to naught. As one French paper boasted, "The Exhibition has brought to France much foreign money, but, what is better, is the change that has taken place in the opinions of foreigners with respect to France. . . . They have seen perfect order in the streets. . . . [W]hen M. de Bismarck tells them that France is on the eve of a bloody revolution, foreigners will smile."

There were many tallies to measure the fair's success: By one reckoning the world had come in droves: 90,000 Americans; 32,000 Austrians; 12,000 Africans; 8,000 Asiatics; 3,000 Australians; 225,000 Belgians; 380,000 English; 160,000 Germans; 5,000 Greeks, Romanians, and Turks; 38,000 Italians; 3,500 Portuguese; 7,000 Russians; 25,000 South Americans; 56,000 Spaniards; 3,000 Swedes and Norwegians; and 52,000 Swiss. In total, they had shelled out an estimated $324 million.

Not all who came to Paris during those last weeks of the fair were of good cheer. W. D. Baldwin had arrived to check on the Otis Brothers' ongoing lawsuit against Eiffel. Baldwin was not hopeful, he said, writing Charles Otis: "The Eiffel suit comes up on Monday next and I am going over to be present at the argument. . . . [We have] but little if any chance against Eiffel." After the acrimonious relations, it was no surprise that Eiffel had refused to pay Otis the firm's final $14,700 balance. His argument was simple: the Otis elevators were not working when promised.

The close of the Exposition Universelle left Parisians feeling somewhat bereft. A week after the fair's close, Rastignac of *L'Illustration* lamented, "The boulevards no longer look as they did eight days ago. In place of the rolling flood of cabs and hackneys, the taxi stands have long lines of empty carriages and here and there a single shivering fare waiting in the backseat while the driver makes himself hoarse shouting, 'Let's go, let's go, off to *Buffalo!*'"

Yes, the World's Fair had closed, but Buffalo Bill and his Wild West show had lingered on, playing only one three o'clock show each day. To spice up what was now a familiar series of acts, Cody had introduced the pursuit and hanging of a horse thief, as well as a re-creation of his own dramatic fight to the death with Yellow Hand back in June of 1876. That Cheyenne's purported scalp had been a much-commented-upon souvenir

Wild West performers pose before the Western backdrop.

on prominent display in Cody's luxurious tent. As reenacted in the Neuilly arena, Cody and an Indian charged each other on horseback, fell to the ground, and lunged into hand-to-hand combat with bowie knives. "The act is well-played," reported *Galignani's Messenger*, "and the vast audiences are daily thrilled by its actuality." One of those watching from the grandstands was the young Nor+wegian painter Edvard Munch, who wrote his father, "Sunday I was at Bilbao Bill's [*sic*]. Bilbao Bill is the most renowned trapper in America. He has come here with a large number of Indians and trappers and has set up an entire Indian village outside Paris with many Indian tents. Bilbao Bill took part in several Indian wars . . . among other things in a big fight with a well-known Indian chief and took his scalp with a knife. The knife and scalp are displayed in his tent. Many of the Indians that took part in the battle are here now and re-enact how it took place."

Munch's father, who was very ill, wrote, "It must be fun to see Indians, but I am doubtful if Mr. Bill really is an old trapper and that there is any trace of truth in knife's and scalp's authenticity."

As the weather grew wintry, Nate Salsbury departed to southern France and Spain to arrange the troupe's next engagements. The crowds still filled the stands for the single afternoon show, for not only were there the two new acts, but "Miss Oakley and Johnny Baker are both shooting splendidly, and so, too, is Daly. The charming Farrell sisters ride better than ever, and 'Marm Whittaker' is a decided success in her log cabin scene. It is said that a fashionable modiste of the Rue de la Paix is anxious to borrow Mrs. Whittaker's sun-bonnet, as she wishes to introduce the fashion among Parisians."

Wednesday, November 13, was announced as the final Wild West show, and on that day, all of Paris—American and French—overflowed the stands. "Colonel Cody's Wild West show closed its Paris engagement most brilliantly yesterday afternoon," reported the Paris *Herald*. "The American colony turned out in force to see the last of the Colonel and his gallant cowboys, of Miss Annie Oakley, of 'Marm' Whittaker, of Buck Taylor, of 'good old' Rocky Bear, and the other Indians, chiefs, braves, squaws, and papooses, of the bucking horses, baby buffalo and their other friends from the Far West. . . . Each member of the programme was greeted with hearty and prolonged applause, which became a veritable ovation when, after his shooting on horseback act, Colonel Cody was presented with a superb wreath of flowers from 'His Paris Friends.'"

After tumultuous applause, the show came to its end, and those who strolled over to the Wild West camp for one last visit were not disappointed. That evening, as the cold autumnal breezes blew, the Indians hosted a religious ceremony, a farewell to the camp and Paris. "At half-past nine a great fire was lighted," reported the *Herald* man, "over which a whole bullock and a number of dogs were roasted, while the Indians, with no other clothing than their war paint, danced solemnly around. Speeches were made by Red Shirt and Rocky Bear, the latter saying that in Colonel Cody God had sent the red man first an enemy and then a friend who had proved the best friend they had ever known." Cody responded with his own praise of the Indians. Then the roast bullock and dogs were cut up, and portions handed out to those "who cared to partake." With much handshaking and farewells, this "unique ceremony" closed. The next morning, the Wild West members would strike their tents and board their train for Marseilles, the next stop on their grand European tour.

*   *   *

The Washington Post declared the Exposition Universelle "the most successful affair of this kind that has ever been organized. . . . Not only has this great show reflected great credit on those who conceived it and carried it out, pouring millions into the pockets of thrifty Frenchmen, but it has put the French republic on a more secure foundation than it has hitherto rested on, and has driven its enemies into exile. In all respects it has exceeded the most sanguine expectations of its promoters. And yet we expect that the [American] World's Fair of 1892 will beat it."

Gustave Eiffel

CHAPTER ELEVEN

Afterword

On January 11, 1893, Gustave Eiffel once again found himself very much in the public eye—this time not in the familiar role of heroic engineer atop his incomparable *Tour en Fer*, but as a criminal defendant. In a jammed Paris courtroom deep inside the fortress-like Palais de Justice, the dour chief magistrate Samuel Périvier was grilling Eiffel, who along with four officers of the bankrupt Panama Canal Company had been charged with defrauding the now-ruined shareholders.

In the hush of the courtroom Eiffel reluctantly acknowledged to the judge that he had made a $6.6 million profit on his $13.8 million lock contract.

The spectators gasped amid angry murmurings. At Eiffel's admission of his huge profit, the judge declared: "'I consider such transaction void. The Prosecutor General will tell you more about this tomorrow and at the subsequent sittings of this court.'

"Mr. Eiffel," reported *The New York Times*, "quailed visibly under these words, and the audience rose from their seats to get a better view of the manner in which he bore the reproof."

The Panama Canal Company, having lost $280 million since 1880 on a doomed sea-level canal, had turned to Eiffel in December 1887 as a desperate last resort. He had overcome his qualms and had begun construction of a system of "liquid" locks. But the company had hemorrhaged too many millions, and in February 1889, only months before the opening of the fair, Eiffel had been ordered to stop building, while all over France investors saw their shares become so much worthless paper.

The Paris World's Fair had been so beguiling, and such a triumph for the republican government, that it had taken some time for French outrage over the collapse of the Panama Canal Company to boil over. The Americans had long been skeptics. "It may seem passing strange," the Paris correspondent for *The New York Times* had written on December 20, 1888, "almost funny indeed, that any one still believed in the Panama Canal speculation under its present manipulators. Hosts of people did and thousands of people do. I have myself heard within the last few days positively aggressive assertion, that the actual state of things is all owing to the jealousy of the United States. I know of a clerk who only this morning borrowed money—3,000 francs—to put into the stock, with the profound, earnest conviction that it would be just so much treasured gold for his children."

Now, with the Exposition Universelle just a memory, French investors wanted to know how almost $300 million of their money had disappeared into a tropical quagmire. The Panama Affair became one of the great scandals of modern French history, for it slowly emerged that even as the Canal Company wasted vast sums excavating a sea-level canal that could not work, it had paid $4.4 million in bribes to politicians and members of the French press to support its increasingly shaky stock and bond offerings, thus encouraging French families to throw good money after bad. So much money had been wasted on the initial hopeless design that not enough remained to complete Eiffel's version. On November 20, 1892, one of the company's chief promoters, Baron Jacques de Reinach, had been discovered dead in his luxurious apartment, apparently a suicide, while another promoter fled to England. And so it was that Charles de Lesseps (his revered father, Ferdinand, builder of the Suez Canal, was by now senile and feeble), three other company officers, and contractor Gustave Eiffel found themselves in a Paris courtroom where an angry audience relished their comeuppance.

As David McCullough wrote in his history of the Panama Canal, "No one ever got to the bottom of the Panama Affair and no one ever will." Certainly there were official inquiries, including 158 depositions and a final report filling "three ponderous volumes. But time and again the fact-finding stopped short of facts that might prove too embarrassing or destructive." On February 9, 1893, restive crowds surrounded the Palais de Justice and filled the courtroom to hear the verdict in this first trial. Eiffel and his fellow defendants sat stunned when the judge pronounced them, one by one, guilty. Eiffel listened to his sentence of two years in prison and a \$4,000 fine, stood up, and departed with his lawyers. Wrote the Paris *Herald*: "Real French patriots are chagrined to see two men like De Lesseps and Eiffel, whose names are known over the whole universe, abused and condemned to imprisonment while other political culprits escape."

Eiffel's tower had made him world-famous, one of the most admired men in France, and—by the end of the Exposition Universelle—richer than ever. But the very public that had so delighted in his triumph, lauding him as the beau ideal of a modern titan, now assumed that Eiffel must in fact be a venal scoundrel. His fall from grace was as utter as it was swift. Eiffel had argued that his locks were but a patriotic effort to actually build a workable canal of great national importance. But he had made far too much money on the venture when all around tens of thousands lost their meager savings. An aged silk maker in Versailles spoke for many when he described his helpless fury at the loss of savings scrimped together through a half-century of labor and frugality, declaring, "I am a man of order, but I say strongly that if a chance presents itself, I will secure justice myself." Another ruined shareholder threatened in a note to Eiffel, "Your house will be blown up by dynamite."

Four months later, at 10:00 a.m., on Thursday, June 8, Eiffel, his hair and beard gone visibly whiter, presented himself at the Conciergerie in the Palais de Justice to serve his prison sentence. This proud engineer, so accustomed to complete autonomy in his daily affairs, soon found himself walking through the grim corridors of France's most famous dungeon, where Marie Antoinette spent her final weeks. And then came his first glimpse of Cell 74, where he would pass the next two years: a small room with stone walls and a plank floor, furnished with only a bed, a table, and a chair. From a high barred window, Eiffel could see only the Seine with its passing barges. Every morning the guards would awaken him at 6:30 a.m. and each night they would check at 10:00 p.m. to be sure his candle was extinguished. Eiffel was allowed the solace of providing his own meals, as well as visits every day.

One week later, on Thursday, June 15, Eiffel awoke in his small cell as usual at six thirty. Later that morning he and another Panama Canal prisoner were brought out to a waiting room where Eiffel saw his lawyers, his son, Édouard, with his wife and her mother, as well as his son-in-law,

Monsieur Salles. They all cried out joyfully to Eiffel that a higher court had just voided his guilty verdict and prohibited further prosecution, noting that the three-year statute of limitations had been ignored. Eiffel, already pale from his week of incarceration, looked stunned and then, clutching his son, began to weep. The group departed the prison for his mansion on rue Rabelais, where his daughter, Claire, stood waiting. The two fell into each other's arms, and more tears were shed.

Subsequently, the Legion of Honor also investigated Eiffel's role. While he had earned a gigantic profit, he had built the locks as agreed until ordered to stop. He had had no position at all in the company, had opposed the original sea-level canal, and had played no part in the vast network of bribes to government officials and newspapers. The Legion of Honor therefore found no act worthy of censure, much less punishment. Yet Eiffel's reputation remained irrevocably tarnished. He removed his name from his company, and undertook no further high-profile engineering projects.

A full decade after the Panama scandal, an admiring journalist wrote of Eiffel: "A great many people who lost their money in the Panama Canal Scheme have very bitter things to say about him; even his complete downfall and disgrace have not satisfied their rancours; they are pleased that with his own hands he raised to himself, so high that all the world may see it, a memorial tower which none looks at without remembering a certain verdict and a certain judgment. For my part, I can only say that Monsieur Eiffel always impressed me as being a straightforward, plain-spoken business man, as full of energy as he seemed devoid of cunning."

For the van Gogh brothers, the years following the fair were rife with triumph and tragedy alike. Six of Vincent's Provence paintings were shown in Brussels with Les Vingtistes, where the critic Albert Aurier praised his swirling sunflowers, wheat fields, and vineyard as "brilliant and dazzling symphonies of color and lines. . . ." "What makes his entire body of work unique is excess, excess of power, excess of nervousness, and violence in the expression." Not only were the paintings admired, but one sold for four hundred francs. Vincent, however, had begun suffering from seizures again, leaving him too ill to paint much or attend the March Salon des Indépendants, where Gauguin, Pissarro, and Monet all hailed his paintings as the best in the show. Still, by May 16, 1890, Vincent had sufficiently recovered to depart the asylum at St.-Rémy for good, stopping first in Paris to visit with Theo, Jo, and their new three-month-old child, Vincent.

Vincent could tolerate only three days of Parisian noise and bustle before setting off for his new home in Auvers-sur-Oise, a bucolic village north of Paris long popular with painters. Dr. Paul Gachet, a patron of artists and art who amused the locals by walking a pet goat named Henriette, had agreed to supervise his case. Vincent would board in a local inn, where Dutch painter Anton Hirschig could also keep an eye on him. Inspired by the spring landscape with its multi-hued farm fields and rolling hills, van Gogh arose early to spend long, fruitful hours *en plein air*, turning out seventy-six paintings in the next two months. When Theo, Jo, and the baby came to visit on June 8, they passed a sunny Sunday ambling about the countryside and conversing before taking a leisurely lunch under the trees at Dr. Gachet's house.

That summer, even as Vincent seemed comfortably settled, Theo's health was deteriorating. He became tired and sickly, frustrated that his longtime employers, Boussod, Valadon and Company, seemed so little interested in modern art or appreciative of Theo's years of faithful work. Vincent, hearing of Theo's discontents, worried that his younger brother's job, and therefore his own monthly stipend, was in jeopardy. He felt guilty about being a financial burden. And he was disappointed that Theo and Jo were not coming to see him again in July, but were traveling instead to Holland for vacation and to introduce their six-month-old son to their families.

On Monday, July 28, not long after his return from his holiday, Theo was busy in the Paris gallery when Anton Hirschig appeared with a letter from Dr. Gachet urging him to come immediately. Alarmed, Theo set out for Auvers and the inn. When he mounted the stairs to Vincent's small room and opened the door, he burst into tears: Vincent lay there swaddled in bloody bandages, deathly pale. The day before, he had hiked out into the fields to paint, taking a revolver, ostensibly to scare off crows. Instead, he had tried unsuccessfully to commit suicide by shooting himself in the chest. Dr. Gachet had patched him up, and Theo remembered how Vincent had come through the earlier ear slashing. Yet even as Theo expressed his optimism, Vincent announced his intention to try to take his life again. Theo wrote to Jo: "You could not imagine there was so much sorrow in life." At 1:30 in the morning, Vincent, thirty-seven years old, died in the arms of his brother.

The next afternoon, a weeping Theo led the funeral procession from the inn. Gachet was present, as were numerous artists, including Émile Bernard, who described the event to Aurier: "The sun was terribly hot outside. We climbed the hill outside Auvers talking about him, about the daring impulse he had given to art, of the great projects he was always thinking about, and of the good he had done to all of us." The cemetery was a new one. "It is on the little hill above the fields that were ripe for harvest under the wide blue sky that he would still have loved. . . . [T]he day was too much made for him for one not to imagine that he was still alive and enjoying it."

Paul Gauguin, stuck in Le Pouldu as he sought a way to get to Tahiti, responded to another letter from Bernard: "Sad though his death may be, I am not very grieved, for I knew it was coming and I knew how this poor fellow suffered in his struggles with madness. To die at this time is a great happiness for him, for it puts an end to his sufferings and if he returns in another life he will harvest the fruit of his fine conduct in this world (according to the law of the Buddha)."

When Theo returned to Paris, he devoted a great deal of energy to finding a gallery to mount an exhibition of Vincent's work. Turned down again and again, he decided to move his family into a larger apartment and, with Émile Bernard's help, create a museum of sorts there by hanging Vincent's paintings on every wall. "These canvases are not the work of a sick mind," he wrote, "but of the ardor and humanity of a great man."

For a few weeks Theo slept better, and his chronic cough eased up. But in October, his health collapsed, and in an eerie echo of Vincent, he began to suffer bouts of insanity. He sent Gauguin a telegram: "Departure to tropics assured, money follows–Theo, Director." When an initially overjoyed Gauguin discovered that Theo had in fact become as mad as his dead brother, he was angry and disappointed. Soon Theo's violent, erratic behavior was carried over to his relationship with his wife and child, which led to his confinement in a nursing home. When he briefly recovered, Jo took him home to Holland, but by mid-November, Theo was again confined, for he had become disoriented, incontinent at times, wracked by pain, and prone to furious fits of destroying furniture–and he no longer recognized Jo. Speechless and paralyzed, he died on January 25, 1891, at age thirty-three from what was later recognized as tertiary syphilis. It was left to his widow to become the keeper of his brother's artistic flame.

With Theo, his dealer, lost to illness, Gauguin marshaled all his considerable energies toward one goal: reaching Tahiti, where he felt his art could flourish. He moved back to Paris and threw himself into cultivating cultural leaders such as Stéphane Mallarmé and author Charles Morice. Their prestige helped Gauguin secure a spot as an official government artist in Tahiti, while their admiration for his Symbolist paintings cast Gauguin as a big talent. He courted anyone who might be a patron, and a month after Theo's death held a successful sale of his art. He could now afford to make a visit to Denmark to see his estranged wife and their five children before setting sail in April 1891 for the South Pacific.

Buffalo Bill, capitalizing on the Wild West show's success, had departed Paris to barnstorm with his company through southern Europe, opening first in Marseilles. Then it was on to Spain and Barcelona, where an epidemic of Spanish influenza wrought havoc, laying low half the company. Just as Annie Oakley was recovering, orator Frank Richmond died. With that, Cody and Nate Salsbury secured the only steamer they could and fled in mid-January 1890 with their performers and animals to Naples. A convalescing Oakley reveled in the warm sun and the sights. "Of course I visited Vesuvius," she wrote, "Pompeii and Herculaneum. Standing on the shaking top of Vesuvius, I had the desire to look down into the crater though the lava was falling thick about me.

"Pompeii interested me. One house had undoubtedly been the home of a sportsman, as every inch of the walls was covered with the finest paintings representing a game scene. . . . One picture . . . represented a marsh scene with rushes, out of which birds that looked like English snipe were rising."

The poverty of these old Mediterranean ports could be startling. When Oakley's husband ventured into Barcelona to buy a Christmas turkey, the butcher "could not believe that anybody would buy a whole turkey. Two hundred beggars followed them and the turkey and the butcher sent an armed guard along with them." Far worse, local outbreaks of smallpox and typhoid carried off several Indians, starting with Featherman and Chief

Hawick, both of whom died in Marseilles. In Naples, the company lost Goes Flying, forty-five, and then Little Ring, thirty-three, apparently from a bad heart. Despite such calamities, the show went on.

When the troupe arrived in Rome in late February, Cody rode over to survey the ancient Coliseum, where he had long dreamed of performing. Under the blue Roman sky, he climbed about the crumbling galleries of seats and stared down into the arena. The prospect of bringing the show there was enticing, but the practical showman in him had to concede that the venue was ill-suited and decrepit. His cowboys and Indians instead performed in their tented arena elsewhere in the Eternal City.

Throughout the mild Italian spring, the Wild West company wended its way north, playing in Florence, Bologna, and Milan. In picturesque Verona, Cody finally satisfied his ambition of playing in a Roman amphitheater, this one built almost two millennia earlier by Emperor Augustus. The Italian tour ended with a day of pleasure in Venice, where Buffalo Bill and all the cowboys and Indians (the chiefs in full ceremonial headdresses) boarded gondolas for a languorous trip up and down the Grand Canal past the faded splendor of the pastel palazzos. From there, they departed for Austro-Hungary and Germany.

Even as the Wild West show enjoyed sold-out houses and lavish gifts from the local aristocracy (Oakley especially treasured her diamond bracelet from the regent of Bavaria), some of the Indians had had enough. Red Shirt and his family had sailed back home after the dispiriting run in Barcelona, followed that summer by several small bands. The first were five Wild West Sioux who debarked the S.S. *Saale* in New York on June 14, 1890, including Kills Plenty, whose right arm had been crushed when a horse fell on him in Germany. When he died from blood poisoning within days of landing in New York, the press paid attention. Disaffected and homesick, two other small groups of returning Indians were happy to vent their discontents to the newspapers.

Cody, Burke, and Salsbury knew that the new regime at the Interior Department's Bureau of Indian Affairs was avidly following the Wild West's Indian woes. These federal officials, who had long been eager to put an end to Indian performances promoting "savagery" and the old way of life, pointed to the five Indian deaths, various injuries, sundry complaints of ill treatment, and the persistent rumors (largely true) about Cody's Indians

Buffalo Bill and Indians taking a gondola ride in Venice, spring 1890

carousing and tomcatting about the Continent. All, they insisted, were proof of "the evil resulting from [Indians] connecting themselves with such shows." To counter the bad press, in late July Major Burke dispatched home to refute the bad-mouthers No Neck, a strapping charmer who carried a fancy black umbrella and whose raven locks were perfumed by the finest Paris musk.

That autumn, when yet two more Wild West Indians died in Germany, one after falling off a horse and being trampled by a buffalo, the Bureau of Indian Affairs announced a formal investigation and issued a ban on further work permits. The Wild West higher-ups were now genuinely alarmed, for without the Sioux performers there would be no show. As soon as the company settled into its winter quarters in Benfeld, a small town near Strasbourg, Germany, Major Burke departed immediately for the United States with the remaining thirty-eight Indians in tow, to prove that all were in fine fettle, and to fight the new ruling. On November 13, 1890, Burke and the Indians steamed into Philadelphia, and they had barely docked when Major Burke, his wild muttonchop whiskers trimmed back to a respectable length, assembled the press in a forward saloon so that Rocky Bear, with Bronco Bill Irving serving as his interpreter, could testify on behalf of the Wild West, while the remaining Indians stood by to exude good health and fine spirits.

As soon as the press conference concluded, Burke and the Indians boarded a train to Washington, and by the next day the Indians were testifying at the Bureau. Nate Salsbury had also sailed home to be present at the hearing, for the Wild West's $20,000 bond was at stake if the Bureau of Indian Affairs could prove mistreatment. Black Heart explained that Cody and Salsbury "furnished us the same work we were raised to. . . . At the end of every month we drew our salary. What we eat is just the same as the whites eat, and we sit in the camp with them just the same exactly. . . . The company have spent lots of money on us, certainly; that is what we went with them for." Rocky Bear also spoke and displayed a purse filled with $300 in gold coins, proof that the Indians were gainfully employed. Moreover, they all indicated that they hoped to return to Europe after visiting their relatives back at the Pine Ridge Agency.

A few days later, on November 18, Colonel Cody himself could be spied on the deck of the French liner *La Normandie*, waiting impatiently to debark in New York after having received a reassuring telegram from Major Burke summing up the Washington testimony. A quarantine inspector's discovery of a steerage passenger with smallpox meant an eighteen-hour delay before Cody could finally walk down the gangplank and emerge from the tumult of U.S. Customs to make his case to the horde of waiting reporters. Cody said that the Sioux all wished to return to work on the show. "The theory of the government's management of the Indian," Cody pointed out, "is that he should be made self-supporting." Further, Cody wanted contrition from his critics, who should "now come out and openly and publicly admit the injustice of the charges made against us." Yet there was no such sign from the Bureau of Indian Affairs.

Even as Cody was brooding about how best to get his Indian performers back, he received a telegram from Gen. Nelson Miles, the famous Indian fighter whose forces had captured Geronimo. That confidential missive summoned Buffalo Bill west, setting in motion one of the stranger episodes of his later career. Since 1884, Buffalo Bill had been making a handsome living off the Wild West show, but he had not actually worked as an Indian scout in fourteen years. The fact was, he and his Wild West Sioux had all come home at a grim moment in the Indians' history. The treaty the Indians had declined to sign in Paris had gone into effect, opening eleven million acres of Sioux land to white miners and settlers. Three years of drought had undermined official plans for nomadic Sioux tribes to settle down as farmers. Even as crops withered, the government cut food rations at the reservations Standing Rock and Pine Ridge, which led to widespread starvation and illness. At this desperate juncture, Chief Sitting Bull had joined tribes across the Plains in embracing the new Ghost Dances, frenzied rituals to usher in the coming of an Indian messiah, a savior from white perfidy who "would bring with him all of the Indians who had died, and all of the departed horses and buffalo. As he started walking from west to east, a wave of new earth many feet deep would accompany him, covering the white man and all his works and returning to the living Indian and his departed ancestors the world as it had been before Columbus." Ghost Dancing was seen as a prelude to war.

General Miles, for whom a far-younger Cody had once scouted, had now requested that Cody undertake a secret official mission to talk sense into and urge peace with Sitting Bull. The old chief, who had toured with the Wild West during its first season, still rode a gray horse Cody had given him. Cody opined to *The New York Herald* that he doubted the Indians would be fighting immediately because it was winter: "Indians dread winter warfare. If it were spring there would be a general uprising. They are discontented, and claim that the Government has not kept its agreements with them in rations or by paying for their land. These Indians know that the harder they fight the more presents they will get from the Government when peace is proclaimed." *The Herald* noted that experience had taught Cody that "whites invariably break a promise."

Buffalo Bill was soon riding the train west to the Dakotas. During a brief Chicago stopover where he met with General Miles, he confided to a *New York Times* reporter, "Of all the bad Indians, Sitting Bull is the worst. . . . He is a dangerous Indian and his conduct now portends trouble."

He also said that Rocky Bear and other veterans of the Wild West were going home to the Pine Ridge reservation and "will do whatever is necessary to defeat Sitting Bull." Cody did not fail to appreciate his odd position should there be an Indian war, confessing to another journalist, "I don't yet know whether I shall fight them or not. It might not look exactly right for me to do so, for I have made a fortune out of them, but if they get to shedding innocent blood I may, if I can be any service, go up there."

And in fact, within days Cody could be seen stepping off the Northern Pacific Railroad in snowy Bismarck, capital of the year-old state of North Dakota, wrapped in a buffalo robe against the searing cold and accompanied by two old western pals. He rented a livery rig in the rugged frontier town and headed south through the magnificent snow-covered hills and big western sky to Fort Yates and the Indian Standing Rock Agency, a part of the world he had not been in since 1876. The Standing Rock Indian agent, James McLaughlin, was none too happy at Cody's presence, for he had intended to deal with Sitting Bull himself.

McLaughlin telegraphed immediately to Washington for someone to countermand Miles's orders, while the soldiers engaged the ever-convivial Cody in an epic drinking contest, hoping to derail him. The next day, Cody, not visibly worse for wear, loaded up a mule-drawn spring wagon with hundreds of dollars' worth of gifts and candy for Sitting Bull and, with his two companions, set out in the bitter weather to visit him. Cody had not yet reached the old chief's camp on the Grand River when he was overtaken and presented a telegram from President Benjamin Harrison rescinding his mission. An annoyed Cody dutifully turned around his laden wagon, returned to Fort Yates, and set off for Scout's Rest, in North Platte, Nebraska, for a planned family reunion with his sisters.

Two weeks later, on December 18, 1890, McLaughlin's Indian Police launched a predawn raid on Sitting Bull's cabin, intending to arrest the old chief. Sitting Bull's 150 followers leapt into combat, and during the ensuing gun battle, the Indian Police killed Sitting Bull and seven of his warriors while suffering five fatalities of their own. In a bizarre note, when the shooting broke out, Sitting Bull's gray horse, which had been trained for the Wild West arena, reportedly took the sound of gunfire as a cue to begin a choreographed prancing number that culminated in its sitting down and raising one hoof. The Indian Police were terrified at this exhibition, for they believed the spirit of Sitting Bull was coming back to life through his favorite horse.

In the wake of Sitting Bull's death, the Pine Ridge Agency bustled with newly arriving troops and cavalry, as well as twenty-five war correspondents who had come to cover the Ghost Dancing, the possible Indian uprising, and now the killing of Sitting Bull. Major Burke, having squired the Wild West Indians back home, remained to curry favor with the local Indian agent, who was about to launch yet another investigation of the Wild West group and how they had been treated. The latter did their part by enlisting in the Indian Police, all hoping to persuade the government to issue new show permits in time for the Wild West's spring European tour. Meanwhile tensions were building in the surrounding plains and valleys, where five thousand Sioux were camped out in their teepees, and three thousand American troops were slowly encircling them, presumably prepared to use their overwhelming firepower. It was the largest assemblage of army troops since the Civil War.

Eleven days after Sitting Bull's death, on December 29, the 450 members of the Seventh Cavalry massed near the frozen banks of Wounded Knee Creek on the Nebraska border. They were to accept the surrender of a band of armed Sioux warriors and escort their families back to the nearby Pine Ridge reservation. When one Indian balked at handing over his gun, a melee broke out and soon turned into hand-to-hand combat. The soldiers trained their Hotchkiss rapid-fire guns on the camp and opened fire. When the shooting ended, the snowy winter landscape lay covered with almost two hundred dead and dying Indians, mainly women and children, mowed down as they tried to flee. Twenty-five soldiers lay dead, while thirty-seven were wounded. General Miles, appalled by this massacre, began arresting leaders of the Ghost Dancers to fend off further violence.

A week later Buffalo Bill rode his white horse into the tense atmosphere of Pine Ridge, dispatched by Nebraska governor John Thayer to calm apprehensive settlers along the state's border and to advise Miles, as "[his] superior knowledge of Indian character and mode of warfare [might] enable [him] to make suggestions of importance." Major Burke was delighted to welcome his world-famous boss (now promoted to Brigadier General Cody in the Nebraska Militia) to the scene. Was a great Indian war imminent, or was this the poignant finale of Native Americans reduced to penury and powerlessness by the whites? While Cody made himself useful as an aide-de-camp to General Miles, Major Burke churned out lurid dispatches under Cody's byline for the front pages of Bennett's *New York Herald*: "At the moment, as far as words go, I would say it will be peace, but the smoldering spark is visible that may precipitate a terrible conflict any time in the next few days."

On January 16, the outgunned Ghost Dancers and their followers formally surrendered to Miles, who rode through the camp near Pine Ridge on his black horse accompanied by Cody. Miles had spent his career fighting Indians, yet found the surrender of this proud and warlike people "weird and in some respects desolate." For Cody it was a strange gift: he and his Indians had been spared any actual warfare, even as his own credentials as a bona fide Indian fighter and frontiersman had been nicely burnished.

More fortuitous yet, when the general returned to Fort Sheridan outside Chicago with twenty-three Ghost Dancing ringleaders as prisoners, he proposed exiling them all to Europe with Buffalo Bill's Wild West show. Under relentless political pressure, the Bureau of Indian Affairs grudgingly lifted its performance ban in March, giving permission not only to the prisoners, but to another seventy-five Sioux who wished to sign on with Cody. By April 1, 1891, a jubilant Major Burke was busy at the Philadelphia docks hustling the Indians on to the Red Star steamer *Switzerland* before the permits could be revoked.

Nate Salsbury, who had been left in charge of the Wild West all that winter in Benfeld in Alsace-Lorraine, had had no reason to believe that the Sioux would be allowed to return, and had therefore been busy assembling a gigantic new spectacle, an equestrian extravaganza of the highest order, showcasing the most exotic and colorful horsemen he could engage: Russian Cossacks, Argentine gauchos, and English, German, and U.S. cavalry. The Mexican vaqueros and American cowboys and cowgirls had all remained with the show, as had star sharpshooters Annie Oakley and Johnny Baker. When Major Burke and the Indians arrived, the company swelled to an amazing 640 people.

The familiar Wild West show was now interwoven with astounding feats of foreign horsemanship, above all by the bearded Cossacks. Outfitted with high conical hats, knee-length belted coats crisscrossed with ammunition sashes, and tall leather boots sporting huge silver spurs, these soldiers of the Russian steppes looked exotic and ferocious with their great curved daggers, thirty-two-inch muzzle-loading pistols, and long rifles. When the Cossacks raced into the arena, artist Frederic Remington, who was in the audience, marveled to see the acrobatics they performed atop their horses. "They stand on their heads, vault on and off, chase each other in a game called chasing the handkerchief." The Argentine gauchos astounded by hurling *bolas*, iron balls on rawhide thongs, across the arena with a deadly accuracy. The new show, billed as "Buffalo Bill's Wild West and Congress of Rough Riders of the World," was an immense success, playing to sold-out houses in Germany, Holland, and the British Isles. It would establish the Wild West format for the next decade.

By late August, Cody was in Nottingham, England, writing his brother-in-law back at Scout's Rest, "From the time I enter my grounds in the morning until I leave after the night show it's a continual strain, and I am becoming very nervous, although stranger to say I am shooting better than I ever did in my life." Wherever he was traveling, Cody was always thinking of his ranch and how to improve it. He now dreamed of an additional barn: "All I want is shelter enough to keep all our stock home this winter. I thought I would like to have the new Barn painted white. Then in the

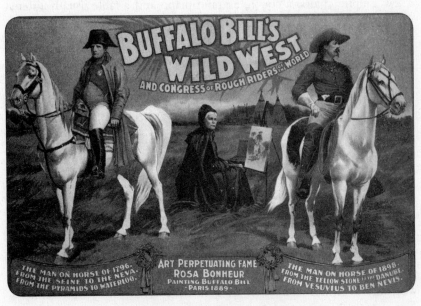

The poster for the show in the 1890s

spring we could put a fresh coat of red paint on the Big Barn, and paint the House blue with green borders and it would look nice. Red White & blue. . . . I want to try a hundred acres of Alfalfa. Do you know of a good farmer I can hire by the year?"

Three years after the 1889 Exposition Universelle, James McNeill Whistler and his wife had relocated to Paris, swayed in part by official French *hommage.* "The dreariness and dullness of London was at last too depressing for anything," Whistler wrote a friend; ". . . I could at last come to this land of light and joy where honors are heaped upon me, and Peace threatens to take up her abode in the garden of our pretty pavilion." The republican government had not only "knighted" Whistler, by making him a chevalier in the Legion of Honor, but they had also purchased, at the urging of Stéphane Mallarmé and other artists, his painting *Arrangement in Grey and Black, No. 1: Portrait of the Artist's Mother* to hang in the Louvre. Whistler finally had the official acclaim for which he had yearned.

The Master and Trixie happily nested at 110 rue du Bac in the ground floor of a seventeenth-century house, where a "reception room, painted blue and white and with a carpeting of blue matting, [was] furnished with a few Empire chairs, a couch, a grand piano and a table usually littered with newspapers. On a wall was an early Whistler. Near the fireplace was a writing table with inkwell, papers, and pens, where Whistler would often sit with a cup of coffee and a cigarette while he pondered a barbed note to an editor." When the couple needed fresh air and greenery, they merely had to open the French doors and step out into a spacious old garden with huge trees and graveled paths. At its far end, beyond a high stone wall, a seminary's muted bells marked the hours, while in the evening the faint sounds of a chanting choir floated over. Ever the social butterfly, Whistler often sat under the trees holding court for his many visitors. Among a certain set, Whistler had now become the most famous American in Paris.

At fifty-seven, he basked in his new status and renown. And to his glee, for the first time in his career his work commanded big prices. The city of Glasgow had purchased his portrait of Carlyle for a thousand guineas, while the American millionaire Charles Freer eagerly paid top dollar to assemble a serious collection of Whistler's art, from oil paintings to lithographs. Isabella Stewart Gardner of Boston came calling to The Master's new studio on rue Nôtre Dame des Champs, determined to own *Harmony in Blue and Silver*, a portrait of the beach at Trouville. Whistler was invited to show three paintings with the British at the upcoming Chicago World's Fair. Of course, he still relished verbal sparring and contretemps, though Edgar Degas wondered why, saying, "What a pity! He should paint with his tongue: then he might be a genius."

And what, in these years after the fair, had come of all the talk about "Out-Eiffeling Eiffel" with a structure taller than his *Tour en Fer*? The English got so far as starting construction in June of 1893 of an iron tower in Wembley Park, near London, but when it reached several hundred feet, it rose no farther. It was in the United States, where Chicago had won the right to host America's Columbian Exposition, that the contest heated up. The *Chicago Tribune* held a competition that attracted all manner of unpromising proposals, including one from the Chicago-Tower Spiral-Spring Ascension and Toboggan Transportation Company, which envisioned "a tower with a height of 8,947 feet, nearly nine times the height of the Eiffel Tower, with a base one thousand feet in diameter sunk two thousand feet into the earth. Elevated rails would lead from the top of the tower all the way to New York, Boston, Baltimore, and other cities. Visitors ready to conclude their visit to the fair and daring enough to ride elevators to the top would then toboggan all the way back home." Stranger yet was a proposed four-thousand-foot tower anchoring a two-thousand-foot rubber cable with a car attached to its end. "The car and its passengers would be shoved off a platform and fall without restraint to the end of the cable. . . . The engineer urged that as a precaution the ground 'be covered with eight feet of feather bedding.'"

Before Gustave Eiffel had been engulfed by the Panama scandal, he had proposed to out-Eiffel himself, contacting the Chicago fair's directors in August 1891 to see if they would be receptive to a taller version of his Paris monument. As word of the inquiry raced around, American engineers expressed outrage that a Frenchman should dare try to claim so American a prize, and Eiffel's offer was politely declined. Other strange and impractical proposals filtered in, including a log-cabin tower constructed of tremendous trees, like some giant's creation. The men running the Chicago fair were getting worried. They had designed a classical, ethereal Beaux Arts White City set in a verdant landscape of elegant lakes and canals, but where was the American engineering marvel to equal, much less eclipse, the Eiffel Tower?

In mid-December of 1892, they had their answer: George Washington Ferris proposed erecting not a tower but a gigantic revolving wheel. "This wheel would carry thirty-six cars, each about the size of a Pullman, each holding sixty people and equipped with its own lunch counter, and when filled to capacity the wheel would propel 2,160 people at a time three hundred feet into the sky over Jackson Park, a bit higher than the crown of the now-six-year-old Statue of Liberty."

When the Ferris wheel was up and running, it did not, in truth, out-Eiffel Eiffel. It never came close to rivaling the tower's elegance, much less its almost instant fame and iconic status. Still, the towering device had the inherent charm of the gigantic, and its novelty and originality provided its own enchantments. At night, it glittered in the sky, its slowly revolving structure and shiny Pullman cabins outlined with three thousand shimmering lights. More than a million fair visitors (less than half of Eiffel's gate) paid fifty cents to board and make two stately revolutions high up in the air, enjoying the views of nearby smog-enshrouded Chicago and, beneath their feet, the fair's fairy-tale grounds. As they circled slowly up and then down, the Ferris wheel riders could see just below the exotic Turkish village, the delightful German beer garden, and the Cairo street (shades of Paris 1889) with its camels, minareted mosque, and Egyptian tombs.

The Chicago fair's directors had rejected not only a larger tower by Eiffel, but also Buffalo Bill's bid for a spot inside the fairgrounds. In response, Salsbury secured fourteen strategic acres opposite the fair's main entrance, and by late March 1893 Cody had arrived to set up camp and build an arena. He reported that summer to his sister, "I am doing the business of my life," and indeed, the Chicago World's Fair run would be one of the most successful seasons of Cody's career. A North Dakotan named P. B. Wickham had managed to obtain Sitting Bull's cabin, with its bullet-riddled front door, as well as his sweat lodge, and had Chief Rain-in-the-Face living there, a prime authentic Midway attraction.

When the fair managers, struggling to recoup construction costs, refused Chicago mayor Carter Harrison's request to allow the city's poor children free admission for one day to the fair, it was once again Buffalo Bill to the rescue. He proclaimed Waif's Day at the Wild West. As Erik Larson recounts in *The Devil in the White City*, his wonderful history of the 1893 fair, Cody "offered any kid in Chicago a free train ticket, free admission to the show, and free access to the whole Wild West encampment, plus all the candy and ice cream the children could eat.

"Fifteen thousand showed up."

It is probably safe to say that while the Chicago run was Cody's most lucrative—he reportedly cleared $1 million in profits—the Paris World's Fair still remained the high point of his professional life. Not only had he been the toast of the world's most cosmopolitan city, the darling of aristocratic French hostesses, and the most lionized American in Paris (at least until Edison appeared), he also had served all through the fair as a genuine cultural ambassador, introducing the American frontier (however sanitized) to enthralled audiences from around the globe. In Chicago, Cody's role was more that of a familiar and lovable showman, there to make money.

Annie Oakley's conquest of Europe only amplified her celebrity at home. Now thirty-three, she had become a huge star. At the fair, on June 28, Ohio governor William McKinley presided over a reception at the Ohio State Building in honor of this local girl made good. Like Buffalo Bill, Oakley exemplified the American Dream: an individual of humble origins who had achieved the heights of success by hard work and talent. Oakley also personified the emerging spunky modern woman—self-reliant, as good as (in fact, far better than) most men at guns and shooting. In Glasgow, she had purchased and begun riding a bicycle, thus adding to her image as an up-to-the-minute new woman. She had always encouraged women to master shooting, hunting, and other outdoor pursuits, personally instructing thousands in gun skills over the years.

At the same time, in her home life Oakley remained the happily married Mrs. Butler. Part of her considerable charm was the simplicity of her ways and person. "There is not a nicer wife or woman in the land than Annie Oakley," wrote one Chicago reporter. "When she was in Europe royalty courted her and she accepted it as she would the complacent attentions of the village quilting party." She liked nothing better than being out in nature. "Truly, I long for the day when . . . I can take to the field and stream as often as true inclination may lead me there."

On August 30, 1893, Paul Gauguin returned to France from Tahiti, hoping for the fame and success that had eluded him at the 1889 fair. He debarked the steamer *Armand Béhic* onto the dock in Marseilles with four francs in his pocket and sixty-six paintings. His disciple Sérusier wired 250 francs to pay for his hotel and a train ticket to Paris, where other old friends rallied round with loans, a tiny apartment, the share of a studio, and meals on credit at the local *crémerie*. After several rebuffs at other galleries, Durand-Ruel agreed to give Gauguin a show, but only if he fronted the considerable costs of framing and publicity. On November 9 the aesthetes and artists of Paris streamed in to see the forty-four paintings and many wooden sculptures they had heard so many rumors about. Gauguin, very much the rebel artist in a long navy blue cape, bold-checked trousers, and a pleated astrakhan hat, yearned to make a sensation. Instead, the show yielded respectful notices and meager sales. His main solace was Degas's purchase of two paintings.

Once the Durand-Ruel show ended, Gauguin followed the example of Theo van Gogh and in early 1894 created his own permanent one-man exhibit on the bright yellow walls of his spacious new studio at 6 rue Vercingétorix, south of the Gare Montparnasse. There ensued a jumbled period of love affairs, one with an odd Javanese girl; an interest in wooden sculptures and a new rough style of woodblock prints; street brawls that left Gauguin with an injured ankle; and the loss of his Pont-Aven paintings, which had been entrusted to his old landlady. Any dealings with his wife, Mette, in Denmark just resulted in mutual rancor. Gauguin concluded that the life of a Paris artist was not for him, and on September 5, 1895, he set sail again to work in Polynesia.

Whistler's charmed Paris period did not last long. In the spring of 1894, Trixie's health had begun to decline, even as Whistler was threatening lawsuits against George du Maurier for the Whistler-like character in his popular novella *Trilby*. Some days that summer and fall, Trixie was so fatigued that she did not leave their wondrous sleigh bed, a carved-and-lacquered Louis XVI Empire antique with swans' heads ornamenting each corner. The bedstead had been partial payment for Whistler's full-length portrait of their friend Count Robert Montesquiou. By Christmas Whistler had decided Trixie needed further medical attention and the company of her family. They accordingly closed up the rue du Bac apartment and sailed across to England, where London doctors diagnosed her with cancer.

For the next two years, as Whistler wrote to one friend, "We have wandered from home and work—going from town to country, and from doctor to doctor. Living in hotels, and leaving behind us the beautiful place you know so well in Paris." By spring of 1896 they were staying out in the pure air of Hampstead Heath, but Whistler acknowledged, "We are very, very bad." By mid-May, Trixie was dead. Devastated, Whistler buried his grief in his work, even starting an art atelier in Paris for a few seasons. By 1899 he had drifted back to London and taken up residence in the spacious, fashionable flat of his publisher, William Heinemann. Though only in his mid-fifties, Whistler found that his artistic drive and ambition had ebbed, and he was often ill. His friends watched sadly as he faded, succumbing at age fifty-nine to a final bout of pneumonia on July 17, 1903.

Whistler outlived Paul Gauguin, fifty-four, by a mere two months. After Gauguin's return to the Pacific, despite steady bouts of poor health he turned out large ambitious paintings. Isolated and desperate for money, he wrote to a friend in Paris, "If I can no longer paint, I who love only that—neither wife nor children—my heart is empty. Am I a criminal? I don't know. I seem condemned to live when I have lost all moral reasons for living." Gauguin was as yet unaware that he had become the toast of artistic Paris for a show of his Tahitian paintings at the gallery of dealer Ambrose Vollard.

Having failed to make any real mark at the 1889 Paris fair, Gauguin then hoped to ride his new prominence at long last to a place of artistic honor at the Paris Exposition Universelle of 1900. Instead, his large shipment of paintings was waylaid and not retrieved until the fair was over. Close to an invalid now and seeking a change, he moved to the tiny island of Hivaoa, in the Marquesas. Vollard was sending a monthly stipend, but Gauguin was rarely well enough to paint or create art. He was found dead in the squalor of his house on May 8, 1903, like Theo van Gogh, a victim of tertiary syphilis.

Back in the halcyon days of the 1889 Paris World's Fair, Thomas Edison had often bragged that Americans were certain to best Eiffel by building a tower twice as tall, a boast he repeated while regaling the New York reporters about his triumphant visit to Paris. But once back at the laboratory in West Orange, Edison found himself beset by troubles. J. P. Morgan, his biggest Wall Street backer, had been busy machinating to sell Edison's electric company out from under him, and by 1892, without so much as a word to the great inventor, Morgan merged Edison Electric into a more profitable entity he rechristened General Electric.

Edison sought escape from these business travails out in the wilds of Ogden, New Jersey, where he was happily perfecting a giant ore-crushing

Thomas Edison and his new, improved phonograph

plant that pulverized rock into powder, enabling a super-powerful magnet to extract the valuable iron ore. Outfitted in a filthy old duster coat, a broken-down hat, and a dust filter mask, which he occasionally lifted up to spit out chewing tobacco, Edison was convinced he was on the brink of a huge success. From time to time, he pulled himself away from his bleak nineteen thousand acres (and what would turn out to be the worst boondoggle of his career) to return to West Orange to work on other inventions.

There he and his assistants were continually improving the phonograph to make it a truly commercial entity. He was also developing the Kinetoscope, a primitive motion picture machine that played a short scene for a nickel. In 1893 Edison wrote that he was "very doubtful if there is any commercial feature in it, and fear that they will not even earn their cost." On April 14, 1894, he was proven utterly wrong when the first small Kinetoscope parlor with five machines opened on lower Broadway, where patrons inserted a nickel to watch a ninety-second short of prizefighting. As word spread about *moving* pictures, customers mobbed the street, becoming so unruly that police had to control the lines of those waiting to enter.

Edison quickly built a movie studio in West Orange, a ramshackle structure called the Black Maria, which was encased in black tar paper to control the lighting. In that stifling space, his men set to churning out frenetic short films for the suddenly booming Kinetoscope market. A steady flow of luminaries—pugilists, dancers, strong men, anyone with a highly visual act or silly skit—made the pilgrimage to West Orange on the ferry and trolley to be recorded for the Wizard's latest sensation. And so it was that once again the two most beloved Americans in the Paris of 1889—Buffalo Bill and Thomas Edison—reunited briefly in New Jersey.

Buffalo Bill's touring company was finishing up a run in Ambrose Park, Brooklyn, and he led fifteen of the Wild West Indians in fullest war paint out to West Orange to reenact famous frontier scenes before the battery-operated camera. Some weeks later, Annie Oakley had her turn. Edison was delighted to see how the camera captured the way her guns smoked and the glass balls shattered during her sharpshooting act. Little did Cody imagine that day in the stifling Black Maria studio that motion pictures would slowly lure away the audience for the live extravaganzas that had made him so much money.

In the coming years, Edison had to concede that his "Ogden Baby" was a hopeless white elephant, but he was rich enough not to be overly concerned with its failure. By 1904 he was selling 113,000 phonographs and seven million cylinder recordings. The motion picture business was also booming. By 1909, 8,000 theaters were featuring "movies," typically fourteen minutes of wrecked trains, ladies rescued from villains, and terrible calamities and tragedies. Edison cheerfully informed a friend, "My three companies, the Phonograph Works, the National Phonograph Company, and the Edison Manufacturing Company (making motion picture machines and films), are making a great amount of money, which gives me a large income."

Not long after the 1889 Exposition Universelle, James Gordon Bennett, Jr., shut down his brief-lived London *Herald*—English libel laws were too strict for his tastes. But the Paris *Herald* flourished and, once the flood tide of Americans had receded, its yearly losses of $100,000 were a matter of pride. Bennett could easily absorb the French shortfall with *The New York Herald* earning a million a year in profits back in the United States. As a boss, the Commodore was unchanged: imperious, terrifying, utterly erratic. The Paris staff resorted to bribing Bennett's butler to sound the alarm whenever Bennett "left his apartment breathing fire and heading for the Rue du Louvre," writes biographer Richard O'Connor. "The doorman downstairs was similarly alerted to warn them before he entered the premises. One night the warning system failed. . . . [T]he staff heard his heavy tread in the corridor outside and the terrible man was surveying the editorial department with blood and brandy in his eye." Someone had placed many empty beer bottles on the sports editor's desk as a joke. It was an infamous fact that Bennett did not tolerate employee drinking and he sternly asked about the bottles. The editor gamely claimed them as his, no doubt expecting immediate dismissal. Instead, Bennett summoned the city editor and snapped, "I want you to raise Mr. Bishop's salary fifty francs a week. He needs it to pay his beer bills."

One of the more oft-repeated of the Bennett the Irrational Autocrat stories took place in his luxurious apartment. Bennett was standing before his fireplace wrestling to extricate something from one of his pockets. He pulled out a thick roll of banknotes and, as they were not what he was seeking, flung them in irritation into the crackling flames of his fireplace. A guest retrieved the large sum of money, waited while Bennett located what he wanted from his pocket, and then handed it back to his host.

"Perhaps that is where I wanted the roll," said Bennett, as he consigned the bills once again to the fireplace, this time to be consumed by the flames.

Bennett, who loved speed in all its forms, was an early enthusiast of the horseless carriage. Consequently, the Paris *Herald* covered these new machines in breathless detail, featuring lavish illustrations of Messieurs Peugeot's Petroleum Phaeton and Petroleum Victoria, Messieurs De Dion and Bouton's Remorqueur, and M. E. Roger's Petroleum "Vis-à-vis." Asserted one *Herald* story, "Not to be a 'chauffeur' nowadays is to be nobody. . . . 'I never see any one driving horses nowadays without thinking of Louis XIV,' said one of the wittiest and prettiest women in Paris society." Among those who found the new machines an abomination was none other than Hugues Le Roux, the first writer to ascend to the top of the Eiffel Tower with Gustave Eiffel. Le Roux "said his life, and those of his wife and children, had been so often imperiled by automobiles that he now promenaded the streets of Paris with a revolver in his pocket. 'The next chauffeur who refuses to stop after nearly running me over will get shot.'"

Bennett was so enamored of the automobile and the new races featuring fast machines careening across the French countryside that he could not resist sponsoring one, and naming it after himself.

If living well is the best revenge, then Gustave Eiffel, in the years after the Panama Canal scandal and his brief incarceration, could certainly console himself. His Paris domicile was a splendid Second Empire mansion, built by the Duc d'Angoulême, son of Charles X, at 1 rue Rabelais, opposite the fashionable Jockey Club and near the Champs-Élysées. He continued to live with his favorite daughter, Claire (who remained completely devoted to her *cher papa*), her husband, Adolphe Salles, and their children. The pedigreed mansion had an austere but elaborate façade enclosing a cobblestone courtyard. The spacious entry hall was lavish, featuring sculpted wooden paneling, towering polished marble columns, and a two-story oval skylight. The high-ceilinged salon and library were equally ornate, with tall gilded mirrors above carved mantels, antique furnishings, crystal chandeliers, Oriental rugs, and Eiffel's collection of tapestries.

Upstairs in his study, Eiffel could often be found tending to his affairs or writing one of his scientific papers, seated at "his monumental oak desk riddled with secret drawers, bibelots such as a delicate white porcelain pipe with tooled silver cap, a book cover of fine red velvet bearing his initials in silver, an expensive amber cigar holder with 'GE' marked in gold, several gilt statuettes of Buddha, paying homage to the French bourgeoisie's transient turn of the century enthusiasm for chinoiserie." Eiffel had begun composing portions of what would eventually be a personal memoir (some of it written in the third person), titled *Biographie Industrielle et Scientifique.* His library lined the walls, shelf after shelf of leatherbound complete works of Voltaire, Hugo, Labiche, Zola, the de Goncourt brothers, and de Maupassant.

Never a man to be idle, Eiffel now had the time and wherewithal to devote himself to a subject that had long fascinated him: the weather. "During my engineering career the wind was always one of my preoccupations due to the exceptional dimensions of my structures," he would write in his memoir. "It was an enemy against which I had to struggle constantly. My studies to determine its force led me progressively to investigate other aspects of meteorology and eventually to set up a complete weather station." When the Eiffel Tower opened, the station Eiffel installed monitored temperature, humidity, wind speed and direction, rain, mist, snow, and hail. In subsequent years, he would set up (at his own expense) another twenty-five such weather stations all across France, and even one in Algiers. Above all, Eiffel studied the wind, devising ever more precise instruments for recording the wind's direction, strength, and changing temperature. Starting in 1903, he "published at his own expense a series of weather atlases . . . the first synoptic charts to appear in France and the foundation of modern meteorology in that country."

As a longtime student of the dynamics of wind, Eiffel naturally gravitated toward its role in aviation. Ever the methodical engineer, he sought to discover how best to determine air's resistance and what shapes moved most easily through it. On many days, Eiffel could be seen, attired in bowler hat, his beard now gray and white, at the foot of the Eiffel Tower observing and calculating as varied shaped objects came hurtling down a wire apparatus that hung down 377 feet from his lab. By 1905, he had dropped hundreds of objects from the tower, confirming "experimentally that the generally accepted physical law that air resistance increased as the square of the surface of the object moving through it. Further, the tests showed that the coefficient figure used by many scientists to calculate air resistance . . . was off by as much as 56 percent."

Eiffel had long owned a country place, a château outside Paris in Sèvres, but soon after his disgrace he seemed to derive pleasure in collecting sumptuous properties in Brittany, in Bordeaux, in Vevey on Lake Léman, and in Beaulieu-sur-Mer on the French Riviera. He may have encountered James Gordon Bennett in Beaulieu, for both men kept their steam-powered yachts in the harbor there. In these years Eiffel became a grandfather and enjoyed his role as paterfamilias, gathering his offspring for holidays at his various estates and teaching his young grandchildren how to swim and fence, activities he himself still enjoyed. His birthday, on December 15, was always a command performance, a formal gala event featuring famous classical singers and musicians.

The matter almost certainly uppermost on Gustave Eiffel's mind in the period after the 1889 fair was the ultimate fate of his beloved *Tour en Fer*. While it served as a major attraction of the 1900 Paris World's Fair, it was by no means the centerpiece. Those who had never liked the Eiffel Tower—including the architect Jules Bourdais of the proposed Sun Tower—happily contemplated its demolition in 1909, when Eiffel's twenty-year contract expired. Public ardor for the tower had certainly cooled: half as many sightseers—a million—had ascended its heights during the 1900 fair, and otherwise it attracted about two hundred thousand visitors a year. From the start, Eiffel had labored to portray his creation as an indispensable aid to scientific study, and even the original scoffers had to concede that in that respect it had indeed proved its value.

But Eiffel had also from the first invoked the tower's military potential, its great height offering an incomparable bird's-eye view of distant maneuvers. As early as 1898, he had also glimpsed its possible salvation in the nascent technology of radio and wireless telegraphy. He invited French radio pioneer Eugène Ducretet to experiment with placing a transmitter on the tower. When Marconi galvanized the world the following year with cross-Channel transmissions, Eiffel instantly recognized the tower's strategic potential. Yet not until 1903 was he able to persuade the French military command to install Capt. Gustave Ferrié of the French Corps of Engineers with a telegraphy unit atop the tower, and only because Eiffel paid for it.

Meanwhile, Paris officialdom had convened a committee to advise on tearing down the tower. In 1903, just as Captain Ferrié began spending his days in a wooden shack atop it, "with a single antenna guyed from the tower to a tree on the Champ de Mars . . . sending and receiving over distances of 250 miles," the tower committee engaged in fierce debates pro and con. It conceded that some still found the tower an eyesore ("one would wish it were more beautiful"), but also acknowledged its proven value to meteorology, aviation, and telegraphy. "Should all this be sacrificed to a harsh aesthetic evaluation," the committee asked, "and should this colossal building be destroyed, perhaps at great expense, with no compensation for the city?" Moreover, the committee worried about foreign opinion: "Do you not think that the world would be astonished to see us destroy something in our city which continues to be a subject of astonishment for others?" And so, the City of Paris remained ambivalent about its controversial landmark.

In spring of 1905, the big news in Paris was not the fate of the Eiffel Tower but the return of Guillaume Buffalo and his show on his last European tour. On April 2, Buffalo Bill, now fifty-nine, and his Wild West show and Congress of Rough Riders opened a triumphant two-month run to huge and ecstatic crowds. For this visit Cody's giant arena was built on the Champ de Mars in the very shadow of the Eiffel Tower. The Rough Riders camp was artfully landscaped, with the hundreds of large tents arrayed along broad sandy walkways. "In these paths I saw all of Paris strolling!" rhapsodized Monsieur Davenay of *Le Figaro*: "There was official Paris, diplomatic Paris, worldly Paris, theatrical Paris, artistic Paris, rubbernecking Paris, fashionable Paris, and those who were just curious. With all these Parisians convened in one place, it is a lot of people!"

As for the new show, Monsieur Davenay was almost speechless: "The Buffalo Bill who has returned to see us is a Buffalo considerably augmented, amplified, and multiplied. Where to begin, Sir? . . . With the marvelous maneuvers of the American cavalry? Or the fantastic equestrian exercises from the heroes of Fenimore Cooper? With the Cossacks? With the cowboys lassoing and riding wild horses? Perhaps you prefer the marvels of the Japanese fighters? . . . Buffalo is open! That is the cry heard everywhere yesterday in Paris."

As for the dapper Nate Salsbury, who had died the year before, his equestrian extravaganza lived on, enthralling the French. The artist Rosa Bonheur, who had painted Cody's favorite portrait, was also gone, having died of the flu in 1899 at age seventy-seven. But Cody had immortalized her in his own way by featuring Bonheur at her easel on one of his most famous show posters. On June 4, Cody's ad in *The Herald* declared his last performance in Paris: "Positively Farewell to Paris" and "Never Again in Paris." Despite rain and hail and thunder, the final shows were packed. The next morning Cody and his eight hundred players and horses boarded fifty railcars, each fifty-four feet long and eight feet wide, and headed for the French provinces, starting with two nights in the cathedral town of Chartres and then on to Cherbourg, Calais, and Lille, among others.

It so happened that on the day Buffalo Bill played his last shows in Paris, across the Channel, *New York Tribune* publisher Whitelaw Reid was arriving in London to become the new U.S. ambassador to the Court of St. James's. Sixteen years after he had dutifully served as U.S. minister to France during the 1889 World's Fair, Reid had finally secured the diplomatic post he truly desired. The family's new residence in London, Dorchester House on Park Lane, would also serve as the U.S. embassy, for its splendor was renowned. The London mansion had a famous interior white marble staircase, a magnificent ballroom and reception rooms, and a picture gallery. Its previous resident had been Shahzada, son of the Emir of Afghanistan.

While the Parisians still adored him, Buffalo Bill's star power was much diminished from the glory days of 1889. The American colony had not embraced him with the same patriotic fervor, for his show was no longer really concerned with the American frontier, nor was it the folkloric novelty it had once been. People were now more fascinated by motor cars and motion pictures. Even the Paris *Herald*, which had so passionately embraced Cody in 1889, gave him only perfunctory coverage. While this Paris run had been lucrative, a few subsequent weeks of inclement weather and the necessity of putting down two thirds of the show's horses stricken with glanders had wrought fiscal havoc. From Verdun, Cody would write on July 16 to his sister Julia: "I hope you are happy in your own home. Don't worry sister mine about paying for it. I am haveing hard times just now but I will win out—Can't down a man—that won't be downed. Can they Dear?"

Despite making huge sums in these years, Cody was in a perennial financial bind, for he was pouring money into his greatest pipe dream yet. Out in the new state of Wyoming, he and various partners were developing the sixty-thousand-acre Big Horn Basin farming and irrigation canal scheme. Ever the optimist, Cody rhapsodized that the Big Horn Basin was "the greatest land deal ever" and that he and his partners would retire there to "a big farm of our own that will . . . support us in our old age and we can lay under the trees and swap lies." Instead, the parched Wyoming projects sucked up far more money than water.

The centerpiece of Big Horn Basin was a new town at the fork of the Shoshone River that the colonel founded and named after himself: Cody, Wyoming. He was also underwriting a newspaper and various mining companies, and had dispatched his sister, Julia, sixty-two, to manage his elegant (and largely empty) new Irma Hotel. It did not become the boomtown he had envisioned, and one pastor's wife described it as having "only 1000 inhabitants and fully two miles away from the railroad station; hardly a tree and mostly one story buildings, wooden sidewalks, and a few lights at night. . . . Only two stores seem to keep everything. . . . No one ever knows when some man will be suddenly thrown out on the street from one of the saloons."

Notably absent from Paris and the European tour was Annie Oakley, now fifty-five. Injured when a Wild West train derailed in 1901, she had not returned to Cody's show, which more and more entailed long stretches of grueling one-night stands. She opted instead for a more leisurely life, performing only occasionally, competing in shooting meets, and visiting family and friends. Then, on August 11, 1903, she opened the Chicago Hearst newspaper to see the headline "ANNIE OAKLEY ASKS COURT FOR MERCY Famous Woman Crack Shot . . . Steals to Secure Cocaine." The article was picked up throughout the country, and while the offending newspapers ran journalistic mea culpas and apologies once the story was refuted, Oakley was not assuaged. She became embroiled in libel suits against fifty-five newspapers, testifying at one trial after another over the next five years until all had paid up.

In the spring of 1906, Gustave Eiffel rejoiced to learn that his beloved tower would receive a reprieve from the City of Paris, which extended his contract to 1915. The city's committee expressed no great enthusiasm, however, stating, "If [the Eiffel Tower] did not exist, one would probably not contemplate building it there, or even perhaps anywhere else; but it does exist." The attitude was very much a resigned "Since it is there, let it stay"—at least for an additional five years.

Energized by this victory, Eiffel expanded his investigations into the nature of wind and aviation. Seeking more control and precision, he built a large wind tunnel at the foot of the tower. There, he used the tower's generators to operate a fan system that blew a steady, powerful wind of up to forty miles an hour. He conducted thousands of experiments that helped in the redesign of the wings and propellers of airplanes. His book *The Resistance of the Air and Aviation* earned him the Smithsonian Institution's prestigious Langley Gold Medal in 1913.

By then, Eiffel no longer worried about the future of his tower. In early 1908 the French War Department had finally come around to his point of view. "The Government has begun the installation of an elaborate apparatus for wireless telegraphy in the Eiffel Tower," reported *The New York Times*, further describing "splendid results attained . . . messages were sent here direct from Morocco, a distance of about 2,000 kilometers. . . . [A]n instrument in [the] Eiffel Tower would prove most useful as a part of the national defense in time of war."

In August of 1911 Thomas Edison returned to Paris for the first time in twenty-two years. He, Mina, and their children, Madeleine and Charles, were embarked on that rare Edison activity: a family vacation. "I have just finished something new," he told the inevitable horde of reporters, "my talking pictures are complete; two hundred sets of them have been made and they are wonderful." Among the many subjects the usually loquacious Edison did *not* address was the Eiffel Tower and why America had not yet built something taller and better.

At one chic Paris restaurant, a fashionable woman asked, "Who is that shabby little man with the crowd around him?" When told it was Le Grand Edison, she said, "His clothes look as though they had cost about fifty francs, but he has a brain great enough to make him Emperor of France." The Edisons spent two busy months motoring through France, Switzerland, and Germany, and the great inventor had plenty to say about his experiences. As for Paris, it "impresses me favorably as the city of beautiful prospects, but not as a city of lights. New York is far more impressive at night." Edison reckoned he had covered almost two thousand miles during his travels, and thus felt well qualified to proclaim: "In France, the roads are the finest in the world. The fact is, France is one great park. The farms are splendid, and the people get twice as much out of an acre as we do in America." More ominously, when asked if he saw any signs of war, he confirmed what many feared, answering, "Yes, at every little mountain pass there was a fort with wire entanglements. The military was in evidence everywhere, in cities, villages, the countryside, and all."

Edison would never return to Paris, and spent his remaining two decades lionized in America as a national hero whose genius had bequeathed to the world the incandescent light, the delights of the phonograph, and, to a lesser degree, the marvels of the moving pictures.

In early August 1914 war came, as feared, to Europe. James Gordon Bennett's many automobiles, horses, and carriages (and the Jersey dairy cow from his Versailles estate) were requisitioned for the Gallic war effort, as were those of every French resident. Bennett, seventy-three, had no intention of abandoning Paris, and he could be seen walking daily to the offices of the Paris *Herald*, which he turned into a lifeline of information for the thousands of Americans initially stranded by the chaos of war. The reading room at 49 avenue de l'Opéra became the center for "Americans in Paris [to find] salient news of the war and the European situation."

Gustave Eiffel had long argued the strategic value of his thousand-foot tower, and during the early weeks of war he was vindicated. "In August 1914," recounts Eiffel Tower historian Joseph Harriss, "the tower's receiver captured a radio message from [German] General von der Marwitz," whose cavalry division was bearing down on Paris, except that he "had run out of feed for his horses and was unable to advance—intelligence that helped convince the French General Staff that the time had come for a decisive counterattack on the Marne."

In *The Herald*'s newsroom, "an editor kept track of the armies by sticking pins in a map, but when they came too close to Paris the editor fled." Not the pugnacious Bennett, however, for with almost all his staff gone by September, he simply took over as managing editor, while also working as a reporter. A great student of military strategy, he did not believe the Germans would take Paris, but he told his London correspondents that "he would keep on printing his paper . . . and if the Germans ever did get into Paris he would keep on printing it if they would let him. His example had a fine effect on the courage of the people." As the war dragged on and many Paris papers ceased publication altogether, Bennett began printing two front pages for *The Herald*—one in French and one in English. Back in America, he put the full might of *The New York Herald* into urging the United States to enter the war against Germany.

In these early years of the war, the Paris *Herald* was losing ever-greater sums, and though few were aware of it, Bennett could no longer easily absorb such losses. The sad truth was that by 1914 the glory days of *The New York Herald* were behind it. During the 1890s, when Joseph Pulitzer's *World* and William Randolph Hearst's *Journal-American* had been battling it out in downtown Park Row, Bennett's *Herald*, largely *hors de combat*, flourished. In 1893, he had moved the paper north to West Thirty-fifth Street, to a two-story Veronese palace designed by Stanford White. *The Herald*, with its uptown location and high-toned readership, captured much of the splashy advertising of the new nearby Macy's and Gimbel's department stores.

In 1906, however, Bennett decreed that *The New York Herald* would oppose rival publisher William Randolph Hearst's Democratic candidacy for governor of New York. When Hearst lost, he sought to punish Bennett. For years, *The Herald*'s personals columns had been known along Park Row as "the Whores' Daily Guide and Compendium." Bennett's editors had often warned their boss that "some day the personals would get him in trouble with the postal laws, that they were a constant affront to decent people. . . . The Commodore swept aside their warning memos. Those little ads kept him in yachts, champagne, and country estates, as well as helping to pay for the *Herald*'s costly foreign correspondence." Now avenging Hearst lieutenant S. S. Carvalho persuaded a federal grand jury to investigate.

The grand jurors had little trouble deciphering the intent of such typical *Herald* personals as: "A woman finds paddling her own canoe dreary task, seeks manly pilot," "Young lady, good figure, wants to pose for artists," or the dollar-a-line come-ons such as "chic Parisian ladies with cozy suites," "masseuses with highly magnetic manners," and "witty, affectionate ladies possessing beautiful figures, hair, teeth" seek "jolly sports" in search of "pleasant possibilities." On April 10, 1907, James Gordon Bennett and his newspaper were convicted and fined $25,000. The "indecent" personals were ordered halted, causing a great drop-off in revenue and circulation. Bennett's Gilded Age had come to an end.

The Herald was still profitable but was no longer the cash cow that had sustained Bennett's many extravagances. In 1915, a *Herald* reporter who had recently returned from wartime Paris was asked how Bennett was. "The old, drunken, money-spending Jim Bennett is dead. In his place had come a Scotch miser." Equally surprising had been Bennett's marriage on September 10, 1914, to Maud, the American widow of Baron de Reuter, a European news magnate.

Bennett was no longer young, and his stalwart publishing of the Paris *Herald* during the war years took its toll. However, not even World War I could persuade him to give up one of his more peculiar editorial whims—the daily appearance in the Paris *Herald* since December 24, 1899, of the exact same letter from "Old Philadelphia Lady": "I am anxious to find out the way to figure the temperature from Centigrade to Fahrenheit and vice-versa. In other words, I want to know, whenever I see the temperature designated on Centigrade's thermometer, how to find out what it would be on Fahrenheit's thermometer."

James Gordon Bennett did, however, give up a number of his other indulgences. In 1916, he sold his luxurious yacht *Lysistrata* to the Russian Red Cross. Perhaps he could no longer afford to maintain the one-hundred-man crew, or perhaps on a continent mired in trench warfare and slaughter, pleasure cruising was considered bad form. In the fall of 1917, Bennett went to visit the war wounded in a hospital in Paris and caught the flu. He and his wife retreated to the Villa Namouna on the Côte d'Azur in Beaulieu, where he could convalesce among the rose gardens, the lawn cluttered with ceramic and iron animal sculptures, and his beloved herd of tiny dogs. Bennett recovered, only to be stricken with pneumonia. He would remain at his villa, bedridden, until his death on May 14, 1918, at five thirty in the morning. James Gordon Bennett, Jr., died at the age of seventy-six with the great story of his final years—World War I—still unfinished.

The French newspapers genuinely mourned the loss of this noted American Francophile: "All Paris knew his tall, slim figure," declared an editorial in *Excelsior*, but what "stood out most prominently, especially at this time of universal upheaval, was his fervent friendship for France, which never failed and which strengthened in our hours of trial." "Gordon Bennett!" exclaimed *L'Heure*. "What an original figure and what memories! Never again shall we see the Napoleonic director of the *New York Herald*, the inventor of the 'grand reportage,' the man who sent Stanley in search of Livingstone. . . . It is a great pity, in all sincerity. And what a friend of France! What sound judgment! His Paris edition of the *Herald* was always a little chef-d'oeuvre of elegance."

While year after year, Cody's Rough Rider and Wild West show earned decent and sometimes even immense profits, Cody himself teetered, as ever, on the brink of fiscal calamity. When he failed to repay a $20,000 six-month loan from a ruthless scalawag named Henry Tammen, owner of the *Denver Post*, Buffalo Bill found himself in a kind of indentured servitude, working for Tammen's Sells-Floto Circus. On October 22, 1915, he reported to his sister Julia from Bryan, Texas: "This has been another long season 183 days given 366 performances traveled 16,878 miles. And with God's help I haven't missed a performance."

By the spring of 1916, Cody was his own boss once again, out in the hustings with "The Military Pageant Preparedness, 'Buffalo Bill' (himself) Combined with the 101 Ranch Shows." Some days, Johnny Baker worried that Cody, who wore a hairpiece to hide his baldness, would not manage to mount his horse, McKinley. But Cody was the quintessential trouper. "For four weeks we have had the hottest sweltering mucky sticky heat I ever experienced," he wrote Julia on August 1, 1916, from Amsterdam, New York. "And the epidemic among the children just paralised business. But I am still alive."

When the tour wrapped up on November 11 in Portsmouth, Virginia, Cody gratefully caught the train to Denver to visit his sister May, then continued on to Wyoming to pass Christmas at his beloved TE Ranch, before returning to Denver to seek new financing for his show. Although he was not well, he could not resist granting an interview to reporter Chauncey Thomas, who wrote, "The old scout was in pajamas and slippers, and over them was drawn a house coat. . . . Just the man himself standing there, waxen pale, his silver hair flowing down over his straight, square shoulders, his hand out in a last farewell. . . . It was the last time. I knew it; he knew it; we all knew it. But on the surface not a sign." On January 10, a few minutes after the noon hour, at the age of seventy, Buffalo Bill Cody died at his sister May's house, surrounded by his family. His passing was big news, and the occasion for national mourning. Twenty-five thousand people, including cowboys, Indians, and grizzled old scouts, paid their respects as he lay in state in the Colorado State Capitol.

Even in death, Buffalo Bill's fate was shaped by debt. He had reportedly wanted to be buried in the hills near Cody, Wyoming, but when Henry Tammen offered free burial and a grand monument atop Lookout Mountain, twenty miles from Denver, Mrs. Cody and Johnny Baker quickly agreed. That June the Cody family and friends reconvened in Denver to make the trek out to Lookout Mountain, where Cody would be interred in a vault blasted from solid rock. "For hours before the ceremony at the grave there was a steady procession of automobiles winding up the mountainside toward the summit. Several thousand persons, who came by trolley to Golden, at the foot of the mountain, climbed steep foot trails or trudged along the automobile road to Wildcat Point, where the burial was held. . . . At the conclusion of the service, a bugler sounded taps." The view, indeed, was magnificent, and from the peak one could see the plains of Colorado, Nebraska, Kansas, and Wyoming. But Tammen, true to form, never delivered on his promise of a monument.

As Cody's most recent and thorough biographer, Louis S. Warren, sums up his career: "In a time when America represented the future of the modern world in its exploding cities and its industrial power, Buffalo Bill brought together the wild, primitive parts of the American frontier—buffalo, elk, staged prairie fires, real Indians—and the astonishing promise of a technological future, in his show's modern gunplay, its glowing electric lights and brilliantly colored publicity. He represented the coming together of the old and new, nature and culture, the past and the future. He straddled the yawning chasms between worlds, and in doing so, rose to greater heights of fame than any American could have dreamed."

Annie Oakley was not in attendance for Buffalo Bill's final appearance, but she wrote the following appreciation: "William F. Cody was the kindest hearted, simplest, most loyal man I ever knew. He was the staunch-est friend. . . . I traveled with him for seventeen years. . . . It may seem strange that after the wonderful success attained that he should have died a poor man. But it wasn't a matter of any wonder to those that knew and worked with him . . . he never seemed to lose his trust in the nature of all men, and until his dying day was the easiest mark above ground for every kind of sneak and gold brick vender." Perhaps Cody was more of an average American than she thought—a decent man whose pie-in-the-sky dreams, optimism, and gullibility left him broke.

Annie Oakley and Frank Butler, financially comfortable from their glory days, had now settled into a good life working at two fashionable resorts—the Lakeview Hotel in Leesburg, Florida, and the Carolina Hotel in Pinehurst, North Carolina. "Annie enjoyed getting up at four in the morning and heading down to the stables for a fox hunt," writes biographer Shirl Kasper of these years. "She wore a tweed jacket, high boots, and a black, broad-brimmed hat. . . . The weekly hunts, Annie said, kept her 'vi-tal.' She raced at the Pinehurst jockey club, entered a setter named Roy in a dog show (and took first place in the pointer class), and, of course, went after the quail." She taught many women guests how to shoot, engaged in shooting matches from time to time, and enjoyed the convivial atmosphere of these busy holiday places. In the spring of 1926, she and Frank went home to Ohio and family, where Oakley died peacefully at age sixty-six in Greenville on November 3.

When armistice finally came to a war-weary Europe, Gustave Eiffel, eighty-six, watched with satisfaction as the public once again flocked to his famous tower, which had been closed for military use through 1918. Now half a million visitors ascended its heights each year, more than double the prewar number. Above all, the great engineer relished the fact that despite so many boasts, no individual or nation had managed to construct a struc-ture that came close to topping his beloved tower in height. Nor could it be asserted any longer that the tower was impractical or useless.

"The tower," he wrote in his memoir, "is the principal work of M. Eiffel and appears as a symbol of force and difficulties overcome. [The tower's] construction itself was a marvel of precision, all the more important since its height surpassed by a great deal that of all the edifices built till this time. . . . This monument, constructed on the Champ de Mars on the occasion of the Exposition Universelle of 1889, was the main attraction of that fair, as it was again for the fair of 1900. Millions of people from all the countries visited it, and reproductions of every kind are spread all over the world." Eiffel finished this memoir in September of 1923, and presented a typed copy to each of his five grown children. Three months later, two days after Christmas, he succumbed to a series of strokes at the age of ninety-one.

"I ought to be jealous of the tower," he once protested half seriously. "It is much more famous than I am. People seem to think it is my only work, whereas I have done other things after all."

Before we bid adieu to the dramatis personae of the Paris World's Fair of 1889, let us examine how time has dealt with some of them.

Did Vincent and Theo van Gogh ever envision that Vincent's paintings from his years in Provence and Auvers would become some of the most beloved, familiar, and valuable images in the world? Could Dr. Gachet have dreamed, as he sat for two portraits by van Gogh, that one day, in the final years of the twentieth century, one of them would sell at auction for $82.5 million?

One can more easily imagine Paul Gauguin concluding that the exalted status and stratospheric prices of his art were long overdue.

As for James McNeill Whistler, he would have expected his art to be sought after and admired, as it indeed is. But he would be furious to learn that contemporaries such as van Gogh and Gauguin had so eclipsed him—in status, prestige, and prices.

After James Gordon Bennett's death, Ogden Mills Reid, son of Whitelaw Reid and by then publisher of *The New York Tribune*, eventually came into ownership of *The New York Herald* and, of course, its European edition. No one would have been more amused and pleased than the imperious Commodore to see the Paris-based *International Herald-Tribune* outlast every New York paper of his day except *The New York Times*, which came to own it. The *International Herald-Tribune*'s readership of 240,000 is not huge, but it is very influential.

One suspects that Annie Oakley might object somewhat to her brassy portrayal in the Broadway musical and Hollywood movie that have most famously preserved her fame and legend, *Annie Get Your Gun*. But as a longtime star, she could only have approved of her story becoming a classic in American entertainment.

As for Buffalo Bill, he remains an amazingly enduring American icon, hugely popular, much loved, his myth and persona kept alive over the decades through television, movies, and his very own town. Cody, Wyoming, population nine thousand, is "a small western town with a big city attitude" that keeps the memory and spirit of Buffalo Bill alive through its museums, horse culture, rodeos, and Irma Hotel. Fittingly, the Wild West show lives on in Paris at EuroDisney, while the French love affair with the American West is undiminished.

And Gustave Eiffel, as he predicted, is now largely forgotten, while his *Tour en Fer* has become only more famous with the passing years. It is probably safe to proclaim Eiffel's tower the most celebrated and instantly recognizable structure in the world, as well as the ubiquitous and undisputed symbol of Paris and French culture. All this would undoubtedly have pleased Eiffel the engineer—as would knowing that it took four decades before another building topped his 1,000-foot tower. In 1929, the skyscraping Chrysler Building in New York surpassed the Eiffel Tower, at 1,046 feet. Chrysler's reign proved to be short-lived, for two years later the Empire State Building became the tallest building in the world, at 1,250 feet.

Eiffel was sufficiently the patriot that he, above all others, would have gloried in how completely his tower became the symbol of France. Nothing better illustrates this than the story of the final days of World War II in Paris.

"Lucien Sarniguet, a forty-five-year-old captain in the Paris fire department," relates Joseph Harriss, "had had the duty of lowering the French flag from the tower's mast for the last time the morning of June 13, 1940. At that time he had vowed to himself to be the first to raise the tricolor when the occupation ended. Now, having eagerly followed, through the clandestine radio broadcasts of the Resistance, the advance of Leclerc's Second Armored, Sarniguet judged that August 25 would be the crucial battle for Paris and he intended to boost French morale the best way he knew." He prepared by fashioning a large *tricoleur* from old bedsheets dyed with "weak wartime dyes of red and blue."

On the morning of August 25, as a battle raged around the nearby

The Eiffel Tower in 1932, an iconic symbol of Paris

École Militaire, Sarniguet and three fellow firemen arrived at the foot of the Eiffel Tower and began their ascent of the 1,671 steps. "When the Germans [at the École Militaire] saw Sarniguet's group climbing the stairs they opened fire on them, sending bullets ricocheting through the tower's iron beams. But what Sarniguet saw above him was worse, in a very personal sense, than the danger from German rifle fire: two other men were already halfway up the stairs with a flag in their arms. He bounded up the steps three at a time but could not catch the others, personnel from the nearby French Naval Museum. Trembling with fatigue and frustration just below the top, Sarniguet watched as the two raised the French flag on the Eiffel Tower for the first time in four years. Then, suddenly forgetting his disappointment, he found himself grinning and hugging the men who had beat him to the top—the occupation was over, as every Parisian knew who saw the tricolor snapping defiantly that afternoon atop their proud tower."

Strikingly, the Eiffel Tower's fame and allure have only grown with the passing decades. In 1889, the year when Monsieur Eiffel so triumphantly first held court high in his aerie, more than two million people came to ascend the tower. That figure would not be matched again until 1965. And yet, as the tower marks its 120th anniversary, six million visitors annually wait in long lines for the pleasure of communing with the landmark. What accounts for its enduring glamor and popularity, for its mystique and ubiquity as a globalized image?

Mega-skyscrapers long ago overshadowed the Eiffel Tower's status as the world's tallest structure. Yet no other man-made artifact has ever rivaled the tower's potent mixture of spare elegance, amazing enormity and complexity when experienced firsthand. The gargantuan wrought-iron skeleton provokes awe as it lays bare the details of Eiffel's practical engineering genius. The Eiffel Tower, with its sheer aerial playfulness and charm, literally comes to life as crowds clamber up and down its stairs and elevators, and dine and eat and flirt aloft on its platforms high in the sky. And, of course, when visitors feel that frisson of unease as they gaze far below to the panorama of Paris. The tower still serves as a lofty stage for all manner of stunts and derring-do, the occasional starting point for the Tour de France bicycle race, and the ultimate launching pad for Gallic celebratory pyrotechnics. The Eiffel Tower still speaks uniquely to the human fascination with science and technology *and* to the human desire for pleasure and joie de vivre. In 1889, Jules Simon, the republican politician and philosopher, declared, "We are all citizens of the Eiffel Tower," a sentiment as true today as it was then.

ACKNOWLEDGMENTS

Working on *Eiffel's Tower* has been a pleasure from start to finish. So many people have been helpful in so many ways. As ever, I have enjoyed working with Rick Kot, my delightful editor at Viking, and my always wonderful agent, Eric Simonoff of Janklow & Nesbit.

In Cody, Wyoming, home of the excellent Buffalo Bill Historical Center and McCracken Research Library, I first met Paul Fees, world expert on Buffalo Bill and Annie Oakley. We spent a lovely day visiting Yellowstone and various Cody sites, as he answered innumerable questions. Subsequently, Paul Fees graciously continued to share his knowledge, and kindly reviewed my manuscript. Thanks to his efforts, collector Michael Del Castello generously lent me Buffalo Bill's personal Paris scrapbook.

At the McCracken Research Library, Juti Winchester shared her files and enthusiasm, while Ann Marie Donoghue helped with photos.

In Cody, Jim and Mary Crow at the Lambright Place Bed and Breakfast could not have been kinder, serving not only breakfast but evening cocktails and dinner, too.

Before I traveled to Paris, our family friend Harold Lubell engaged in advance research in the Eiffel Archives at the Musée d'Orsay. Madame Caroline Mathieu, chief conservator at the Musée d'Orsay, was most welcoming and helpful, as was archivist Fabrice Golec. There, fellow researchers Pascale Copart and Mirek Malevski were amusing companions whom I thank for a memorable champagne lunch.

While I do not know the names of the research librarians who assisted me in the Bibliothèque Nationale de France, their help was invaluable. My Paris research sojourn was made especially enjoyable by the comings and goings of family and friends. I thank them for all the meals together and treasured memories.

Once again, I had the pleasure of working with Thomas Edison expert Paul Israel. This time I finally met him in person while visiting the archive at Rutgers, which he supervises. Over the course of this book, Israel answered multiple queries, and again helped me navigate the vast collection of Edison material in the extraordinary online Edison archive. And finally, he kindly read the whole manuscript and offered very useful criticism. I feel fortunate to have worked on two books with such a generous scholar.

Much of my day-in and day-out library work is accomplished at the Milton S. Eisenhower Library at Johns Hopkins University, where I received my Ph.D. So, once again I am very indebted to the dedicated librarians there who over the years have always gone out of their way to secure books, articles, and information. Librarian Paul A. Espinosa helped me time and again when I was working at Hopkins's magnificent Peabody Library.

Many first-class librarians at the Library of Congress exerted themselves on my behalf in the newspaper room, the Prints and Photograph Division, the Rare Books and Manuscripts Division, and the reading rooms. Likewise, at the University of Pennsylvania Dental School's Leon Levy Library, librarian Patricia Heller went above and beyond as I researched Dr. Thomas Evans, dentist to royalty.

My old friend Judith Weinstein came to my rescue when I needed articles from 1889 French newspapers available only at the Center for Research Libraries in Chicago. Gioia Diliberto, another Chicago friend, offered advice garnered from research for her Parisian novels. Anne Bolton, old friend and expert on French sculpture, educated me on the world of *animalier* art. Steve Showers, corporate archivist at Otis, was very helpful with materials concerning their Eiffel Tower elevators, including many old photographs. At the Garst Museum in Greenville, Ohio, Brenda Arnett kindly provided one of their Annie Oakley photos. My friend and neighbor Cyndy Serfas generously helped organize my many digital photos. I deeply appreciated this act of efficiency and kindness, as did Laura Tisdel, the Viking editorial assistant whom I thank for keeping all things running smoothly as the manuscript became a book.

I'd like to thank another friend and neighbor, artist Ellen Burchenal, who read an early version of *Eiffel's Tower* and offered advice. Eiffel scholar Professor Miriam Levin of Case Western Reserve also critiqued the first draft, and I much appreciated her suggestions. And, of course, my husband, Christopher Ross, read the manuscript, and made me happy by laughing quite a bit as he did. When *Eiffel's Tower* was in a near final form, Jenna Dolan was its able copy editor.

And final thanks to old friends Bob and Peggy Sarlin, who continue to be gracious hosts when I go to Manhattan.

I should also note that I have translated the French articles and books into English.

NOTES

CHAPTER ONE: *We Meet Our Characters, Who Intend to Dazzle the World at the Paris Exposition*

1 *"The sitting-room"*: "The Woman Rifle Expert," *Chicago Tribune*, Jan. 13, 1888, p. 6.

2 *"I rolled under an iron gate"*: Ibid.

2 *"She looked innocent"*: Shirl Kasper, *Annie Oakley* (Oklahoma City: University of Oklahoma Press, 1992), p. 22.

2 *"I will practice"*: "The Woman Rifle Expert."

2 *"We will show our sons"*: Joseph Harriss, *The Tallest Tower* (Boston: Houghton-Mifflin, 1975), p. 10.

2 *"an advertisement for the Republican"*: Jean Gatot, "The Magnificent Exposition Universelle of 1889," *World's Fair* (Winter 1984): 16.

4 *"You elected me"*: Stanley Weintraub, *Whistler: A Biography* (New York: Weybright and Talley, 1974), pp. 318–19.

5 *"The few works I have sold"*: *Gauguin by Himself*, Belinda Thomson, ed. (Boston: Little, Brown, 1993), p. 75.

5 *"Not Greek, not Gothic"*: Michel Carmona, *Eiffel* (Paris: Fayard, 2002), p. 296.

6 *"frictionless floating ring"*: Harriss, *The Tallest Tower*, p. 10.

6 *"one of the most extraordinary"*: Daniel Bermond, *Gustave Eiffel* (Paris: Perrin, 2002), p. 249.

6 *"Politics have done much"*: "The Paris Exhibition," *Engineering*, May 3, 1889, p. 415.

7 *"as an abomination"*: "The French Exposition," *Chicago Tribune*, Aug. 6, 1888, p. 4.

7 *"as educator, benefactor"*: Gatot, "The Magnificent Exposition Universelle of 1889," p. 14.

7 *"We will celebrate"*: Gustave Eiffel, "The Eiffel Tower," *Annual Report of the Board of Regents of the Smithsonian Institution* (Washington, D.C.: GPO, 1890), p. 736.

8 *"For a long time"*: Max de Nansouty, "Centenaire de 1789," *Le génie civil: Revue générale des industries françaises et étrangères* 6, no. 7 (Dec. 13, 1884): 108–9.

8 *"eight thousand kinds of chemicals"*: Matthew Josephson, *Edison: A Biography* (New York: McGraw-Hill, 1959), p. 315.

8 *"Have nothing to do with them"*: Ibid., p. 318.

9 *"The 'talking machine'"*: "Another Edison Triumph," *New York Times*, May 12, 1888, p. 8.

9 *"New Shirt yesterday devoured"*: "Where Dogs Are Disappearing," *New York Times*, June 28, 1888, p. 2.

9 *"I am tired out"*: *Letters from Buffalo Bill*, Stella Foote, ed. (Billings, Mont.: Foote Publishing, 1954), p. 14.

10 *"fine equipages"*: A. A. Anderson, *Experiences and Impressions* (New York: Macmillan Co., 1933), p. 21.

11 *"Draw a thousand pounds"*: Charles L. Robertson, *The International Herald Tribune* (New York: Columbia University Press, 1987), pp. 15–16.

11 *"down the aisle, yanking"*: Richard O'Connor, *The Scandalous Mr. Bennett* (Garden City, N.Y.: Doubleday, 1962), p. 153.

12 *"Beneath his thin veneer of civilization"*: Don Seitz, *The James Gordon Bennetts* (New York: Bobbs-Merrill Co., 1928), p. 270.

13 *"a national exhibition as the world"*: "The Paris Exhibition of 1889," *Engineering*, Dec. 16, 1887, p. 627.

13 *"finds Europeans very ignorant"*: Henry James, "Americans . . ." *The Nation*, Oct. 3, 1878, p. 209.

13 *"to put American ideas"*: Al Laney, *Paris Herald* (New York: Appleton-Century, 1947), p. 19.

14 *"France has neither winter"*: Albert Bigelow Paine, *Mark Twain* (New York: Harper and Bros., 1912), p. 642.

14 *"I think that you should make a display"*: Letter from Francis Upton to Thomas Edison, dated Aug. 1, 1888, Thomas A. Edison Papers Digital Edition, D8842AAK, Rutgers University.

CHAPTER TWO: *Gustave Eiffel and "the Odious Column of Bolted Metal"*

15 *"magnificent panorama"*: Gustave Eiffel, "The Eiffel Tower," *Annual Report of the Board of Regents of the Smithsonian Institution* (Washington, D.C.: GPO, 1890), p. 734.

15 *"infinitesimally out of plane"*: Harriss, *The Tallest Tower*, p. 60.

16 *"an inartistic . . . scaffolding"*: Bermond, *Gustave Eiffel*, p. 256.

16 *"a man of taste"*: Ibid., pp. 258–59.

18 *"nothing more nor less than a German Jew"*: Ibid., p. 267.

19 *"Please be good enough"*: Harriss, *The Tallest Tower*, p. 60.

19 *"I would be satisfied with a girl"*: Ibid., p. 37.

20 *"Just in two or three days"*: Bermond, *Gustave Eiffel*, pp. 135–36.

20 *"Our poor Laure"*: Ibid., p. 136.

20 *"Marguerite is"*: Ibid., p. 193.

21 *"a distinctive character"*: Henri Loyrette, *Gustave Eiffel* (New York: Rizzoli, 1985), p. 116.

21 *"The interior was richly"*: Robert H. Sherard, *Twenty Years in Paris* (London: Hutchinson and Co., 1906), p. 166.

21 *"A program has already been"*: Eiffel, "The Eiffel Tower," *Annual Report of the Board of Regents*, p. 735.

22 *"Was it sensible"*: Loyrette, *Gustave Eiffel*, p. 119.

22 *"These foundations"*: Gustave Eiffel to Édouard Lockroy, Dec. 22, 1886, ARO 1981 1253 (5) Eiffel Archives, Musée d'Orsay, Paris.

23 *"anti-artistic"*: Bermond, *Gustave Eiffel*, p. 263.

23 *"an extraordinary thing"*: Ibid., p. 265.

23 *"wild only about the giddy"*: Rastignac, "Eiffel," *L'Illustration*, Nov. 13, 1886, p. 3.

23 *"She holds that the building"*: "To Cease Building the Tower," *New York Times*, Nov. 29, 1886, p. 2.

25 *"Today I must tell you"*: Gustave Eiffel to Édouard Lockroy, Dec. 22, 1886, ARO 1981 1253 (5) Eiffel Archive, Musée d'Orsay, Paris.

25 *"showed that the subsoil"*: Eiffel, "The Eiffel Tower," *Annual Report of the Board of Regents*, p. 731.

26 *"I watched an army"*: *The Eiffel Tower: A Tour de Force, Its Centennial Exhibition*, Phillip Dennis Cate, ed. (New York: Grolier Club, 1989), p. 28.

26 *"a lighthouse, a nail"*: "La Tour Eiffel," *L'Illustration*, Feb. 5, 1887, p. 3.

26 *"dizzily ridiculous tower"*: Harriss, *The Tallest Tower*, p. 21.

27 *"I believe that the tower"*: "The Big Tower for Paris," *New York Times*, March 3, 1887, p. 2.

28 *"may be used as a pretext"*: Harriss, *The Tallest Tower*, p. 24.

28 *"each pier would rest"*: Ibid., p. 58.

29 *"The descent is a strange experience"*: Gaston Tissandier, *The Eiffel Tower* (London: Sampson Low, Marston, Searle, and Rivington, 1889), p. 27.

30 *"By means of these"*: Eiffel, "The Eiffel Tower," *Annual Report of the Board of Regents*, p. 731.

30 *"Soon the elephant's"*: Loyrette, *Gustave Eiffel*, p. 138.

31 *"250 workmen came"*: Rene Poirier, *Fifteen Wonders of the World* (New York: Random House, 1961), p. 252.

31 *"The position of each"*: William A. Eddy, "The Highest Structure in the World," *Atlantic Monthly*, June 1889, pp. 726–27.

31 *"When we approach it"*: Tissandier, *The Eiffel Tower*, p. 94.

32 *"there was virtually no experience"*: Robert M. Vogel, "Elevator Systems of the Eiffel Tower, 1889," *United States National Museum Bulletin* 228 (Washington, D.C.: Smithsonian, 1961), p. 2.

32 *"Young man, your future career"*: Robertson, *The International Herald Tribune*, p. 19.

33 *"Who but Chamberlain"*: O'Connor, *The Scandalous Mr. Bennett*, p. 209.

33 *"I want you fellows"*: Robertson, *The International Herald Tribune*, p. 20.

33 *"watching the never-ending procession"*: Raymond Rudorff, *Belle Époque: Paris in the Nineties* (London: Hamish Hamilton, 1972), p. 32.

35 *"This is not a new newspaper"*: Robertson, *The International Herald Tribune*, p. 3.

36 *"predicted flatly"*: Harriss, *The Tallest Tower*, p. 69.

36 *"I had never believed"*: Ibid., p. 157.

37 *"The Tower Is Sinking"*: Ibid., pp. 69–70.

38 *"If a column"*: Ibid., p. 68.

38 *"Despite all the snowfalls"*: "Visit to the Eiffel Tower Work," *L'Illustration*, March 3, 1888, p. 31.

38 *"Joined by a belt"*: Harriss, *The Tallest Tower*, p. 76.

CHAPTER THREE: *Troubles on the Tower*

41 *"the oyster peddler"*: Norma Evenson, *Paris: City of Change, 1878–1978* (New Haven, Conn.: Yale University Press, 1979), p. 20.

41 *"so frisky, so affable"*: Mark Twain, *The Travels of Mark Twain* (New York: Howard-McCann, 1961), pp. 155–56.

41 *"M. Eiffel's Tower of Babel"*: "M. Eiffel's Big Tower," *New York Times*, May 18, 1888, p. 6.

42 *"The four cranes"*: Poirier, *Fifteen Wonders of the World*, p. 252.

42 *"Each piece"*: Harriss, *The Tallest Tower*, p. 62.

42 *"a chunk of coarse bread"*: "Boulanger's New Contest," *New York Times*, Jan. 27, 1889, p. 10.

43 *"People who have watched"*: Harriss, *The Tallest Tower*, p. 69.

43 *"Paris is making great preparations"*: "Jennie June Abroad," *Godey's Lady's Book* 117, no. 699 (Sept. 1888): 240.

44 *"it will be, when completed"*: Ibid.

45 *"On the Left Bank"*: Caroline Mathieu, *Paris in the Age of Impressionism* (New York: Harry Abrams, 2003), p. 22.

45 *"The beginning was difficult"*: Eiffel, "The Eiffel Tower," *Annual Report of the Board of Regents*, p. 735.

46 *"a grandiose marvel"*: "Next Year's Big Show," *New York Times*, May 6, 1888, p. 10.

47 *"Friend Gouraud"*: Letter from Thomas Edison to George Gouraud, dated June 12, 1888, Thomas A. Edison Papers Digital Edition [TAED], Rutgers University.

48 *"Rumors were afloat"*: "Work on the Eiffel Tower," *New York Times*, Sept. 8, 1888, p. 16.

48 *"There was snow"*: Bermond, *Gustave Eiffel*, p. 296.

49 *"After the second platform"*: Eugène-Melchior de Vogüé, *Remarques sur l'exposition du centenaire* (Paris: Librairie Plon, 1889), p. 15.

49 *"The professional risks remained"*: Loyrette, *Gustave Eiffel*, p. 149.

51 *"Were those workmen specially trained?"*: Tissandier, *The Eiffel Tower*, pp. 38–39.

51 *"Their workmates laughed"*: Loyrette, *Gustave Eiffel*, p. 149.

51 *"the Americans"*: Eiffel, "The Eiffel Tower," *Annual Report of the Board of Regents*, p. 729.

52 *"the Washington shaft"*: "Big Bait for Yankees," *New York Times*, Feb. 25, 1889, p. 4.

52 *"The public may go up"*: "Next Year's Big Show," p. 10.

52 *"Your role herein"*: *Whistler on Art*, Nigel Thorp, ed. (Manchester, U.K.: Fyfield Books, 1994), pp. 111–12.

52 *"I am burning with desire"*: Letter from J. M. Whistler to Robert de Montesquiou-Fezensac, dated May 24/25, 1888, Centre for Whistler Studies, Glasgow University Library, Online Archive, Glasgow University, http://www.whistler.arts.gla.ac.uk/correspondence.

53 *"cultivated upward-pointed mustaches"*: Weintraub, *Whistler*, p. 347.

53 *"The room of all shades of red"*: Edgar Munhall, *Whistler and Montesquiou: The Butterfly and the Bat* (Paris: Flammarion, 1995), p. 36.

54 *"I want a side board"*: *Letters from Buffalo Bill*, p. 24.

54 *"Lulu has got most"*: Ibid., p. 18.

55 *"unerring aim"*: Kasper, *Annie Oakley*, pp. 100–101.

55 *"Annie Oakley defeats John Lavett"*: Annie Oakley, *The Autobiography of Annie Oakley* (Greenville, Ohio: Darke County Historical Society, 2006), p. 36.

56 *"It's strange"*: *Gauguin by Himself*, pp. 97–99.

56 *"It is amazing"*: Chris Stolwijk and Richard Thomson, *Theo van Gogh* (Zwolle: Waanders, 1999), p. 45.

56 *"You can ask Pissarro"*: *Gauguin by Himself*, p. 95.

57 *"All things considered"*: Ibid., pp. 94–95.

57 *"My situation here"*: Martin Gayford, *The Yellow House* (Boston: Little, Brown, 2006), p. 271.

58 *"sunflowers against a yellow background"*: *Gauguin by Himself*, pp. 97–99.

58 *"picturesque, rat-infested street"*: O'Connor, *The Scandalous Mr. Bennett*, p. 185.

58 *"a glittering cortège"*: Rudorff, *Belle Époque*, p. 34.

59 *"His hot temper"*: Joseph I. C. Clarke, *My Life and Memories* (New York: Dodd, Mead and Co., 1925), p. 143.

59 *"What in hell"*: O'Connor, *The Scandalous Mr. Bennett*, p. 166.

59 *"was handsome, he had fine whiskers"*: Rudorff, *Belle Époque*, p. 23.

60 *"We enjoy having you"*: Laney, *Paris Herald*, pp. 28–29.

61 *"huge crowds gathered"*: Rudorff, *Belle Époque*, pp. 25–26.

61 *"the late cold snap"*: "Boulanger's New Contest," p. 10.

62 *"It is impossible!"*: David McCullough, *The Path Between the Seas* (New York: Touchstone, 1977), p. 202.

CHAPTER FOUR: *"The First Elevator of Its Kind"*

65 *"Desolation on desolation!"*: Hugues Le Roux, "The First Ascent of the Eiffel Tower," *Current Literature* 2, no. 5 (May 1889): 386.

68 *"congratulations were coming in"*: Ibid.

69 *"The curvature of the Tower's legs"*: Vogel, "Elevator Systems of the Eiffel Tower," p. 24.

70 *"[We] have shipped our products"*: Jason Goodwin, *Otis: Giving Rise to the Modern City* (Chicago: Ivan R. Dee, 2001), pp. 66–67.

70 *"Yes, this is the first elevator"*: Vogel, "Elevator Systems of the Eiffel Tower," p. 24.

71 *"the perfect safety"*: Ibid.

71 *"Meantime . . . we examined the Tower"*: Report of Chief Otis Engineer Thomas Brown, 1888, Otis Corporate Archives, Farmington, Conn.

72 *"I should favor"*: Letter from W. E. Hale to Charles Otis, dated Feb. 16, 1888, Otis Corporate Archives, Farmington, Conn.

73 *"You forget that"*: Letter from Charles Otis to Gustave Eiffel, dated Feb. 18, 1889, Otis Corporate Archives, Farmington, Conn.

73 *"an ingenious modification"*: Vogel, "Elevator Systems of the Eiffel Tower," p. 24.

74 *"Keep right ahead"*: O'Connor, *The Scandalous Mr. Bennett*, pp. 214–15.

75 *"you have lost all confidence"*: Letter from Charles Otis to Gustave Eiffel, dated Feb. 18, 1889, Otis Corporate Archives, Farmington, Conn.

77 *"Fine! Wonderful!"*: Oakley, *The Autobiography of Annie Oakley*, p. 19.

77 *"I had Jerry, the big moose"*: Ibid., p. 26.

77 *"Tons of beautiful flowers"*: Ibid., pp. 28–30.

79 *"On the highest point reached"*: "Eiffel's Tower of Babel," p. 12.

79 *"a rumor that [the Eiffel Tower]"*: "The Eiffel Tower," *The Engineer*, Jan. 11, 1889, p. 39.

80 *"thick coal tar smoke"*: Bertrand Lemoine, *La Tour de Monsieur Eiffel* (Paris: Gallimard, 1989), p. 45.

80 *"As soon as it was possible"*: de Vogüé, *Remarques sur l'Exposition du centenaire*, pp. 16–17. This translation is from *The Eiffel Tower: A Tour de Force*, Phillip Dennis Cate, ed. (New York: Grolier, 1989), p. 50.

81 *"merits, or otherwise"*: "Fritz," *The Eiffel Tower* (London: F. C. Hagen and Co., 1889), Box 60/brochures/Eiffel Archives, Musée d'Orsay, Paris.

81 *"How many times"*: Tissandier, *The Eiffel Tower*, pp. 82–83.

82 *"pen, pencil, and brush"*: Richard Kaufman, *Paris of To-day*, excerpted in Cate, ed., *The Eiffel Tower: A Tour de Force*, p. 51.

82 *"the Eiffel Tower mania"*: Ibid.

82 *"the practicality and methodical* sang-froid*"*: Max de Nansouty, "Gustave Eiffel," *Revue illustrée* 6, no. 62 (July 1, 1888): 6.

82–83 *"The form suggested the ugliest"*: "The Eiffel Tower," *Times* (London), April 1, 1889, p. 5.

84 *"Their idea of the American"*: "The Paris Exposition, III," *New York Daily Tribune*, June 23, 1889, p. 14.

CHAPTER FIVE: **In Which the Artists Quarrel and the Tower Opens**

86 *"Whistler, if you were not a genius"*: Weintraub, *Whistler*, p. 345.

86 *"I am Mr. Whistler"*: James M. Whistler, *The Gentle Art of Making Enemies* (New York: G. P. Putnam and Sons, 1904), pp. 266–67.

89 *"Mounts Valérien, Montmartre"*: "Sur La Tour Eiffel," *Le Figaro*, April 1, 1889, p. 1.

90 *"We salute the flag"*: "Above the World," *New York Herald*, European edition, April 1, 1889, p. 1.

90 *"an elegant little lunch"*: "Upon the Eiffel Tower," *New York Herald*, European edition, April 2, 1889, p. 1.

91 *"decided to inscribe in letters of gold"*: Eiffel, "The Eiffel Tower," *Annual Report of the Board of Regents*, p. 733.

92 *"Bravo!"*: *Gauguin by Himself*, p. 102.

92 *"At first"*: John Rewald, *Post-Impressionism* (New York: MOMA, 1978), p. 258.

93 *"excessive drinking"*: Gayford, *The Yellow House*, p. 296.

93 *"moods of indescribable"*: Ibid., p. 298.

93 *"Only remember"*: *Gauguin by Himself*, p. 102.

93 *"the State increasingly protected"*: Ibid., p. 108.

93 *"The fear and horror"*: The Complete Letters of Vincent van Gogh* (Boston: New York Graphic Society, 1978), pp. 170 and 173.

94 *"'making a great deal of money'"*: Letter from Samuel Insull to Alfred O. Tate, dated Oct. 16, 1888, TAED (D8850AD01), Rutgers University.

94 *"I am astonished"*: Josephson, *Edison*, p. 326.

95 *"Without doubt"*: Letter from Thomas Edison to George Gouraud, dated March 5, 1889, TAED (LB028520), Rutgers University.

95 *"I have placed Mr. W. J. Hammer"*: Letter from Thomas Edison to George Gouraud, dated Dec. 19, 1888, TAED (LB027491), Rutgers University.

95 *"anyone who wishes"*: Letter from George Gouraud to Thomas Edison, dated March 26, 1889, TAED (D8946AAW), Rutgers University.

95 *"Refuse absolutely"*: Cablegram from Thomas Edison to George Gouraud, dated April 8, 1889, TAED (LB029010), Rutgers University.

95 *"a small charge of admission"*: Letter from George Gouraud to Thomas Edison, dated April 12, 1889, TAED (LB029076), Rutgers University.

95 *"Make no arrangement"*: Cablegram from Thomas Edison to W. J. Hammer, dated April 19, 1889, TAED (LB029155), Rutgers University.

95 *"threatens to bring the enterprise"*: Letter from Thomas Edison to George Gouraud, dated April 20, 1889, TAED (LB029180), Rutgers University.

96 *"congregate at the Palais de l'Industrie"*: Edward Simmons, *From Seven to Seventy* (New York: Harper's, 1922), pp. 125–26.

96 *"Everyone of importance"*: Ibid.

97 *"Whenever Chauchard's"*: Rudorff, *Belle Époque*, p. 105.

97 *"I never in my life"*: *Americans in Paris* (Oklahoma City: Oklahoma City Museum of Art, 2003), pp. 22–23.

98 *"three prying scribblers"*: "Music in the Air," *New York Herald*, European edition, Oct. 7, 1889, p. 1; "Hawkins Hits Back," *New York Herald*, European edition, Oct. 8, 1889, p. 1.

99 *"Paris is going into raptures"*: "The Eiffel Tower," *New York Tribune*, May 9, 1889, p. 1.

99 *"Eiffel Towers of every size"*: "The Eiffel Tower," *New York Times*, Aug. 11, 1889, p. 11.

99 *"As an enormous and skillful monument"*: "The Show That Paris Is," *New York Times*, May 26, 1889, p. 12.

100 *"monstrous erection"*: "The Completion of the Eiffel Tower," *Times* (London), April 2, 1889, p. 9.

100 *"fever of festivity"*: "The French Exposition," *New York Tribune*, May 5, 1889, p. 1.

100 *"Haven't we had enough"*: "Buffalo Bill in Paris," no date, Buffalo Bill's Wild West Paris scrapbook, McCracken Research Library, Buffalo Bill Historical Center, Cody, Wyoming.

101 *"We were there early"*: "Observations Abroad," *Christian Advocate* 64, no. 22 (May 30, 1889): p. 342.

101 *"[British ambassador] Lord Lytton"*: "The Paris Exhibition," *New York Tribune*, May 5, 1889, p. 1.

102 *"the exhibits in an imperfect state"*: "Observations Abroad," p. 342.

102 *"humanistic, philanthropic"*: Gatot, "The Magnificent Exposition Universelle of 1889," p. 15.

102 *"palace of the Argentine Republic"*: Edyth Kirkwood, "The Paris Exposition," *Arthur's Home Magazine* 59 (Sept. 1889): 799.

102 *"There are fifty or sixty Egyptian donkeys"*: "Observations Abroad," p. 342.

104 *"all aspects of French industry"*: John W. Stamper, "The Galerie des Machines of the 1889 Paris World's Fair," *Technology and Culture* 30, no. 2 (April 1989): 347.

104 *"The Exposition has been opened"*: Letter from W. J. Hammer to Francis Upton, dated May 13, 1889, TAED (D8946ABo), Rutgers University.

104 *"as his solitary picture"*: "American Art in Paris," *New York Times*, June 16, 1889, p. 11.

105 *"The walks are broad"*: "Paris and the Great Fair," *New York Times*, Aug. 3, 1889, p. 5.

105 *"We stood before a grating"*: Twain, *Travels of Mark Twain*, p. 161.

106 *"actors and singers"*: Rudorff, *Belle Époque*, p. 72.

106 *"He would gaze"*: Ibid., p. 77.

106 *"an arrogant and brutal voice"*: Ibid.

106 *"and the hint"*: Ibid., p. 65.

107 *"antique furniture"*: Ibid., p. 67.

107 *"might drop off where"*: Rita Napier, "Across the Big Water: American Indians' Perceptions of Europe and Europeans, 1887–1906," in *Indians and Europe: An*

Interdisciplinary Collection of Essays, Christian F. Feest, ed. (Aachen, Germany: Herodot, 1987), p. 386.

107 *"an elegant cold collation"*: "Wild West Here," *New York Herald*, European edition, May 11, 1889, p. 1.

108–9 *"There must have been fifty thousand"*: "Colonel Cody in Camp," *New York Herald*, European edition, May 13, 1889, p. 1.

109 *"crowded with strange"*: "Buffalo Bill on French Soil," *Chicago Tribune*, May 12, 1889, p. 15.

109 *"twenty hands"*: "Buffalo Bill à Paris," *Le Figaro*, May 12, 1889, p. 1.

111 *"We sure did attract some attention"*: Kasper, *Annie Oakley*, p. 105.

111 *"curious cavalcade"*: "Colonel Cody in Camp," p. 1.

112 *"Buffalo Bill was one of the world's great men"*: Larry McMurtry, *The Colonel and Little Missie* (New York: Simon and Schuster, 2005), p. 12.

112 *"In nine times out of ten"*: Louis S. Warren, *Buffalo Bill's America: William Cody and the Wild West Show* (New York: Knopf, 2005), pp. 195–96.

113 *"Where did the money go?"*: Ibid., p. 346.

113 *"wildly in mines"*: McMurtry, *The Colonel and Little Missie*, p. 9.

113 "Midi moins neuf, ouf!: Charles Braibant, *Histoire de la Tour Eiffel* (Paris: Plon, 1964), p. 138.

114 *"We have put together this number"*: "Inauguration," *Le Figaro de la Tour*, May 15, 1889, p. 1.

114 *"remained all day"*: "The Great French Show," *New York Times*, May 19, 1889, p. 1.

115 *"it's not more"*: "Échos de la Tour," *Le Figaro*, May 16, 1889, microfilm, Bibliothèque Nationale Mitterand, Paris.

115 *"What Eiffel is to the externals"*: "America at the Big Show," *New York Times*, June 10, 1889, p. 2.

115 *"for business purposes only"*: Josephson, *Edison*, p. 326.

116 *"A girl in half-nude dress"*: "At the Paris World's Fair," *New York Times*, June 23, 1889, p. 16.

116 *"half a dozen grimy cafés"*: W. C. Brownell, "The Paris Exposition," *Scribner's* 7, no. 1 (Jan. 1890): 28.

117 *"A very wobbly, rock-a-bye"*: Kirkwood, "The Paris Exposition," p. 800.

118 *"the Arabic, Moorish and Turkish"*: Susan Hayes Ward, "With the Crowd at the Exposition," *Christian Union* 40, no. 3 (July 18, 1889): 74.

118 *"I think you were right"*: *The Complete Letters of Vincent van Gogh*, p. 182.

119 *"Of course this exhibition"*: *Gauguin by Himself*, p. 103.

119 *"a troupe of temple dancers"*: David Sweetman, *Paul Gauguin* (London: Hodder and Stoughton, 1995), p. 227.

119 *"You missed something"*: *Gauguin by Himself*, p. 104.

119–20 *"all of artistic Paris"*: Brownell, "The Paris Exposition," pp. 29–30.

CHAPTER SIX: *Buffalo Bill and Annie Oakley Triumphant*

122 *"Last—but not by any means"*: "Carnot Among the Cowboys," *New York Herald*, European edition, May 19, 1889, p. 1.

122 "L'attaque d'un convoi": *"Programme de la Buffalo Bill's Wild West Company,"* Ms. 6,

Series 6A/Box 1, Folder 9, McCracken Research Library, Buffalo Bill Historical Center, Cody, Wyoming.

124 *"a very pretty one":* Don Russell, *The Lives and Legends of Buffalo Bill* (Norman: University of Oklahoma Press, 1960), p. 314.

124 *"They sat like icebergs":* Kasper, *Annie Oakley,* pp. 104–5.

125 *"As the cheers":* Oakley, *Autobiography of Annie Oakley,* p. 37.

125 *"fashionable young men":* L. G. Moses, *Wild West Shows and the Images of American Indians, 1883–1933* (Albuquerque: University of New Mexico Press, 1996), p. 22.

125 *an American Corn Palace:* "A People's Work," *New York Herald,* European edition, May 7, 1889, p. 7.

126 *"Carrying his rifle lightly":* Warren, *Buffalo Bill's America,* p. 146.

127 *"I have tried and used":* John F. Sears, "Bierstadt, Buffalo Bill, and the Wild West in Europe," paper from the Franklin and Eleanor Roosevelt Institute, p. 9, files of Buffalo Bill Historical Center, Cody, Wyoming.

127 *"We laughed a lot":* "Échos de la Tour," p. 1. Other information on painting mishap from Eiffel documents in ARO 1981 1271 1–27, Eiffel Archives, Musée d'Orsay, Paris.

127 *"The platform was at that moment":* Ibid., p. 1.

129 *"What was to be done":* "The Otis Lift in the Eiffel Tower," *Times* (London), May 30, 1889, p. 5.

130 *"I was at Buffalo":* Lettres de Paul Gauguin à Émile Bernard, 1888–1891 (Geneva: Pierre Cailler, 1954), p. 75.

130 *"white men have eaten":* Daniele Fiorentino, "Those Red-Brick Faces: European Press Reactions to the Indians of Buffalo Bill's Wild West Show," p. 407, in Feest, ed., *Indians and Europe.*

131 *"hideous scenes of initiations":* Hugh Honour, *The New Golden Land: European Images of America from the Discoveries to the Present Time* (New York: Pantheon, 1975), pp. 237–38.

131 *"The Parisians appear to take":* Untitled, *Home Journal New York,* July 12, 1889, Buffalo Bill Wild West Paris 1889 Scrapbook, McCracken Research Library, Buffalo Bill Historical Center, Cody, Wyoming.

131 *"The Indian tents":* "The Great French Show," *New York Times,* May 19, 1889, p. 1.

131 *"for the benefit of the Berck Hospital":* "Cabby and the Paris Show," *New York Times,* June 16, 1889, p. 1.

132 *"The irate husband":* "The Buffalo Bill Rage in Paris," *York Weekly Post,* June 22, 1889, p. 5.

132 *"I am delighted with my reception":* "Carnot Among the Cowboys," *New York Herald,* European edition, May 19, 1889, p. 1.

133 *"She is not even 25":* Clipping from *Écho de Paris,* dated May 20, 1889, in Annie Oakley Paris 1889 Scrapbook, McCracken Research Library, Buffalo Bill Historical Center, Cody, Wyoming.

133 *"Many of the Indians":* "Astonished Redskins," *New York Herald,* European edition, May 25, 1889, p. 1.

134 *"Had they tomahawked":* "Paris and Its Big Show," *New York Times,* May 25, 1889, p. 9.

134 *"waved their hands":* "Astonished Redskins," p. 1.

134 *"some of the petty Balkan states":* Montezuma, "My NoteBook," *The Art Amateur* 21, no. 3 (Aug. 1889): 46.

134–35 *"It is not surprising"*: Annette Blaugrund, *Paris 1889* (New York: Abrams, 1989), p. 22.

135 *"knows very little"*: "Art and Artfulness," *New York Herald*, European edition, June 1, 1889, p. 5.

135 *"through the transparent tower"*: "The Eiffel Tower," *Times* (London), June 3, 1889, p. 5.

136 *"have flocked to Paris"*: "American Types at the Paris Exposition," *Harper's Weekly*, June 22, 1889, p. 499.

136 *"to which the Eiffel Tower"*: Royal Cortissoz, *The Life of Whitelaw Reid*, vol. 2 (New York: Scribner's, 1921), p. 128.

136 *"surmounted by a figure"*: "At the Mayor's Office," *New York Times*, July 31, 1889, p. 8.

137 *"These voitures Tonkinoises"*: Susan Hayes Ward, "With the Crowd at the Exposition," *Christian Union* 40, no. 3 (July 18, 1889): 74.

138 *"Only a Yankee"*: Blaugrund, *Paris 1889*, p. 77.

138 *"It is American!"*: Letter to the editor from W. J. Hammer, *New York Herald*, European edition, July 28, 1889, p. 5.

139 *"when the card of a visitor"*: Alfred O. Tate, *Edison's Open Door* (New York: E. P. Dutton, 1938), p. 232.

139 *"He does not intend"*: Letter from Alfred O. Tate to Samuel Insull, dated July 27, 1889, Thomas Edison Archives website, Rutgers University.

140 *"received his guests"*: "Carnot Among the Cowboys," p. 1.

140 *"Go see her"*: "Annie Oakley," *Écho de Paris*, May 20, 1889, from Annie Oakley Scrapbook, McCracken Research Library, Buffalo Bill Historical Center, Cody, Wyoming.

140 *"I attribute her masterly shooting skill"*: "La vie en plein air," undated clipping from Annie Oakley Scrapbook, McCracken Research Library, Buffalo Bill Historical Center, Cody, Wyoming.

141 *"We could always have hot water"*: Oakley, *The Autobiography of Annie Oakley*, p. 20.

141 *"Pahuska . . . was in town again"*: John G. Neihardt, *Black Elk Speaks: Being the Life Story of a Holy Man of the Oglala Sioux* (Lincoln: University of Nebraska Press, 1993; orig. 1932), pp. 228–29.

142 *"The American traveller"*: "The American Colony in France," *The Nation*, April 18, 1878, p. 258.

142 *"During our travels"*: Oakley, *The Autobiography of Annie Oakley*, p. 58.

144 *"he entertains handsomely"*: "Personals," *Chicago Tribune*, Sept. 23, 1889, p. 4.

144 *"the halo of glory"*: Untitled clipping, *Sunday Morning News*, July 14, 1889, Buffalo Bill's Wild West Paris 1889 Scrapbook, McCracken Research Library, Buffalo Bill Historical Center, Cody, Wyoming.

144 *"The fact that a man"*: Cortissoz, *The Life of Whitelaw Reid*, vol. 2, p. 137.

145 *"a kindly feeling"*: Ibid.

145 *"We do not forget"*: "Mr. Reid Presented," *New York Tribune*, May 22, 1889, p. 1.

145 *"to enfeeble a hated"*: Ron Chernow, *Alexander Hamilton* (New York: Penguin, 2004), p. 119.

145 *"Americans have been swarming here"*: Cortissoz, *The Life of Whitelaw Reid*, vol. 2, p. 127.

145 *"serried files"*: "From the Top of a Coach," *Harper's Weekly*, Nov. 15, 1890, p. 576.

145 *"We do not intend to permit":* "Letters," *New York Herald,* European edition, Oct. 6, 1887, p. 1.

146 *"This is simply excruciating":* "A French Paper," *New York Herald,* June 16, 1889, p. 14.

146 *"I love America":* O'Connor, *The Scandalous Mr. Bennett,* p. 185.

147 *"I've held four kings":* Christopher Corbett, *Orphans Preferred* (New York: Broadway Books, 2003), p. 164.

147 *"The Russian, the German":* Letter from Minister Reid to Secretary of State James G. Blaine, dated June 20, 1889, Despatches from U.S. Ministers to France, M34 Roll T105 RG 59, Records of the U.S. Department of State, National Archives, College Park, Md.

148 *"it is not easy to approach":* Rewald, *Post-Impressionism,* p. 261.

148 *"You want my news?":* *Lettres de Gauguin à sa femme et ses amis* (Paris: Bernard Grasset, 1946), p. 19.

148 *"Schuff has written":* *Gauguin by Himself,* p. 104.

CHAPTER SEVEN: *Gustave Eiffel Holds Court amid the Art Wars*

151 *"From the second floor":* "Up the Tower," *New York Herald,* European edition, June 25, 1889, p. 1.

151 *"great triumph of American skill":* "Climbing the Eiffel Tower," *Chicago Tribune,* June 5, 1889, p. 3.

152 *"the violence of atmospheric currents":* "1,000 Feet Above Paris," *Chicago Tribune,* July 31, 1889, p. 9. Uses *World* reporting.

152 *"My request may seem odd":* Bermond, *Gustave Eiffel,* p. 311.

153 *"a hundred Congo sailors":* "1,000 Feet Above Paris," p. 9.

153 *"Spotted at 11 o'clock":* "Échos de la Tour," p. 1.

153 *"Women selling cigarettes":* Kaufman, *Paris of To-day,* p. 57.

155 *"We gave the monarchies":* Bermond, *Gustave Eiffel,* p. 322.

155 *"an interesting group of buildings":* Ward, "With the Crowd at the Exposition," p. 74.

156 *"I should so have liked":* The Complete Letters of Vincent van Gogh, pp. 179–80.

156 *"Esquimaux, Laplanders":* Ward, "With the Crowd at the Exposition," p. 74.

156 *"an African coastal king":* de Vogüé, *Remarques sur l'exposition du centenaire,* pp. 171.

157 *"feelings of pride":* Ibid., pp. 172–73.

157 *"All these exotic peoples":* Ibid., pp. 188–90.

158 *"The inevitable Tsiganes":* "Exhibition Dinners," *New York Herald,* European edition, June 20, 1889, p. 5.

158 *"The plates were cold":* "Exhibition Dinners," *New York Herald,* European edition, June 25, 1889, p. 5.

160 *"In France, the American":* Blaugrund, *Paris 1889,* p. 81.

160 *"I would never have believed":* Americans in Paris, p. 13.

161 *"the thrilling story":* Rush C. Hawkins, Commissioner, "Report on the Fine Arts," U.S. Commissioner Reports on the Universal Exposition of 1889 (Washington, D.C.: GPO, 1890), p. 19.

161 *"a moment of intense satisfaction":* "At the Secrétan Sale," *New York Times,* July 14, 1889, p. 5.

162 *"saw across the wide stretch of autumn fields"*: "The Angelus," *Washington Post*, July 5, 1889, p. 4.

162 *"They thought . . . the Louvre"*: "At the Secrétan Sale," p. 5.

163 *"Today we see a canvas"*: Hawkins, "Report on the Fine Arts," p. 18.

163 *"What a business, that Secrétan sale!"*: *The Complete Letters of Vincent van Gogh*, p. 194.

163 *"I left Paris"*: Guy de Maupassant, *La vie errante* (Paris: Louis, Conair, 1939), p. 1.

164 *"Homage to M. Eiffel"*: Harriss, *The Tallest Tower*, pp. 125–26.

165 *"The madame of a whorehouse"*: Édmond and Jules de Goncourt, *Journal: Mémoires de la vie littéraire*, vol. 16 (Monaco: Fasquelle et Flammarion, 1956), p. 71.

165 *"The ascent on the elevator"*: Ibid., p. 100.

166 *"the bracing air"*: "Exhibition Dinner," July 5, 1889, *New York Herald*, European edition, p. 5.

166 *"the art (not very difficult in Paris)"*: "A Sensible American," *New York Herald*, European edition, July 7, 1889.

167 *"where refreshments"*: Kirkwood, "The Paris Exposition," p. 799.

168 *"Altogether, Paris"*: "1,000 Feet Above Paris," p. 9. Uses *World* reporting.

170 *"Well, Doctor, we certainly"*: Gerald Carson, *The Dentist and the Empress* (Boston: Houghton-Mifflin, 1983), p. 145.

170 *"We offer our hearty congratulations"*: "At the United States Legation," *New York Herald*, European edition, July 5, 1889.

171 *"Miss Eames"*: "1,000 Feet Above Paris," p. 9.

171 *"Yesterday was a busy day for me"*: *Letters from Buffalo Bill*, pp. 35–36.

171 *"was tall"*: Carson, *The Dentist and the Empress*, p. 154.

172 *"would be a wicked thing"*: Ibid.

173 *"the strange, odd idea"*: Blaugrund, *Paris 1889*, p. 81.

173 *"would materially help"*: Letter from Whitelaw Reid to Secretary James Blaine, dated June 28, 1889, Despatches from U.S. Ministers to France, M34, Roll T105 RG 59, U.S. State Department, National Archives, College Park, Md.

173 *"I want you to capture him"*: "Gossip from Gay Paris," *Chicago Tribune*, July 28, 1889, p. 26.

174 *"No other horse"*: Ibid.

174 *"When you feel like changing your nationality"*: Kasper, *Annie Oakley*, p. 104.

174 *"How much do you want for her?"*: Courtney Ryley Cooper, *Annie Oakley* (New York: Duffield and Co., 1927), pp. 213–14.

176 *"I was eight years old"*: Kasper, *Annie Oakley*, p. 4.

176 *"All went well for a month"*: Oakley, *Autobiography of Annie Oakley*, pp. 7–11.

179 *"the only and original painter"*: "Whistler," *Washington Post*, Sept. 23, 1889, p. 4.

179 *"He might just as well"*: Letter from Alfred Tate to Samuel Insull, dated July 23, 1889, TAED (D8959ACS), Rutgers University.

180 *"I have always insisted"*: Letter from Samuel Insull to Alfred Tate, dated July 30, 1889, TAED (LB031451), Rutgers University.

180 *"truly Whistlerian"*: Hawkins, "Report on the Fine Arts," p. 81.

CHAPTER EIGHT: *The Monarchs of the World Ascend the Republican Tower*

183 *"His Majesty"*: "Honoring the Shah," *New York Herald*, European edition, Aug. 1, 1889, p. 1.

185 *"To my astonishment"*: L.K., "At the Big Exposition," *New York Times*, Aug. 18, 1889, p. 9.

185 *"The king climbed"*: St.-Jacques, "Dernière heure," *Le Figaro de la Tour*, Aug. 3, 1889, p. 1.

186 *"The truth is"*: Rudorff, *Belle Époque*, p. 41.

186 *"everyone was waiting for him"*: L.K., "At the Big Exposition," p. 9.

187 *"lacked application and tenacity"*: E. Yarshater, "Observations on Nasir al-Din Shah," in Edmond Bosworth and Carole Hillenbrand, eds., *Qajar Iran* (Costa Mesa, Calif.: Mazda Publishers, 1992), p. 7.

188 *"I readily assented"*: Richard J. Walsh, *The Making of Buffalo Bill* (Indianapolis: Bobbs-Merrill, 1928), p. 277.

189 *"obvious. . . . And"*: R. Parent, "Chez Buffalo-Bill," *Le Gil Blas*, Aug. 3, 1889, Buffalo Bill Wild West Show 1889 Paris Scrapbook, McCracken Research Library, Buffalo Bill Historical Center, Cody, Wyoming.

189 *"When you learn"*: Yarshater, "Observations on Nasir al-Din Shah," p. 6.

189 *"with an intense, almost childish"*: "Fêting the Shah," *New York Herald*, European edition, Aug. 2, 1889, p. 1.

190 *"made an amusing speech"*: "A Brilliant Dinner," *New York Herald*, European edition, Aug. 1, 1889.

190 *"One little Indian boy"*: "Fêting the Shah," p. 1.

192 *"Their religious services"*: William Walton, *Chefs-d'oeuvre de l'Exposition Universelle* (Philadelphia: G. Barrie, 1889), p. xlii.

192 *"Do you think this exhibition"*: *Gauguin by Himself*, p. 104.

192 *"What annoys me"*: Jan Hulsker, *Vincent and Theo van Gogh: A Dual Biography* (Ann Arbor, Mich.: Fuller Publications, 1990), p. 376.

193 *"When I think"*: Marie-Angélique Ozanne and Frédérique de Jode, *Theo: The Other van Gogh* (New York: Vendôme Press, 2004), p. 164.

193 *"a five week Paris engagement"*: Oakley, *The Autobiography of Annie Oakley*, pp. 33 and 39.

194 *"The Indians are very bitter"*: "Sioux Nation Consents," *New York Herald*, Aug. 21, 1889, p. 1.

194 *"told his Indians"*: Sam A. Maddra, *Hostiles? The Lakota Ghost Dance and Buffalo Bill's Wild West* (Norman: University of Oklahoma Press, 2006), p. 70.

195 *"Such a breakfast"*: "Les Gaillard de Paris," *New York Herald*, July 28, 1889, p. 7.

195–96 *Le Cercle des Patineurs*: Oakley, *The Autobiography of Annie Oakley*, pp. 37 and 38.

196 *"there were 12 days"*: Ibid., p. 33.

196 *"The American jury"*: Walter E. Smith, "An Explanation Wanted," *New York Herald*, European edition, Aug. 5, 1889, p. 5.

197 *"very picturesquely costumed"*: Richard Thomson, "Camille Pissarro, 'Turpitudes Sociales,' and the Universal Exhibition of 1889," *Arts Magazine* 56, no. 8 (April 1982): 85.

198 *"There's no beating John Mackay"*: Robertson, *The International Herald Tribune*, p. 16.

199 *"news empire"*: Laney, *Paris Herald*, p. 15.

199 *"I will have no indispensable"*: Seitz, *The James Gordon Bennetts*, p. 243.

199 *"A wealthy bachelor"*: Stephen Fiske, *Off-hand Portraits of Prominent New Yorkers* (New York: Arno, 1975; reprint 1884), p. 37.

200 *"With their large dark coats"*: "Les Buffalo Bill," *Le Figaro de la Tour*, Aug. 9, 1889, p. 3.

200 *"all around, the many other visitors":* Ibid.

200 *"Paris is again Paris":* Kirkwood, "The Paris Exposition," p. 799.

202 *"Ah, Saint Virgin Mary":* Henri Rousseau, *Une visite à l'Exposition, 1889* (Geneva: P. Cailler, 1947).

202 *"Neuilly, the Isle of La Grande Jatte":* Rudorff, *Belle Époque,* p. 31.

203 *"Before the Persian shah's visit":* Édmond and Jules de Goncourt, *Journal,* vol. 16, p. 127.

CHAPTER NINE: *In Which Thomas Edison Hails the Eiffel Tower and Becomes an Italian Count*

205 *"I have come to Europe":* Bermond, *Gustave Eiffel,* p. 304.

205 *"The famous inventor":* "Edison," *Le Journal Illustré,* from website of Thomas A. Edison Digital (TAED), Rutgers University, http://edison.rutgers.edu/images/fp/fp0559.jpg.

205 *"The French public":* "Edison Is Enjoying Himself," *Chicago Tribune,* Sept. 13, 1889, p. 9.

206 *"strolling down the long platform":* Alfred O. Tate, *Edison's Open Door* (New York: E. P. Dutton, 1938), pp. 233–34.

207 *"How do you like Paris?":* "Edison's Millennium," *New York Herald,* European edition, Aug. 13, 1889, p. 1.

208 *"This was done":* Tate, *Edison's Open Door,* pp. 235–36 and 241.

208 *"some hard work":* "Edison's Millennium," p. 2.

209 *"When we reached the place":* Tate, *Edison's Open Door,* p. 166.

209 *"An elevator was reserved for us":* Letter from Margaret Upton to her mother, dated Aug. 14, 1889, Margaret Upton Papers, New Jersey Historical Society, Newark, N.J.

210 *"saluted him":* St.-Jacques, "Edison à la Tour Eiffel," p. 1.

210 *"Mr. Edison was not quite prepared":* "Edison's Pleasant Day," *New York Herald,* European edition, Aug. 14, 1889, p. 3.

211 *"Toasts of all kinds":* Letter from Margaret Upton, dated Aug. 14, 1889.

211 *"Miss Annie Oakley":* Kasper, *Annie Oakley,* p. 104.

211 *"If I spend one dollar foolishly":* Oakley, *The Autobiography of Annie Oakley,* pp. 11 and 60.

212 *"The Exhibition is immense":* Sherard, *Twenty Years in Paris,* pp. 178–79.

213 *"My déjeuner with Edison":* Sherard, *Twenty Years in Paris,* pp. 183–85.

214 *"The work of a bridge builder":* Richard Sherard, "With Mr. Edison on the Eiffel Tower," *Scientific American* 61, no. 11 (Sept. 14, 1889): 166.

214 *"There is a great deal of humbug":* Sherard, *Twenty Years in Paris,* pp. 185–88.

215 *"They are all clamoring for you":* Letter from J. S. Sargent to James McNeill Whistler, from early May 1889, Centre for Whistler Studies, Glasgow University Library, Online Archive, Glasgow University, http://www.whistler.arts.gla.ac.uk/correspondence.

215 *"I would very much like to be":* Letter from J. M. Whistler to Stéphane Mallarmé, dated early July, Centre for Whistler Studies, Glasgow University Library, Online Archive, Glasgow University, http://www.whistler.arts.gla.ac.uk/correspondence.

215 *"I fear that I have an inherent objection":* Letter from J. M. Whistler to Sheridan Ford, dated August 18, 1889, Centre for Whistler Studies, Glasgow University Library, Online Archive, Glasgow University, http://www.whistler.arts.gla.ac.uk/correspondence.

216 *"But Paris is so lovely":* Letter from Lady Gertrude Campbell to Beatrix Whistler,

dated Aug. 18, 1889, Centre for Whistler Studies, Glasgow University Library, Online Archive, Glasgow University, http://www.whistler.arts.gla.ac.uk/correspondence.

216 *"a more enthusiastic welcome"*: "An American Abroad," *New York Tribune*, Aug. 18, 1889, p. 6.

216–17 *"seated at a banquet"*: Helen Cody Wetmore, *Buffalo Bill* (Lincoln: University of Nebraska Press, 2003), p. 191.

217 *"Edison has had a reception"*: "Edison Is Enjoying Himself."

217 *"Dinners, dinners, dinners"*: Josephson, *Edison*, p. 334.

217 *"Like every American abroad"*: "At Home in France," *New York Herald*, European edition, Aug. 23, 1889, p. 1.

218 *"police agents at Mentone"*: Telegram (in cipher) from Minister Whitelaw Reid to Secretary of State James Blaine, dated Aug. 7, 1889, RG 59, Dispatches from Minister Whitelaw Reid, U.S. State Department, National Archives, College Park, Md.

218 *"I have repeatedly"*: Letter from John Burke to Minister Whitelaw Reid, dated Aug. 15, 1889, RG 59, Dispatches from Minister Whitelaw Reid, U.S. State Department, National Archives, College Park, Md.

219 *"I stated what was expected of them"*: Letter from Minister Whitelaw Reid to Secretary of State James Blaine, dated Aug. 17, 1889, RG 59, Dispatches from Minister Whitelaw Reid, U.S. State Department, National Archives, College Park, Md.

219 *"It came from a multitude of throats"*: Tate, *Edison's Open Door*, p. 234.

219 *"The managers took great pleasure"*: from F. L. Dyer and T. C. Martin, *Edison: His Life and Inventions*, vol. II (New York: Harper and Brothers, 1910), pp. 747–48.

220 *"the grand orchestra played"*: Letter from Margaret Upton to her mother, dated Aug. 20, 1889, Margaret Upton Papers, New Jersey Historical Society, Newark, N.J.

220 *"the manager came around"*: Dyer and Martin, *Edison*, vol. II, p. 748.

220 *"It must be cute"*: Neil Baldwin, *Edison* (New York: Hyperion, 1995), p. 207.

220 *"the enormous number of cranks and crooks"*: Sherard, *Twenty Years in Paris*, p. 175.

221 *"Oh, yes . . . they are grand art"*: Ibid., p. 185.

222 *"To my mind the Old Masters"*: Josephson, *Edison*, p. 336.

222 *"the exhibit of the Kimberley diamond mines"*: Dyer and Martin, *Edison*, vol. II, p. 750.

222 *"We had a good library"*: Anderson, *Experiences and Impressions*, p. 47.

223 *"To avoid the crowd"*: Ibid., p. 32.

224 *"It represents nothing"*: "An Interesting Talk with Inventor Edison in Paris," *Chicago Tribune*, Sept. 9, 1889, p. 5.

224 *"Oh, they don't have inventors"*: Sherard, *Twenty Years in Paris*, p. 190.

224 *"The fact is this"*: "Troubles of a Millionaire," *Chicago Tribune*, July 2, 1888, p. 2.

225 *"the usual panicky reaction"*: O'Connor, *The Scandalous Mr. Bennett*, pp. 206–7.

225 *"This last trip"*: "Troubles of a Millionaire," p. 2.

225 *"Then, blazing in diamonds and gold lace"*: Tate, *Edison's Open Door*, p. 23

226 Coquelin the Younger, who *"mounted the stage"*: Ibid.

226 *"It reproduced speeches"*: "Sa Majesté Edison," *New York Herald*, European edition, Aug. 27, 1889, p. 1.

228 *"with special permission"*: Tate, *Edison's Open Door*, pp. 242–43.

229 *"To the loveliest"*: Kasper, *Annie Oakley*, p. 106.

230 *"Is Manet . . . in Paris"*: *Paul Gauguin: 45 Lettres à Vincent, Théo et Jo van Gogh*, Douglas Cooper, ed. (Staatsuitgeverij: La Bibliothèque des Arts, 1983), pp. 124–25.

230 *"I am working like one actually possessed":* The Complete Letters of Vincent van Gogh, vol. 3 (Boston: New York Graphic Society, 1978), p. 203.

230 *"Who is it who interprets":* Ozanne and de Jode, *Theo: The Other van Gogh,* p. 168.

231 *"He occupied three rooms":* Dyer and Martin, *Edison: His Life and Inventions,* p. 749.

231 *"with its powerful electric lamp":* "Scientific Use of Eiffel's Tower," *New York Times,* July 6, 1889, p. 2.

231 *"the master of the cable system":* Dyer and Martin, *Edison: His Life and Inventions,* pp. 752–53.

232 *"Pasteur invited me":* Ibid., p. 750.

232 *The Paris* Herald *reported:* "The Pasteur Institute," *New York Herald,* European edition, Sept. 28, 1889.

233 *"would complicate his life":* Josephson, *Edison,* p. 336.

233 *"At first it was my head":* Sherard, *Twenty Years in Paris,* p. 189.

223 *"I think Eiffel":* "An Interesting Talk with Inventor Edison in Paris," p. 5.

234 *"In our little pavilion":* "Échos de la Tour," p. 1.

234 *"to walk on a cable":* "Blondin's Daring Proposition," *Washington Post,* Aug. 11, 1889, p. 12.

236 *"Our dear and illustrious master":* "Eiffel's Toast to Edison," ARO 1981 IIII a&b, Eiffel Archive, Musée d'Orsay, Paris.

236 *"Seventy-five of us":* "Not Spoiled by Honors," *New York World,* Oct. 10, 1889.

237 *"To M. Eiffel":* Harriss, *The Tallest Tower,* p. 119.

237 *"The man who could":* Ibid., p. 140.

237 *"The Eiffel Tower":* Ibid.

237 *"I am glad to hear it":* Sherard, *Twenty Years in Paris,* p. 173.

239 *"Paris, in the Hotel de Ville":* Anderson, *Experiences and Impressions,* pp. 31–32.

239 *"a feeble mark of his gratitude":* "He Enjoyed His Stay Here," *New York Herald,* European edition, Sept. 12, 1889, p. 1.

240 *"Hold on there":* "Reminiscences," in William J. Hammer Collection, National Museum of American History Archives Center, Smithsonian Institution, Washington, D.C.; also online at TAED (X098A001).

240 *"Every man in the company":* "Honoring Mr. Edison," *New York Tribune,* Oct. 7, 1889, p. 1.

CHAPTER TEN: *Rosa Bonheur Meets Buffalo Bill*

243 *"'Why do you want me'":* Anna Klumpke, *Rosa Bonheur: The Artist's (Auto)biography* (Ann Arbor: University of Michigan Press, 1997), p. 24.

244 *"Observing them at close range":* Ibid., pp. 193 and 24.

244–45 *"the barking of numerous dogs":* Henry Bacon, "Rosa Bonheur," *Century Illustrated Magazine* 28, no. 6 (Oct. 1884): 886.

245 *"a huge chimney":* Ibid., p. 887.

245 *"Behind the house":* Ibid.

245 *"Because of his frequent shows":* Klumpke, *Rosa Bonheur: The Artist's (Auto)biography,* p. 193.

245 *"more interesting things of French kings":* "Buffalo Bill and Rosa Bonheur," *Galignani's Messenger,* Sept. 26, 1889, from the Wild West Company's Paris 1889 Scrap-

book, McCracken Research Library, Buffalo Bill Historical Center, Cody, Wyoming.

246 *"I hope you will not be cross"*: Klumpke, *Rosa Bonheur: The Artist's (Auto)biography*, p. 8.

246 *"The princes Saïd and Omar"*: *Le Figaro, Édition Spéciale Imprimée dans la Tour Eiffel*, Sept. 30, 1889, p. 1.

246 *"Tomorrow begins the last month"*: Ibid.

247 *"Paris was like some lovely"*: Art Young, *Art Young: His Art and Times* (New York: Sheridan House, 1939), p. 3.

248 *"It has become the true crown"*: Eugène de Rastignac, "Courrier de Paris," *L'Illustration*, Sept. 21, 1889, p. 26.

248 *"Just as our driver"*: Klumpke, *Rosa Bonheur: The Artist's (Auto)biography*, pp. 8–11.

250 *"Eight days on the ocean liner"*: Robert Conot, *A Streak of Luck* (New York: Seaview Books, 1979), p. 286.

250 *"I went over to see"*: "Not Spoiled by Honors," *New York World*, Oct. 7, 1889, p. 1.

250 *"I am just as much"*: "Edison Back from Paris," *New York Times*, Oct. 7, 1889, p. 5.

251 *"Edison . . . says"*: Ibid.

251 *"I did not mind the fact"*: "By the Zuyder-Zee," *New York Herald*, European edition, Oct. 3, 1889, p. 1.

251 *"I have never in my life"*: "Whacking Whistler," *New York Herald*, European edition, Oct. 4, 1889, p. 1.

251 *"We can endure"*: "A Question of Taste," *New York Herald*, European edition, Oct. 5, 1889, p. 5.

252 *"I never allow myself"*: "Hawkins Hits Back," *New York Herald*, European edition, Oct. 8, 1889, p. 1.

252 *"It is a sad shock"*: "Whistler's Grievance," *New York Herald*, European edition, Oct. 9, 1889, p. 5.

252 *"The truth is"*: "A Refusé Speaks Out," *New York Herald*, European edition, Oct. 9, 1889, p. 5.

252 *"the first papoose"*: "Little 'Red Shirt,'" *New York Herald*, European edition, Sept. 29, 1889, p. 5.

253 *"We had never cared"*: Pattie Miller Stocking, "The Big Show in Paris," *Washington Post*, Oct. 6, 1889, p. 16.

253 *"a splendid trotter"*: Theodore Stanton, ed., *Reminiscences of Rosa Bonheur* (London: Andrew Melrose, 1910), p. 246.

253 *"gave me time to study their tents"*: Klumpke, *Rosa Bonheur: The Artist's (Auto)biography*, p. 24.

255 *"the hand of the white man"*: "French Talk of the Time," *New York Times*, Oct. 1, 1889, p. 9.

255 *"Mr. Bierstadt, a veteran"*: H. Barbara Weinberg, *Paris 1889: American Artists at the Universal Exposition* (New York: Abrams, 1989), p. 20.

256 *"Among other things"*: *Gauguin by Himself*, p. 106.

256 *"From time to time"*: *The Complete Letters of Vincent van Gogh*, p. 222.

256 *"I like the wheat field"*: Ozanne and de Jode, *Theo: The Other van Gogh*, p. 170.

256 *"The main thing"*: *The Complete Letters of Vincent van Gogh*, p. 220.

257 *"the perfect healthfulness of the meat"*: Letter from Whitelaw Reid to Secretary of State

James Blaine, dated Oct. 19, 1889, Despatches from U.S. Ministers to France, M34, Roll T105 RG 59, U.S. State Department, National Archives, College Park, Md.

257 *"Business had been bad"*: Oakley, *The Autobiography of Annie Oakley*, p. 58.

258 *"A few days ago he spent"*: "Notes from Paris," Annie Oakley Paris Scrapbook, McCracken Research Library, Buffalo Bill Historical Center, Cody, Wyo.

258 *"In the front of the Tonkin village"*: Rastignac, "Courrier de Paris," p. 186.

259 *"have given vent to their disappointment"*: "The Exhibition," *American Register*, Oct. 5, 1889.

259 *"For me, it was truly like"*: Édmond and Jules de Goncourt, *Journal: Mémoires de la vie littéraire*, vol. 16, p. 154.

259 *"We have the Exposition"*: Rastignac, "Courrier de Paris," p. 326.

260 *"Cambodian antiquities"*: Édmond and Jules de Goncourt, *Journal: Mémoires de la vie littéraire*, vol. 16, p. 156.

260 *"A head the size"*: Ibid., p. 158.

260 *"The Javanese kampong"*: "Paris Local," *American Register*, Oct. 26, 1889.

260 *"strange plants of Mexico"*: Édmond and Jules de Goncourt, *Journal: Mémoires de la vie littéraire*, vol. 16, pp. 160–61.

260 *"I relented in regard"*: The Letters of Henry James, Percy Lubbock, ed. (New York: Charles Scribner's Sons, 1920), pp. 154–55.

261 *"In this monumental chaos"*: Eugène-Melchior de Vögué, "Impressions Made by the Paris Exposition," *The Chautauquan* 10, no. 1 (Oct. 1889): 66.

261 *"Here all is truth"*: Ibid.

262 *"The designs must show a tower"*: "London's Tall Tower," *New York Herald*, European edition, Oct. 23, 1889, p. 1.

262 *"which will cause the Eiffel Tower"*: "To Overtop the Eiffel": *Chicago Tribune*, Oct. 24, 1889, p. 2.

262 *"To put the comparison in a nutshell"*: "Tower to the Clouds," *Chicago Tribune*, Oct. 26, 1889, p. 9.

262 *"The rush for the Decauville trains"*: "Exhibition Notes," *New York Herald*, European edition, Nov. 5, 1889, p. 1.

263 *"The [fair] grounds"*: Ibid.

263 *"With a last thank-you"*: Eiffel's Livre d'Or Scrapbook, Eiffel Archives, Musée d'Orsay, Paris.

263 *"crowds of people"*: "Parisiana," *New York Herald*, European edition, Nov. 6, 1889, p. 1.

264 *"What a crush there was!"*: "The Exhibition Closes," *New York Herald*, European edition, Nov. 7, 1889, p. 1.

265 *"It was a curious experience"*: Young, *His Life and Times*, p. 14.

265 *"shed over Paris a shower of gold"*: Editorial, *American Register*, Nov. 30, 1889.

266 *"The Exhibition has brought to France"*: "Closing of Exhibition," *American Register*, Nov. 30, 1889, p. 5, quoting an unnamed French publication.

266 *"The Eiffel suit"*: Letter from W. D. Baldwin to Charles Otis, dated November 20, 1889, Otis Corporate Archives, Farmington, Conn.

266 *"The boulevards no longer look"*: Rastignac, "Courrier de Paris," p. 418.

267 *"Sunday I was at Bilbao Bill's"*: Dore Ashton, *Rosa Bonheur* (New York: Viking, 1981), p. 156.

268 *"Miss Oakley and Johnny Baker"*: "The Wild West," *Galignani's Messenger*, Oct. 23, 1889.

268 *"Colonel Cody's Wild West show"*: "A Brilliant Close," *New York Herald*, European edition, Nov. 14, 1889, p. 1.

269 *"the most successful affair"*: "The Paris Exposition," *Washington Post*, Nov. 6, 1889, p. 4.

CHAPTER ELEVEN: *Afterword*

271 *"I consider such transaction void."*: "Millions Paid in Bribes," *New York Times*, Jan. 12, 1893, p. 3.

272 *"It may seem passing strange"*: "Confidence in the Canal," *New York Times*, Jan. 6, 1889, p. 12.

272 *"No one ever got to the bottom"*: McCullough, *The Path Between the Seas*, p. 213.

273 *"Real French patriots"*: "Five Years for De Lesseps," *Chicago Tribune*, Feb. 10, 1893, p. 5.

273 *"I am a man of order"*: Bermond, *Gustave Eiffel*, p. 337.

273 *"Your house will be blown up"*: Ibid., p. 338.

274 *"A great many people who lost their money"*: Sherard, *Twenty Years in Paris*, p. 165.

274 *"brilliant and dazzling symphonies"*: Gayford, *The Yellow House*, p. 303.

274 *"What makes his entire body of work"*: Ozanne and de Jode, *Theo: The Other van Gogh*, p. 172.

275 *"You could not imagine"*: Gayford, *The Yellow House*, p. 305.

276 *"The sun was terribly hot"*: Ozanne and de Jode, *Theo: The Other van Gogh*, p. 196.

276 *"Sad though his death"*: Gayford, *The Yellow House*, pp. 305–6.

276 *"These canvases are not the work"*: Ozanne and de Jode, *Theo: The Other van Gogh*, p. 203.

276 *"Departure to tropics"*: Ibid., p. 205.

277 *"Of course I visited Vesuvius"*: Oakley, *The Autobiography of Annie Oakley*, p. 42.

277 *"could not believe"*: Ibid., p. 40.

279 *"the evil resulting"*: Maddra, *Hostiles? The Lakota Ghost Dance and Buffalo Bill's Wild West*, p. 63.

280 *"furnished us the same work"*: Ibid., p. 79.

280 *"The theory of the government's management"*: Ibid., p. 81.

281 *"would bring with him"*: Russell, *The Lives and Legends of Buffalo Bill*, p. 354.

281 *"whites invariably break"*: "Buffalo Bill on the Indian War," *New York Herald*, Nov. 19, 1890, p. 5.

281 *"Of all the bad Indians"*: "The Worst Indian of Them All," *New York Times*, Nov. 25, 1890, p. 5.

282 *"I don't yet know"*: Warren, *Buffalo Bill's America*, p. 378.

283 *"[his] superior knowledge of Indian character"*: Russell, *The Lives and Legends of Buffalo Bill*, p. 354.

284 *"At the moment, as far as words go"*: Ibid., p. 290.

285 *"They stand on their heads"*: Walsh, *The Making of Buffalo Bill*, p. 296.

285 *"From the time I enter my grounds"*: *Letters from Buffalo Bill*, pp. 37–38.

286 *"reception room"*: Weintraub, *Whistler: A Biography*, p. 174.

287 *"What a pity!"*: Ibid., p. 345.

287 *"a tower with a height of 8,947 feet"*: Erik Larson, *The Devil in the White City* (New York: Crown, 2003), pp. 134–35.

288 *"This wheel would carry"*: Ibid., p. 185.

288 *"I am doing the business": Letters from Buffalo Bill*, p. 41.

289 *"offered any kid in Chicago":* Larson, *The Devil in the White City*, p. 251.

289 *"When she was in Europe":* Kasper, *Annie Oakley*, p. 126.

290 *"Truly, I long for the day":* Ibid.

291 *"We have wandered from home":* Weintraub, *Whistler: A Biography*, p. 403.

291 *"If I can no longer paint":* David Sweetman, *Paul Gauguin: A Life* (New York: Simon and Schuster, 1995), p. 466.

293 *"very doubtful":* Josephson, *Edison: A Biography*, p. 392.

294 *"My three companies":* Jill Jonnes, *Empires of Light* (New York: Random House, 2003), p. 351.

294 *"left his apartment":* O'Connor, *The Scandalous Mr. Bennett*, pp. 203–4.

295 *"Not to be a 'chauffeur'":* Hebe Dorsey, *The Belle Époque in the Paris Herald* (London: Thames and Hudson, 1986), p. 179.

296 *"During my engineering career":* Harriss, *The Tallest Tower*, p. 165.

296 *"published at his own expense":* Ibid., p. 166.

296 *"experimentally that the generally accepted":* Ibid., pp. 167–68.

298 *"with a single antenna":* Harriss, *The Tallest Tower*, p. 173.

298 *"one would wish it were more beautiful":* Loyrette, *Gustave Eiffel*, p. 168.

298 *"In these paths":* "Le Gala de Buffalo Bill," *Le Figaro*, April 2, 1905, p. 1.

299 *"I hope you are happy": Letters from Buffalo Bill*, p. 63.

300 *"the greatest land deal ever":* Warren, *Buffalo Bill's America*, p. 472.

300 *"only 1000 inhabitants":* Ibid., p. 487.

301 *"If [the Eiffel Tower] did not exist":* Loyrette, *Gustave Eiffel*, p. 168.

301 *"The Government has begun":* "Wireless to New York," *New York Times*, Jan. 26, 1908, p. 1.

301 *"I have just finished something new":* "Edison Off for Holiday," *Los Angeles Times*, Aug. 3, 1911, p. 17.

301 *"Who is that shabby little man":* "The Great American in Europe Is Thomas Edison," *Los Angeles Times*, Sept. 17, 1911, p. 15.

302 *"impresses me favorably":* "Edison Returns Home," *Washington Post*, Oct. 8, 1891, p. 3.

302 *"In France, the roads":* "We're Still Ahead," *New York Times*, Oct. 8, 1911, p. 5.

302 *"Americans in Paris":* "War News," *New York Herald*, European edition, Aug. 3, 1914, p. 2.

302 *"In August 1914":* Harriss, *The Tallest Tower*, p. 173.

302 *"an editor kept track":* Seitz, *The James Gordon Bennetts*, p. 376.

303 *"he would keep on printing":* "Bennett a Figure in Many Anecdotes," *New York Times*, May 15, 1918, p. 6.

303 *"the Whores' Daily Guide and Compendium":* O'Connor, *The Scandalous Mr. Bennett*, p. 272.

303 *"A woman finds":* Ibid., p. 273.

304 *"The old, drunken":* Seitz, *The James Gordon Bennetts*, p. 376.

304 *"I am anxious":* "From Centigrade to Fahrenheit," *New York Herald*, Aug. 3, 1914, p. 2.

305 *"All Paris knew":* "French Press Laments Loss of a Friend," *New York Herald*, European edition, May 15, 1918, p. 1.

305 *"This has been another long season": Letters from Buffalo Bill*, p. 77.

305 *"For four weeks we have had":* Ibid.

305 *"The old scout":* Walsh, *The Making of Buffalo Bill*, p. 359.

306 *"For hours before the ceremony"*: "Cody Now Rests on Lookout Mountain," *Washington Post*, June 4, 1917, p. 10.

306 *"In a time when America"*: Warren, *Buffalo Bill's America*, p. x.

306–7 *"William F. Cody was the kindest hearted"*: Oakley, *The Autobiography of Annie Oakley*, pp. 57–58.

307 *"Annie enjoyed getting up"*: Kasper, *Annie Oakley*, p. 205.

307 *"The tower . . . is the principal work"*: Gustave Eiffel, *Biographie industrielle et scientifique de Gustave Eiffel*, vol. 1, ARO 1981 977(c), p. 44, Eiffel Archive, Musée d'Orsay, Paris.

309 *"Lucien Sarniguet, a forty-five-year-old captain"*: Harriss, *The Tallest Tower*, p. 181.

311 *"We are all citizens of the Eiffel Tower"*: Braibant, *Histoire de la Tour Eiffel*, p. 158.

PHOTOGRAPH CREDITS

INDEX

Page numbers in *italics* refer to illustrations.

Conquering Gotham
Building Penn Station and Its Tunnels

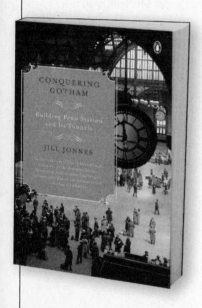

Conquering Gotham re-creates the riveting struggle waged by the great Pennsylvania Railroad to build Penn Station and the monumental system of tunnels that would connect water-bound Manhattan to the rest of the continent by rail. Historian Jill Jonnes tells a ravishing tale of snarling plutocrats, engineering feats, and backroom politicking packed with the most colorful figures of Gilded Age New York.

ISBN 978-0-14-311324-9

"Superb. [A] first-rate narrative."
—*The Wall Street Journal*

"The kind of precision attained only by hard research."
—*The Economist*

PENGUIN
BOOKS